BREAKFAST

THE
COOKBOOK

EMILY ELYSE
MILLER

THE
COOKBOOK

BREAKFAST

CONTENTS

DAIRY-FREE

GLUTEN-FREE

VG

VEGAN

VT

VEGETARIAN

15

**LESS THAN
15 MINUTES**

5

**LESS THAN
5 INGREDIENTS**

INTRODUCTION

I was raised in both Arizona and Hawaii in a family for which breakfast is sacred. On weekends, my late grandfather Shelly would call out from the kitchen, with a thick New York accent: "You want eggs?" He owned an appetizing store in The Bronx, and the shop specialized in smoked and cured fish, such as salmon, sable, whitefish, and herring, plus a vast assortment of cream cheeses and spreads; cold appetizers including whitefish salad, chopped liver, and egg and tuna salads; and all the other fixings for bagels. This coveted call from him to my dad, then to my sister and me, was always followed by a peek around the doorway to make sure we were awake and had heard his important question. We would gather around the table and devour Lox, Eggs, and Onions (page 32) with toasted bagels and cream cheese. Sometimes there would be Egg-in-a-Hole (page 31) or French Toast (page 140), the first breakfast my dad taught me to make.

When I wake up at the crack of dawn, the only thought keeping me from going back to sleep is a subliminal display of flashing images featuring everything I could make for breakfast. I think about whether I have invited a friend over for a morning meal, if I should make Cornetti (page 364) for my neighbor or a Breakfast Burrito (page 158) for my sister, or if I should simply prepare Avocado Toast (page 144), as a gesture for myself. Breakfast is often hastily thrown together or eaten on the go, yet it is a meal steeped with tradition and rituals. It happens at the most intimate time of the day and displays our need for comfort through food.

I realized early on, and especially as my career developed, that what I enjoy most is exploring other cultures through food, and specifically through breakfast. Enamored by the relationships forged over a shared meal, I became fascinated with the ritualistic steps of peoples' morning routines. Breakfast is a mealtime when your brain and palate are a clean slate. Thoughts and foods enjoyed first thing in the morning determine your mindset for the rest of the day.

I had many conversations about and around breakfasts and I created spaces where chefs, artists, designers, and thinkers could continue exchanging ideas in a creative way. In 2015, I founded BreakfastClub, a global series that brings people together to share a one-time-only breakfast menu at restaurants typically closed in the morning. The food the chefs made was innovative, delicious, and personal. I noticed it was often driven by nostalgia: the experience encouraged them to go back to their roots, to think creatively about humble ingredients.

To continue my exploration of breakfast around the world, I curated guided breakfast walking tours, inviting international guests to experience a city's neighborhood and its culinary treasures and traditions. It is incredible that in Manhattan's Lower East Side neighborhood Jewish, Mexican, Dominican, Chinese, and American Southern dishes can all be enjoyed in one morning. Guests discover that Wonton Soup (page 258) is a typical breakfast from Shanghai, learn the tragically romantic translation behind the Dominican breakfast drink Morir Soñando (page 432), and enjoy a classic New York Bacon, Egg, and Cheese (page 172), reinvented by a Louisiana native. From London to Lisbon, Singapore to Bangkok, Tel Aviv to Beirut, and Los Angeles to Mexico City, I spent hundreds of hours listening to stories, searching for recipes, and sharing meals with people from different countries.

I became a student, eager to soak up traditional and modern techniques. Strangers became friends after revealing their morning routines. During long drives to the airport, taxi drivers shared their favorite places to enjoy traditional dishes from their homelands and neighborhoods. I obsessively searched online, sifting sites and videos of local bloggers, home cooks, and street food vendors. When talking about breakfast, borders were dropped, talk quickly became candid, and friends asked friends, called aunts, and reconnected with distant cousins to recall an ingredient, technique, or story from a precious morning food memory. I witnessed heated conversations from an impassioned audience, recounting slight variances in spelling, ingredients, origins, and techniques of their favorite dishes.

After three years of researching, I had a list of about 1,000 breakfast options that turned into 650 recipes, then to the nearly 400 tested dishes and drinks in this book. *Breakfast: The Cookbook* is meant to offer an extensive variety of global cuisines—with iconic and lesser-known regional breakfast specialties—of sweet and savory, healthy and decadent. I wanted the recipes included to be authentic and faithful in their representation of different cultures. Every country, region, and kitchen has its own way of preparing breakfast. From the dozens of ways to cook eggs, to the "correct" toppings for a bowl of congee, most recipes have too many variations to count. These recipes lay a foundation for your kitchen. The magic of breakfast is in how endlessly adaptable it is. You can play with these recipes without judgment.

It felt like a tremendous responsibility to document culinary traditions from so many places. The recipes in this book are a summary of the research, stories, and notes from people representing each of the countries included. Breakfast as a category is limitless and the preparation of one's breakfast is a truly personal experience. For example, Shakshuka—a stewed, spiced tomato and pepper dish with poached eggs—has become synonymous with Israeli breakfast culture, though it is thought to have originated in Yemen (and I've included both the Israeli Shakshuka, page 66, and the Yemeni version, page 68). Israel's diverse diaspora of Moroccan, Tunisian, Iraqi, and Yemeni descent has led to countless variations in spelling and technique to make this simple dish, yet all are "correct" and delicious. The freedom to represent your identifying culture wherever you are in the world has developed some tasty combinations. The popular Hawaiian Noodle Soup (page 248) is melded with Japanese, Chinese, and Filipino ingredients. Kedgeree (page 276), a spiced rice and flaked haddock dish in the United Kingdom, fuses Indian spices and cooking techniques with the addition of local British comfort foods. The cuisine of Singapore is made up of Malaysian, Indian, and Chinese roots, and their breakfast tables have Roti Prata (page 207), *chai tow kway* (Carrot Cake, page 52), and Toast with Coconut Jam and Soft-Boiled Eggs (page 150). America's breakfasts are a summary of global cuisine adopted by immigrants from the first settlers to modern day. Grits (page 83) came from Native American tribes in the southern United States, Frittata (page 65) from Italy, and Açaí (page 444) from Brazil.

Because it is often prepared in the morning, breakfast can be scrappy, resourceful, and inventive. It can also be the humblest of meals, and perfectly acceptable to concoct out of leftovers from the night before. Put an egg on it and it can be breakfast. In Korea, leftover protein is turned into a soup or stew, while day-old rice is fried to perfection and enjoyed with *banchan*, or side dishes, such as Cabbage Kimchi (page 270). In Colombia, stale bread is revived in a Milk Soup called *changua* (page 248). In America, Scrapple (page 347) is a cornmeal and meat loaf made from less desirable cuts of pork, then sliced, fried, and served with eggs and toast. Even a cold slice of pizza from the night before can be considered breakfast.

The recipes in this book evoke simple, shared meals and conversations around breakfast. They keep me daydreaming about what goes on in the early hours around the world. In Tunis, you might be deciding what toppings to include on your *leblebi*, or Chickpea and Torn Bread Soup (page 262). Mid-morning in Madrid, it is time for a *tortilla Española* (Potato and Egg Omelet, page 50). In Beirut, people enjoy an Instant Coffee (page 412) with powdered milk and a Flatbread with Za'atar or Keshek (pages 202–3) from their favorite street vendor. In Havana, there is a line outside a frankfurter stand, which also sells a great Cafecito (page 416). In Los Angeles, a bowl of fresh picked guava, avocado, pomegranate, and other seasonal fruits is getting a squeeze of lime. In Manila, a pot of *champorado* (Chocolate Rice Porridge, page 102) is simmering on the stove. While in Singapore, a hawker-center vendor is selling *bak kut teh* (Pork and White Pepper Soup, page 259) in a melamine bowl to their regular breakfast customers.

These recipes should encourage everyone to explore and travel the world through breakfast, connecting us at breakfast tables near and far.

EGGS

FRIED EGG
GLOBAL

This recipe is for "sunny-side up" (not flipped with a runny yolk) eggs. To prepare an "over easy" fried egg (flipped with a runny yolk), simply flip the egg in the last 20 seconds of the cooking process. For "over medium" (flipped with slightly runny yolk), flip the egg and cook for an additional 20 seconds, and for "over hard" (flipped with solid yolk), flip and cook an additional 40 seconds.

Cooking time: 5 minutes
Makes: 1 egg

· ½ tablespoon (7 g) butter or olive oil
· 1 egg
· Salt and freshly ground pepper

In a medium nonstick skillet, heat the butter or olive oil over medium heat. Crack in the egg and season with salt and pepper. Cook for 1 minute and reduce the heat to low. Cook until the white is set and the edges are golden and crispy, about 2 minutes more. In the last 30 seconds of cooking, use a spoon to baste the egg white with hot butter or oil, helping to finish cooking the white. Use a thin spatula to transfer the egg to a plate for serving.

BOILED EGG
GLOBAL

Boiled eggs are submerged in boiling water for varying amounts of time depending on the desired softness of the yolk. A hard-boiled egg has a fully cooked yolk. The egg can be sliced and put on toast or knäckebröd *(Crispbread with Smoked Cod Roe Spread, page 152). A medium- to soft-boiled egg has a creamy yolk and is enjoyed with Eggs and Soldiers (page 50). An extra soft-boiled egg (see Variation) has a runny yolk and barely opaque white, and is often eaten in Southeast Asia, as kaya toast (Toast with Coconut Jam and Soft-Boiled Eggs, page 150) or as khai luak (Soft-Boiled Egg Shot, page 55).*

Cooking time: 10 minutes
Makes: 1 egg

· 1 egg

Set up a bowl of ice and water. Bring a small pot of water to a gentle boil. Carefully lower the egg into the boiling water and cook for 5 minutes for a runny yolk, 7 minutes for a custardy yolk, and 10 minutes for a hard yolk. Using a slotted spoon, transfer the egg to the ice bath to stop them from cooking further.

To eat/serve a 5- or 7-minute egg, use a spoon to delicately crack the shell. Remove the shell carefully as to not break into the egg and break the yolk. For a 10-minute egg, use a spoon to crack the shell and peel the shell under running water for easy removal.

Variation
For an extra-soft egg, bring a small saucepan of water to a boil. Remove from the heat and add the eggs. Set aside, uncovered, for 15 minutes. Carefully crack the eggs into a small bowl. The consistency should be very runny with barely opaque whites.

POACHED EGG
GLOBAL

The whites of a poached egg should be soft and opaque, and the yolk still runny. These are found in Eggs Benedict (page 58). Poached eggs can be made in advance. Simply reheat in simmering water for about 1 minute, taking care not to overcook the yolk.

Cooking time: 10 minutes
Makes: 1 egg

· 1 egg

Fill a large saucepan or deep skillet with water and bring to a simmer, making sure the water doesn't boil. Crack the egg into a small ramekin or bowl. Use a spoon to create a whirlpool in the simmering water and immediately slide the egg into the center of the whirlpool. Gently use the spoon to rein in the whites and nestle around the yolk. Cook until the white is set and the yolk is runny, about 3 minutes. Use a slotted spoon to transfer the egg to a plate. Serve warm.

SCRAMBLED EGGS
GLOBAL

Scrambled eggs can be enjoyed on their own or have a variety of mix-ins and toppings like migas *(Scrambled Eggs with Crushed Tortilla Chips, page 36), Lebanese eggs* awarma *(Fried Eggs with Ground-Lamb Confit, page 43), or Turkish* menemen *(Scrambled Eggs with Tomato and Peppers, page 46). This recipe produces traditional scrambled eggs with a medium curd; see Variations for other consistencies.*

Cooking time: 5 minutes
Makes: 2 eggs

· 2 eggs
· Salt and freshly ground pepper
· ½ tablespoon (7 g) butter or olive oil

In a bowl, beat the eggs with a fork. Make sure the yolk and white are fully incorporated. Season with salt and pepper. In a medium nonstick skillet, heat the butter or olive oil over low heat. Pour the eggs into the pan and, with a wooden spoon, immediately begin to pull the edges toward the center until curds begin to form. Continue to stir until scrambled, about 40 seconds. The eggs should appear curdled and slightly glossy. Transfer to a plate and serve warm.

Variations
Small-curd scrambled eggs: Have the pan over low heat and stir the beaten eggs constantly, making sure to break up any curds that begin to form, for 30 seconds. Remove from the heat and continue to stir for 5 seconds. Repeat, returning on and off the heat, stirring constantly until the mixture thickens, 8 minutes. The consistency should appear silky and glossy.

Stirred eggs: Do not beat the egg. Heat the butter in the pan over medium heat, then crack in the egg and season with salt and pepper. With a wooden spoon immediately begin to stir up the whites, leaving the yolk intact. Pull the whites around the pan until they begin to form curds, about 20 seconds. Break the yolk in the pan and stir in with the whites. Cook for about 20 seconds before transferring to a plate.

THE DINER BREAKFAST

UNITED STATES

Diners, popular all-day eateries in the United States, are a mainstay for locals and travelers stopping in for bite. They are especially known for the American classic morning staples, such as a plate with "eggs any style" served alongside Diner Toast (page 142) and homemade bacon (page 322), as well as a choice of hash browns (shredded potato that is crisped on a griddle or cast-iron pan) or home fries (cubed potato crisped on a griddle or steamed in a pan with onions and sometimes bell peppers).

Preparation time: 20 minutes
Cooking time: 20 minutes
Serves: 2

· 4 slices (rashers) bacon, homemade (page 322) or store-bought
· 4 eggs: fried (page 14), poached (page 15), or scrambled (page 15)
· Hash Browns or Home Fries (recipes follow)
· Salt and freshly ground pepper
· Diner Toast (page 142), for serving
· Ketchup and/or hot sauce, for serving (optional)

Start with a cold cast-iron skillet or frying pan and place the bacon in flat. Slowly bring the heat to medium to let the fat render and result in crispy bacon. Cook on both sides until crispy, about 10 minutes. Transfer the bacon to paper towels to drain.

Pour off all but about 2 tablespoons of bacon fat from the pan and set over low heat. Use the bacon fat in lieu of butter or oil to cook desired egg preparation, unless poached or boiled.

Transfer the eggs to a plate along with the bacon and hash browns or home fries. Serve with ketchup and/or hot sauce and diner toast.

HASH BROWNS

Preparation time: 10 minutes
Cooking time: 10 minutes
Serves: 2

· ½ lb (115 g) russet (baking) potatoes (about 1 medium), peeled
· 2 tablespoons olive oil
· 1 tablespoon (15 g) unsalted butter
· Salt and freshly ground pepper

Grate the potatoes using the large holes of a box grater. Soak in a bowl of water to remove extra starch, tossing the mixture for about 30 seconds. Drain and transfer the shredded potatoes to a tea towel and wring out water from the potatoes. Transfer the potatoes to a bowl, season with salt and pepper, and toss with your hands.

In a cast-iron skillet or frying pan, heat the olive oil and butter over medium heat. When it begins to sizzle, add the potatoes. Spread in an even layer and allow the potatoes to cook until golden, 7 minutes. Flip with a spatula and cook until browned, 4 minutes. Transfer to paper towels to drain.

HOME FRIES

Preparation time: 15 minutes
Cooking time: 20 minutes
Serves: 2

· ½ lb (115 g) russet (baking) potatoes (about 1 medium), diced
· 1 tablespoon olive oil
· ½ small yellow onion, thinly sliced
· 1 tablespoon (15 g) unsalted butter
· Salt and freshly ground pepper

In a saucepan, combine the potatoes with water to cover. Bring to a boil over medium-high heat and cook until the potatoes are fork-tender, about 5 minutes. The potatoes shouldn't be too mushy in the center. Drain the potatoes and allow them to cool.

Meanwhile, in a cast-iron skillet or frying pan, heat oil over medium heat. Add the onion and cook until soft and translucent, about 5 minutes. Transfer the onion to a bowl.

Add the butter to the pan. Once the butter has melted, add the potatoes. Season with salt and pepper. Allow the potatoes to sear in the pan, resisting the initial temptation to stir, until the bottoms are browned, 5 minutes. Stir the potatoes in the pan and allow to cook for another 3 minutes. Return the onion to the pan and scrape the bottom of the pan, stirring gently to combine. Season with more salt and pepper to taste.

See picture on the next page.

The Diner Breakfast (page 16–17)

FRIED TORTILLAS WITH FRIED EGGS, HAM, AND PEAS

MEXICO

Primarily found in the city of Motul on the Yucatán Peninsula, huevos motuleños *are fried tortillas topped with various combinations of the following ingredients: beans, Cotija cheese, ham, peas,* salsa roja *(page 21), fried plantains, and a fried egg.*

Preparation time: 10 minutes
Cooking time: 25 minutes
Serves: 2

· 6 tablespoons vegetable oil
· 4 corn tortillas
· 1 small ripe plantain, sliced on a diagonal
· ¼ cup (40 g) diced ham
· ¼ cup (35 g) peas
· 4 eggs
· ½ cup (130) refried black beans, warmed
· ¼ cup (30 g) crumbled Cotija cheese
· ¼ cup (60 ml/2 fl oz) Salsa Verde or Salsa Roja (pages 20–21) (optional)
· Chopped fresh chives, for garnish

In a medium frying pan, heat 4 tablespoons of the oil over medium-high heat until very hot. Test if the oil is hot enough for frying by adding a piece of tortilla: if it sizzles, the oil is ready. Fry the tortillas, 1 or 2 at a time, until golden brown on both sides, flipping halfway through, about 1 minute. Transfer the tortillas to paper towels to drain.

Carefully add the plantain slices to the pan and cook until golden brown on both sides, 4 minutes. Transfer to paper towels to drain.

Pour most of the oil out of the pan and set over low heat. Add the ham and cook until lightly browned, about 4 minutes. Transfer to paper towels.

If using fresh peas, cook them in a medium saucepan of boiling salted water until tender, about 3 minutes.

In the frying pan, heat the remaining 2 tablespoons oil over medium heat, swirling to coat the pan. Crack in the eggs and season with salt. Cook for 1 minute and reduce the heat to low. Cook until the white is set and the edges are golden and crispy, about 2 minutes more. In the last 30 seconds of cooking, use a spoon to baste the egg white with the hot oil, helping to finish cooking the white. Transfer the fried eggs to a plate using a spatula.

Spread the refried black beans on the fried tortillas (about 2 tablespoons each) and divide between two plates. Top each tortilla with a fried egg, peas, ham, Cotija, salsa, if desired, and chives. Serve with fried plantains on the side.

CHILAQUILES
MEXICO

Chilaquiles are torn corn tortillas soaked in salsa verde *or* salsa roja *and topped with a combination of* crema, *chopped onion, shredded chicken, or a fried egg. Typically served with a* bolillo *(large hero roll), chilaquiles can also be stuffed inside the bread to create a* torta de chilaquiles. *These two salsas are used to top an array of Mexican and American Southwestern breakfast items such as:* Huevos Rancheros *(page 23),* enchiladas montadas *(Fried Tortillas with Fried Eggs and Salsa, page 23), and more.*

Preparation time: 10 minutes
Cooking time: 1 hour 20 minutes
Serves: 2

· 4 tablespoons vegetable oil
· 8 corn tortillas, quartered (see Note)
· 1 cup (240 ml/8 fl oz) Salsa Verde or Salsa Roja (recipes follow)
· 2 eggs
· Salt and freshly ground pepper
· 4 tablespoons crema (see Note)
· 2 tablespoons crumbled Cotija cheese
· ¼ small onion, diced
· ½ avocado, sliced (optional)
· Cilantro (coriander) leaves, for garnish

In a large frying pan, heat 2 tablespoons of the oil over medium-high heat. Working in two batches, add the tortilla quarters and fry until the chips are golden brown on both sides, about 1 minute per side. Transfer the chips to paper towels to drain.

In a saucepan over medium heat, add 1 tablespoon of the oil. Add the salsa and cook to warm through. Add the chips and stir to coat with the salsa.

Meanwhile, in a small frying pan, heat the remaining 1 tablespoon oil. Crack in the eggs and season with salt and pepper. Cook for 1 minute and reduce the heat to low. Cook until the white is set and the edges are golden and crispy, about 2 minutes more. In the last 30 seconds of cooking, use a spoon to baste the egg white with the hot oil, helping to finish cooking the white. Transfer the fried eggs to a plate using a spatula.

To serve, spoon the chips and salsa on 2 plates. Top each with a fried egg, crema, Cotija, onion, avocado (if using), and cilantro (coriander).

Notes: You could use 20 store-bought unsalted thick-cut tortilla chips in place of the tortillas. Just skip the first frying step and warm the chips in the salsa as directed. As a substitute for *crema*, combine 2 tablespoons sour cream and 2 tablespoons heavy (whipping) cream, ½ teaspoon of lime juice, and a pinch of salt.

SALSA VERDE

Preparation time: 15 minutes
Cooking time: 1 hour 10 minutes
Makes: 2½ cups (590 ml/20 fl oz)

· ½ lb (225 g) tomatillos, husked and rinsed
· ½ medium white onion, sliced into rings 1 inch (2.5 cm) thick, separated
· 1 clove garlic (unpeeled)
· 1 jalapeño chili, seeded
· 4 serrano chilies, seeded
· 1 poblano chili, seeded
· 5 large sprigs cilantro (coriander), chopped, stems included
· 1 tablespoon olive oil
· Juice of ½ lime
· Salt

Preheat the oven to 350°F (180°C/Gas Mark 4). Lightly oil a rimmed baking sheet.

Halve the tomatillos. Arrange the tomatillos (cut-side down), onion rings, garlic, and chilies on the baking sheet. Bake the vegetables until they're softened, 35 minutes.

Peel the garlic. Transfer the vegetables to a blender. Add the cilantro (coriander) and 2 cups (4475 ml/16 fl oz) water. Blend until combined and finely chopped.

In a medium saucepan, heat the olive oil over medium-low heat. Add the salsa and simmer until the sauce is thickened, 25 minutes.

Stir in the lime juice and season to taste with salt. Store the salsa in an airtight container in the refrigerator for up to 5 days.

SALSA ROJA

Preparation time: 10 minutes
Cooking time: 1 hour
Makes: 2 cups (495 ml/16 fl oz)

· ½ small white onion, cut in half
· 2 cloves garlic (peeled)
· 3 Roma (plum) tomatoes, quartered
· 1 ancho chili, seeded
· 1 jalepeño chili, seeded
· ½ teaspoon dried oregano
· 5 large sprigs cilantro (coriander), chopped, stems included
· 2 tablespoons lime juice
· 1 tablespoon olive oil
· 1 tablespoon plus 2 teaspoons brown sugar
· Salt

In a dry frying pan, cook the onion, garlic, ancho chili, jalapeño, and tomatoes over medium heat until browned and aromatic, about 5 minutes.

In a saucepan over medium-high heat add the onion/chili/tomato mixture, oregano, and 3 cups (710 ml/24 fl oz) water. Stir and bring to a boil. Remove the pan from the heat and cover, allowing the chilies to soak until softened, about 10 minutes. Reserving the soaking liquid, drain the vegetables and transfer to a blender. Add 2 cups (495 ml/16 fl oz) of the reserved soaking liquid. Add the lime juice and cilantro (coriander) and blend until smooth.

Wipe out the saucepan and heat the olive oil over medium-low heat. Add the sauce, bring to a simmer, and cook until the sauce is thickened, 25 minutes. Stir in the brown sugar and season to taste with salt. Store the sauce in an airtight container and keep in the refrigerator for up to 5 days.

See picture on the next page.

Chilaquiles (page 20–21)

HUEVOS RANCHEROS

MEXICO

A common breakfast in the United States as well as in Mexico, huevos rancheros is a lightly fried tortilla topped with salsa verde, salsa roja, or half of each (called divorciados), and a fried egg.

Preparation time: 5 minutes
Cooking time: 1 hour 20 minutes
Serves: 1

· 2 tablespoons vegetable oil
· 2 corn tortillas
· 2 eggs
· Salt
· Cilantro (coriander) leaves, for garnish
· Crumbled queso fresco or Cotija cheese (optional)
· ¼ cup (60 ml/2 fl oz) Salsa Verde, Salsa Roja (pages 20–21), or both

In a saucepan, warm the salsa over medium heat. (If making *divorciados*, warm the salsas in separate pans.)

In a frying pan, heat the oil over medium-high heat. Test if the oil is ready to fry by adding a small piece of tortilla: if it sizzles, the oil is ready. Fry the tortillas until golden brown on both sides, flipping halfway through, about 1 minute. Transfer to paper towels to drain.

Reduce the heat to low and crack the eggs into the pan. Season with salt and pepper. Cook for 1 minute and reduce the heat to low. Cook until the white is set and the edges are golden and crispy, about 2 minutes more. In the last 30 seconds of cooking, use a spoon to baste the egg white with the hot oil, helping to finish cooking the white. Transfer the fried eggs to a plate using a spatula.

To serve, top each tortilla with an egg and spoon the salsa (or both salsas) around each yolk to create a nest. Season with salt and sprinkle with cilantro (coriander) leaves and crumbled cheese.

FRIED TORTILLAS WITH FRIED EGGS AND SALSA

UNITED STATES

Enchiladas montadas is a morning meal in New Mexico. A stack of crispy corn tortillas is topped with salsa verde and/or salsa roja and fried eggs. Make it "Christmas," also known as "divorciados" style, by using half salsa verde, half salsa roja equally down the plate.

Preparation time: 10 minutes
Cooking time: 1 hour 20 minutes
Serves: 1

· 4 tablespoons vegetable oil
· 3 corn tortillas
· ½ cup (125 g) Salsa Verde (page 20) or Salsa Roja (page 21)
· ¼ cup (30 g) shredded queso fresco
· ¼ small yellow onion, chopped
· ½ green Hatch chili, chopped (optional)
· 1 Fried Egg (page 14)
· 1 tablespoon chopped cilantro (coriander)

In a small frying pan, heat the oil over medium-high heat. Test if the oil is ready by adding a small piece of tortilla: if it sizzles, the oil is ready. Fry the tortillas until golden brown, flipping halfway through, about 1 minute. Transfer the tortillas to paper towels to drain.

In a saucepan, warm the salsa over medium heat. (If making *divorciados*, warm the salsas in separate pans.)

Heat the broiler (grill) to low.

Dollop about 2 tablespoons of the salsa into a small ovenproof baking dish or plate. In a single stack, layer in 1 tortilla, top with 2 tablespoons salsa, a sprinkling of cheese, half the onion, and half the chili (if using). Repeat to make the second layer. Add the final tortilla and top with the remaining salsa and cheese. Place the enchilada under the broiler until the cheese is melted, taking care to not let it burn.

Serve the enchilada topped with a fried egg and cilantro (coriander).

EGGS

EGGS WITH MASHED PLANTAINS, FRIED SALAMI, AND FRIED CHEESE
DOMINICAN REPUBLIC

Mangú (mashed plantains) is a staple dish in Dominican culture. It is enjoyed throughout the day but in the morning, mangú is topped with pickled onions and served alongside Los Tres Golpes *("The Three Hits"): a fried egg, fried salami, and* queso frito *(fried cheese).*

Preparation time: 10 minutes, plus 2 hours pickling time
Cooking time: 30 minutes
Serves: 2

For the pickled red onion:
· ½ cup (120 ml/4 fl oz) white vinegar
· ¼ teaspoon fine sea salt
· ½ red onion
· 1 clove garlic, peeled
· 4 black peppercorns

For the mangú:
· 2 green plantains, peeled, quartered and sliced lengthwise
· Salt
· 2 teaspoons (10 g) unsalted butter, at room temperature

For the queso frito:
· ½ cup (120 ml/4 fl oz) vegetable oil, for frying
· 4 slices queso de freir (cheese for frying)
· 4 tablespoons all-purpose (plain) flour or cornstarch (cornflour)

For the salami:
· 4 slices Dominican salami, ¼ inch (6 mm) thick
· 2 Fried Eggs (page 14)

Make the pickled red onions:
In a saucepan, combine the vinegar, 4 tablespoons water, and salt and heat over medium heat, stirring until the salt is dissolved. Use a mandoline or sharp knife to thinly slice the onion into half-moon slivers. Put the onion slices and garlic clove in a glass jar and top with the vinegar solution. Add peppercorns to the jar and let cool before sealing with a lid and letting the mixture sit for at least 2 hours before using. Pickled onions can keep in the refrigerator for up to 2 weeks.

Make the *mangú*:
In a medium saucepan, cover the plantains with 1 inch (2.5 cm) water. Add salt to taste and bring to a boil over medium-high heat. Reduce the heat to low, cover, and cook until the plantains are tender, 20 minutes.
 Reserving the cooking liquid, use a slotted spoon to transfer the plantains to a bowl. With a fork or potato masher, mash the plantains with the butter, salt to taste, and a few tablespoons of the cooking liquid. Add more water as needed until smooth.

Make the *queso frito*:
In a medium frying pan, heat the oil over medium-high heat. Test if it is ready for frying by adding a small piece of cheese. If it sizzles, the oil is ready. Spread the flour or cornstarch (cornflour) in a shallow bowl. Lightly dredge the cheese slices in the flour or cornstarch, allowing the excess to fall back into the bowl. Carefully lower the cheese into the hot oil and fry until golden brown on both sides, flipping once, about 2 minutes. Transfer to paper towels to drain.

Make the salami:
Make 1 small cut, about ½ inch (1.25 cm) deep, on each of the salami rounds to prevent them from curling up when fried.
 Heat a small frying pan over medium-high heat. Add the salami and cook until browned and crispy on both sides, about 6 minutes.
 Serve *mangú* topped with pickled red onions alongside *queso frito*, salami, and fried eggs.

Eggs with Mashed Plantains, Fried Salami, and Fried Cheese

ISRAELI BREAKFAST PLATE
ISRAEL

An Israeli breakfast table can be expanded and contracted with ease to fit your morning mood. Labneh (page 74), a fresh cheese made from straining yogurt, is served alongside olives, eggs, smoked salmon or Lox (page 351), Middle Eastern chopped salad (below), and spicy schug (a staple condiment made from fresh herbs and chilies, below). Challah (page 234) is used to swipe up the last bits of labneh and egg yolk, and it is all washed down with freshly squeezed orange or pomegranate juice (pages 432 and 434).

Preparation time: 40 minutes
Cooking time: 5 minutes
Serves: 2

· 4 Fried Eggs (page 14)
· 2 tablespoons Schug (recipe follows)
· ½ cup (115 g) labneh, store-bought or homemade (page 74)
· 1 cup (135 g) Middle Eastern Chopped Salad (recipe follows)
· 4 tablespoons olives
· 4 slices smoked salmon or lox, store-bought or homemade (page 351) (optional)
· 2 slices challah, store-bought or homemade (page 234)

Serve the fried eggs with *schug*, labneh, Middle Eastern chopped salad, olives, smoked salmon or lox (if using), and challah.

Variation
Israeli Breakfast Plate with Shakshuka: Omit the fried eggs and prepare the eggs in *shakshuka* (page 66).

SCHUG

Preparation time: 15 minutes
Serves: 2

· 1 jalapeño chili, seeded
· 1 poblano chili, seeded
· ½ cup (10 g) cilantro (coriander), coarsely chopped
· ½ cup (10 g) parsley, coarsely chopped
· 2 cloves garlic, mashed
· ½ teaspoon ground cardamom (or seeds from 2 cardamom pods)
· Salt and freshly ground pepper
· 3 tablespoons olive oil

In a food processor, combine the jalapeño, poblano, cilantro (coriander), parsley, garlic, cardamom, and salt and pepper to taste. Pulse the mixture until chopped, then add the olive oil gradually as you pulse to emulsify the mixture. Pulse until the mixture is combined and completely smooth. Serve with everything.

MIDDLE EASTERN CHOPPED SALAD

Preparation time: 15 minutes
Serves: 2

· 1 medium tomato, diced
· 2 mini cucumbers, diced
· ¼ red onion, finely diced
· 2 tablespoons finely chopped parsley
· 2 tablespoons lemon juice
· 3 tablespoons olive oil
· Salt and freshly ground pepper

In a bowl, combine the tomato, cucumbers, onion, and parsley. Toss with the lemon juice and olive oil. Season with salt and pepper to taste.

Israeli Breakfast Plate

FULL ENGLISH
UNITED KINGDOM

Breakfast in the UK and Ireland is an example of breakfast at its most hearty. Nicknamed a "Full" English, Scottish, Welsh, or Irish, or a "Fry Up," this is a morning meal with many components. The combinations vary depending on the country and region, but are mostly assembled based on personal preference. Here are the components for a Full English, including: broiled tomatoes and mushrooms, beans, fried, buttered, or toasted bread, bacon, chipolatas (thin pork sausage), and/or black pudding (blood sausage), and eggs, usually fried.

Preparation time: 15 minutes
Cooking time: 30 minutes
Serves: 1

For the broiled tomato:
· ½ Roma (plum) tomato
· Salt and freshly ground pepper
· Olive oil, for drizzling

For the broiled mushrooms (optional):
· 4 button mushrooms or 1 medium portobello, stemmed and left whole
· ½ tablespoon (7 g) unsalted butter, melted
· Salt and freshly ground pepper

For serving:
· 1 slice Fried Bread (page 147)
· 2 tablespoons canned baked beans in tomato sauce
· 2 slices (rashers) back bacon or Canadian Bacon (page 323)
· Chipolatas or black pudding
· 1 Fried Egg (page 14)

Make the broiled tomato:
Position a rack in the center of the oven and preheat the broiler (grill) to high. In a baking dish, place the tomato cut-side up and season with salt and pepper. Drizzle with olive oil. Broil (grill) until the tomato has released its juices and begins to brown, 5 minutes. Serve warm.

Make the broiled mushroom(s), if serving:
Preheat the broiler (grill) to high. Toss the mushroom(s) with the melted butter and season with salt and pepper. Distribute on a lined baking sheet. Broil (grill) until lightly browned and soft, 5 minutes.

Make the bacon:
Start with a cold cast-iron skillet or frying pan and place the bacon in flat. Slowly bring the heat to medium to let the fat render and result in crispy bacon. Cook on both sides until browned, about 10 minutes.

Make the chipolatas or black pudding:
Place the chipolatas or black pudding in a cast-iron skillet or frying pan over medium heat. Cook until golden, about 3 minutes on each side.

To serve:
Top the fried bread with the beans. On a large plate, arrange the fried bread with beans, broiled tomato, broiled mushroom(s), bacon, sausage and/or black pudding, and fried egg.

See image on page 30

Variations

Scottish Fry Up/Full Scottish: Serve the fried egg with the broiled tomato and broiled mushrooms, baked beans, 1 slice Lorne Sausage (page 327), 2 Tattie Scones (page 201), and an oatcake.

Welsh Fry Up/Full Welsh: Serve the fried egg with the broiled tomato, broiled mushrooms, baked beans, 2 slices (rashers) streaky bacon, 2 sausage links, and Laverbread and Cockles (page 353).

Ulster Fry (Northern Ireland Breakfast): Serve the fried egg with the broiled tomato, broiled mushrooms, baked beans, 2 slices (rashers) back bacon, 2 sausage links, Potato Farl (page 201), and 1 slice brown bread.

Irish Fry Up: Serve the fried egg with the broiled tomato, broiled mushrooms, baked beans, 2 slices (rashers) back bacon, 2 slices white and/or black pudding, 2 Grated Potato Pancakes (page 120), and 1 slice brown bread or soda bread.

BREAKFAST ROLL

As an alternative to a Fry Up plate, the classic elements (except beans) can be stacked into a sandwich for a more portable option. One or more fillings such as a fried egg, tattie scone, lorne sausage, bacon, white or black pudding, mushrooms, tomatoes, and ketchup or brown sauce can be added. Though this recipe variation is for a Scottish Breakfast Roll, Irish comedian Pat Shortt created a song called "Jumbo Breakfast Roll," dedicated to the sandwich.

Preparation time: 10 minutes
Cooking time: 20 minutes
Serves: 1

· 1 bread roll or Scottish Morning Roll (page 213)
· ½ tablespoon (7 g) unsalted butter, at room temperature
· 1 slice Lorne Sausage (page 327), sliced and pan-fried
· 1 Tattie Scone (page 201)
· 1 Fried Egg (page 14)
· Brown sauce or ketchup, to serve (optional)

Spread the roll with the butter. Layer the bottom half of the roll with the sausage, a Tattie Scone, and a fried egg. Spread brown sauce or ketchup on the top of the roll (if using). Top the egg with the other half of the roll and serve warm.

Full English (page 28–29)

EGG-IN-A-HOLE
UNITED STATES

Also known as egg in the middle, egg in a basket, and many other endearing nicknames, this comfort food is a slice of toast with a round hole cut out of the center, fried in a pan with an egg perfectly nestled inside. Enjoy the cutout spread with butter or cream cheese as a snack while cooking.

Preparation time: 5 minutes
Cooking time: 5 minutes
Serves: 1

· ½ tablespoon (7 g) butter, plus more for serving
· 1 slices white or whole wheat (wholemeal) bread
· 1 egg
· Salt and freshly ground pepper

In a medium frying pan, melt the butter over medium heat, swirling to coat evenly. Using a small round cookie cutter or the rim of a wineglass, about 2 ½ inches (6.5 cm) in diameter, cut out a hole in the center of bread. Place the bread slice in the frying pan. Crack an egg into the hole and season with salt and pepper. Turn the heat to low and allow the egg white to set, about 2 minutes. Using a spatula, carefully flip the bread to cook on the other side for 1 minute. Transfer to a plate and enjoy.

NIGERIAN FRIED EGGS
NIGERIA

Morning street vendors at mai shai *stalls serve tea and breakfast dishes like this one, along with Instant Noodles (page 281). These fried eggs are enjoyed with sliced bread, white rice, fried or boiled potatoes, and yams or plantains.*

Preparation time: 10 minutes
Cooking time: 15 minutes
Serves: 2

· 1 tablespoon olive oil
· 1 small onion, chopped
· 2 small tomatoes, chopped
· ⅛ teaspoon onion powder
· ⅛ teaspoon garlic powder
· ¼ teaspoon ground ginger
· Salt and freshly ground pepper
· 4 eggs

In a medium frying pan, heat the oil over medium heat. Stir in the onion and cook until soft and translucent, about 5 minutes. Stir in the tomatoes and cook, stirring frequently, until the liquid evaporates, about 7 minutes.

Stir in the onion powder, garlic powder, ground ginger, and salt and pepper to taste. In a small bowl, beat the eggs together with a fork. Add to the pan and allow them to set for at least 30 seconds. When the eggs are just set, pull the edges in toward the center until curds begin to form. Continue to stir until the eggs have set and are scrambled, about 1 minute. Serve warm.

LOX, EGGS, AND ONIONS
UNITED STATES

Preparation time: 10 minutes
Cooking time: 35 minutes
Serves: 2

· 1 tablespoon (15 g) butter, plus more if needed
· 1 small onion, chopped
· 4 slices Nova lox, cut into small pieces
· 4 eggs
· Salt and freshly ground pepper
· 4 slices American cheese
· 2 bagels, toasted (see Everything Bagel, page 190)
· ½ tablespoon butter, for serving
· 1 tablespoon cream cheese (page 75), for serving

Lox, eggs, and onions, known as LEO, is a common breakfast dish in the American Northeast. The eggs are gently scrambled over low heat with lox (page 351) and caramelized onions. In the Pacific Northwest, you might find baked or smoked salmon instead of lox.

In a frying pan, melt the butter over low heat, swirling around the pan to evenly coat. Add the onion and cook, stirring with a wooden spoon, until caramelized, about 20 minutes.

In a small bowl, beat the eggs together with a fork. Season the eggs with salt and pepper. Distribute the cut pieces of lox evenly in the pan. Pour in the egg and allow it to set for a few seconds. With a wooden spoon, pull the edges of the eggs in toward the center of the pan until the eggs begin to curd, about 30 seconds. Continue to stir until the eggs have just set, but still have a glossy finish about 1 minute. Blanket the eggs with slices of American cheese and cover the pan until the cheese has melted, about 1 minute. Serve with a toasted bagel spread with butter or cream cheese.

FRIED MATZO
UNITED STATES

Preparation time: 5 minutes
Cooking time: 5 minutes
Serves: 1

· 1 sheet matzo
· 2 eggs
· Salt
· 2 tablespoons (30 g) unsalted butter
· Cinnamon sugar: ½ teaspoon sugar plus ¼ teaspoon ground cinnamon
· Applesauce and/or sour cream, for serving

Matzo Brei is a dish enjoyed during the spring Jewish holiday of Passover, when unleavened bread, or matzo, is typically in the pantry. Matzo, also spelled matzah, is dipped in egg, fried until golden, and seasoned with salt and served with sour cream and/or applesauce as a savory option or topped with cinnamon sugar for a sweet variation.

Break the matzo into pieces and put in a bowl. Rinse the pieces under cold tap water and soak for 10 seconds until soft. Meanwhile, in a medium bowl, use a fork to beat together the eggs and ¼ teaspoon salt. Drain the matzo and add to the bowl with the beaten eggs.

In a small frying pan, melt the butter over medium heat, swirling around the pan to coat evenly. Pour the egg and matzo mixture into the pan and stir constantly until the eggs are set, about 2 minutes.

Serve warm topped with either salt or cinnamon sugar and with applesauce and/or sour cream on the side.

HOPPEL POPPEL

UNITED STATES

A Midwestern dish featuring a mountain of scrambled eggs, potatoes, veggies, and available protein: typically, leftover ham, salami, or sausage.

Preparation time: 10 minutes
Cooking time: 30 minutes
Serves: 2

· 1 Yukon Gold potato, peeled and cubed
· 2 tablespoons (30 g) unsalted butter, plus more if needed
· ½ medium shallot, diced
· ½ small red bell pepper, diced
· ¾ cup (125 g) torn pieces of salami, ham, or leftover meat
· 4 eggs
· 1 teaspoon minced fresh thyme
· Salt and freshly ground pepper
· ¾ cup (85 g) grated aged Wisconsin cheddar

In a medium saucepan, combine the potato with water to cover and bring to a boil over medium-high heat. Reduce to a simmer and cook until tender, about 10 minutes. Drain the potato.

In a cast-iron skillet, melt 1 tablespoon of butter over medium-high heat. Add the potato and cook until the cubes begin to brown, about 10 minutes. Add the remaining 1 tablespoon butter to the pan. Stir in the shallot, bell pepper, and meat. Cook, stirring occasionally, until the shallot and bell pepper are softened, about 7 minutes.

Meanwhile, in a small bowl, use a fork to beat together the eggs and thyme. Season with salt and black pepper.

Add more butter to the pan if it seems dry. Reduce the heat to low and pour the beaten eggs into the pan. Allow the eggs to set over the vegetables, pulling in from the edges toward the center of the pan as curds begin to form, about 30 seconds. Sprinkle the cheddar over the setting eggs and stir occasionally until the eggs are just set and the cheese is melted, about 2 minutes more. Season with salt and pepper.

Serve with toast.

HANGTOWN FRY
UNITED STATES

The American Pacific Northwest is home to this fried-oyster omelet studded with crispy bacon. This dish became popular during the California Gold Rush in the 1840's as a way for successful miners to show off their wealth. The city was then called Hangtown, later renamed Placerville.

Preparation time: 15 minutes
Cooking time: 20 minutes
Serves: 2

· 4 tablespoons all-purpose (plain) flour
· 4 tablespoons cornmeal
· ¼ teaspoon cayenne pepper
· Salt and freshly ground pepper
· 8 medium to large oysters, shucked
· 2 slices (rashers) bacon (streaky)
· 1 tablespoons (30 g) unsalted butter
· 6 eggs
· Sliced fresh chives, for garnish
· Hot sauce, for serving

In a shallow bowl, whisk together the flour, cornmeal, and cayenne and season with salt and black pepper. Dredge both sides of the oysters in the mixture until nicely coated and then transfer to a plate.

Start with a cold cast-iron skillet or frying pan and place the bacon in flat. Slowly bring the heat to medium to let the fat render and result in crispy bacon. Cook on both sides until crispy, about 10 minutes. Transfer the bacon to paper towels to drain.

Pour most of the bacon fat out of the frying pan, leaving some behind. Add the butter to the pan and heat over medium-high heat. Add the oysters and fry, flipping once, until browned and crisp, about 2 minutes per side.

Meanwhile, in a bowl, beat the eggs with a fork. Make sure the yolk and white are fully incorporated. Season with salt and pepper. Reduce the heat to low and pour the eggs into the pan over the oysters. Crumble the bacon into the pan. With a wooden spoon, pull the eggs in toward the center of the pan until they form small curds, 30 seconds. Swirl the runny eggs around the pan to fill evenly. Cover and let cook until the omelet is just set, about 2 minutes. Use a spatula to slide onto a plate.

Garnish with fresh chives and serve with hot sauce.

SPAM AND EGGS
UNITED STATES

This Hawaiian breakfast features cubed Spam (a canned pork product popularized during World War II) mixed with eggs and served with rice or put in a sandwich. Spam can also be sliced, grilled, and served on the side with rice and eggs.

Preparation time: 5 minutes
Cooking time: 10 minutes
Serves: 2

· 4 eggs
· Salt and freshly ground pepper
· 1 tablespoon (15 g) butter
· ½ can (170 g) Spam, diced

In a frying pan, melt the butter over medium heat, swirling it around the pan to coat. Add the Spam and cook until slightly browned, stirring occasionally, about 3 minutes.

In a small bowl, beat the eggs with a fork. Make sure the yolk and white are fully incorporated. Season with salt and pepper. Reduce the heat to low and pour the eggs into the pan over the Spam. With a wooden spoon, immediately begin to pull the edges toward the center until curds begin to form, about 30 seconds. Continue to scramble, stirring constantly, until eggs are just set, about 2 minutes.

SHREDDED DRIED BEEF WITH EGGS
MEXICO / UNITED STATES

Popular in the American Southwest and Northern Mexico, machaca *or* carne seca *is shredded dried beef often mixed with eggs, and in New Mexico, wrapped into a burrito.*

Preparation time: 10 minutes
Cooking time: 30 minutes
Serves: 2

· 2 tablespoons olive oil
· ½ small yellow onion, diced
· ½ small jalapeño chili, diced
· ½ small tomato, roughly chopped
· Pinch of cayenne pepper
· Salt and freshly ground pepper
· 1 cup (170 g) carne seca (dried meat) or shredded brisket
· 4 eggs
· 4 tablespoons refried beans
· 4 tablespoons crumbled queso fresco

For serving:
· Salsa Verde or Salsa Roja (pages 20–21)
· Avocado slices
· 2 burrito-size (10-inch/25 cm) flour tortillas (optional)

In a frying pan, heat 1 tablespoon of oil over medium heat. Add the onion and sauté until soft and translucent, about 5 minutes. Stir in the jalapeño, tomato, cayenne, and salt and black pepper to taste. Cook, stirring, until the vegetables are beginning to soften, about 5 minutes. Stir in the shredded meat and cook until heated through, 2 minutes.

In a bowl, beat the eggs with a fork. Make sure the yolk and white are fully incorporated. Season with salt and pepper. Reduce the heat to low and pour the eggs into the pan over the meat and vegetables. With a wooden spoon, pull the edges of the egg in toward the center until the egg begins to form curds, about 30 seconds. Continue to stir constantly until the eggs are just set, about 2 minutes. Transfer to 2 plates.

Set the same frying pan over medium-high heat with 1 tablespoon oil and add the refried beans. Cook until warmed through, about 2 minutes.

With a spatula, slide half the beans onto each plate with the eggs and top the beans with crumbled cheese. Garnish the plate with fresh salsa and avocado slices. If desired, wrap everything in a flour tortilla to make a burrito.

SCRAMBLED EGGS WITH CRUSHED TORTILLA CHIPS
MEXICO / UNITED STATES

Migas, *meaning "crumbs," carries a diverse meaning in different countries. In Spain, leftover bread is torn and soaked in water, garlic, and paprika, then cooked in a skillet with chorizo. In Mexico,* migas *is fried corn tortillas, often leftover from dinner the night before. The tortilla chips are then broken into pieces and scrambled with eggs in a skillet. In the American Southwest, the Tex-Mex version is the same as Mexico but often includes the addition of chopped tomato, onion, chili, and cheese, and served in fresh corn tortillas as tacos.*

Preparation time: 10 minutes
Cooking time: 15 minutes
Serves: 1

· ½ tablespoon olive oil
· ½ cup (35 g) crushed tortilla chips
· ½ small onion, diced
· 1 tablespoon chopped cilantro (coriander)
· ½ small tomato, diced
· ½ jalapeño chili, diced (optional)
· 3 eggs
· Salt and freshly ground pepper
· 4 tablespoons crumbled Cotija cheese

For serving:
· Salsa verde (page 20)
· Chopped cilantro (coriander), for garnish
· Lime slices
· Avocado slices
· 3 corn tortillas, warmed (optional)

In a medium frying pan, heat the oil over medium-high heat. Add the tortilla chips, onion, cilantro (coriander), tomato, and jalapeño. Cook until the onion is soft and translucent, about 5 minutes.

In a bowl, beat the eggs with a fork. Make sure the yolk and white are fully incorporated. Season with salt and pepper. Reduce the heat to low and pour the eggs into the pan over the tortilla-chip mixture. With a wooden spoon, pull the edges of the egg in toward the center until the egg begins to form curds, 30 seconds. Continue to stir until the eggs are just set, about 2 minutes. Sprinkle with the cheese.

Transfer the egg mixture to a plate and top with salsa verde and cilantro (coriander), with sliced lime and avocado on the side. To make *migas* tacos, serve in warmed tortillas.

Scrambled Eggs with Crushed Tortilla Chips

CHAYA EGGS
BELIZE

Chaya *is a Mayan leafy green superfood high in protein, calcium, iron, and vitamin A, served mixed with scrambled eggs and with Fry Jacks (page 296) on the side. Raw leaves have a high content of toxic hydrocyanic acid, which requires them to be precooked.*

Preparation time: 10 minutes
Cooking time: 30 minutes
Serves: 2

· 4 cups (300 g) chaya leaves (about 2 large leaves), fresh Swiss chard, or baby spinach, coarsely chopped
· 1 tablespoon coconut oil or olive oil
· ½ medium onion, diced
· 1 clove garlic, minced
· 6 eggs
· Salt and freshly ground pepper
· Hot sauce, for serving
· Fry Jacks (page 296), for serving

If using *chaya* leaves, precook them: Combine in a pot with cold water to cover, bring to a simmer over medium-high heat, and cook, 20 minutes. Drain and chop. This step is important as chaya leaves carry a toxic hydrocyanic acid that should not be consumed raw.

In a frying pan, heat the oil over medium heat. Mix in the blanched *chaya*, chard, or spinach leaves, onion, and garlic. Cook, stirring, until the onion is soft and translucent, about 5 minutes.

In a medium bowl, use a fork to beat the eggs and season with salt and pepper. Pour into the pan over the onion mixture. Allow the eggs to set, about 30 seconds. With a wooden spoon, pull the edges of the eggs toward the center until curds begin to form. Cook until the eggs are just set, 2 minutes. Serve with hot sauce and Fry Jacks.

SCRAMBLED EGGS WITH TOMATOES AND SCALLIONS
COLOMBIA / VENEZUELA

Huevos pericos *is a simple scrambled egg dish literally translating to "parrot eggs" as the tomato, scallion, and eggs playfully mimic the colors of a parrot. Popular in Colombia and Venezuela,* huevos pericos *can be served with or stuffed into an arepa.*

Preparation time: 10 minutes
Cooking time: 15 minutes
Serves: 2

· 1 tablespoon (15 g) butter
· 2 medium tomatoes, diced
· 2 scallions (spring onions), diced
· 4 eggs
· Salt and freshly ground pepper
· 2 Arepas (page 314), for serving

In a medium frying pan, melt the butter over medium-high heat. Add the tomatoes and scallions and cook, stirring occasionally, until the tomatoes are soft, about 3 minutes.

In a small bowl, use a fork to beat the eggs, and season with salt and pepper. Reduce the heat to medium and pour the eggs over the vegetables. Allow the eggs to set, about 30 seconds. Using a wooden spoon, gently pull the eggs in toward the center of the pan, stirring occasionally, until lightly scrambled and just set, about 2 minutes. Serve with arepas.

EGGS AND PLANTAIN SCRAMBLE

HAITI

A plantain and egg scramble, or ze ak bannann, *is simply overripe plantains scrambled with eggs and a selection of other spices and veggies, often adjusted based on the household.*

Preparation time: 10 minutes
Cooking time: 35 minutes
Serves: 1

· ½ tablespoon (7 g) unsalted butter
· 1 very ripe plantain, peeled and sliced
· 1 tablespoon olive oil
· ¼ medium yellow onion, diced
· ¼ red bell pepper, chopped
· 1 jalapeño chili, chopped
· ½ teaspoon sweet paprika
· ¼ teaspoon chili powder
· ¼ teaspoon ground cumin
· Salt and freshly ground pepper
· 3 eggs

In a small frying pan, melt the butter over medium-high heat, swirling it around the pan to coat evenly. Add the sliced plantain and cook until the plantain is golden brown on all sides, 4 minutes. Transfer the plantains to a plate.

Meanwhile, in a medium frying pan, heat the olive oil over medium heat. Add the onion and cook until soft and translucent, about 5 minutes. Stir in the bell pepper and jalapeño and cook until softened, about 5 minutes. Add the paprika, chili powder, and ground cumin and season with salt, stirring until everything is thoroughly combined.

In a bowl, beat the eggs with a fork. Make sure the yolk and white are fully incorporated. Season with salt and pepper. Reduce the heat to low and pour the eggs into the pan. With a wooden spoon immediately begin to pull the edges toward the center until curds begin to form, 30 seconds. Continue to stir until scrambled, about 30 seconds more. The eggs should appear curdled and slightly glossy. Transfer to a plate and serve warm with plantains.

HOMINY AND EGGS

ECUADOR

Mote *is hominy, dried nixtamalized corn kernels, which here is sautéed with eggs, chives, and* achiote *(also called* annato, *used for color and a nutty, peppery flavor). This dish is best served with hot black coffee and slices of fresh cheese like* queso blanco *or mozzarella.*

Preparation time: 10 minutes
Cooking time: 15 minutes
Serves: 2

· 1 tablespoon olive oil
· ½ medium onion, diced
· 2 cloves garlic, minced
· ¼ teaspoon achiote paste
· ¼ teaspoon ground cumin
· Salt and freshly ground pepper
· 1 can (15 oz/425 g) mote (hominy), drained
· 4 eggs
· 4 tablespoons full-fat milk
· Cilantro (coriander) leaves, for garnish

In a frying pan, heat the oil over medium heat. Stir in the onion and cook until translucent, about 5 minutes. Stir in the garlic, achiote, and cumin, and season with salt and pepper. Stir in the hominy until everything is incorporated.

In a bowl, beat the eggs with a fork. Make sure the yolk and white are fully incorporated. Season with salt and pepper. Reduce the heat to low and pour the eggs into the pan over the hominy and onions. With a wooden spoon immediately begin to pull the edges toward the center until curds begin to form, 30 seconds. Continue to stir until scrambled, about 1 minute more. The eggs should appear curdled and slightly glossy. Serve warm topped with cilantro (coriander) leaves.

EGGS WITH CURED BEEF

EGYPT

Known as beid bel basterma, *this cured beef is heavily spiced with* chaimen *(cumin, smoky paprika, fenugreek, Turkish chili, and garlic). Typically purchased sliced thin,* basterma *can be enjoyed simply with bread (pita) or served with scrambled or fried eggs. Eggs with* basterma *is always served with pita, which is used as a vessel to scoop up the eggs, sans fork. The Armenian diaspora in the Middle East popularized* basterma *in Egypt, where it is now as common a breakfast as bacon and eggs in the United States.*

Preparation time: 5 minutes
Cooking time: 5 minutes
Serves: 2

· ½ tablespoon (7 g) ghee or butter
· 6 slices basterma or pastrami, torn to bits
· 6 eggs
· Salt and freshly ground pepper
· 2 pitas

In a frying pan, melt the butter over medium heat. Add the *bastermu* and cook, stirring occasionally and making sure not to burn the cured meat, until warmed, 1 minute.

In a bowl, beat the eggs with a fork. Make sure the yolk and white are fully incorporated. Season with salt and pepper. Reduce the heat to low and pour the eggs into the pan over the basterma. With a wooden spoon, immediately begin to pull the edges toward the center until curds begin to form, 30 seconds. Continue to stir until scrambled, about 1 minute more. The eggs should appear curdled and slightly glossy. Serve warm with pita.

FRIED EGG WITH CUMIN

MOROCCO

Moroccans take their olives very seriously. Different colored olives (red, green, and black) are harvested from the same trees but are preserved differently; they can be brine-cured, oil-cured, or dry-cured. Serve with oil-cured black olives.

Cooking time: 5 minutes
Serves: 1

· 1 tablespoon olive oil
· 2 eggs
· Salt
· ¼ teaspoon ground cumin
· Black olives, for serving

In a medium nonstick skillet, heat the olive oil over medium heat. Crack in the eggs and season with salt. Cook for 1 minute and reduce the heat to low. Cook until the white is set and the edges are golden and crispy, about 2 minutes more. In the last 30 seconds of cooking, use a spoon to baste the egg white with the hot oil, helping to finish cooking the white. Transfer the fried eggs to a plate using a spatula and sprinkle with the cumin. Serve with black olives.

FRIED EGG WITH LEMON

GREECE

Sunny-side up eggs drizzled with lemon juice is a typical late-morning breakfast in Crete.

Preparation time: 5 minutes
Cooking time: 5 minutes
Serves: 1

· 1 tablespoon olive oil
· 2 eggs
· 1 tablespoon lemon juice, or to taste
· Salt and freshly ground pepper

In a medium nonstick skillet, heat the olive oil over medium heat. Crack in the eggs and season with salt and pepper. Cook for 1 minute and reduce the heat to low. Cook until the white is set and the edges are golden and crispy, about 2 minutes more. In the last 30 seconds of cooking, use a spoon to baste the egg white with the hot oil, helping to finish cooking the white. Transfer the fried eggs to a plate using a spatula and drizzle with lemon juice.

EGGS WITH FRIED PLANTAINS AND REFRIED BEANS

EL SALVADOR

A tipico Salvadoreño *or "typical" break-fast in El Salvador: Scrambled eggs served with fried plantains, refried beans,* crema, queso fresco, *and tortillas.*

Preparation time: 15 minutes
Cooking time: 30 minutes
Serves: 1

· 4 tablespoons cooked black beans
· ½ cup (120 ml/4 fl oz) plus 2 tablespoons vegetable oil
· 1 very ripe plantain, peeled and quartered lengthwise
· ¼ small onion, diced
· ¼ green bell pepper, diced
· ½ small tomato, diced
· 2 eggs
· Salt and freshly ground pepper
· 4 tablespoons crema (see Note)
· 1 tablespoon queso fresco, crumbled
· 2 corn tortillas, warmed

In a small blender, purée the beans with 1 tablespoon of water until silky smooth. In a medium frying pan, heat 1 tablespoon of the oil over medium-high heat. Add the bean purée and cook to dry out and evaporate some excess water, about 5 minutes. Set aside.

In a separate medium frying pan, heat ½ cup (120 ml/4 fl oz) oil over medium-high heat. To test if the oil is ready for frying, carefully add a small piece of plantain. If it sizzles, the oil is ready. Using tongs, carefully lower the quartered plantain into the oil. Fry well until all sides are deeply golden brown, about 2 minutes. Transfer to paper towels to drain. Discard the oil.

Add the remaining 1 tablespoon of oil to the frying pan over medium heat. Add the onion and pepper and cook until soft and translucent, about 5 minutes. Add the tomato and cook until softened, 3 minutes.

In a bowl, beat the eggs with a fork. Make sure the yolk and white are fully incorporated. Season with salt and pepper. Reduce the heat to low and pour the eggs into the pan over the vegetables. With a wooden spoon, immediately begin to pull the edges toward the center until curds begin to form, 30 seconds. Continue to stir until scrambled, about 1 minute more. The eggs should appear curdled and slightly glossy. Serve warm fried plantains with the beans, cheese, *crema*, and tortillas on the side.

Note: As a substitute for *crema*, combine 2 tablespoons sour cream and 2 tablespoons heavy (whipping) cream, ½ teaspoon of lime juice, and a pinch of salt.

FRIED EGGS WITH GROUND LAMB CONFIT

LEBANON

Awarma, *a ground-lamb confit, is stored in jars for use throughout the year as a source of protein for mountain villagers in the winter. Now common across the country for anytime of the year, eggs with* awarma *is a scrambled-egg dish, typically cooked in a clay skillet (*fakhar*) with the lamb confit. The* awarma *features ground lamb cooked and preserved in the tail-fat of the* awassi *(fat-tailed sheep), a native breed to the Middle East.*

Preparation time: 10 minutes
Cooking time: 40 minutes
Serves: 1

· 2 tablespoons Awarma (recipe follows)
· 3 eggs
· Salt

In a nonstick frying pan, heat the *awarma* over medium heat. In a small bowl, use a fork to beat the eggs. Make sure the yolk and white are fully incorporated. Add the beaten eggs and season with salt to taste. Allow the eggs to set for about 30 seconds. With a wooden spoon, pull the edge of the eggs in toward the center until the egg begins to form curds. Continue to stir until the eggs are done, about 1 minute. Serve warm.

AWARMA

Preparation time: 5 minutes
Cooking time: 35 minutes
Makes: 1 ¼ pounds (680 g)

· ½ lb (225 g) lamb fat, preferably from the tail
· 1 lb (455 g) ground (minced) lamb meat, broken up
· 2 teaspoons fine sea salt
· 1 teaspoon ground allspice

In a pot, slowly melt the lamb fat over low heat. Add the ground lamb to the pot and season with 1½ teaspoons of the salt and the allspice. Cook, stirring frequently with a wooden spoon or spatula, until the meat is cooked through, about 30 minutes, stirring in the remaining ½ teaspoon salt halfway through. Store the *awarma* in sterilized jars in the refrigerator for 2 weeks.

EGGS WITH SPICED CLARIFIED BUTTER

ETHIOPIA

Called enqulal tibs *in Ethiopia, enqulal refers to a dish fried in a pan. Prepare the eggs scrambled in* niter kibbeh, *a spiced clarified butter, topped with berbere, an essential Ethiopian spice mixture consisting of paprika, cayenne pepper, fenugreek, coriander, cumin, cardamom, cinnamon, cloves, allspice, ginger, and turmeric. As here, the dish sometimes includes fresh green and red bell peppers and tomatoes.*

Preparation time: 15 minutes
Cooking time: 45 minutes
Serves: 2

· 1 tablespoon Spiced Clarified Butter (recipe follows) or ghee
· ½ medium onion, diced
· 4 tablespoons green or red bell peppers, chopped (optional)
· 4 tablespoons tomatoes, chopped (optional)
· 1 small jalapeño chili, chopped
· ½ teaspoon berbere
· Salt and freshly ground pepper
· 4 eggs

In a medium frying pan, melt the spiced clarified butter or ghee over medium heat. Add the onion and cook until soft and translucent, about 5 minutes. Add the bell peppers and tomatoes, if using, and cook until they begin to soften, about 5 minutes. Stir in the jalapeño, berbere, and salt and pepper to taste.

In a bowl, beat the eggs with a fork. Make sure the yolk and white are fully incorporated. Reduce the heat to low and pour the eggs into the pan over the vegetables. With a wooden spoon, immediately begin to pull the edges toward the center until curds begin to form, 30 seconds. Continue to stir until scrambled, about 1 minute. The eggs should appear curdled and slightly glossy. Serve warm.

SPICED CLARIFIED BUTTER (NITER KIBBEH)

Preparation time: 5 minutes
Cooking time: 30 minutes

· 4 tablespoons (60 g) unsalted butter
· 2 cloves garlic, chopped
· 1 tablespoon minced onion
· ¼-inch (6 mm) slice fresh ginger, peeled and chopped
· ¼ teaspoon fenugreek seeds
· ¼ teaspoon cardamom seeds
· 1 whole clove

In a small saucepan, melt the butter over low heat. Add the garlic, onion, ginger, fenugreek, cardamom, and clove and cook for 30 minutes, stirring occasionally. Strain the butter through a fine-mesh sieve and store in the refrigerator for up to 6 months.

Eggs with Spiced Clarified Butter

SCRAMBLED EGGS WITH TOMATO AND PEPPERS

TURKEY

Breakfast in Turkey typically consists of a sizable main dish like this menemen. In some regions this recipe is made without onions or shakshuka-style (see Israeli Shakshuka, page 66). On the side, you'll find an assortment of small plates such as clotted cream (Kaymak, page 78), white cheese (similar to feta), Mihalic or Kelle cheese (salty white cheese with holes), yellow cheese (kaşar peyniri), black and/or green olives (zeytin), butter, honey, jam, sliced tomatoes and/or cucumbers, sliced green peppers, dried apricots, cured meat, sumac for sprinkling, and chopped fresh parsley for garnish.

Preparation time: 10 minutes
Cooking time: 20 minutes
Serves: 2

· 2 tablespoons olive oil
· ½ medium yellow onion, diced
· 4 Bull's Horn peppers (long thin green peppers), cut into thin rings, or 1 green bell pepper, diced
· 4 medium tomatoes, finely chopped
· 1 teaspoon crushed chili flakes
· Salt and freshly ground pepper
· 4 eggs
· Finely chopped parsley, for garnish (optional)

In a medium frying pan, heat the oil over medium-high heat. Add the onion and cook until soft and translucent, about 5 minutes. Stir in the green pepper and tomatoes. Cook until the liquid from the tomatoes has reduced by half, about 10 minutes. Stir in the chili flakes and season with salt and pepper.

Crack the eggs into the pan, season with salt and pepper, and stir constantly to scramble with the vegetables. Cook until the eggs are scrambled and glossy, 2 minutes. Serve warm garnished with parsley, if desired.

FARMERS' MARKET OMELET

UNITED STATES

This is an omelet made with seasonal vegetables and herbs found at the local farmers' market. You can add a tablespoon of milk for a smoother, silkier texture.

Preparation time: 15 minutes
Cooking time: 10 minutes
Serves: 1

· 1 tablespoon olive oil
· ½ cup chopped squash or zucchini (courgette)
· ½ small red bell pepper or tomato, diced
· ½ small onion, diced
· 1 cup (45 g) chopped Swiss chard or kale
· 3 eggs
· 1 tablespoon full-fat milk (optional)
· Salt and freshly ground pepper
· ½ tablespoon (7 g) butter
· 1 tablespoon goat cheese

In a medium frying pan or omelet pan, heat the oil over medium heat. Add the squash or zucchini, bell pepper or tomato, onion, and Swiss chard or kale, and sauté until the onion is soft and translucent and the Swiss chard is wilted, about 7 minutes. Transfer to a bowl.

In a small bowl, beat the eggs and milk (if using) with a fork. Make sure the yolk and white are fully incorporated. Season with salt and pepper. Add the butter to the frying pan and melt over low heat. Pour in the egg mixture, letting the eggs set for about 30 seconds. With a wooden spoon, gently pull the edges of the eggs slightly toward the middle to form curds. Swirl the runny eggs around the pan to fill evenly. Cook until the eggs have set, about 1 minute. Spoon the cooked vegetables over half of the omelet and crumble the goat cheese on top. Tilt the pan to the side and flip the plain half of the omelet over the filling. Gently slide omelet onto a plate and serve warm.

SOUTHWESTERN OMELET

UNITED STATES

An omelet style popular in the Southwestern United States for its use of peppers, onions, Monterey Jack cheese, and salsa.

Preparation time: 10 minutes
Cooking time: 15 minutes
Serves: 1

· ½ tablespoon (7 g) butter
· ½ red bell pepper, chopped
· ¼ small yellow onion, diced
· 3 eggs
· 1 tablespoon full-fat milk (optional)
· Salt and freshly ground pepper
· ½ cup (55 g) shredded Monterey Jack cheese
· ½ cup (120 ml/4 fl oz) medium salsa

In a medium nonstick frying pan, melt the butter over medium heat, swirling it around the pan to coat evenly. Add the bell pepper and onion and cook until the onion is translucent and the pepper is soft, about 10 minutes.

In a small bowl, use a fork to beat the eggs and milk (if using) and season with salt and pepper. Spread the vegetables in an even layer in the pan and pour the eggs over. Allow the eggs to set, about 30 seconds. Using a wooden spoon, pull the edges slightly in toward the center and swirl the pan around so that the eggs fill the edges. Stir the eggs and swirl the pan until the eggs set, about 1 minute more. Sprinkle the cheese over the eggs. Tilt the pan and flip one half of the omelet over the other, letting the eggs in the center set slightly.

Slide the omelet onto a plate. Serve with salsa and season to taste with salt and pepper.

DATE OMELET

IRAN

Dates are an essential ingredient in Persian cooking. The dates provide an unexpected sweetness to a simple omelet and the addition of turmeric adds a bright color and an earthy note.

Preparation time: 5 minutes
Cooking time: 5 minutes
Serves: 1

· 3 eggs
· ¼ teaspoon ground turmeric
· Salt and freshly ground pepper
· ½ tablespoon (7 g) unsalted butter
· 2 Medjool dates, pitted and diced

In a small bowl, use a fork to beat the eggs and turmeric and season with salt and pepper.

In a medium nonstick frying pan, melt the butter over medium heat, swirling it around the pan to coat evenly. Add the dates and cook until lightly fried, 2 minutes. Reduce the heat to low and pour the eggs over the dates. Allow the eggs to set, about 30 seconds. Using a wooden spoon, pull the edges slightly in toward the center and swirl the pan around so that the eggs fill the pan. Stir the eggs and swirl the pan until the eggs set, about 1 minute more. Tilt the pan and flip one half of the omelet over the other, letting the eggs in the center set slightly.

Slide the omelet onto a plate and serve.

FRIED OMELET
THAILAND

Khai jiao is a Thai omelet that is deep fried in a wok, with excess oil soaked up by a bed of jasmine rice. This classic Thai comfort food has a pillowy appearance, aided by the addition of cornstarch, which gives the omelet a smooth texture and even surface coating of golden brown.

Preparation time: 5 minutes
Cooking time: 5 minutes
Serves: 1

· 3 eggs
· 2 teaspoons fish sauce
· ¾ teaspoon lime juice or distilled white vinegar
· 1 tablespoon cornstarch (cornflour)
· ¾ cup (175 ml/6 fl oz) vegetable oil
· Cooked jasmine rice, for serving
· Thai Sriracha sauce, for serving

In a bowl, use a fork to whisk the eggs with the fish sauce, lime juice, and cornstarch (cornflour) until frothy.

In a wok, heat the oil over medium-high heat. Test if the oil is ready to fry by adding a drop of egg. If it sizzles, the oil is ready. Pour the eggs into the oil and allow them to puff up and fry, about 20 seconds. Flip and fry on the other side, about 20 seconds.

Serve warm with jasmine rice and Thai Sriracha sauce.

ROLLED OMELET
JAPAN

Tamagoyaki involves cooking beaten eggs in thin paper layers, rolled into an omelet using a special rectangular tamagoyaki *pan (see Note). The omelet is sliced and served alongside a bowl of rice or Rice with Raw Egg (page 68), yakizakana (Grilled Fish, page 348), Miso Soup (page 260), and asazuke (Quick Pickled Vegetables, page 348).*

Preparation time: 5 minutes
Cooking time: 15 minutes
Serves: 2

· 4 eggs
· 1 tablespoon soy sauce
· 1½ tablespoon mirin
· 1 teaspoon sugar
· ½ teaspoon fine sea salt
· Vegetable oil, for the pan

In a bowl, whisk the eggs, soy sauce, mirin, sugar, and salt, taking care not to incorporate too much air into the eggs as you mix.

Set a lightly oiled *tamagoyaki* pan over medium heat, then pour in a thin layer of egg, using only a small amount of the egg mixture. Swirl it around the pan to coat the bottom. Cook the egg until it is just set but still a bit moist and glossy on top, about 30 seconds. Using chopsticks or a flat spatula, starting at the far end of the pan, roll the egg toward you by flipping it over a few times, then push it to the far end of the pan.

Lightly oil the pan again and pour in another small amount of the mixture, swirling it around the pan to coat, including under the roll. Once it is set but glossy on top, roll the egg mixture—including the first roll—toward you, layering the eggs. Push the egg roll to the back of the pan and continue to oil, cook, and roll the layers like this until all the egg mixture is used up. The omelet should come out like a rectangular log with slightly flat sides. Let cool and slice crosswise to serve.

Note: For a similar result, you can use a nonstick frying pan, but it will be difficult to achieve the intended firm, structured roll shape.

Rolled Omelet

EGGS AND SOLDIERS
UNITED KINGDOM

In this British breakfast staple, also called "dippy eggs and soldiers," soft-boiled eggs are served with long, narrow fingers of toasted and buttered bread (the "soldiers"), used to scoop and soak up the soft-boiled egg.

Preparation time: 5 minutes
Cooking time: 5 minutes
Serves: 1

· 1 Soft-Boiled Egg (page 14)
· 1 slice whole wheat (wholemeal) bread, toasted
· ½ tablespoon (7 g) unsalted or salted butter

Transfer the soft-boiled egg to an egg cup.

Spread the toast with butter and slice it into thin fingers or "soldiers." Use a spoon to delicately crack and peel off the top quarter of the egg shell to expose the runny yolk. Dip the bread into the egg to enjoy.

See image on page 170

POTATO AND EGG OMELET
SPAIN

This potato and egg omelet, a tortilla Española, *is fried in a pan and sliced like a cake. It is typically enjoyed at home or at a café counter before or during work as a quick break.*

Preparation time: 15 minutes
Cooking time: 35 minutes
Serves: 4

· 2 lb (910 g) Yukon Gold potatoes (about 4 medium)
· 1½ cups (240 g) diced yellow onion
· Salt
· ¾ cup (175 ml/6 fl oz) olive oil, plus more as needed
· 10 eggs

Peel the potatoes and slice them lengthwise, then thinly slice crosswise into half-circles about ¼ inch (6 mm) thick. Place them in a large bowl with the onion. Season with a generous pinch of salt and toss to combine.

In a 10-inch (25 cm) cast-iron skillet or nonstick frying pan, heat the oil over medium heat. Add the potato mixture to the oil and bring to a simmer, adjusting the heat as needed to maintain a gentle simmer, until the potatoes are tender, about 20 minutes. Remove the pan from the heat.

In a large bowl, beat the eggs and season generously with salt. Using a slotted spoon, transfer the potatoes and onion to the eggs and stir to combine.

Set the same pan with the leftover oil over medium heat. Pour in the egg/potato mixture. Cook the eggs, swirling the pan until they settle and begin to set, about 2 minutes. With a wooden spoon or spatula, press the edges of the egg into a thick cake-like shape. Cook until the eggs begin to firm, 4 minutes. Protecting your hands with an oven mitt or tea towel, place a large plate or a baking sheet over the pan and quickly and carefully invert the *tortilla* onto the plate. Add 1 tablespoon of oil to the pan if it's dry. Slide the egg carefully back into the pan and cook the other side until set, 5 minutes more.

Transfer to a plate and let cool slightly. Serve warm or at room temperature.

CRAB OMELET

UNITED STATES

Typical in the Northeast and Pacific Northwest, Dungeness crab (West Coast) and Blue Crab (East Coast) is a regional ingredient often folded into an omelet with cheese for breakfast.

Preparation time: 10 minutes
Cooking time: 15 minutes
Serves: 1

· ½ tablespoon (15 g) unsalted butter
· ½ cup (80 g) diced onion
· 3 eggs
· Salt and freshly ground pepper
· ½ cup (80 g) Dungeness or Blue Crab meat, picked over
· 2 tablespoons finely diced tomato
· 2 slices American cheese (optional)

In a medium frying pan, melt the butter over medium heat. Add the onion and cook, stirring occasionally, until soft and translucent, about 5 minutes.

In a small bowl, use a fork to beat the eggs. Season with salt and pepper. Pour in the egg mixture, letting the eggs set, 30 seconds. With a wooden spoon, gently pull the edges of the egg slightly toward the middle to form curds. Swirl the runny eggs around the pan to fill evenly. Cook for 1 minute more or until the eggs have just set but are still glossy. Spoon the crabmeat and tomatoes over half of the omelet. Top the crab with the cheese slices (if using). Tilt the pan and flip one half of the omelet over the filling with a heatproof spatula. Allow the cheese to melt slightly, 30 seconds.

Gently push the folded omelet out of the pan and onto your plate.

DENVER OMELET

UNITED STATES

Also known as a Western omelet, this classic diner dish is studded with bell peppers, diced ham, and cheese. It is believed to have been invented in sandwich form by Chinese cooks working on the transcontinental railroad, or as a way to mask the taste of spoiled eggs. When the railroad made its way to Denver, the bread was dropped, and the Western sandwich turned into a Denver omelet after the titular city.

Preparation time: 10 minutes
Cooking time: 30 minutes
Serves: 2

· ½ tablespoon (7 g) unsalted butter
· ½ medium white onion, diced
· ¼ red bell pepper, diced
· ¼ green bell pepper, diced
· 2 slices deli ham, diced
· Salt and freshly ground pepper
· 3 eggs
· ½ cup (60 g) grated cheddar cheese
· Hot sauce or ketchup, for serving (optional)

In a medium frying pan, melt the butter over medium heat. Add the onion and bell peppers and cook until the onions are soft and translucent, about 5 minutes. Add the ham and stir until slightly browned. Season with salt and pepper.

In a small bowl, use a fork to beat the eggs. Reduce the heat to low and pour the egg mixture over the vegetables. Allow the eggs to set for 30 seconds. With a wooden spoon, pull the edges of the eggs in toward the center slightly and then swirl the eggs around to fill the pan's sides. Allow the eggs to cook until almost set, about 2 minutes. Sprinkle with the cheddar. Tilting the pan, use a spatula to carefully fold the omelet over. Allow the cheese to melt slightly, 30 seconds. Transfer the omelet to a plate.

If desired, serve with hot sauce or ketchup.

CARROT CAKE

SINGAPORE

Chai tow kway *is an omelet made with Chinese turnip cake. In Singapore the dish is nicknamed "Carrot Cake" and can be made in white (plain) or black (with dark soy sauce) versions. The cake can be made at home, but is often available in Asian food markets. This dish was introduced to Singapore through the diaspora of Chinese people from the Chaoshan region. In Teochew (the dialect of Chaoshan),* chai tow *translates to radish or carrot and* Kway *to cake. When non-speaking visitors arrived to Singapore, "carrot" was a more recognizable translation so the name "Carrot Cake" stuck as a misnomer.*

Preparation time: 10 minutes
Cooking time: 20 minutes
Serves: 1

· 3 tablespoons oil or lard
· 9 oz (255 g) luo buo gao (Chinese turnip cake), store-bought or homemade (page 403), cut into 1-inch (2.5 cm) cubes
· 1 clove garlic, minced
· 2 teaspoons chye poh (preserved radish)
· 1 teaspoon chili paste (optional)
· ½ teaspoon fish sauce (optional)
· 2 eggs
· 1 scallion (spring onion), chopped

In a medium frying pan, head 2 tablespoons of the oil or lard over medium heat. Add the turnip cake and stir, breaking it up. Pan-fry the turnip cake until browned, about 3 minutes. Stir and continue to brown the cake, 3 more minutes.

Pushing the cake to one side of the pan, add the remaining 1 tablespoon oil or lard. Stir in the garlic and *chye poh* and cook until fragrant, about 4 minutes. Stir in the chili paste and fish sauce, if using.

In a small bowl, use a fork to beat the eggs. Reduce the heat to low and pour the eggs over the stir-fried turnip cake. Allow the eggs to set, about 2 minutes. Flip the omelet and cook until set, about 1 minute. (It is okay if it falls apart a bit.)

Serve warm, garnished with scallion (spring onion).

Black Carrot Cake: After adding the beaten eggs, allow them to set slightly, then pull the sides in toward the center to scramble them. Stir in 1½ tablespoons Thick/Dark Soy Sauce (Cheong Chan Thick Caramel Sauce) and cook until the eggs and turnip cake are coated evenly.

MIDDLE EASTERN OMELET

EGYPT

Eggah *is a Middle Eastern omelet also known as an Arab omelet, or* ijjeh *in Palestine. Flour is added to the omelet for a fluffy appearance, smooth texture, and even browning.*

Preparation time: 10 minutes
Cooking time: 5 minutes
Serves: 1

· 2 eggs
· 2 teaspoons all-purpose flour
· 3 tablespoons finely chopped parsley
· ½ medium yellow onion, chopped
· Salt and freshly ground pepper
· 1 tablespoon olive oil

In a bowl, whisk the eggs with the flour until smooth. Add the parsley and onion, season with salt and pepper, and whisk until combined.

In a small nonstick frying pan, heat the oil over medium heat. Pour in the egg and swirl the pan to evenly distribute it. Allow the underside of the *eggah* to cook until golden, about 2 minutes. With a wide spatula, flip the *eggah* and cook the other side until golden, about 1 minute more. Serve warm.

Carrot Cake

PORK AND EGGPLANT OMELET

PHILIPPINES

Tortang Talong with Giniling is a ground-pork omelet pan-fried on a whole smashed eggplant (aubergine) and served with a sweet, spiced banana ketchup.

Preparation time: 20 minutes
Cooking time: 40 minutes
Serves: 2

· 2 small Asian eggplants (aubergines)
· 4 eggs
· 1 tablespoon coconut milk
· 3 tablespoons olive oil
· ¼ medium yellow onion, diced
· Salt and freshly ground pepper
· ½ medium tomato, diced
· ¼ small green bell pepper, diced
· 2 cloves garlic, minced
· ¼ lb (115 g) ground (minced) pork
· Banana Ketchup (recipe follows), for serving

Char the eggplants (aubergines) directly over the low flame of a stove burner, turning carefully with tongs, until all sides are blackened and the eggplants are very soft, 10 minutes. Transfer to a resealable plastic bag, seal shut, and let steam for 5 minutes. When cool enough to touch, peel the eggplant and flatten the flesh with a fork or your hand. Repeat with the second eggplant.

Whisk an egg in each of two small bowls, with ½ tablespoon of coconut milk in each.

In a frying pan or wok, heat 1 tablespoon of the oil over medium heat. Add the onion, season with salt and pepper, and cook, stirring, until the onion is soft and translucent, about 5 minutes. Stir in the tomato, bell pepper, and garlic and cook until aromatic, about 2 minutes. Stir in the pork and cook, stirring occasionally, until cooked through and browned, about 5 minutes. Transfer the mixture to a bowl. Once it has cooled, divide the mixture among the egg bowls.

In a frying pan, heat 1 tablespoon oil over medium-high heat. Add one eggplant and pour one bowl of egg/pork mixture on top. Cook until the eggs have set and encased the eggplant, about 2 minutes. Flip and cook for 2 minutes more, then transfer to a plate. Add the remaining tablespoon of oil and repeat with the second eggplant.

BANANA KETCHUP

Preparation time: 10 minutes
Cooking time: 20 minutes
Makes: 1 cup (250 ml/8 fl oz)

· 2 tablespoons vegetable oil
· 1 small shallot, diced
· 1 clove garlic, minced
· 1½ teaspoons grated fresh peeled ginger
· ¼ teaspoon ground turmeric
· ⅛ teaspoon ground cinnamon
· Pinch of ground nutmeg
· 2 large bananas, mashed
· 3 tablespoons distilled white vinegar
· 1 tablespoon tomato paste (purée)
· 1 tablespoon honey
· ½ tablespoon light brown sugar
· Salt and freshly ground pepper

In a saucepan, heat the oil over medium heat. Add the shallot and cook until translucent, about 5 minutes. Add the garlic, ginger, turmeric, cinnamon, and nutmeg and cook until fragrant, 2 minutes. Stir in the mashed bananas, vinegar, tomato paste (purée), honey, brown sugar, and 2 tablespoons water. Season with salt and pepper. Bring to a simmer, reduce the heat to low, cover, and cook for 10 minutes. Transfer to a food processor and purée until smooth. Store in the refrigerator for up to 1 week.

SOFT-BOILED EGG SHOT
THAILAND

Khai luak is a street food breakfast served in a cup, often enjoyed in one bite. An extra-soft egg is topped with Maggi seasoning sauce, a popular condiment in Thailand, and white pepper.

Preparation time: 5 minutes
Cooking time: 10 minutes
Serves: 2

· 2 extra-soft-boiled eggs (page 14)
· Maggi seasoning sauce
· White pepper and soy sauce, for seasoning (optional)

Bring a small saucepan of water to a boil. Remove from the heat and add the eggs. Set aside, uncovered, for 15 minutes. Carefully crack the eggs into a small bowl. The consistency should be very runny with barely opaque whites.

Crack each egg into two glasses and season with Maggi and, if using, white pepper and soy sauce. Stir to incorporate and enjoy.

ESPRESSO MACHINE EGGS
UNITED STATES

Light and fluffy scrambled eggs cooked with the steamer wand of an espresso machine has been popularized in cafes and coffee shops with little to no kitchen space as a way to offer breakfast and maximize counterspace. The steam cooks the eggs while infusing air to create a pillowy texture of fine egg curds.

Preparation time: 5 minutes
Cooking time: 1–2 minutes
Serves: 1

· 2 eggs
· Salt and freshly ground pepper
· ½ tablespoon (7 g) unsalted butter (optional)

Beat the eggs in a jar or milk steamer. Wrap the jar with a tea towel to avoid burning your hand. Dip the steamer wand into the eggs and swirl it around, making sure to reach the bottom, until the eggs are steamed and fluffy, about 1 minute. Season with salt and pepper and stir in the butter (if using).

EGGS IN A GLASS
AUSTRIA / GERMANY

A simple morning meal in Austria and Germany is Ei im Glas: *two soft-boiled eggs placed in a wide-rimmed glass or mason jar, sprinkled with herbs, and in Germany, set atop* schmand *(a higher-fat version of sour cream), and eaten with a spoon.*

Preparation time: 5 minutes
Cooking time: 10 minutes
Serves: 1

· 2 Soft-Boiled Eggs (page 14), peeled
· 4 tablespoons schmand
· 1 tablespoon chopped chives, dill, and/or parsley

Scoop the schmand into a glass. Top with peeled eggs. Sprinkle with the herbs and enjoy with a spoon.

FAVA BEANS WITH FLATBREAD AND EGGS
IRAQ

A popular morning meal in Baghdad, this dish is a soaked flatbread topped with fava (broad) beans (bragilla) and an omelet.

Preparation time: 5 minutes
Cooking time: 15 minutes
Serves: 4

· 1 cup (100 g) dried fava (broad) beans, soaked overnight, drained, and rinsed
· 2 khubz (flatbreads), quartered or roughly torn
· Salt and freshly ground pepper
· 2 tablespoons olive oil
· 4 eggs
· ½ small white onion, chopped
· 1 teaspoon dried wild mint (butnuj), to serve

Transfer the drained beans to a medium saucepan and add fresh water to cover the beans by about 2 inches (5 cm). Bring to a boil over medium-high heat, then reduce the heat to low and cook, covered, until the beans are very soft, about 1 hour 30 minutes. With a slotted spoon, transfer the beans to a bowl and reserve the cooking liquid.

Turn the heat on low and soak the bread in the bean liquid for 1 minute. Transfer the soaked bread to a platter, top with the beans, and season with salt and pepper.

In a medium frying pan, heat the oil over low heat. In a small bowl, use a fork to beat the eggs, and season with salt and pepper. Add the eggs to the pan and allow them to set, about 30 seconds. Pull the eggs to the center of the pan and stir occasionally until the eggs are just set, about 2 minutes.

Spoon the eggs over the beans and drizzle with hot oil from the frying pan, then top with onion and dried mint to serve.

Eggs in a Glass

EGGS BENEDICT
UNITED STATES

A typical weekend brunch dish, eggs Benedict comes in many forms. Most traditionally it consists of an English muffin sliced in half, each side topped with Canadian bacon and a poached egg, and doused in hollandaise sauce. Alternate options to the English muffins can include latkes (page 59) or crab cakes (page 64), and spinach (Eggs Florentine, page 65) or lox (page 351) can take the place of the Canadian bacon.

Preparation time: 15 minutes
Cooking time: 20 minutes
Serves: 2

· 4 Poached Eggs (page 15)
· ½ cup (120 ml/4 fl oz) Hollandaise Sauce (recipe follows)
· 2 English muffins, store-bought or homemade (page 200)
· 1 teaspoon vegetable oil
· 4 slices Canadian bacon (page 323)

Prepare the poached eggs and hollandaise sauce.

For Canadian Bacon: Start with a cold cast-iron skillet or frying pan and add the oil. Place the bacon in flat. Slowly bring the heat to medium to let the fat render and result in crispy bacon. Cook on both sides until crispy, about 10 minutes.

Meanwhile, split the muffins in half and toast. Spread with butter.

Top each muffin half with a slice of bacon. Top each with a poached egg and spoon about 2 tablespoons (or desired amount) of hollandaise sauce over. Serve warm.

HOLLANDAISE SAUCE

Preparation time: 10 minutes
Cooking time: 5 minutes
Makes: ½ cup (120 ml/4 fl oz)

· 2 egg yolks
· 1 ½ teaspoons lemon juice
· 6 tablespoons (85 g) unsalted butter, warm but not hot
· Salt and freshly ground pepper
· Pinch of cayenne pepper

In a large heatproof bowl, whisk together the egg yolks, lemon juice, and 1 ½ teaspoons cold water until the eggs are pale and frothy.
Set the bowl over a pan with 1 inch (2.5 cm) simmering water. Whisk constantly and vigorously for about 2 minutes, until the eggs are pale, frothy, and thick, making sure to avoid cooking the eggs. If the eggs start to scramble instead of thicken, tip the eggs into another bowl to cool as quickly as possible, then return to the heat and continue.

Whisk in the warm melted butter a little at a time, until all the butter has been added and the sauce is thickened and rich, 1 to 2 minutes. Remove from the heat and season with a pinch each of salt, black pepper, and cayenne pepper.

Serve immediately, or to keep the sauce warm, set the sauce over a bowl of hot water (not the pan, as this will be too hot, even off the stovetop). If the sauce thickens as it stands, add a dash of hot water and whisk well.

EGGS BENEDICT WITH LATKES

UNITED STATES

In this version of Eggs Benedict (page 58), latkes (crispy potato pancakes) replace the English muffin and lox (page 351) stands in for the Canadian bacon. Popularized during the brunch craze in New York City in the early 2000's, this dish is now a staple variation of the classic Benedict.

Preparation time: 30 minutes
Cooking time: 50 minutes
Serves: 2

· 4 Poached Eggs (page 15)
· ½ cup (120 ml/4 fl oz) Hollandaise Sauce (page 58)
· 4 large slices lox (page 351)

For the latkes:
· 1 lb/455 g russet (baking) potatoes (about 2 medium), peeled
· ½ small yellow onion, diced
· 1 egg
· 4 tablespoons matzo meal
· Salt
· ¼ cup (60 ml/2 fl oz) vegetable oil

Make the latkes:
Grate the potatoes using the large holes of a box grater. Soak in a bowl of water to remove extra starch, tossing the mixture for about 30 seconds. Drain the potatoes and transfer the pile of shredded potatoes to a tea towel. Wring out water from the potatoes.

In a small bowl, mix the potatoes and onion together. Mix in the egg and matzo meal with a wooden spoon or spatula. Season with salt and form the mixture into 4 patties.

In a medium cast-iron skillet, heat the oil over medium-high. Add the latke patties and cook until browned, 3 minutes per side. Transfer to paper towels to drain.

Prepare the poached eggs and hollandaise sauce.

To serve:
Put two latkes on each plate and top each with a slice of lox and a poached egg. Drizzle with hollandaise sauce.

REEM KASSIS
MIDDLE EASTERN BREAKFAST

Reem Kassis is a cook and a writer. Her love of food stems from an upbringing in a family revered for its cooks. From a very young age, she spent weekends in her grandmothers', mother's, and aunts' kitchens observing, learning, and soaking up everything there was to know about Palestinian cooking.

It has been almost fifteen years since I left Palestine—the place I still, and always will, fondly refer to as "home"—in pursuit of big opportunities and even bigger dreams. In the tapestry of experiences I lived through and countries I inhabited, food remained the unifying thread tying me to my family, my roots, and my country of birth. Nowhere has this been more obvious than at breakfast, which to this day remains my favorite meal. Not only because of its vibrant constellation of dishes, but because it is the embodiment of the immigrant experience: it holds the promise of a fresh start, yet reminds us of the past we cherish most.

If I close my eyes, I can picture my parents' and grandparents' breakfast tables: a bowl of labneh with a well of olive oil in the middle, a plate of sliced cucumbers and tomatoes, a ramekin of za'atar, a pot of olives, and a pile of freshly baked pita bread. When I open my eyes, I see on my own kitchen table today, oceans away from Jerusalem, a ramekin of za'atar next to one of olive oil. It is ever present on the table and often refilled. Across the Middle East, and the Levant in particular, bread dipped in za'atar and olive oil is the breakfast of choice for the hurried weekday, and part of a much larger spread during a leisurely weekend breakfast.

Throughout my childhood, this is what we ate on a daily basis, with some alternating additions depending on the season and generosity of the land. Home-cooked tomato spread, chili-and-walnut-stuffed aubergines pickled in oil, apricot jam, mulberry preserve, humus, avocados from our trees, pickled labaneh, boiled eggs, cheese, and tahini spreads also made the rounds. Weekend breakfasts were, of course, a more elaborate affair with fried halloumi cheese, falafel, ka'ak, or Palestinian frittata.

But the Middle East is such a wide and diverse region that we often borrowed dishes from neighbouring countries to enrich our breakfast table, especially if we had guests or were celebrating something: *ful medames* from Egypt, *shakshuka* from Tunisia, *malawah* with *schug* from Yemen, even stretching as far as Turkey to enjoy cheese *borek*. As a child, I didn't understand the vastness and richness of this experience, thinking of these foods simply as breakfast. Only when I was far removed from my homeland did I grasp the expansive history of our region's food, and how it tells a tale of unique culinary transformation and transmission.

Breakfast is the meal where foods from across the region can sit side by side in harmony, reminding us of our glorious past, of our connection to the land and its cherished bounty, and of the abundance of things we have to unite rather than separate us. Indeed, the Middle East was once one land, "the land where the sun rises" (*al-mashriq* / The Levant) and "the land where the sun sets" (*al-maghreb* / North Africa). When we look at a Middle Eastern breakfast table, when we see the dishes hailing from across the region, when we learn their history and taste the flavors that complement each other so well, it's hard to ignore that whether we are Palestinian, Lebanese, or Syrian, whether we are Egyptian, Moroccan, or Tunisian, we are all different threads of the same tapestry. Our food offers a glimpse into how we can weave our way back to a beautiful image, just like this tablescape, where the day starts with a harmony of dishes that come together to sketch a scene that is much greater than the sum of its parts.

01. Israeli Breakfast Plate PAGE 26   02. Schug PAGE 26   03. Israeli Shakshuka PAGE 66
04. Knafeh Sandwich with Kataifi Crust PAGE 178

05. Cheese-Stuffed Puff Pastry PAGE 378   06. Pomegranate Juice PAGE 434   07. Egyptian Fava Bean Stew PAGE 267
08. Flatbreads with Za'atar and Keshek PAGES 202-3

CRAB CAKES BENEDICT

UNITED STATES

A common ingredient in the Northeast, crab makes its way onto the breakfast table by replacing the English muffin in Eggs Benedict (page 58) with a crab cake.

Preparation time: 25 minutes
Cooking time: 50 minutes
Serves: 2

· 4 Poached Eggs (page 15)
· ½ cup (120 ml/4 fl oz) Hollandaise Sauce (page 58)

For the crab cakes:
· ½ lb (455 g) jumbo lump crabmeat, picked over
· 2 tablespoons (55 g) crushed oyster crackers or breadcrumbs
· 1 egg, beaten
· 2 tablespoons mayonnaise
· 1 teaspoon Worcestershire sauce
· 1 teaspoon Dijon mustard
· 1 teaspoon hot sauce, or to taste
· 2 teaspoons minced fresh parsley
· ½ teaspoon fine sea salt
· ½ teaspoon freshly ground pepper
· ½ teaspoon sweet paprika
· 2 tablespoons vegetable oil

Prepare the poached eggs and hollandaise sauce.

Make the crab cakes: Place the crabmeat in a large bowl. In a separate bowl, whisk together the crushed oyster crackers or breadcrumbs, egg, mayonnaise, Worcestershire sauce, mustard, hot sauce, parsley, salt, pepper, and paprika until thoroughly combined. Fold the mixture into the crabmeat carefully. Divide the mixture into quarters and form each into a patty.

In a large cast-iron skillet, heat the vegetable oil over medium-high heat. Fry the crab cakes until golden brown, about 5 minutes per side.

To serve, place a poached egg on top of a crab cake and drizzle with hollandaise sauce.

EGGS FLORENTINE
UNITED STATES

Serving a poached egg on a bed of cooked spinach is a popular vegetarian alternative to a traditional Eggs Benedict made with Canadian bacon (page 58). À la Florentine simply refers to the addition of spinach, said to have been introduced to the French by Catherine de Medicis of Florence. In this recipe, grated Gruyère cheese is added to the hollandaise. Another variation would be to use a Mornay sauce (béchamel sauce with the addition of grated Gruyère cheese).

Preparation time: 25 minutes
Cooking time: 50 minutes
Serves: 2

· 2 Poached Eggs (page 15)
· ½ cup (120 ml/4 fl oz) Hollandaise Sauce (page 58)
· 2 English muffins, store-bought or homemade (page 200)
· 2 tablespoons olive oil
· 3 cups (85 g) spinach, stemmed
· Salt and freshly ground pepper
· 4 tablespoons grated Gruyère cheese

Prepare the poached eggs and hollandaise sauce. Split the English muffin in half and toast.

In a frying pan, heat the olive oil over medium heat. Add the spinach, season with salt and pepper, and cook until wilted, 2 minutes.

Heat the hollandaise in a small saucepan over low heat and stir in the grated Gruyère cheese until incorporated, 1 minute.

To serve, top each English muffin with spinach and a poached egg. Douse with the hollandaise cheese sauce.

FRITTATA
UNITED STATES

A baked egg dish that can be made with any savory leftovers you have in the refrigerator or fresh vegetables and herbs from the farmers' market. Frittata is derived from the Italian verb meaning "to fry." American frittatas tend to be studded with cheese, meat, and vegetables, whereas Egyptians enjoy a paired down version called eggah *(Middle Eastern Omelet, page 52).*

Preparation time: 10 minutes
Cooking time: 30 minutes
Serves: 2

· 1 tablespoon olive oil, plus more as needed
· ½ small onion or 1 leek, chopped
· 4 oz (115 g) cremini (chestnut) mushrooms, thinly sliced
· Salt and freshly ground pepper
· 6 eggs
· 4 tablespoons full-fat yogurt or milk
· 1 teaspoon fresh thyme
· 4 tablespoons goat cheese or ½ cup (55 g) grated cheese, such as cheddar
· 4 tablespoons grated Parmesan cheese
· Brioche, for serving (optional)

Preheat the oven to 350°F (180°C/Gas Mark 4).

In a medium cast-iron or ovenproof frying pan, heat the oil over medium heat. Add the onion or leek and cook until soft and translucent, about 5 minutes. Add the mushrooms and season with salt and pepper. Cook the mushrooms, stirring occasionally, until browned, 5 minutes.

Meanwhile, in a medium bowl, whisk together the eggs, yogurt or milk, and thyme, and season with salt and pepper.

Add a little extra oil to the pan if needed and pour the egg evenly over the mushrooms and onion. Sprinkle the cheese over the eggs and transfer the skillet to the oven. Cook until the eggs are set, 10 minutes.

Allow the frittata to cool and then slice into wedges. It can be served on a soft brioche bun.

ISRAELI SHAKSHUKA

ISRAEL

A dish of baked eggs in tomato sauce is a popular breakfast dish in Israel. Meaning "all mixed up," different versions of the dish exist across the Middle East, such as Yemeni Shakshouka (page 68) or Turkish menemen (Scrambled Eggs with Tomato and Peppers, page 46). Shakshuka can be served with other Israeli breakfast staples (See Israeli Breakfast Plate, page 26) or enjoyed on its own with Challah *(page 234) or pita.*

Preparation time: 10 minutes
Cooking time: 35 minutes
Serves: 2

For the sauce:
· 2 tablespoons olive oil
· 1 medium yellow onion, diced
· 1 medium red or orange bell pepper, chopped
· 3 cloves garlic, minced
· 3 tablespoons tomato paste (purée)
· 1 can (28 oz/565 g) crushed (finely chopped) tomatoes, with juices, or 4 medium tomatoes, chopped
· ½ tablespoon sweet paprika
· 1 tablespoon crushed chili flakes, 1 teaspoon cayenne pepper, or 1 fresh chili, minced
· ½ teaspoon ground cumin
· 1 teaspoon sugar
· 1 teaspoon fine sea salt
· ½ teaspoon freshly ground pepper

For the eggs and serving:
· 4 eggs
· 4 tablespoons tahini
· 2 tablespoons lemon juice
· Salt, to taste
· ½ cup (75 g) crumbled feta cheese (optional)
· Chopped parsley leaves

Make the sauce:
In a 10-inch (25 cm) cast-iron skillet or frying pan, heat the oil over medium heat. Add the onion and cook, stirring occasionally, until soft and translucent, about 5 minutes.

Add the bell pepper and garlic, cover, and cook, stirring occasionally, until the pepper is soft, about 5 minutes.

Add the tomato paste (purée) and stir to thoroughly combine. Add the crushed (chopped) tomatoes with their juices, paprika, chili flakes, cumin, sugar, salt, and pepper. Stir and reduce the heat to low. Cover and bring the tomato mixture to a simmer, stirring occasionally to avoid burning, until the mixture has thickened, 15 minutes.

Cook the eggs:
With a wooden spoon, press 4 wells into the thickened tomato sauce. Crack an egg into each well and season with salt. Reduce the heat to low, cover, and cook until the egg whites have set, 7 minutes more. Remove from the heat.

In a small bowl, stir the tahini, lemon juice, and water until thoroughly combined. The mixture will turn lighter in color and the texture should be silky smooth.

To serve, drizzle the tahini over the *shakshuka* and top with feta (if using) and parsley. Scoop out 2 eggs and sauce into each bowl. Serve warm.

Israeli Shakshuka

YEMENI SHAKSHOUKA

YEMEN

The Yemeni Shakshouka is similar to the Israeli one (page 66), but is made with scrambled eggs and hawaij—a popular Yemeni spice blend of cumin, coriander, cloves, turmeric, and black pepper. Serve with Malawah (page 237), a laminated flatbread.

Preparation time: 10 minutes
Cooking time: 25 minutes
Serves: 2

· 2 tablespoons olive oil
· 1 medium yellow onion, diced
· 1 small green chili, chopped
· 1 clove garlic, minced
· 4 medium Roma (plum) tomatoes, chopped
· ¼ teaspoon hawaij
· ¼ teaspoon sweet paprika
· Salt and freshly ground pepper
· 6 eggs
· Malawah (page 237), for serving

In a medium frying pan, heat the oil over medium-high heat. Add the onion and cook until soft and translucent, about 5 minutes. Add the chili and garlic and cook until fragrant, about 2 minutes. Stir in the tomatoes, *hawaij*, and paprika, and season with salt and pepper. Cook, stirring to combine, until the tomatoes are softened, 5 minutes.

In a medium bowl, use a fork to beat the eggs. Pour the beaten eggs into the pan and let them set over the vegetables, 30 seconds. Using a wooden spoon, gently pull the eggs in toward the center of the pan and cook until evenly scrambled, about 2 minutes.

Serve warm with *malawah*.

RICE WITH RAW EGGS

JAPAN

A simple comfort food breakfast in Japan, TKG—Tamago Kake Gohan—is a raw egg (tamago) vigorously frothed into a bowl of steamed rice (gohan) and seasoned with soy sauce and furikake, which translates to "sprinkle over," a range of seasonings meant for topping rice. A simple blend would be toasted sesame seeds and nori flakes with sugar and salt. TKG is often enjoyed at breakfast along with Yakizakana (Grilled Fish, page 348), miso soup (page 260), and Asazuke (Quick Pickled Vegetables, page 348).

Preparation time: 5 minutes
Cooking time: 20 minutes
Serves: 2

· 2 cups (370 g) freshly cooked short-grain white rice, very hot
· 2 eggs
· Soy sauce
· Furikake

Divide the rice between two bowls. Make an indentation in the center of the cooked rice and crack 1 egg into the dent per bowl. Season with soy sauce and *furikake* and stir vigorously with chopsticks until the egg is thoroughly combined with the rice and the mixture appears frothy.

Rice with Raw Eggs

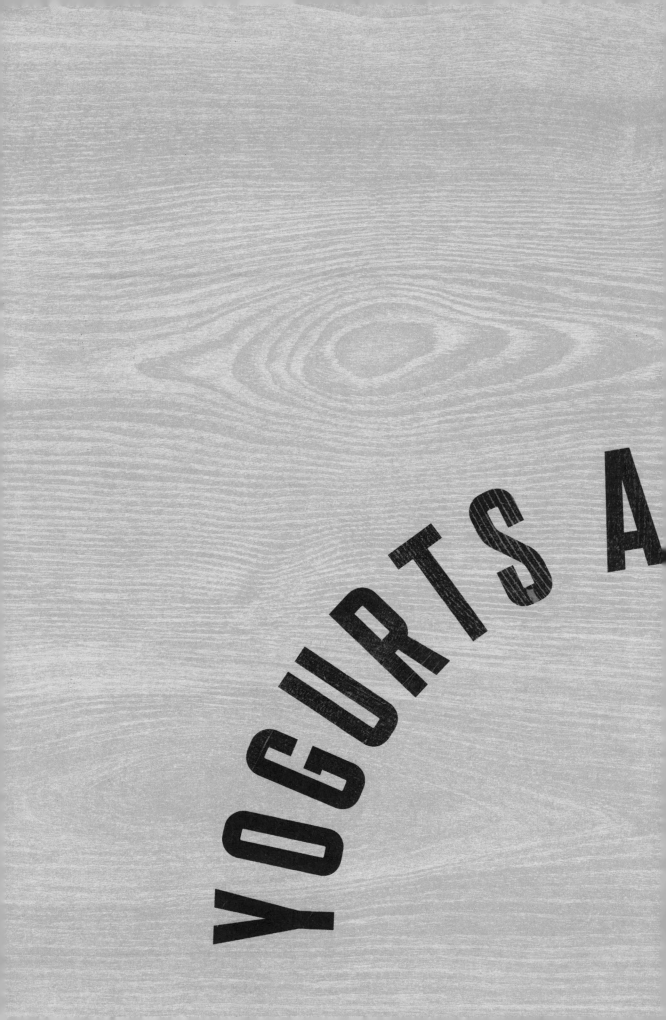

ND CHEESES

YOGURT PARFAIT

UNITED STATES

Often served in a clear glass, this healthy breakfast option features layers of colored berries, fruits, and granola.

Preparation time: 5 minutes, plus 15 minutes cooling time
Cooking time: 5 minutes
Serves: 1

· 1 cup (150 g) chopped strawberries or fresh fruit of your choice
· 1 teaspoon sugar (optional)
· 1 cup (285 g) yogurt or Greek Yogurt (see below)
· 4 tablespoons granola, store-bought or homemade (page 110)

In a small saucepan, combine the fruit and sugar (if using), cover, and cook over medium heat until the fruit softens, about 5 minutes. Remove the sauce from the heat. Using a fork, muddle the fruit slightly to create a chunky sauce. Let cool completely and store in the refrigerator until ready to use.

Spoon half the yogurt into a small bowl, ideally glass so the layers will show. Top with half of the fruit mixture and 2 tablespoons granola. Repeat the layers and serve.

GREEK YOGURT AND HONEY

GREECE

For authentic Greek yogurt, use a base of goat or sheep's milk yogurt. A simple drizzle of Greek honey is all that is needed, thyme-infused if available. The wild flowering plants across the Greek islands make it an ideal ecosystem for bees to create hyper-local, distinctly flavored honeys that vary with the seasons.

Preparation time: 5 minutes, plus up to 18 hours incubating and draining time
Cooking time: 10 minutes
Serves: 4

· 4 cups (950 ml/32 fl oz) pasteurized full-fat milk
· 2 tablespoons plain, goat, or sheep's milk yogurt
· Thyme honey (or any available Greek honey), for serving

In a medium saucepan, bring the milk to a simmer over medium heat until it reaches about 180°–200°F (82°–93°C), stirring occasionally to avoid scorching the milk. Remove the saucepan from the heat and allow the milk to cool slightly to about 100°–120°F (38°–49°C). The milk should be warm to the touch. Stir in the yogurt until it is combined thoroughly with the milk.

Divide the mixture into two 1-pint (500 ml) mason jars, screw on the lid, and wrap in a warm blanket. Store in a warm, draft-free place, like an oven or close to a radiator, to incubate for up to 12 hours, until the desired tartness is achieved.

Line a sieve with a double layer of cheesecloth set over a bowl so the whey can easily drain out. Spoon the yogurt into the cheesecloth. Set in the refrigerator and allow the whey to drain until the yogurt is thick, 4-6 hours.

Serve the Greek yogurt in a bowl with a helping of honey.

Yogurt Parfait

ARISHÉ WITH HONEY
LEBANON

Arishé, *a fresh cheese similar to ricotta cheese or farmer cheese, is often served drizzled with honey and rolled up in a soft, thin flatbread called* saj, *named after the dome-shaped grill it is cooked over.* Arishé *is found at laiterie shops (convenience stores specializing in fresh dairy products) along the freeway to the fertile farmlands in eastern Lebanon called the Beqaa Valley. If saj is not available, man'oushe (Flatbread with Za'ater or Keshek, pages 202–3) can be used.*

Preparation time: 5 minutes
Serves: 1

· ¼ cup (65 g) arishé (if available), ricotta cheese, or farmer cheese
· 1 tablespoons honey
· 1 saj, or available flatbread, warmed

Spread the cheese on the warm saj and drizzle with honey. Roll up into a wrap and serve warm.
Note: If *saj* is not available (though not traditional), *man'oushe* (Flatbread with Za'atar or Keshek, pages 202–3).

LABNEH
ISRAEL

A fresh cheese made by straining yogurt, this is typically seen spread on a plate topped with olive oil and za'atar or rolled into balls, sometimes coated in crushed chili flakes or za'atar. Serve as part of an Israeli Breakfast Plate (page 26).

Preparation time: 5 minutes, plus up to 48 hours for draining
Makes: ½ cup (110 g)

· ½ teaspoon fine sea salt
· 4 cups (910 g) plain (natural) whole-milk yogurt
· Olive oil, for drizzling
· Za'atar, for serving

Stir the salt into the yogurt. Line a sieve with a double layer of cheesecloth and set over a bowl. Pour the yogurt into the sieve. Twist the cheesecloth tightly over the yogurt and cover the bowl with plastic wrap (cling film). Transfer to the refrigerator to drain the whey for at least 8 hours and up to 48. The longer the labneh drains, the thicker it will be. Serve the labneh drizzled with olive oil and sprinkled with za'atar.

CREAM CHEESE
UNITED STATES

Cream cheese is most often used as a "schmear" (generous spread) on bagels. Recipes for cream cheese date back to the late 1700s in Philadelphia, a century before a New York dairyman, William Lawrence, began distributing the cheese in foil wrappers, now known as Philadelphia brand cream cheese. Today, cream cheese comes in many flavors, from plain to vegetable, chive, smoked salmon; even vegan versions have become commonplace.

Preparation time: 5 minutes, plus 4 hours draining time
Cooking time: 10 minutes
Makes: 1 cup (150 g)

· 2 cups (475 ml/16 fl oz) heavy (whipping) cream
· 2 cups (475 ml/16 fl oz) full-fat milk
· 1 tablespoon cultured buttermilk
· 2 tablespoons lemon juice
· Salt

In a heavy-bottomed pot, bring the cream and full-fat milk to a gentle boil over medium heat. Reduce the heat to low and stir in the buttermilk. Cook for 1 minute, then stir in 1 tablespoon of the lemon juice. Cook for 1 more minute and stir in the remaining 1 tablespoon lemon juice. Stir occasionally until curds begin to form, 3 minutes.

Line a sieve with a double layer of cheesecloth and set it over a bowl, so the whey can easily drain out. Pour the curds into the sieve and refrigerate until the cheese is thick, 6–8 hours.

Put the strained cream cheese in a bowl or airtight container, add the salt, and stir until smooth. Store the cream cheese in a covered bowl or airtight container in the refrigerator for up to 1 week.

SKYR
ICELAND

Brought to Iceland by Norwegian Vikings, skyr is a thick, strained yogurt with a mild tang. In Iceland, the curds created during the process technically place skyr in the fresh cheese or quark category. The best way to mimic the cultures found in skyr is to incorporate a portion of a finished skyr (available in most specialty grocery stores). Once one batch is made, the homemade batch will then become the starter needed for the next—a similar process is used for all yogurt-making.

Preparation time: 5 minutes, plus up to 20 hours incubating and draining time
Cooking time: 10 minutes
Makes: 1 cup (225 g)

· 4 cups (950 ml/32 fl oz) fat-free (skimmed) milk
· 5 tablespoons skyr yogurt
· 2 drops liquid vegetable rennet

In a medium saucepan, bring the milk to a steady simmer over medium heat, stirring to prevent scorching the milk. Once the milk has reached 190°F (88°C), remove it from the heat and allow it to cool until it is just warm to the touch, 110°–115°F (43°–46°C). Stir in the yogurt until thoroughly combined. Mix the drops of rennet and 2 tablespoons water together, then stir into the milk until thoroughly combined. Cover the pot with a tea towel and incubate for up to 12 hours in a warm, draft-free place.

Line a sieve with a double layer of cheesecloth and set over a bowl to collect the whey. Spoon the curds into the sieve and refrigerate to allow the whey to drain until the skyr is thick, 6–8 hours.

Whisk 1 tablespoon of the drained whey back into the skyr until smooth. Add more whey, 1 tablespoon at a time, until the desired silky consistency is achieved. Store in the refrigerator, in a mason or glass jar, for up to 1 month.

FILMJÖLK
SWEDEN

Similar to kefir, this fermented milk can be drunk on its own but is more often served in a bowl topped with Muesli (page 108), Granola (page 110), or crushed knäckebröd.

Preparation time: 5 minutes, plus up to 2 days fermenting and chilling time
Serves: 2

· 3 cups (355 ml/12 fl oz) full-fat milk
· 4 tablespoons *filmjölk* or kefir
· ½ cup knäckebröd, crushed, to taste (optional)

In a 1-pint (500 ml) mason jar, add the milk and *filmjölk* or kefir and stir to incorporate. Screw on the lid and let the milk sit in a warm place for up to 48 hours. Check after at least 8 hours. The texture should start to change, becoming thicker, but still liquid-y. To test if the mixture is ready, tilt the jar to the side: the *filmjölk* should cleanly pull away from the jar as one solid mass. Refrigerate the *filmjölk* for at least 8 hours before eating. To make future batches, save at least 4 tablespoons to mix into milk.

YMER WITH YMERDRYS

DENMARK

Ymer *(Danish fermented milk) is typically eaten topped with* ymerdrys, *a mixture of toasted rye breadcrumbs and brown sugar. You can buy* ymerdrys *or make it from scratch.* Ymer *can be substituted with* filmjölk *(page 76) or* kefir, *a similar fermented milk drink.*

Preparation time: 5 minutes
Cooking time: 10 minutes
Serves: 2

· 2 cups (455 g) ymer
· 8 tablespoons Ymerdrys (recipe follows), or to taste

Pour the *ymer* into 2 bowls and top each with 4 tablespoons *ymerdrys*, or to taste.

YMERDRYS

Makes: ½ cup

· 2 slices (3.5 oz/100 g) dark rye bread, torn into large pieces
· 1 tablespoon brown sugar

Preheat the oven to 375°F (190°C/Gas Mark 5). Line a baking sheet with parchment paper.

In a food processor, combine the bread and brown sugar and pulse until coarse crumbs have formed. Spread the breadcrumb mixture evenly on the baking sheet and bake until toasted, about 10 minutes, watching closely so as not to burn.

See image on page 372

KAYMAK

TURKEY

Clotted cream made with buffalo milk,
kaymak is often served with honey on
pide, Turkish flatbread.

Preparation time: 5 minutes, plus 24 hours chilling time
Cooking time: 2 hours
Serves: 2–4

· 4 cups (950 ml/2 pints) water buffalo or goat milk (or 3 cups/710 ml heavy/whipping cream plus 1 cup/240 ml full-fat milk)

In a 10-inch (25 cm) frying pan, heat the milk (or cream and milk) over low heat. Bring to a gentle simmer and cook at a slow, steady simmer until the mixture turns yellow and begins to separate, about 1 hour and 30 minutes. Remove from the heat, let cool completely, then cover the pan with plastic wrap (cling film) and refrigerate for 24 hours. Spoon off the kaymak (clotted cream) that has risen to the top, discard the whey and store the kaymak in the refrigerator in an airtight container for up to 3 days.

FATTEH

LEBANON

Fatteh is the Arabic word for "crushed"
or "crumbs," referring to the way this
stewed chickpea dish is served: layered
with crunchy Lebanese bread (similar
to a traditional pita, but thinner and
larger) and garlicky yogurt, topped with
toasted, slivered nuts cooked in lamb fat.

Preparation time: 5 minutes (see Note)
Cooking time: 10 minutes (see Note)
Serves: 2

· 2 Lebanese flatbreads or pita, torn, or 2 cups (300 g) store-bought pita chips
· ½ tablespoon olive oil
· 1 tablespoon lamb fat or butter
· ½ cup (55 g) slivered almonds
· 4 tablespoons pine nuts
· 1 clove garlic, minced
· 1 cup (225 g) plain full-fat yogurt
· ½ teaspoon ground cumin
· 2 tablespoons lemon juice
· Salt
· 1 (16 oz/455 g) can chickpeas (see Note), rinsed and drained

Preheat the oven to 350°F (180°C/Gas Mark).
Toss the torn Lebanese bread with the olive oil on a baking sheet and bake until the bread is crisp and crunchy, about 8 minutes (skip if using store-bought pita chips).
In a small frying pan, heat the lamb fat or butter over medium heat. Add the almonds and pine nuts and toast, stirring, until lightly browned and nutty smelling, about 3 minutes. Remove the nuts from the hot pan to keep them from overcooking.
In a bowl, combine the garlic and yogurt. Stir in the cumin and lemon juice and season with salt.
Divide the toasted bread between two bowls. Top each with half of the cooked chickpeas. Divide the yogurt mixture between the bowls and sprinkle with toasted almonds and pine nuts.

Note: To make this with home-cooked chickpeas, add overnight soaking to the prep time and 1 hour to the cook time. Start with ¾ cup (150 g) dried chickpeas, soaked overnight then cooked, covered in water by at least 2 inches (5 cm), until tender, about 1 hour.

Fatteh

CEREALS AND

PORRIDGES

HAITIAN CORNMEAL

HAITI

This cornmeal porridge, or Mayi Moulin ak Fèy *in Haitian Creole, features* epis, *a popular herb/spice blend in Haitian cooking. This combination, along with cooked spinach, creates a flavorful, hearty meal out of simple ingredients.*

Preparation time: 15 minutes
Cooking time: 25 minutes
Serves: 2

· 3 tablespoons vegetable oil
· 4 tablespoons diced onion
· 1 tablespoon Epis (recipe follows)
· 1 large tomato, diced
· ½ chicken bouillon (stock) cube
· Salt
· ½ Scotch bonnet pepper, chopped
· ½ cup (20 g) finely chopped spinach
· ½ cup (70 g) coarse cornmeal or polenta
· ½ avocado, sliced

In a small saucepan, heat the oil over medium heat. Add the onion and *epis* and cook until the onion is soft and translucent, about 5 minutes. Stir in the tomato. Cook, stirring occasionally until the tomato has softened, about 2 minutes. Add the bouillon (stock) cube and season with salt to taste. Pour in 2 cups (475 ml/16 fl oz) water and stir in the Scotch bonnet pepper. Bring the water to a simmer, add the spinach, and cook until wilted, about 1 minute. Stir in the cornmeal and cook, stirring constantly to avoid clumps from forming, about 5 minutes. Reduce the heat to medium and cook, covered, until the cornmeal has thickened, about 10 minutes. Serve in a bowl topped with sliced avocado.

EPIS

Preparation time: 10 minutes
Makes: ½ cup

· ¼ small onion, chopped
· ¼ cup (5 g) parsley leaves
· ¼ cup (5 g) cilantro (coriander) leaves
· ¼ green bell pepper, chopped
· 2 scallions (spring onions), white parts only, chopped
· 2 cloves garlic
· 2 tablespoons olive oil
· ½ tablespoon lime juice
· 1 teaspoon white vinegar
· ¼ chicken bouillon (stock) cube

In a food processor or blender, process all the ingredients until smooth. Store in an airtight jar in the refrigerator for up to 3 days.

GRITS
UNITED STATES

This ground cornmeal porridge is a specialty of the American South, served alone topped with a pat of butter or as part of a meal such as Shrimp and Grits (page 352) or Country Ham with Red-Eye Gravy and Grits (page 324).

Preparation time: 5 minutes
Cooking time: 40 minutes
Serves: 2

- 1 cup (240 ml/8 fl oz) full-fat milk
- 1 cup (240 ml/8 fl oz) heavy (whipping) cream
- ½ cup (70 g) corn grits
- 1 tablespoon (15 g) unsalted butter
- ¼ teaspoon fine sea salt
- ½ cup (2 oz/57 g) grated cheddar cheese

In a heavy pot, combine the milk and cream and bring to a boil over medium-high heat, stirring occasionally to avoid burning. Stirring constantly, gradually stream in the corn grits. When the mixture returns to a boil, reduce the heat to low and stir frequently with a wooden spoon until the mixture thickens, about 30 minutes. Once the the grits are thick, remove the pot from the heat and stir in the butter and salt. Sprinkle with the cheddar and serve.

COUSH-COUSH
UNITED STATES

Brought over from Africa, this griddled cornmeal porridge was inspired by North African couscous (small granules of pasta made with semolina). It was adapted by Creole people (mixed African and European descendants living in New Orleans) utilizing local ingredients such as cornmeal. Coush-Coush gets crisped in a pan, broken up into pieces, and served in a bowl with milk, like cereal, or topped with butter, sugar, or cane syrup.

Preparation time: 5 minutes
Cooking time: 15 minutes
Serves: 2

- 1 cup (100 g) yellow cornmeal
- 1 teaspoon baking powder
- ¾ teaspoon fine sea salt
- ¾ cup (175 ml/6 fl oz) hot water or milk
- 4 tablespoons (60 g) butter or rendered fat
- ½ cup (120 ml/4 fl oz) full-fat milk or to taste (optional)
- ½ tablespoon salted butter, or to taste (optional)
- ½ tablespoon cane syrup or granulated sugar or to taste (optional)

In a bowl, stir together the cornmeal, baking powder, salt, and hot water or milk. In a cast-iron frying pan, heat the butter over medium heat. Scrape the cornmeal mixture into the pan and cook until the bottom has browned and crisped, about 10 minutes. Reduce the heat to low. With a spatula, break up the cornmeal and toss, cooking until browned all over, about 10 more minutes. Serve hot topped with butter, milk, and cane syrup or sugar, if using.

BILL GRANGER
AUSTRALIAN BREAKFAST

Australian restaurateur Bill Granger opened his first restaurant in Sydney in 1993. It quickly became famous for the best scrambled eggs and ricotta hotcakes in town, served at a communal table. In 2011, he opened his first London café, in Notting Hill. Granger now owns eighteen eateries across London, Sydney, Seoul, Honolulu, and Japan.

I guess it always comes back to that first, all-important meal of the day—breakfast.

One of my earliest memories of taking it into my own hands was making breakfast-in-bed for my parents when I was about nine years old. Even then, it had to be a combination of healthy and indulgent, and of course it had to look appetizing. I remember painstakingly cutting up fresh fruit and attempting to make pancakes. There was probably some toast with Vegemite, too.

I'll never forget my first hotel breakfasts as a kid, going on road trips with my parents and staying at motels where food was delivered through a hatch in the wall. Those packs of assorted cereals always seemed the height of sophistication to me. I still love a good hotel breakfast, but my standards are slightly higher now.

Pellegrini's Espresso Bar in Melbourne, where I grew up, was probably one of the first places that inspired me to dream about owning my own restaurants one day. I've always loved that buzzy chatter in Italian cafes, especially in the morning. When I moved to Sydney for art college, I used to go to an Italian place next to the ABC Television studios. I loved seeing all the journalists come in, discussing stories over coffee and those rosetta rolls filled with prosciutto.

I've always been an early riser, so Sydney felt like it was made for me; it's so light and bright. I'd go for a 5am swim at the Andrew (Boy) Charlton pool or Bondi, then hit the food and flower markets. It's also where I discovered and fell in love with having early morning phở.

When I opened my first restaurant, bills, 25 years ago in Darlinghurst, Sydney, the idea was to create a simply designed space where people could gather in a totally relaxed way and catch up over something delicious. At the time, I could only open between 7 am and 4 pm (thanks to my landlord). So I decided I'd make it my 'thing' to serve really good coffee—not something you could find much of at the time in Australia—alongside freshly cooked, inviting food that matched the Sydney lifestyle and that time of day.

Scrambled eggs quickly became the most popular dish on the menu. In the morning, while I got the place ready for our first customers, I'd have an avocado smashed onto sourdough toast as a simple, virtually instant snack I could eat with one hand. I'd stick some chopped chili on top, a few grinds of salt, and lots of citrus. I decided to feature it in my first cookbook, *Bill's Sydney Food*, just for fun, and now there's talk that this was where the avocado toast obsession began.

I think we'd all agree that for many years Australia wasn't really applauded for its cuisine, so it's great that we're now known for creating vibrant and fresh dishes, often artfully thrown together, suited to any time of day. And if I've contributed to making breakfast that little bit more inspiring, and encouraged people to get together and enjoy it a bit more often, then I'm good with that.

01. Toast with Vegemite PAGE 146   02. Flat White PAGE 420   03. Green Juice PAGE 435   04. Banana Bread PAGE 390

TOM BROWN

GHANA

Tom Brown is a nickname given to any porridge made of roasted corn flour with a golden brown color. The name's origin is unclear, but some believe it is inspired by the golden brown cover of Tom Brown's Schooldays, *a book read to children in international schools in Ghana during the 1960's. Administered by the Ministry of Health to enhance nutrient-rich foods in the Ghanaian diet, Tom Brown was given to children during weaning. It was nicknamed weanimix as it is fortified with varying ingredients: cow peas (black-eyes peas), soybeans, and peanuts (groundnuts).*

Preparation time: 5 minutes
Cooking time: 10 minutes
Serves: 2

· ½ cup (60 g) roasted corn flour or weanimix
· 1 teaspoon light brown sugar (optional)
· Evaporated milk, for drizzling, to taste

In a small saucepan, bring 1 cup (240 ml/8 fl oz) water to a simmer over medium-high heat. Whisk ½ cup (120 ml/4 fl oz) water into the roasted corn flour until thoroughly combined. Add the moistened corn flour to the simmering water and stir to combine. Reduce the heat to low. Stir constantly to avoid lumps until the porridge is thickened, about 2 minutes. Add brown sugar (if using) and stir for 1 minute. Serve warm with a drizzle of milk.

CORNMEAL PORRIDGE WITH CINNAMON AND BUTTER

PUERTO RICO

Cremita de maíz is a cornmeal porridge similar to Farina (a wheat-based porridge, page 89). It is a Puerto Rican comfort food often sweetened and served topped with cinnamon and butter.

Preparation time: 5 minutes
Cooking time: 15 minutes
Serves: 1

· 1½ cups (355 ml/12 fl oz) full-fat milk
· 1 tablespoon (15 g) unsalted butter, plus more for serving
· Pinch of salt
· 2 tablespoons granulated sugar
· ½ cup (140 g) coarse yellow cornmeal (polenta)
· Ground cinnamon, for serving

In a small saucepan, bring the milk to a boil over medium-high heat. Stir in the butter and salt. Reduce the heat to low and, stirring constantly, gradually stream in the cornmeal. Simmer, stirring occasionally, until the cornmeal has thickened into a smooth consistency, about 3 minutes. Add the sugar and stir for 1 minute. Serve warm with generous amounts of cinnamon dusted on top and an extra pat of butter.

FARINA

UNITED STATES

Farina (semolina) is a milled wheat often enjoyed cooked into a porridge. There are many versions of this wheat porridge served around the world. In the United States, Cream of Wheat (a popular brand name of farina) is typically served with a splash of cold milk and/or cinnamon sugar.

Preparation time: 5 minutes
Cooking time: 10 minutes
Serves: 1

· 1 cup (240 ml/8 fl oz) full-fat milk or water
· 4 tablespoons farina (semolina)
· 1 teaspoon sugar (optional)
· Salt

For serving:
· Ground cinnamon (optional)
· 1 tablespoon butter, or to taste
· Full-fat milk or heavy (whipping) cream

In a small saucepan, bring the milk or water to a boil. Stirring constantly, stream in the farina (semolina). Reduce the heat to low and stir constantly to avoid forming lumps. Stir in the sugar (if using) and salt to taste. Simmer until thickened, 4 minutes.

Serve topped with cinnamon (if using), a pat of butter, and a splash of cold milk or cream.

SLICED CORNMEAL PORRIDGE

ROMANIA

Mămăligă is a firm cornmeal porridge that is meant to be sliced and served with sour cream. This morning meal is featured in Bram Stoker's novel Dracula: *"I had for breakfast more paprika, and a sort of porridge of maize flour which they said was 'mamaliga.'"*

Preparation time: 5 minutes
Cooking time: 20 minutes
Serves: 2

· 1 tablespoon (15 g) butter
· ¼ teaspoon fine sea salt
· ½ cup (70 g) coarse yellow cornmeal
· Sour cream or yogurt, for serving (optional)

In a small frying pan or cast-iron skillet, bring 1½ cups (355 ml/12 fl oz) water to a boil over medium-high heat. Stir in the butter and salt with a wooden spoon. Stirring clockwise constantly, gradually stream in the cornmeal. Once it has all been poured in, reduce the heat to low and continue to stir until the porridge is thickened and pulling away from the sides of the pan, 15-20 minutes. Let cool for 5 minutes to set before slicing into quarters and serving warm with sour cream or yogurt, if using.

KASHA

RUSSIA

Kasha simply means porridge and can be made with any kind of grain boiled in water or milk. In Russia and Eastern Europe, kasha *is often made with whole buckwheat or buckwheat groats, but millet, barley, rye, and wheat can also be used. A beaten egg is sometimes added before toasting the groats, to coat each grain and keep them separated and fluffy during cooking.*

Preparation time: 5 minutes
Cooking time: 15 minutes
Serves: 2

· ½ cup (80 g) buckwheat groats, rinsed and dried
· 1 egg
· ½ tablespoon (7 g) unsalted butter
· ½ teaspoon fine sea salt
· ¼ cup (120 ml/4 fl oz) full-fat milk plus more for serving

In a medium bowl beat the egg and stir in the groats to evenly coat.

In a dry cast iron skillet over medium heat, toast the groats until fragrant and golden, stirring occasionally so as not to burn, 5 minutes.

In a small saucepan, combine 1 cup (240 ml/8 fl oz) water, butter, and salt to taste and bring to a boil over medium-high heat. Stir in the toasted groats, reduce the heat to a simmer, and cook covered, stirring occasionally, until the water is absorbed, about 10 minutes. Stir in the milk. Return the grains to a boil over medium-high heat. Stir and cook until thickened, about 3 minutes more. Serve warm with a splash of milk, if using.

Kasha

SLAP PAP
SOUTH AFRICA

Pap, *a general term for porridge, was adopted from Dutch settlers living in South Africa. "Slap" is a slang term meaning "limp," referring here to a soggy or saturated porridge with a runny texture, often served with milk and sugar.* Pap *comes in three variations according to the water to cornmeal ratios:* stywe pap *(stiff),* putu pap *(crumbly), and* slap-pap *(runny).* Pap *is found across Africa with varying preparations, grains, and accompaniments. In Ghana, the fermented porridge (*koko*) is spiced with ground alligator pepper, ginger, and cayenne, and is commonly served with* koose, *a millet-based fritter.* Pap *in Nigeria is a porridge made with* ogi, *a fermented cornmeal.*

Preparation time: 5 minutes
Cooking time: 10 minutes
Serves: 1

· ½ cup (70 g) cornmeal
· Pinch of salt
· 1 tablespoon (15 g) unsalted butter
· Full-fat milk and sugar, for serving

In a small saucepan, bring 1 cup (355 ml/12 fl oz) water to a boil over medium-high heat. In a small bowl, mix ½ cup (120 ml/4 fl oz) of water with the maize meal to form a paste. Add the maize meal to the boiling water and stir. Reduce the heat to low and simmer, covered, stirring occasionally, until thickened, 5 minutes. Once thickened, stir in the butter. Serve with a splash of milk and sugar to taste.

BARLEY PORRIDGE WITH CLARIFIED BUTTER

ETHIOPIA

Known as Genfo *in Ethiopia and* Ga'at *in Eritrea, this is a thick barley porridge spiced with a staple Ethiopian spice blend,* berbere. *A well in the center of the porridge is filled with* niter kibbeh *(Spiced Clarified Butter, page 44). There are many versions of this dish including* fufu, *made from boiled potato and yuca (cassava) and enjoyed in southern Africa and the Caribbean, and* asseda *or* asida, *a broth-filled version from Yemen and other Middle Eastern/North African countries.*

Preparation time: 10 minutes
Cooking time: 40 minutes
Serves: 2

· 1 cup (150 g) barley flour
· ¼ teaspoon ground cardamom
· 2 tablespoons melted Spiced Clarified Butter (page 44)
· ½ teaspoon berbere
· Salt
· ½ cup (140 g) full-fat yogurt, or to taste

Whisk the barley flour together with the ground cardamom. In a medium saucepan, bring 1¾ cups (415 ml/14 fl oz) water to a boil over medium-high heat. Reduce the heat to low slowly stream in the flour mixture, constantly stirring with a wooden spoon until it is a thick smooth paste, 4 minutes.

Heat the *niter kibbeh* in a small saucepan over medium heat until warmed. Mix in the berbere and salt to taste.

Scrape the porridge into a serving bowl and form it into a mound. Using a spoon, make an indent in the center, pour the *niter kibbeh* into the indentation, and spoon the yogurt around the perimeter of the *genfo* and serve.

MILLET PORRIDGE

RWANDA

Igikoma *is commonly known as millet porridge, even though multiple flours are used. Sosoma and Shisha are two name brands of the flour blend that typically combines millet, sorghum, and corn. The watery porridge is often enjoyed out of a mug.*

Preparation time: 5 minutes
Cooking time: 15 minutes
Serves: 2

· ⅓ cup (40 g) sorghum flour
· ⅓ cup (40 g) corn flour
· ⅓ cup (40 g) millet flour
· 2 teaspoons sugar

In a bowl, whisk together the sorghum, corn, and millet flours. Stir in 1 cup (240 ml/8 fl oz) water to create a paste. In a small saucepan, bring 3 cups (710 ml/24 fl oz) water to a boil over medium-high heat. Stir in the flour paste and cook, whisking constantly to avoid clumps, until just thickened, 2 minutes. Stir in the sugar, divide between two mugs or bowls, and serve.

OVERNIGHT OATS

UNITED STATES

This form of muesli is made by soaking a combination of rolled oats with milk, yogurt, nuts, seeds, and spices overnight. Though popular all around the United States, overnight oats is especially popular on the West Coast.

Preparation time: 10 minutes, plus overnight soaking time
Serves: 1

· ⅓ cup (25 g) rolled oats
· ⅓ cup (95 g) Greek yogurt
· ½ cup (120 ml/4 fl oz) unsweetened almond milk
· 2 tablespoons chia seeds (optional)
· 1 tablespoon flaxseeds (linseeds)
· 1 tablespoon almond butter
· 1 teaspoon honey
· ¼ teaspoon ground cinnamon
· Pinch or two of salt

For serving (optional):
· Fresh fruits, sliced
· Nuts, crushed or left whole
· Honey
· Coconut or cane sugar

In a jar or other food-safe container, mix together the oats, yogurt, almond milk, chia seeds, flaxseeds (linseeds), almond butter, honey, cinnamon, and salt to taste. Cover and refrigerate overnight.

Serve topped with fresh fruits, nuts, honey, and/or sugar to taste.

Overnight Oats

BAKED OATMEAL
UNITED STATES

This warm breakfast is made by baking milk-soaked rolled oats with spices and dried fruit. Prepare it the night before and bake in the morning for a warm alternative to Muesli (page 108), or hot Steel-Cut or Rolled-Oats Oatmeal (below and opposite). Baked oatmeal is sliced into servings and enjoyed in a bowl, topped with fresh berries and a splash of cold milk.

Preparation time: 10 minutes
Cooking time: 45 minutes
Serves: 2–4

· 4 tablespoons (60 g) unsalted butter, melted, plus more for the pan
· 1½ cups (120 g) rolled (porridge) oats
· ⅓ cup (65 g) packed light brown sugar
· ¾ teaspoon baking powder
· ½ teaspoon fine sea salt
· ½ teaspoon ground cinnamon
· ¼ teaspoon ground ginger (optional)
· ¾ cup (175 ml/6 fl oz) full-fat milk, plus more for serving
· 1 egg
· Fresh berries, to serve

Preheat the oven to 350°F (180°C/Gas Mark). Grease an 8-inch (20 cm) square baking pan with butter.
　In a large bowl, combine the oats, brown sugar, baking powder, salt, cinnamon, and ginger (if using) and stir to incorporate the ingredients thoroughly. In a separate bowl, whisk together the milk, egg, and melted butter. Pour the wet ingredients into the dry ingredients and stir with a wooden spoon or rubber spatula until thoroughly combined.
　Scrape the oats into the greased baking pan and gently spread into an even layer. Bake until set, about 45 minutes. Serve warm in a bowl with cold milk and berries.

STEEL-CUT OATMEAL
IRELAND / SCOTLAND / UNITED STATES

Different takes on this classic morning meal are served in the United States, United Kingdom, Ireland, and Northern Europe. Sometimes referred to as Irish or Scottish oats, this form of oatmeal has a longer cooking time than rolled oats (opposite) because the whole-oat groat is chopped into pieces rather than steamed and flattened. Optional toppings include: fruit (fresh or dried), nuts, seeds, sugar, butter, maple syrup, jam, milk or cream, even peanut butter (popular in the United States).

Preparation time: 5 minutes
Cooking time: 25 minutes
Serves: 1–2

· 1½ cups (355 ml/12 fl oz) full-fat milk or water
· ½ cut steel-cut (Scottish) oats
· Pinch of salt
· Fruit (fresh or dried), nuts and/or seeds, sugar, butter, maple syrup or jam, milk or cream, peanut butter, for serving (optional)

　In a small saucepan, bring the milk or water to a boil over medium-high heat. Stir in the oats and salt. Reduce the heat to low, cover, and simmer until most of the liquid is absorbed, 15–20 minutes. Serve warm with optional toppings.

ROLLED-OATS OATMEAL
ICELAND / UNITED STATES

Also called old-fashioned oats, rolled (porridge) oats cook are steamed until pliable then flattened to absorb liquid faster. This dish is enjoyed in United States, United Kingdom, and Ireland, and is a definitive breakfast in Iceland. Hafragrautur (Icelandic rolled oats oatmeal) is traditionally topped with Skyr (page 76) or sour milk similar to Swedish Filmjölk (page 76).

Preparation time: 5 minutes
Cooking time: 20 minutes
Serves: 2

· 1 cup (80 g) rolled (porridge) oats
· ½ teaspoon fine sea salt
· Raisins, butter, *skyr, filmjölk,* or brown sugar, for serving (optional)

In a small saucepan, combine the oats, 2 cups (475 ml/16 fl oz) water, and salt and bring to a boil over medium-high heat. Reduce the heat to low and simmer until the water is mostly evaporated and the oats are thick and tender, about 25 minutes. Serve warm with optional toppings.

SPICED SEMOLINA PORRIDGE
INDIA

Rava upma *is a South Indian roasted semolina and vegetable dish, topped with cashews and served with coconut chutney.* Rava *is the name used to refer to toasted flour.*

Preparation time: 10 minutes
Cooking time: 25 minutes
Serves: 1–2

· ½ cup (85 g) semolina flour
· 2 tablespoons ghee
· ½ teaspoon mustard seeds
· ¼ teaspoon cumin seeds
· 1 teaspoon urad dal (black lentils)
· 4 fresh curry leaves
· ½ small red onion, diced
· ½-inch (1.25 cm) piece fresh ginger, peeled and finely chopped
· ½ green chili, diced
· ½ teaspoon fine sea salt, or to taste
· Cashews, for serving
· Coconut Chutney (page 132)

In a medium frying pan, roast the semolina flour over medium heat, stirring often, until it is aromatic and warm but not browned, about 5 minutes. Set aside to cool.

In a small saucepan, heat the ghee over medium-high heat. Add the mustard seeds and cook until they begin to crackle and splatter, about 30 seconds. Add the cumin seeds, urad dal, and curry leaves and cook until beginning to brown, about 2 minutes. Add the red onion, ginger, and chili and cook until the red onion is translucent, about 7 minutes.

Pour in 1½ cups (355 ml/12 fl oz) water. Stir in salt, to taste. Bring the water to a boil, then reduce the heat to low and, stirring constantly, gradually stream in the roaste flour. When all of the water is absorbed, cover the pan, and cook for 2 minutes more.

Serve in a bowl topped with a few cashews and with coconut chutney on the side.

FLATTENED RICE PORRIDGE

INDIA

Poha *is a savory breakfast dish from Northern India, in which the flattened rice is tossed with vegetables and aromatic spices. While the preparation method is the same, each household tends to have a slightly different preference of spices and other ingredients.*

Preparation time: 10 minutes
Cooking time: 25 minutes
Serves: 4

· 2½ cups (400 g) poha (flattened rice)
· 6 tablespoons canola (rapeseed) oil
· 2 teaspoons mustard seeds
· 15 fresh curry leaves
· ¾ medium onion, coarsely chopped
· 1 jalapeño chili, chopped
· ½ cup (75 g) unsalted roasted peanuts
· 4 tablespoons golden raisins (sultanas)
· 1 small potato, boiled and cubed
· 1 teaspoon fine sea salt, plus more to taste
· ½ teaspoon ground turmeric
· ½ teaspoon red chili powder, plus more to taste
· ½ cup (20 g) cilantro (coriander), chopped
· 1 lime, halved

Place the *poha* in a fine-mesh sieve and shake to remove any small pieces. Evenly sprinkle with a little water (about 6 tablespoons) to barely moisten. Set aside.

In a saucepan or wok, heat the oil over medium heat. Add the mustard seeds and cook until they crackle, about 30 seconds. Stir in the curry leaves, onion, and jalapeño, and cook until the onion is soft and translucent, about 5 minutes. Add the peanuts and stir constantly to avoid burning them, about 1 minute. Stir in the raisins and potato.

Stir in the salt, turmeric, chili powder, and *poha*. The dish should have an even yellow color. Add more chili powder and salt to taste. Reduce the heat to low, cover, and cook for 2 minutes. Stir everything together, cover, and cook for 2 minutes longer, adding water by the tablespoon, if needed; the *poha* should not be too dry or too soggy. Serve in a bowl with cilantro and squeezed lime.

See image on page 303

CONGEE
CHINA

This oversaturated rice porridge is the lifeblood of morning culture in China and Southeast Asia. The type of rice, water amount, cooking time, toppings, and add-ins are all customized to fit regional and personal preferences. In Chinese, it's zhou, *and in Cantonese, it's* jook. *It is called* cháo gà *(Chicken and Rice Porridge, page 104) in Vietnam,* borbor sor *(Rice Porridge with Salted Duck Egg, page 104) in Cambodia, and* jok *(Rice Porridge with Pork Meatballs, page 100) in Thailand. Popular Chinese congee toppings include minced fried garlic or shallots, halved century eggs, pickled mustard greens, fresh herbs, chopped scallions, dried baby shrimp, ground chilies, white pepper, soy sauce, fish sauce,* youtiao *(Chinese Cruller, page 306), rice vinegar, chili oil, peanuts, fried wonton papers, ginger matchsticks, and shredded chicken, pork, or shrimp.*

Preparation time: 5 minutes
Cooking time: 1 hour 5 minutes
Serves: 2

· ½ cup (100 g) long-grain white rice, rinsed until the water runs clear

In a medium to large saucepan, combine the rice and 6 cups (1.4 liters/48 fl oz) water and bring to a boil over medium-high heat. Reduce the heat to low and simmer, stirring occasionally and adding more water if the mixture begins to dry, until the rice has broken down, thickened, and turned into a porridge consistency, about 1 hour. Serve in a bowl with any desired add-ins and toppings.

RICE PORRIDGE WITH PORK MEATBALLS

THAILAND

Jok *is a popular Thai version of Congee (page 99) made with small ground pork meatballs (sometimes fish) and jasmine rice. It can be garnished with an array of toppings, includingd chopped scallions (spring onions), ginger, white pepper, white vinegar, soy sauce or fish sauce, fried garlic and/or shallots, as well as additional pork products such as minced-pork meatballs and slices of liver.*

Preparation time: 10 minutes
Cooking time: 1 hour
Serves: 2

· ½ cup (100 g) jasmine rice, rinsed until the water runs clear
· 4 oz (115 g) ground (minced) pork
· ½-inch (1.25 cm) piece fresh ginger, peeled and finely chopped
· ½ tablespoon minced garlic
· 1 teaspoon fish sauce, plus more to taste
· 2 tablespoons soy sauce, plus more to taste
· 2 scallions (spring onions), chopped

In a medium to large saucepan, combine the rice and 6 cups (1.4 liters/48 fl oz) water and bring to a boil over medium-high heat. Reduce to a simmer and cook, stirring occasionally and adding more water if the mixture begins to dry, for 30 minutes.

Meanwhile, in a medium-sized bowl, mix the pork, ginger, garlic, ½ teaspoon of fish sauce, and 1 tablespoon soy sauce until thoroughly combined. Set aside.

Simmer the porridge until the rice has broken down, thickened, and turned into a porridge-like consistency, about 30 minutes.

Form the pork mixture into bite-size balls and add to the simmering rice porridge along with the remaining fish sauce and soy sauce. Cook for an additional 2–3 minutes until the meatballs are cooked through.

Serve in bowls and season with more fish sauce and soy sauce to taste, garnished with scallions and desired toppings.

Rice Porridge with Pork Meatballs

CHOCOLATE RICE PORRIDGE

PHILIPPINES

Champorado *is a chocolate rice porridge typically accompanied by* tuyo *(salty dried fish).*

Preparation time: 5 minutes
Cooking time: 25 minutes
Serves: 2

· 4 oz (115 g) bittersweet (dark) chocolate (60–70% cacao)
· ¾ cup (140 g) glutinous (sticky) rice, rinsed until the water runs clear
· 4 tablespoons granulated sugar
· ½ teaspoon vanilla extract
· ½ teaspoon grated orange zest (optional)
· 2 tablespoons condensed milk, or to taste
· 2 tuyo (dried herring), or to taste

In a heatproof bowl set over a pan filled with 2 inches (5 cm) of simmering water (make sure the water does not touch the bowl), melt the chocolate. Set aside.

In a saucepan, combine the rice and 2½ cups (590 ml/10 fl oz) water, cover, and bring to a boil over medium-high heat. Reduce the heat to a simmer and cook, stirring the rice occasionally, until it begins to thicken, 12–15 minutes. Add the sugar and melted chocolate. Stir to combine and continue to simmer until thickened, 3–4 more minutes. Remove from the heat and stir in the vanilla and orange zest.

Serve in bowls drizzled with condensed milk and with dried herring on the side.

Chocolate Rice Porridge

CHICKEN AND RICE PORRIDGE
VIETNAM

Cháo gà is a popular Vietnamese variation of a Chinese Congee (page 99), often enjoyed as a street-food breakfast.

Preparation time: 5 minutes
Cooking time: 1 hour 10 minutes
Serves: 2

· 2 bone-in, skin-on chicken thighs
· ½ teaspoon salt, plus more to taste
· ½ cup (100 g) jasmine rice, rinsed until the water runs clear
· Fish sauce
· Cilantro (coriander) leaves, for garnish
· Crispy fried shallots, for garnish (optional)

In a medium saucepan, combine the chicken thighs and 5 cups (1.2 liters/40 fl oz) water. Stir in the salt. Bring to a boil over medium-high heat, then reduce the heat to medium and cook until the chicken is tender and cooked through, 25–30 minutes, skimming off any foam that rises to the surface. Reserving the broth in the pan, transfer the chicken to a cutting board. When cool enough to handle, shred the chicken meat (discard the skin and bones).
    Return the broth to a boil. Add the rice to the broth, reduce the heat to low, cover, and simmer, stirring occasionally to keep the rice from sticking to the bottom of the pan, until the rice is thick and creamy, 30–40 minutes. Season with fish sauce and salt to taste. Transfer the *cháo ga* to a serving bowl and top with the shredded chicken, cilantro, and fried shallots (if using).

RICE PORRIDGE WITH SALTED DUCK EGG
CAMBODIA

The most common breakfast in Cambodia, borbor *sor is a rice porridge like Congee (page 99), but slightly looser in consistency and with more defined grains of rice. It is typically topped with a salted duck egg. You can substitute with a soft-boiled egg (page 14) with a generous seasoning of salt.*

Preparation time: 5 minutes
Cooking time: 50 minutes
Serves: 2

· ½ cup (100 g) long-grain white rice, rinsed until the water runs clear
· 4 cups (950 ml/32 fl oz) chicken stock
· 1 scallion (spring onion), chopped
· 2 salted duck eggs, halved, for serving

In a medium saucepan, combine the rice and stock and bring to a boil over medium-high heat. Reduce to a simmer and cook, stirring occasionally to keep the rice from sticking to the bottom of the pan, until the rice has absorbed all the stock, the rice has thickened and the porridge is creamy, about 45 minutes. Serve with a sprinkling of scallion and a salted duck egg.

CHIA PUDDING
UNITED STATES

Chia seeds are considered a superfood rich in omega-3 fatty acid and the B vitamins. The seeds swell when soaked and form a clear viscous outer layer that binds them all together to form a pudding.

Preparation time: 5 minutes, plus 3 hours chilling time
Serves: 1

· 1 cup (240 ml/8 fl oz) Almond Milk (page 440) or coconut milk
· 4 tablespoons chia seeds
· ½ teaspoon vanilla extract
· Fresh fruit or nuts, such as sliced almonds, shredded coconut, fresh berries, mango slices, and/or Granola (page 110), for topping

In a mason jar, combine the milk, chia seeds, and vanilla extract. Stir to combine. Cover and let chill in the refrigerator for 3 hours or up to overnight. The next morning, serve in a bowl, with toppings.

GREEN BANANA PORRIDGE
JAMAICA

A fragrant porridge made of green bananas, a savory departure from traditional sweet, ripe yellow bananas.

Preparation time: 10 minutes
Cooking time: 20 minutes
Serves: 4

· 2 green bananas, peeled and sliced
· 2 cups (475 ml/16 fl oz) unsweetened coconut milk
· 1 tablespoon sugar
· ½ teaspoon ground cinnamon
· ¼ teaspoon ground nutmeg
· Salt
· ½ teaspoon vanilla extract

In a food processor or blender, blend the bananas and 1½ cups (355 ml/12 fl oz) water together. Pour the blended bananas into a small saucepan and stir in the coconut milk. Bring the mixture to a boil and then reduce the heat to low. Stir in the sugar, cinnamon, nutmeg, and salt to taste. Allow the porridge to simmer until thickened, 10–15 minutes, stirring occasionally. Stir in the vanilla and serve warm.

BANANA BREAD PORRIDGE

SAUDI ARABIA / UNITED ARAB EMIRATES / YEMEN

Masoub, *also referred to as* malakia, *is a ground-up flatbread and banana porridge. The flatbread (typically* khubz, *but any flatbread can be used) acts as a binding agent to thicken the bananas into a porridge. Chai Karak (page 429), a cardamom-infused black tea, is the traditional accompaniment.*

Preparation time: 15 minutes
Serves: 2

· ½ khubz or flatbread, torn into pieces
· 2 overripe bananas, peeled and mashed
· 2 tablespoons honey
· 2 tablespoons almonds, coarsely chopped
· Yogurt, for serving
· ¼ banana, sliced, for serving

In a food processor or blender, pulse or blend the flatbread until it is very finely ground. Mix the flatbread crumbs into the mashed bananas and stir until the consistency is thick and slightly firm. Scoop into 2 bowls, smooth the top, and drizzle each with honey, almonds, yogurt, and banana slices.

TOASTED CORNFLAKES

GLOBAL

One of the most significant breakfast items on a global scale is cold cereal, typically store bought and enjoyed in a bowl with milk. The Cornflakes cereal was invented in Michigan in 1894 by John Harvey Kellogg as a healthy meal for patients of the sanitarium where he was superintendent. The bland cornmeal crisps were intended to be a sterilizing breakfast to aid in digestion and to keep the mind balanced and free of sin. Sugar-coated cornflakes became popular in the 1950's and gave way for many of the popular mass-produced cereals on the market today.

Preparation time: 10 minutes
Cooking time: 1 hour 20 minutes
Makes: 1½ cups (200 g)

· Vegetable oil, for greasing
· ¾ cup (100 g) medium-grind yellow cornmeal
· 4 tablespoons finely ground cornmeal (masa harina)
· ¼ teaspoon fine sea salt
· ½ teaspoon vanilla extract
· 2 tablespoons honey
· 2 tablespoons sugar (optional)
· Milk, for serving
· Fresh berries (optional)

Preheat the oven to 350°F (180°C/Gas Mark 4). Line a baking sheet with greased parchment paper.

In a bowl, combine both types of cornmeal with the salt. In a separate bowl, stir the vanilla extract, 6 tablespoons water, and honey together. Gradually stir the water-honey mixture into the dry ingredients with a wooden spoon until thoroughly combined and the mixture has a consistency similar to pancake batter.

Spread the batter into a thin layer about ⅛ inch (3 mm) thick. The batter should be as thin as possible without seeing any parchment paper. To make frosted cereal, sprinkle 2 tablespoons of sugar over the batter just before baking. Bake for 20 minutes, rotating the baking sheet front to back halfway through, and keeping an eye on it to avoid burning. Remove from the oven and allow to cool slightly.

Using a spatula, break up the dough into cereal-size flakes. Lower the oven to 250°F (130°C/Gas Mark ½). Return the pan to the oven and bake until dried out, about 45 minutes.

Let the cereal cool before serving with milk, sugar, and berries, if using.

Toasted Cornflakes

MUESLI
AUSTRALIA / SWITZERLAND

Bircher müesli, or müesli for short, was originally developed in the late 1800's by Swiss-German physician Maximillian Bircher-Brenner as part of a healthy diet treatment for his patients, along with exercise. His beliefs in healing the body through health food and movement were contradictory to the religious and public beliefs of medicine at the time. Müesli has become such a staple portion of a European breakfast around the world, often sold pre-packaged. The various dry ingredient blends make it easy to soak overnight or to simply enjoy with milk or yogurt. In Australia, muesli (without the umlaut) is a staple morning "brekkie" recipe that changes with the seasons, available ingredients, and personal preferences. Australians typically enjoy their muesli baked with honey. Fruit juice can be used as a muesli soak as opposed to the milk-soaked version from Switzerland. Use this recipe as a guide to experiment with a variety of base ingredients such as rolled (porridge) oats (Uncle Toby's Oats are popular in Australia), buckwheat, and/or amaranth, and a wide range of toppings.

Preparation time: 10 minutes, plus overnight soaking time
Serves: 2

· ½ cup (40 g) rolled (porridge) oats
· 4 tablespoons full-fat milk or water
· ½ tablespoon lemon juice

For serving Swiss bircher müesli:
· 4 tablespoons condensed or fresh milk
· 2 tablespoons honey
· 1 apple, cubed, or desired fresh fruit
· 2 tablespoons dried fruit
· 2 tablespoons nuts
· ½ cup (40 g) rolled (porridge) oats
· ½ cup (120 ml/4 fl oz) plus 2 tablespoons apple juice
· 2 dried apricots, chopped
· 1 tablespoon golden raisins (sultanas)
· 1 tablespoon chia seeds

For serving Australian muesli:
· 4 tablespoons almond milk or yogurt
· 2 tablespoon honey
· 4 tablespoons mixed berries
· 2 dried apricots, chopped
· 2 tablespoons golden raisins (sultanas)
· 1 tablespoon chia seeds
· 2 tablespoons macadamia nuts
· 2 tablespoons waddleseeds (a seed native to Australia)
· 2 tablespoons Brazil nuts
· 2 tablespoons rhubarb compote
· 2 tablespoons puréed pumpkin
· 2 tablespoons mango chutney

In a small bowl, combine the oats, milk or water, and lemon. Cover with plastic wrap (cling film) and refrigerate overnight to allow the oats to absorb the milk. The next morning, stir in a spoonful of yogurt or milk. Serve in a bowl topped with desired Swiss or Australian toppings.

Muesli

GRANOLA
UNITED STATES

A form of cereal similar to muesli, granola is a combination rolled (porridge) oats with a variety of sweeteners and add-ins. Granola, however, is baked before being served as a cereal, used as a topping for yogurt (see Yogurt Parfait on page 72), or formed into bars for a quick, portable breakfast or snack.

Preparation time: 10 minutes
Cooking time: 45 minutes
Serves: 4

- 2 cups (160 g) rolled (porridge) oats
- 1 cup (100 g) of seeds and/or nuts, such as sliced almonds, hulled pumpkin seeds, and shredded coconut
- ½ tablespoon mixed spices such as cinnamon, ground ginger, cardamom, nutmeg, and cloves, or any preferred spice blend
- Pinch of salt
- 2 tablespoons olive oil, vegetable oil, or melted coconut oil
- ½ cup (120 ml/4 fl oz) liquid sweetener, such as maple syrup or honey
- ½ teaspoon vanilla extract
- ½ cup (50 g) chopped dried apricots, raisins, or other dried fruit

Preheat the oven to 300°F (150°C/Gas Mark 2).

In a large bowl, combine the oats, seeds/nuts, and spices. Toss until thoroughly combined. In a small bowl, combine the oil, sweetener, and vanilla. Pour the wet ingredients over the dry ingredients and stir to combine until no dry parts remain. Spread the granola, without breaking it up, onto a baking sheet lined with parchment. Bake, rotating the sheet front to back halfway through baking and tossing the granola for an even bake, until golden brown and aromatic, about 45 minutes.

If you want chunky granola, wait for it to cool before breaking it up. Otherwise, stir the granola to break it up into smaller chunks when it is still warm. Once cool, stir in the dried fruit and keep the granola stored in an airtight cereal container for up to 1 month.

Granola

AKES

BLUEBERRY PANCAKES

CANADA / UNITED STATES

This is a classic pancake enjoyed across the United States and Canada. Popular add-ins or batter mix-ins besides blueberry are banana, walnut, and chocolate chips. You can, make silver dollar (mini) pancakes by using just 1 tablespoon of batter per pancake. Serve topped with butter and maple syrup.

Preparation time: 10 minutes
Cooking time: 20 minutes
Serves: 2–4

· 1½ cups (215 g) all-purpose (plain) flour
· 3 tablespoons sugar
· 1½ teaspoons baking powder
· ½ teaspoon fine sea salt
· 1 cup (240 ml/8 fl oz) full-fat milk
· 2 eggs
· 2 tablespoons (30 g) unsalted butter, melted and cooled, plus more for the pan and for serving
· 1 cup (115–150 g) blueberries

In a bowl, combine the flour, sugar, baking powder, and salt. In a separate bowl, whisk together the milk, eggs, and melted butter. Stir the wet ingredients into the dry until no dry spots remain. It's fine if there are a few lumps.

In a medium frying pan, melt ½ tablespoon butter over medium heat. Ladle in ¼ cup of the pancake batter. Cook until bubbles begin to appear on the surface and the edges are beginning to crisp, about 2 minutes—1 minute in, sprinkle ¼ cup (35 g) blueberries onto the batter. Using a metal spatula, flip the pancake. Reduce the heat to low to ensure even cooking. Cook on the other side until golden, about 2 minutes more. Transfer to a plate. Add more butter to the frying pan as needed and repeat with the remaining batter.

Serve warm with butter and maple syrup.

Blueberry Pancakes

BUTTERMILK PANCAKES

CANADA / UNITED STATES

Preparation time: 10 minutes
Cooking time: 20 minutes
Serves: 2–4

Similar to the classic pancake batter (Blueberry Pancakes, page 114), but with the addition of buttermilk, which adds a tangy flavor and baking soda, which creates a fluffier texture. Buttermilk pancakes have interchangeable add-ins and toppings like blueberry, banana, walnut, and chocolate chip. Serve topped with butter and syrup.

· 1½ cups (215 g) all-purpose (plain) flour
· 3 tablespoons sugar
· 1 teaspoon baking soda (bicarbonate of soda)
· ½ teaspoon baking powder
· ½ teaspoon fine sea salt
· 2 eggs
· 1½ cups (355 ml/12 fl oz) buttermilk
· 2 tablespoons (30 g) unsalted butter, melted and cooled, plus more for the griddle
· Toppings (optional), per pancake: 3 tablespoons blueberries; 5 banana slices; 2 tablespoons chopped walnuts and/or chocolate chips
· Butter, for serving
· Maple syrup, for serving

In a bowl, combine the flour, sugar, baking soda (bicarb), baking powder, and salt. In a separate bowl, whisk together the eggs, buttermilk, and melted butter. Stir the wet ingredients into the dry until no dry spots remain. It's fine if there are a few lumps.

Heat a griddle or cast-iron skillet over medium heat. Melt ½ tablespoon butter. Ladle in ¼ cup of the pancake batter. Cook until bubbles begin to appear on the surface and the edges are beginning to crisp, about 2 minutes—1 minute in, sprinkle with desired topping. Using a metal spatula, flip the pancake. Reduce the heat to low to ensure even cooking. Cook on the other side until golden, about 2 minutes more. Add more butter to the frying pan as needed and repeat with the remaining batter.

Serve warm with butter and maple syrup.

WAFFLES
UNITED STATES

Waffle batter is cooked in a special hinged pan that molds to the shape of the waffle iron. Waffle-iron molds can be novelty or traditional, like the shallow square honeycomb pattern of American waffles, the floral motif of an Italian pizzelle, or the Chinese egg waffle emulating the shape of bubble wrap. The Belgian waffle is most similar to an American waffle, but with deeper pockets and semi-perforated quadrants. This is the American version, traditionally spread liberally with butter and doused with maple syrup. The American South has a sweet and savory version with the addition of fried chicken.

Preparation time: 10 minutes
Cooking time: 20 minutes
Serves: 2–4 , makes 4 waffles

· 1 cup (145 g) all-purpose (plain) flour
· 1 tablespoon sugar
· 1 teaspoon baking powder
· ⅛ teaspoon fine sea salt
· 3 tablespoons (45 g) unsalted butter, melted
· ¾ cup (175 ml/6 fl oz) plus 2 tablespoons full-fat milk
· 1 egg
· Butter, for serving
· Maple syrup, for serving

In a medium bowl, combine the flour, sugar, baking powder, and salt. Stir together until thoroughly incorporated. In a separate bowl, whisk together the melted butter, milk, and egg. Pour the wet ingredients into the dry ingredients, stirring together with a wooden spoon until no dry spots remain. It's okay if there are a few lumps.

Preheat a waffle maker according to manufacturer instructions. Coat with cooking spray and dollop ½ cup (120 ml/4 fl oz) batter into the waffle maker. Cook per waffle maker instructions or until the steaming stops, about 5 minutes. Serve hot.

DUTCH BABY
UNITED STATES

This baked pancake dramatically puffs in the oven, then deflates soon after it is taken from the heat. A searing hot cast-iron skillet and whipped eggs give this pancake its unique rise. The recipe is of German origin, but is said to have been popularized in Seattle in the early 1900s.

Preparation time: 10 minutes
Cooking time: 20 minutes
Serves: 2

· ½ cup (70 g) all-purpose (plain) flour
· ½ cup (120 ml/4 fl oz) full-fat milk
· 1 tablespoon sugar
· 3 eggs
· 4 tablespoons (60 g) unsalted butter, plus more for serving
· ⅛ teaspoon fine sea salt
· 1 wedge of lemon, for serving
· Maple syrup, for serving
· Powdered (icing) sugar, for serving

Preheat the oven to 425°F (220°C/Gas Mark 7). Heat a cast-iron skillet in the oven for 10 minutes until piping hot.

Meanwhile, in a blender, combine the flour, milk, sugar, eggs, 3 tablespoons of melted butter, and salt. Blend until the batter is frothy.

Remove the skillet from the oven and add the remaining 1 tablespoon butter, swirling it around to coat the pan, taking care not to burn yourself as the skillet will be very hot. Pour in the batter and return the skillet to the oven. Bake until pancake is puffed up and golden brown, 18–20 minutes.

Serve warm with butter and a squeeze of lemon, or butter and maple syrup, and top with powdered (icing) sugar.

JOHNNY CAKES
UNITED STATES

Similar to a traditional pancake but made with cornmeal, Johnny cakes are a New England breakfast dish also called hoecakes in the Southern United States. The Johnny cakes you would find in the US Virgin Islands, Jamaica, Bahamas, and Belize are deep-fried dumplings (page 383).

Preparation time: 10 minutes
Cooking time: 20 minutes
Serves: 2–4

· 1 cup (130 g) white cornmeal
· ½ teaspoon sugar (optional)
· ½ teaspoon fine sea salt
· ¾ cup (175 ml/6 fl oz) boiling water
· ½ tablespoon vegetable oil or butter, plus more as needed for the pan
· Maple syrup, for serving

In a bowl, combine the cornmeal, sugar (if using), and salt. Gradually pour in the boiling water, stirring constantly. Continue to stir until a thick pancake batter forms. Let the batter rest for 10 minutes.

In a medium skillet, heat the oil or butter over medium heat. Spoon 2 tablespoons of batter into the pan and cook until browned underneath, about 2 minutes. Reduce the heat to low to ensure even cooking. Cook on the other side until golden, about 2 minutes more. Transfer to a plate and repeat with the remaining batter, adding more oil if needed. Serve warm with maple syrup.

Dutch Baby

TAPIOCA-FLOUR CREPES

BRAZIL

These crepes are made with hydrated tapioca flour, which instantly binds into a disk when it hits the pan. Tapioca starch comes pre-hydrated, but this recipe shows how to do this with dry tapioca flour. The crepes are light as air with a toothy bite from the gummy texture of tapioca. They often come filled with everything from shredded coconut and bananas to ham and eggs, cheese, jam, and more.

Preparation time: 5 minutes
Cooking time: 10 minutes
Serves: 2

· ½ cup (60 g) tapioca flour (or ¼ cup hydrated tapioca starch)
· 2 tablespoons shredded coconut, per pancake
· ½ banana, sliced, per pancake
· 1 tablespoon sweetened condensed milk, per pancake

Place the tapioca flour in a bowl and gradually add 3 tablespoons water 1 tablespoon at a time. Mix the water into the flour with your fingertips, massaging until smooth. The hydrated tapioca flour should appear dry and powdery.

Heat a nonstick frying pan over medium heat. Sift the flour through a fine-mesh sieve, dusting an even layer until the pan is fully covered: You should not be able to see the frying pan through the crepe. Cook for 1 minute before loosening the rim of the crepe. Reduce the heat to low, flip the crepe, and cook the other side, pushing down on it to lightly brown, 1 minute more. Transfer to a plate and fill with desired toppings. Repeat with the remaining tapioca flour.

GRATED POTATO PANCAKE

IRELAND

A key element of an Irish Fry Up (page 28), a boxty is a grated potato pancake similar to a latke (page 59). The loose mixture of milk, flour, and potato make this a pancake/hash-brown hybrid, rather a potato bread like Potato Farl (page 201), common in an Ulster Fry (page 28), or Tattie Scones (page 201), common in a Scottish Fry Up (page 28).

Preparation time: 15 minutes
Cooking time: 20 minutes
Serves: 2

· ½ lb (225 g) russet potatoes (1 large), peeled
· 1 egg
· ¼ cup (60 ml) full-fat milk
· 2 tablespoons all-purpose (plain) flour
· Salt and freshly ground pepper
· 2 tablespoons (30 g) unsalted butter, plus more as needed

Grate the potatoes on the large holes of a box grater. Transfer to a bowl of water and toss for about 30 seconds, to remove extra starch. Drain the potatoes, transfer to a tea towel, and wring out the water.

In a bowl, combine the shredded potatoes, egg, milk, and flour. Season with salt and pepper and stir until thoroughly combined. The mixture will be a little runny.

In a medium frying pan, melt the butter over medium heat, swirling the pan to coat it evenly. Pour in the potato mixture and cook until the underside is golden brown, about 8 minutes. Flip, adding more butter if the frying pan is dry, and cook until the other side is golden brown, 8 minutes more. Serve warm.

Tapioca-Flour Crepes

BLINI
RUSSIA

Enjoyed alone or filled with sweet and savory fillings, blintzes, crepes, or blini, are all different ways to order this thin Russian pancake. Fillings and toppings can include jams, honey, caviar, salmon roe, sour cream, or plum spread with butter. Blinis can also be stored in the refrigerator for a quick breakfast throughout the week.

Preparation time: 10 minutes
Cooking time: 5 minutes
Serves: 2

· ¼ cup (35 g) all-purpose (plain) flour
· ¼ cup (35 g) buckwheat flour
· 1 tablespoon sugar
· ½ cup (120 ml/4 fl oz) + 1 tablespoon full-fat milk
· 1 egg
· ⅛ teaspoon fine sea salt
· 1 tablespoon vegetable oil or melted butter

In a blender or food processor, blend the flours, sugar, milk, egg, salt, and vegetable oil or melted butter until smooth and just starting to froth.

Heat a medium nonstick frying pan over medium heat and coat lightly with cooking spray. Pour in 4 tablespoons of the batter and swirl around the pan to coat evenly in a thin layer, about 8 inches (20 cm) in diameter. Cook until the crepe looks dry, about 30 seconds. Using a spatula, loosen the rim of the crepe. Flip and cook for another 10 seconds. Transfer to a plate and repeat with the remaining batter.

PANCAKES WITH BUTTER AND HONEY
MOROCCO

This Moroccan pancake, called baghrir, *is similar to an English muffin or crumpet. It is defined by the many holes that form on its surface. Cooked on one side only, these plush pancakes are topped with butter and honey and eaten for breakfast or as a snack. In the south of Morocco,* baghrir *is served with* amlou, *a mixture of ground almonds, argan oil, honey, and sugar.*

Preparation time: 15 minutes, plus 2 hours resting time
Cooking time: 40 minutes
Serves: 4, makes 8 pancakes

· 2 cups (470 ml/16 fl oz) warm water
· 1½ teaspoons active dry yeast
· A pinch plus 2 teaspoons sugar
· 1 cup (165 g) semolina flour
· 2 tablespoons all-purpose (plain) flour
· 1 teaspoon baking powder
· ¼ teaspoon fine sea salt
· 2 eggs
· Butter, for serving
· Honey, for serving

In a bowl, combine the warm water, yeast, and pinch of sugar. Set the mixture aside until the yeast is frothy, about 10 minutes. (If the yeast doesn't froth, check the expiration date. You may have to start over with fresher yeast.)

In a blender, combine the yeast mixture, both flours, baking powder, 2 teaspoons sugar, salt, and eggs. Blend until frothy. Let sit until bubbles form on the surface of the batter, at least 2 hours. Gently stir the mixture to incorporate the bubbles into the batter.

Heat a nonstick frying pan over medium heat. Pour in ¼ cup of batter. Bubbles on the surface of the pancake should begin to appear immediately. Cook until the pancake is opaque and the batter has cooked through, 4 minutes. Do not flip. Transfer to a plate and repeat with the remaining batter.

Serve with butter and honey.

Pancakes with Butter and Honey

PANCAKES WITH CRUSHED PEANUTS AND SUGAR

MALAYSIA

Popular across Southeast Asia as ban jian kuih, min jiang kueh, *or* apam balik, *this is a yeast-activated griddle cake filled with ground peanuts, sugar, and butter.*

Preparation time: 10 minutes, plus 2 hours resting time
Cooking time: 30 minutes
Serves: 2–4

For the batter:
· ¾ cup (120 ml/54 fl oz) full-fat milk, warmed
· 2 tablespoons sugar
· ½ teaspoon active dry yeast
· 1 cup (145 g) all-purpose (plain) flour
· ¼ teaspoon baking soda (bicarbonate of soda)
· ¼ teaspoon fine sea salt
· 1 egg
· 2 tablespoons unsalted butter

For the filling:
· ¾ cup (110 g) roasted peanuts, coarsely chopped
· 4 tablespoons light brown sugar

Make the batter:
In a small bowl, combine the warm milk, a pinch of sugar, and yeast. Set the mixture aside until the yeast is frothy, about 10 minutes. (If the yeast doesn't froth, check the expiration date. You may have to start over with fresher yeast.)

In a separate bowl, whisk together the flour, baking soda (bicarbonate of soda), salt, and remaining sugar. Add the yeast mixture and egg and whisk until smooth. No lumps should remain.

Cover the bowl with plastic wrap (cling film) and allow it to rest for 2 hours. The batter should be activated and bubbling.

Make the filling:
In a bowl, combine the roasted peanuts and brown sugar and set aside.

In a medium frying pan, heat ½ tablespoon of butter over medium heat. Pour in half of the batter and spread it evenly in the pan. Let cook until bubbles begin to form, 1 minute. Cover with a lid and let the pancake cook until the edges begin to bubble and turn opaque, 1 minute. Use your hands to break up ½ tablespoon of butter over the top of the pancake. Sprinkle half of the peanut mixture over the pancake. Cook, covered, another 2 minutes until the pancake easily releases from the sides of the pan. Fold the pancake over with a spatula and transfer to a plate. Repeat with the remaining batter and filling. Serve warm.

VEGETABLE PANCAKE

SOUTH INDIA

Uttapam *is a South Indian vegetable pancake that often uses the same batter as a Dosa (page 130) but is much thicker. Chopped vegetables are added to the top and it is served with chutneys (pages 131–32).*

Preparation time: 15 minutes plus overnight soaking time and 8 hours fermenting time for dosa batter
Cooking time: 15 minutes
Makes/Serves: 2

· Dosa batter (page 130)
· Ghee, for the pan
· ½ small onion, diced
· 1 carrot, chopped
· ½ tomato, chopped
· 1 small jalapeño chili, seeded and chopped
· Chutneys (pages 131–32), for serving

In a medium bowl mix the onion, carrot, tomato, and jalapeño.

In a frying pan or griddle, melt the ghee over medium heat. Spoon 1 cup (240 ml) of batter into the pan. Sprinkle about 3 tablespoons of the vegetables over the *uttapam* and cook until golden, about 4 minutes. Add ½ tablespoon of ghee to the top of the pancake and flip. Cook on the other side, about 3 minutes more, until golden brown. Repeat with the remaining batter and vegetables. Serve vegetable-side up with chutneys.

HOPPERS

SRI LANKA

Appa *in Sinhalese and* appam *in Tamil, these bowl-shaped pancakes, made with a fermented rice flour and coconut milk batter, are cooked in a small round nonstick pan called a "hopper pan," similar to a small wok. Thin edges will form at the top, with a thicker, fluffier base. Hoppers can be enjoyed plain but are commonly served with a fried egg cooked into the bottom. Similar in shape, string hoppers are another variation that use a special press to create thin nests of toasted rice flour. Serve with sambal (page 278).*

Preparation time: 20 minutes, plus up to overnight resting time
Cooking time: 1 hour
Makes: 12 hoppers

· 4 tablespoons warm water
· 2 teaspoons sugar
· 1 teaspoon active dry yeast
· 1½ cups (235 g) rice flour
· ½ cups (60 g) all-purpose (plain) flour
· 1 teaspoon fine sea salt
· 1 egg, beaten
· 1 cup (240 ml/8 fl oz) coconut milk
· Vegetable oil, for the pan
· 12 eggs (for Egg Hoppers only, optional)
· Sambal (page 278), for serving

In a bowl, combine the warm water, sugar, and yeast. Set the mixture aside until the yeast is frothy, about 10 minutes.

In a separate bowl, combine the flours and salt. Add the yeast mixture, egg, and 1 cup (250 ml/8 fl oz) water and stir to form a thick paste. Cover the batter with plastic wrap (cling film) and leave to rest for at least 8 hours (preferably overnight).

Add the mixture to a blender with coconut milk and blend until smooth. Let rest for 15 minutes.

Heat a small wok over low heat. Grease the wok liberally. Spoon ¼ cup of batter into the wok, let it set for a few seconds, then swirl the batter around to coat the sides, creating a bowl of batter. If making Egg Hoppers, crack 1 egg in the bottom of the pancake and season with salt. Cook, covered, until the pancake is browned and crispy, about 8-10 minutes. Using a flexible spatula, carefully loosen the edges from the pan. Slide onto a plate and serve warm with sambal.

JASON HAMMEL
AMERICAN BREAKFAST

Jason Hammel is the Chicago, Illinois–based chef and owner of Lula Café in historic Logan Square and Marisol Restaurant at the Museum of Contemporary Art. Chef Hammel splits his time between the restaurants and his not-for-profit food-education foundation, Pilot Light Chefs. Through his work in Chicago classrooms and kitchens, Chef Hammel seeks to bring community, creativity, nourishment, and purpose back to the table.

To know how to cook a perfect over-easy egg, you have to know how to catch a baseball with your bare hand. A hardball that your father has thrown you a bit too hard, when you are eight years old. It comes at you fast and unpredictably, with what you worry is an oddly vindictive force. You have to learn not to hold your hand like a shield, but rather like the net into which a trapeze artist falls, giving under the weight then bending back. As the ball speeds toward you and you reach out your hand, it might make sense to close your eyes and grit your teeth. Prepare yourself. Surely it will hurt as it smacks your palm. But this is not how to catch the ball barehanded. And this is not how to cook the egg. Let your hand fall back, don't fight it, give in, pull back.

The man working next to me at the Odyssey Diner in Illinois cannot speak English, so I can't tell him what I'm thinking. Besides, it's busy. I'm calling orders in a stream of stenographic code: "OE, OM, 2 poached, 4 hard, 2 OE, scram fly." These are the words he knows. Small Teflon-coated pans cover the stove, on burners, in between burners, perched on the stainless-steel edge. I organize the pick. OEs (eggs over easy) have to be flipped just as six other plates are coming together on the kitchen's opposite end, so I look to synchronize the egg cook's movements with theirs. I call three minutes to the pass.

The ball goes skidding into dewy grass. I pick it up and throw it back at my dad and watch as he exaggeratedly palms the hardball. "See," he says, "it's not a hard thing to do."

Two minutes to go. The egg cook puts his good pans down on his best flames. The good pans are ones he buys himself and hides in his locker. They are cared for as my father cares for his vinyl. He wants the frictionless surface of a hot, clean pan. He heats them over a medium flame, drizzles a thin skin of oil. Then comes a move I love to watch—he swirls this oil, and then cracks eggs one at a time using a deft motion of a quick right hand. A sharp tap on the pan's edge and a twist of the fingers, and the egg *collapses* into the pan, the oil speaking back with an expectant crackle. It's just enough heat to set the white without any browning at the edge. He rotates the pan again to even out the whites, then sets it down on a flame. Using his thumb and forefinger, he picks at the membrane around the yolk with his fingers until it breaks, then prepares for the flip.

It's the flip that everyone else does wrong. Bad flips break yolks or fold the egg in half—or worse, get some stubborn part of it stuck to the edge of a pan. Bad flips stall the line and create chaos. Bad flips are for Wednesdays, the only day he doesn't work.

"Plating," I say loudly.

The first time I actually catch the ball, I think my middle knuckle has cracked. It stings and swells, but I hold on. I look out at my father, who claps once on my behalf. "Yes," he says. "That's it." But that's not it. My palm is bruised and red and the knuckle smarts for days. I throw the ball back to him, but it hits ground halfway home.

The egg cook swishes the pan around in a circle. The egg rotates effortlessly, in sync with his motions. He spins it two or three times. Then, with an extended and elongated arc, he pushes the pan forward with just the right amount of force and lift, and when it looks like the egg is about to fly forward across the room, he gives the pan a deft and sharp backwards flick of the wrist. The egg goes up and over.

Suspend the moment and you'd see the egg in the air as it flips back upon itself. As it does, you'd see that he was dropping the pan, falling back, giving in. He'd stepped sideways so that he could drop the pan deeply at his side. The exposed, vulnerable yolks don't smack hard against a hard surface. Instead they are caught, as though by a soft bare hand. He slides the eggs onto a plate, then turns to the next. "6 OE, 2 scram, 2 poached, basted, 2 OM," I call. "6 minutes."

I didn't know him before he'd learned to cook an egg like this. He learned it here, on this line, wearing the same dishwashers' shirt and baggy jeans that he's worn on every shift for six years now. Guys said that nobody, not in this city or any other city, has ever been as good.

We leave the ball in the grass and go inside for lunch. My grandmother cracks two eggs with spindly hands and boils them for me. My father eats a sandwich on newspaper to save from wasting water on dishes. He reads the articles through the grease stains and crumbs. I'm pretty sure we never played catch again.

Eventually the egg cook left to go back home. During his last shift he told me that he had bought his jeans with his first ever paycheck from the diner. He said he would never wear them again. He was quitting the job, quitting the uniform, too. Tomorrow he'd be on a plane.

"Do you know how to play baseball?" I asked.
"I never touched a baseball," he said.
"Will you see your father?" I asked.
"Yes," he said. "He is waiting for me with my son."

In the days after he left, the other cooks told me stories saved up over the years. That he had been saving for six years to go home. That his name wasn't Luis but Alejandro. That he was the greatest cook that ever lived.

01. Everything Bagel with Cream Cheese and Lox PAGE 190   02. Toasted Cornflakes PAGE 106
03. Pour-over Coffee PAGE 408   04. Bacon, Egg, and Cheese Sandwich PAGE 172

DOSA
SOUTH INDIA

Dosas are made with a fermented rice batter cooked into thin pancakes, sometimes stuffed with spiced potato (Aloo Masala). They are always served with a spiced lentil and vegetable stew called sambar *and various chutneys (recipes follow). The chutneys are served with many other Indian breakfast items, like* medu vada *(Spiced Lentil Fritter, page 293),* idli *(Fluffy Rice Cakes, page 401),* uttapam *(Vegetable Pancake, page 125), and more. Dosas are best prepared on a flat iron* tawa, *a round crepe-like pan with little to no rim. This makes it easy to spread the batter thinly over a large surface resulting in the crispiest dosas.*

Preparation time: 15 minutes, plus overnight soaking time and 8 hours fermenting time
Cooking time: 10 minutes
Makes/Serves: 4

· 4 tablespoons warm water
· 1 cup (240 ml/8 fl oz) coconut milk
· Vegetable oil, for the pan
· ¾ cup (150 g) long-grain white rice, soaked overnight
· ¼ cup (50 g) urad dal (split dehusked black lentils), soaked overnight
· ¼ teaspoon fine sea salt
· Pinch of sugar
· Ghee, for brushing
· Aloo Masala (optional; recipe follows), for filling

For serving (recipes follow):
· Sambar
· Tomato Chutney
· Coconut Chutney
· Coriander Chutney

Drain and rinse the rice until the water runs clear. Drain the *urad dal*. Grind the rice and *dal* separately, each with ¼ cup (60 ml/2 fl oz) water, into a silky, smooth paste. Mix the two pastes together, making a thin batter. Add another ¼ cup (60 ml/2 fl oz) water and more if needed: the consistency should be slightly thick but pourable. Allow the batter to ferment, covered in plastic wrap (cling film), for a minimum of 8 hours. Add the salt and sugar. The batter can be used immediately or stored in the refrigerator for up to 1 week.

Heat a flat iron *tawa* or frying pan over medium heat. Pour ½ cup (120 ml/4 fl oz) into pan and quickly swirl it around in a circular motion to make the dosa as thin as possible. The dosa should be about 10 inches (25 cm) in diameter. When the edges begin to turn upwards, after about 1 minute, brush the surface of the dosa with ghee. Let cook for 1 minute more until golden brown, then fold over (see Note) and transfer to a plate. Use a water-soaked paper towel to clean the pan before ladling in the next ½ cup (120 ml/4 fl oz) batter.

Serve the dosas with the sambar and chutneys.

Note: If filling the dosa with aloo masala, just before folding over, put 4 tablespoons of the potato mixture in the center of the dosa, then fold.

See image on page 303

ALOO MASALA

This is a spiced potato mixture that gets tucked inside a dosa.

Preparation time: 10 minutes
Cooking time: 20 minutes
Makes: 2 cups (500 ml/18 fl oz)

· 1 ½ lbs (680 g) Yukon Gold potatoes (3 large), peeled and cut into
1-inch (2.5 cm) cubes
· 4 tablespoons ghee
· 2 teaspoon mustard seeds
· 4 small green chilies, chopped
· 1 cup (150 g) chopped onion
· 4 dried red chilies, minced
· 2-inch (5 cm) piece fresh ginger, peeled and grated
· Salt
· 1 teaspoon asafoetida
· 1 teaspoon ground turmeric
· 1 cup (40 g) chopped cilantro (coriander) leaves
· 10 fresh curry leaves

In a large saucepan, combine the potatoes with water to cover and
bring to a boil. Cook until easily pierced with a fork, about 15 minutes.
Drain and lightly mash.

In a frying pan, heat the ghee and mustard seeds over medium
heat. When the mustard seeds start to pop, add the green chilies and
onion. Fry over medium heat until the onion is soft and translucent,
about 5 minutes.

Meanwhile, in a small bowl, mix together the red chilies, ginger,
asafoetida, turmeric, and salt.

Add the mashed potato to the frying pan. Reduce the heat to low.
Add the chili/ginger mixture, cilantro (coriander), and curry leaves
and cook until fragrant, 3 minutes. Remove the pan from the heat and
set aside for the dosa.

See image on page 302

CORIANDER CHUTNEY

Preparation time: 20 minutes
Cooking time: 5 minutes
Makes: 1 cup (240 ml/8 fl oz)

· 2 cups (40 g) cilantro (coriander) leaves, chopped
· 1 cup (20 g) mint leaves, chopped
· 1-inch (2.5 cm) piece fresh ginger, peeled and chopped
· 2 small green chilies, chopped
· 1 teaspoon ground cumin
· 2 tablespoons lime juice
· ¼ teaspoon fine sea salt
· Pinch of sugar

In a blender, combine ¾ cup (175 ml/6 fl oz) water, cilantro (coriander),
mint, ginger, green chilies, cumin, lime juice, and salt. Add water as
needed 1 tablespoon at a time, to assist the blending until a smooth
paste is formed. Stir in sugar and serve.

See image on page 303

TOMATO CHUTNEY

Preparation time: 10 minutes
Cooking time: 20 minutes
Makes: 1 cup (240 ml/8 fl oz)

· 3 teaspoons vegetable oil
· 1 tablespoon chana dal
· ½ teaspoon cumin seeds
· 1 small dried red chili, seeded
· ¼ small white onion, chopped (about 4 tablespoons)
· 2 cloves garlic, chopped
· 3 medium tomatoes, chopped
· ¼ teaspoon fine sea salt
· Pinch of sugar

In a frying pan, heat 1 teaspoon of the oil and toast the chana dal over medium heat until the dal is lightly golden, 3 minutes. Add the cumin seeds and toast until aromatic, 2 minutes more. Transfer to a plate and let cool.

In the same pan, heat the remaining 2 teaspoons vegetable oil over medium heat. Add the onion, red chili, and garlic and cook until the onion is soft and translucent, about 5 minutes. Stir in the tomatoes and cook until soft, about 3 minutes. Carefully transfer the contents of the frying pan to a blender. Add the dal and cumin mixture and blend until a paste forms. Stir in salt and sugar and serve.

See image on page 303

COCONUT CHUTNEY

Preparation time: 10 minutes
Cooking time: 10 minutes
Makes: 1 cup (240 ml/8 fl oz)

· 3 teaspoons vegetable oil
· 2 tablespoons chana dal
· 1 cup (100 g) unsweetened shredded coconut (desiccated)
· 2 small green chilies, chopped
· 1-inch (2.5 cm) piece fresh ginger, peeled and chopped
· ¼ teaspoon fine sea salt, plus more to taste
· ¼ teaspoon sugar
· ¼ teaspoon mustard seeds
· 3 fresh curry leaves
· 1 small dried red chili, seeded

In a frying pan, heat the oil and toast the chana dal and red chili over medium heat until the dal is lightly golden, 5 minutes. Transfer to a plate and let cool.

In a blender, combine 1½ cups (355 ml/12 fl oz) water, coconut, red and green chilies, ginger, salt, sugar, and toasted chana dal. Scrape the chutney into a serving bowl.

In a small frying pan, heat the oil over medium heat. Add the mustard seeds and curry leaves and cook until the mustard seeds pop and the curry leaves are aromatic, 1 minute. Stir into the coconut chutney.

See image on page 302

SAMBAR

Sambar is a loose lentil stew used to accompany dosas and other Indian breakfast items. Each family, restaurant, and region has a variation, as it depends on preferred spices and available vegetables. Often seen in sambar are drumsticks (moringa), a seed pod from a plant called a drumstick tree. The pods are cooked until soft in the sambar and eaten by squeezing the pulp out with your teeth.

Preparation time: 20 minutes
Cooking time: 1 hour
Serves: 4-6

· ¼ cup (25 g) coriander seeds
· 1 tablespoon chana dal
· 1 tablespoon urad dal
· 1 teaspoon cumin seeds
· ½ teaspoon black peppercorns
· ¼ teaspoon fenugreek seeds
· 1 dried red chili
· 8 fresh curry leaves
· ½ tablespoon unsweetened coconut flakes
· ½ teaspoon ground turmeric
· 4 tablespoons toor dal (split pigeon peas)
· 3 tablespoons chopped cilantro (coriander) leaves and stems
· 1 teaspoon fine sea salt, plus more to taste
· ¼ teaspoon ground turmeric
· 1 tablespoon ghee
· 1 small green chili, chopped
· ¼ yellow onion, chopped
· ¼ zucchini (courgette), chopped
· ½ Asian eggplant (aubergine), cubed
· 1 vegetable drumstick (moringa)
· 1 medium tomato, chopped
· ½ tablespoon ginger, grated
· 1 teaspoon tamarind paste
· ½ teaspoon jaggery

In a wok or frying pan, toast the coriander seeds, chana dal, urad dal, cumin seeds, peppercorns, fenugreek, chili, 2 curry leaves, and coconut over medium-low heat until they turn aromatic, about 3 minutes. Transfer to a plate to cool. Transfer to a blender or spice grinder with the turmeric and blend or grind until a powder is formed. Store the powder in an airtight container.

Rinse the dal until the water runs clear. In a medium saucepan, combine 3 cups (710 ml/24 fl oz) water and dal and bring to a boil over medium-high heat. Boil for 10 minutes, then stir in the cilantro (coriander), salt, and turmeric. Lower the heat to medium and let simmer for 30 minutes.

Meanwhile, in a frying pan, heat the ghee over medium heat. Add the chili, remaining 6 curry leaves, onion, and 2 tablespoons of the sambar powder and cook until onion is soft and translucent, about 5 minutes. Add the zucchini (courgette), eggplant (aubergine), drumstick, and tomato and cook until vegetables are beginning to soften, about 5 minutes.

Add the vegetables to the dal and simmer, uncovered, over medium heat until the vegetables and dal are tender, about 20 minutes. Stir in the ginger, tamarind, and jaggery. Season with salt to taste. Serve in a bowl alongside dosas.

See image on page 302

PANCAKES

SOAKED FERMENTED FLATBREAD

ETHIOPIA

Firfir is a common morning meal made from torn injera (fermented flatbread), soaked with spices and Ethiopian niter kibbeh *(Spiced Clarified Butter, page 44).*

Preparation time: 15 minutes, plus fermenting time for the Injera
Cooking time: 40 minutes
Serves: 2

· 2 tablespoons Spiced Clarified Butter (page 44)
· ½ medium yellow onion, diced
· 2 cloves garlic, minced
· ½-inch (1.25 cm) piece fresh ginger, peeled and finely chopped
· 1 tablespoon berbere
· 1 tablespoon tomato paste (purée)
· Salt and freshly ground pepper
· 4 Injera (recipe follows), torn into pieces
· 1 jalapeño chili, sliced, for garnish
· 1 hard-boiled egg (page 14), peeled, left whole, for serving

In a medium frying pan, heat the *niter kibbeh* over medium heat. Add the onion and cook, stirring occasionally, until the onion is soft and translucent, about 5 minutes. Add the garlic, ginger, berbere, and tomato paste (purée). Season with salt and pepper and stir to incorporate all the ingredients evenly. Pour in 1 cup (240 ml/8 fl oz) water and bring the mixture to a boil. Reduce the heat to low and simmer until slightly thickened, about 5 minutes. Turn off the heat and stir in the injera pieces until almost all of the liquid has been absorbed.

Serve in a bowl topped with sliced jalapeño and the boiled egg.

INJERA

Preparation time: 5 minutes, plus 3 days fermenting time
Cooking time: 5 minutes
Makes: 4

· ½ cup (120 ml/4 fl oz) warm water, plus more as needed
· Pinch of sugar
· ¼ teaspoon active dry yeast
· 1 cup (160 g) teff flour
· ½ teaspoon fine sea salt
· Vegetable oil, for cooking

In a medium bowl, combine the warm water, sugar, and yeast. Set the mixture aside until the yeast is frothy, about 10 minutes. (If the yeast doesn't froth, check the expiration date. You may have to start over with fresher yeast.) Slowly add the teff flour to the yeast mixture until combined. The mixture should resemble wet clay. Cover with plastic wrap (cling film) and set aside in a warm kitchen spot to ferment for 3 days. The mixture should have small bubbles and have a tangy aroma.

When ready to use, pour off any liquid that has accumulated at the top of the mixture. Stir in the salt and up to ½ cup (120 ml/4 fl oz) of warm water to achieve a consistency a little thicker than crepe batter.

Heat a crepe pan or nonstick pan over medium heat. Heat ½ tablespoon of oil and pour in about ½ cup (120 ml/4 fl oz) of the teff batter, swirling it around the pan to coat in a very thin layer. Allow the injera to cook until bubbles begin to form, about 30 seconds. Cover and let cook for 4 minutes, until the top looks dry. Do not flip the injera. Use a spatula to transfer the injera to a plate. Repeat with the remaining batter.

ROUND MINI PANCAKES

MADAGASCAR

Mofo Gasy *are small, round pancakes sold on the street and served with sweet coffee. If a* mofo gasy *pan (a cast-iron skillet with about 2½-inch/6.5 cm craters for holding batter) isn't available, a Danish* aebleskiver *pan works as well.*

Preparation time: 15 minutes, plus 1 hour resting time
Cooking time: 10 minutes
Makes: about 16

- ¾ cup (175 ml/6 fl oz) warm water
- 3 teaspoons sugar
- ½ teaspoon active dry yeast
- ½ cup (70 g) all-purpose (plain) flour
- 6 tablespoons cream of rice (or farina/cream of wheat)
- ¼ teaspoon vanilla extract
- 1 teaspoon honey
- Vegetable oil, for the pan

In a small bowl, combine the warm water, a pinch of sugar, and yeast. Set the mixture aside until the yeast is frothy, about 10 minutes. (If the yeast does not froth, check the expiration date. You may have to start over with fresher yeast.)

In a medium bowl, stir together the flour, cream of rice, vanilla, honey, and remaining sugar. Stir in the yeast mixture until no dry spots remain. Cover with a tea towel and allow the batter to sit for at least 1 hour or up to 4 hours in a warm place.

Heat a *mofo gasy* pan or *aebleskiver* pan over medium heat and add a dab of oil into each hole. Pour the batter, filling ¾ of each hole. When the edges begin to crisp and the batter bubbles and rises, 30 seconds, use a chopstick, popsicle stick, or knife to rotate the the *mofo gasy* 90 degrees and add more batter to each pancake, filling the mold. Let cook another 30 seconds. Flip the *mofo gasy* over and cook until the underside is crisped, 30 seconds more, until golden and cooked through. Repeat with remaining batter. Serve warm.

SCALLION PANCAKES

CHINA

Commonplace at dim sum, these laminated scallion (spring onion) flatbreads are shallow-fried. This version of bing *(flatbread) is also a street snack and can be wrapped around a* youtiao *(Chinese Cruller, page 306). The technique of using boiling water to make the dough is what gives the scallion pancakes their gummy bite.*

Preparation time: 30 minutes, plus 30 minutes resting time
Cooking time: 20 minutes
Makes: 4

· 2½ cups (360 g) all-purpose (plain) flour
· ¼ teaspoon fine sea salt
· ¾ cup (175 ml/6 fl oz) boiling water, plus more as needed
· Toasted sesame oil, for brushing
· 1 cup (100 g) thinly sliced scallions (spring onions), plus more for serving

In a large bowl, combine the flour and salt. Pour in the boiling water and stir with a wooden spoon until a shaggy dough forms. If needed, add more water, 1 tablespoon at a time. Knead the dough until smooth, about 2 minutes. Cover with a tea towel and let rest, about 30 minutes.

Turn the dough onto a lightly floured work surface and divide into 4 equal portions. Working with one at a time, leaving the others under the tea towel, roll out into a 5-inch (13 cm) round, about ¼ inch (0.6 cm) thick. Brush the dough with sesame oil. Sprinkle 4 tablespoons of scallions (spring onions) onto the pancake. Roll into a tight log, then twist into a spiral and coil into a ball. This achieves flaky layers in the pancake. Roll it out into a flat round, again ¼ inch (0.6 cm) thick, and brush with more sesame oil. Repeat with the remaining dough to make 3 more pancakes.

Heat a cast-iron skillet over medium heat. Cook the scallion pancake until the bottom is browned, 3 minutes. Flip and cook until the other side is browned, about 3 minutes more. Transfer to a plate. Serve sliced into wedges and topped with sliced scallions.

Scallion Pancakes

FRENCH TOAST
UNITED STATES

In the United States, French toast (bread slices soaked in egg and pan-fried) is typically topped with butter, maple syrup, and sometimes powdered sugar. Cooking bread in this way dates back to the Roman Empire. In England during the reign of King Henry V, stale baguettes were used to make pain perdu *(page 141) or "lost bread." French Toast in America is said to have been invented in the 1700's, by Joseph French, an innkeeper in Albany, New York.*

Preparation time: 10 minutes
Cooking time: 15 minutes
Serves: 2

· 3 eggs
· 2 tablespoons full-fat milk
· 1 tablespoon granulated sugar
· 1 tablespoon (15 g) unsalted butter, plus more for serving
· 4 slices brioche, challah, or sliced white bread (½–1 inch/1.25–2.5 cm thick)
· Powdered (icing) sugar, for serving
· Maple syrup, for serving

In a shallow dish, whisk the eggs, milk, and granulated sugar.

In a medium frying pan, melt ½ tablespoon butter over medium heat, swirling to coat the pan evenly. Submerge 2 slices of bread in the egg mixture, coating both sides evenly and allowing excess egg to drip back into the bowl. Lay the slices in the pan and brown on each side until golden, about 3 minutes per side. Transfer to a plate. Add the remaining ½ tablespoon butter and repeat with the remaining bread slices and egg mixture.

Serve on a plate with, butter, a shower of powdered (icing) sugar, and a drizzle of maple syrup.

HAWAIIAN FRENCH TOAST
UNITED STATES

A strong Portuguese influence in Hawaii has led to the crossbreeding of culinary cultures. In the case of French toast, Portuguese sweet bread rolls or pão doce *are used for their added sweetness and light texture, best for soaking up the egg mixture.*

Preparation time: 10 minutes
Cooking time:15 minutes
Serves: 2

· 3 eggs
· 2 tablespoons full-fat milk
· Pinch of ground cinnamon
· 1 tablespoon (15 g) unsalted butter, plus more for serving
· 4 small King's Hawaiian Rolls, about ½ inch thick or 2 medium pao doce, halved horizontally
· Powdered (icing) sugar, for serving
· Maple syrup, for serving

In a shallow dish, whisk the eggs, milk, and cinnamon.

In a medium frying pan, melt ½ tablespoon butter over medium heat, swirling to coat the pan evenly. Submerge 2 bread rolls in the egg mixture, coating both sides evenly and allowing excess egg to drip back into the bowl. Lay the rolls flat in the pan and brown on each side until golden, about 3 minutes per side. Transfer to a plate. Add the remaining ½ tablespoon butter and repeat with the remaining rolls and egg mixture.

Serve on a plate with butter, a shower of powdered (icing) sugar, and a drizzle of maple syrup.

PAIN PERDU
UNITED STATES

Popular in 15th Century England then brought to New Orleans, Louisiana, this French toast is made with day-old French bread soaked in an egg mixture infused with nutmeg and vanilla, then fried. The name pain perdu *means "lost bread" in French and refers to a last effort to revive hard or stale bread.*

Preparation time: 10 minutes
Cooking time: 15 minutes
Serves: 2

· 1 egg
· 3 tablespoons full-fat milk
· ½ tablespoon granulated sugar
· ¼ teaspoon vanilla extract
· Pinch of ground nutmeg
· 1 tablespoon (15 g) unsalted butter, plus more for serving
· 6 slices stale French bread, 1 inch (2.5 cm) thick
· Powdered (icing) sugar, for serving
· Maple syrup, for serving

In a shallow dish, whisk the eggs, milk, granulated sugar, vanilla, and nutmeg together.

In a medium frying pan, melt ½ tablespoon butter over medium heat, swirling to coat the pan evenly. Submerge 2 slices of French bread in the egg mixture, coating both sides evenly and allowing excess egg to drip back into the bowl. Lay the slices in the pan and brown on each side until golden, about 3 minutes per side. Transfer to a plate. Add the remaining ½ tablespoon butter and repeat with the remaining bread and egg mixture.

Serve on a plate with butter, a shower of powdered (icing) sugar, and a drizzle of maple syrup.

MILO FRENCH TOAST
MALAYSIA

Here is another classic French toast, made with Milo (a chocolate and malt powder made by Nestlé) mixed into the egg batter. Milo was created in Australia in the 1930s and is a popular beverage in Oceania and Southeast Asia, particularly in Malaysia.

Preparation time: 10 minutes
Cooking time: 15 minutes
Serves: 2

· 4 tablespoons full-fat milk
· 3 tablespoons Milo or cocoa powder
· 2 eggs
· 1 tablespoon (15 g) unsalted butter, plus more for serving
· 4 slices white bread
· Powdered (icing) sugar, for serving
· Sweetened condensed milk, for serving

In a shallow bowl, stir the milk and Milo until thoroughly combined. Whisk in the eggs.

In a medium frying pan, melt ½ tablespoon butter over medium heat, swirling to coat the pan evenly. Submerge 2 slices of bread in the egg mixture, coating both sides evenly and allowing excess egg to drip back into the bowl. Lay the slices in the pan and brown on each side until golden, about 3 minutes per side. Transfer to a plate. Add the remaining ½ tablespoon butter and repeat with the remaining bread slices and egg mixture.

Serve with butter, a shower of powdered (icing) sugar, and sweetened condensed milk.

HONG KONG FRENCH TOAST

CHINA

Thickly sliced shokupan (milk bread) is covered in egg batter and fried until golden brown. Peanut butter is sandwiched between the two slices before cooking. The toast is served with butter and condensed milk or maple syrup.

Preparation time: 10 minutes
Cooking time: 15 minutes
Serves: 2

· 3 eggs
· 4 slices shokupan or white bread, ½–1 inch (1.25–2.5 cm) thick, crusts removed
· 2 tablespoons smooth peanut butter
· 4 tablespoons vegetable oil
· Butter and sweetened condensed milk or maple syrup, for serving

In a shallow dish, whisk the eggs. Slather each of 2 slices of bread with 1 tablespoon peanut butter. Top with the remaining bread to make 2 sandwiches.

In a medium frying pan, heat 2 tablespoons of the oil over medium heat. Soak a sandwich in the egg, covering all sides and allowing excess egg to drip back into the bowl. Place one sandwich in the pan. Fry on both sides until golden brown, about 3 minutes on each side. Repeat with the second sandwich, adding the remaining oil to the pan.

Serve warm with butter and condensed milk or syrup.

DINER TOAST

UNITED STATES

This is a common accompaniment for most breakfast orders at diners in the Northeast: White or whole wheat (wholemeal) bread, lightly toasted, then slathered with a generous pat of butter and served with packets of jam or jelly (typically strawberry or grape).

Preparation time: 5 minutes
Cooking time: 5 minutes
Serves: 1

· 2 slices white or whole wheat (wholemeal) bread, ½–1 inch (1.25–2.5 cm) thick
· 1½ tablespoons (20 g) unsalted butter, at room temperature
· Cinnamon sugar (optional)
· Jam or jelly, for serving (optional)

Lightly toast the bread in a toaster or under a broiler, until just golden, about 2 minutes on each side. Spread with butter and cinnamon sugar, if desired. Spread on jam or jelly, if desired, and serve warm.

See image on page 128

(VT) (15) 5

Hong Kong French Toast

AVOCADO TOAST
AUSTRALIA / UNITED STATES

The simplicity of this recipe and commonality of ingredients make this dish difficult to trace. Dating back thousands of years, avocados were often thought of as a replacement for butter due to heir high fat content and smooth texture when smashed. Avocado toast was popularized after being put on restaurant menus in Queensland, Australia in the early 90's and California, Unites States in the mid 00's.

Preparation time: 10 minutes
Cooking time: 10 minutes
Serves: 1

· 1 slice rustic seeded bread or bread of choice, ½ inch (1.25 cm) thick, toasted
· ½ avocado, pitted, peeled, and thinly sliced
· 1 teaspoon olive oil
· Salt and freshly ground pepper
· ¼ teaspoon red chili flakes
· 1 Fried Egg (page 14) (optional)

Fan out the avocado on the toast, or use the back of a fork to smash the avocado onto the toast, spreading it evenly. Drizzle the olive oil over the avocado and season to taste with the salt, pepper, and chili flakes. Place the fried egg on top, if using, and serve.

TOAST WITH VEGEMITE AND AVOCADO
AUSTRALIA

A typical Toast with Vegemite (page 146), minus the butter, and with the addition of sliced or smashed avocado. A healthy replacement, the avocado mimics the fatty components of butter and adds depth of flavor.

Preparation time: 10 minutes
Cooking time: 5 minutes
Serves: 1

· Vegemite, for spreading
· 1 slice rustic seeded bread or bread of choice, ½ inch (1.25 cm) thick, toasted
· ½ avocado, pitted, peeled, and thinly sliced
· Lemon juice, for sprinkling
· Salt, for sprinkling

Spread the Vegemite on the toast. Use the back of a fork to smash the avocado on the toast. Serve topped with a sprinkling of lemon juice and salt.

Toast with Vegemite and Avocado

TOAST WITH VEGEMITE

AUSTRALIA

Vegemite (a salty spread made from yeast extract, similar to British Marmite) is typically enjoyed on rustic seeded toast with a generous helping of butter.

Preparation time: 5 minutes
Cooking time: 5 minutes
Serves: 1

· 2 slices rustic seeded bread (or bread of your choice), ½ inch (1.25 cm) thick, toasted
· 2 tablespoons (30 g) unsalted butter, at room temperature
· Vegemite, to taste

Spread the toast with butter. Spread a layer of Vegemite on top and serve.

See image on page 86

PAN CON TOMATE

SPAIN

Crunchy toast is rubbed with garlic, tomato, and olive oil and enjoyed as a humble breakfast, deliciously disguising day-old bread with flavorful tomato and good-quality olive oil.

Preparation time: 10 minutes
Cooking time: 5 minutes
Serves: 1

· 1 clove garlic, cut in half
· 1 day-old bread slice, toasted
· 1 tablespoon olive oil
· Salt
· 1 medium overripe tomato, halved through the equator

Rub the garlic clove over the toasted bread. Drizzle with olive oil and sprinkle with sea salt. Grate the tomato using a cheese grater set over a flat plate or bowl and discard the skin. Spoon the tomato over the toast, season with more salt, and serve.

FRIED BREAD

UNITED KINGDOM

Fried bread is a staple in a Full English breakfast plate (page 28), similar to Diner Toast (page 142), but pan-fried in butter rather than toasted in an oven or electric toaster.

Preparation time: 5 minutes
Cooking time: 5 minutes
Serves: 2

· 1 tablespoon (15 g) butter or lard
· 2 slices Irish soda bread, ½ inch (1.25 cm) thick

In a medium frying pan, melt the butter over medium heat, swirling to coat the pan evenly. Add the bread and fry until browned on one side, about 2 minutes. Flip and brown on the other side, adding more butter if the pan is dry, another 2 minutes. Serve warm.

BEANS ON TOAST

UNITED KINGDOM

Baked beans in tomato sauce is the classic accompaniment to any "Fry Up" in the UK (see Full English, page 28).

Preparation time: 5 minutes
Cooking time: 10 minutes
Serves: 2

· Half a 13 oz (368 g) can baked beans with tomato sauce
· 2 slices white bread, toasted or pan-fried (Fried Bread, above)

Preheat the broiler (grill) to high. In a frying pan, warm the beans over medium heat. Place the bread on a baking sheet on the top rack for 2 minutes on each side, or until golden brown. Spoon the warmed beans over toast or Fried Bread.

MARMITE AND TOAST

UNITED KINGDOM

Similar to Vegemite (see page 146), Marmite is a thick, deep-brown spread made from yeast extract. The distinct flavor of this condiment leaves people vehemently standing on either side of love and hate.

Preparation time: 5 minutes
Cooking time: 5 minutes
Serves: 1

· ½ tablespoon (7 g) unsalted butter, at room temperature
· 1 slice wholegrain or seeded bread, toasted
· Marmite, for spreading

Smear the butter on the toast. Spread the marmite over the butter and serve.

CHIPPED BEEF ON TOAST

UNITED STATES

Nicknamed "SOS," this now classic diner food in the Northeastern and Mid-Atlantic states was typically served in the armed forces during World War II. Leftover or canned sliced beef, also known as "chipped beef," is turned into a gravy and served over toast. Today it is commonly prepared with ground (minced) beef.

Preparation time: 10 minutes
Cooking time: 20 minutes
Serves: 2

· ½ lb (225 g) ground (minced) beef
· ½ small shallot, diced
· Salt and freshly ground pepper
· 1 tablespoon (15 g) unsalted butter
· 1 tablespoon all-purpose (plain) flour
· ¾ cup (175 ml/6 fl oz) full-fat milk
· ⅛ teaspoon sweet paprika
· 2 slices country loaf, toasted

In a medium saucepan, cook the beef over medium heat, breaking it up with a wooden spoon, 5 minutes. Add the shallot and cook until soft and the beef is browned, 5 minutes. Remove and reserve, leaving the rendered fat in the pan. Add butter to the pan and melt over medium heat. Stir in 1 tablespoon flour to make a roux (a smooth mixture of fat and flour that helps thicken sauces). Cook, stirring with a wooden spoon to create a smooth paste and cook off the flour taste, 2 minutes. Stir in the milk and bring to a simmer. Whisk constantly until thickened, 2 minutes. Add the beef mixture and paprika, and season with salt and pepper. Stir to combine and let simmer on low heat for 1 minute more. Serve heaped over country bread toast.

TOAST WITH SWEET RED BEAN SPREAD
JAPAN

Ogura toast *is made with* shokupan *(milk bread) topped with butter and sweet adzuki (red bean) paste.*

Preparation time: 10 minutes
Cooking time: 25 minutes
Serves: 2

- ½ cup (130 g) canned adzuki beans, drained
- 4 tablespoons sugar
- Pinch of salt
- 2 slices shokupan or any white bread, ½ inch (1.25 cm) thick, toasted
- 1 tablespoon (15 g) butter

In a small saucepan, combine the adzuki beans, ¾ cup (175 ml/6 fl oz) water, sugar, and salt. Bring to a boil over medium heat, then reduce the heat to low and simmer until slightly thickened and reduced by half, about 20 minutes. Blend in a blender or with a hand blender to make a paste.

Spread the bean paste on the toast and top with a pat of butter.

See image on page 257

RUSKS WITH BUTTER AND STRAWBERRIES
THE NETHERLANDS

Beschuit *are rusks (dried white bread rounds) with a small indentation on the side, which makes them more easily be pulled from their tightly packaged sleeve. They are typically enjoyed topped with butter, sugar, strawberries,* hagelslag *(Dutch sprinkles), and a variety of other toppings.*

Preparation time: 10 minutes
Serves: 1

- ½ tablespoon (7 g) unsalted butter, at room temperature
- 2 beschuits
- 4 (40–80 g) sliced strawberries
- ½ tablespoon sugar

Spread the butter on the *beschuits*. Top with strawberries and sprinkle with the sugar.

TOAST WITH COCONUT JAM AND SOFT-BOILED EGGS
SINGAPORE

Kaya *is an amber-colored coconut and egg sugar jam that is sometimes found with a green hue due to the addition of pandan, a tropical-plant leaf commonly used in Southeast Asian cooking. The jam is spread on a charcoal-grilled, crustless toast sandwich with a generous serving of butter. It is accompanied by extra soft-boiled eggs that are topped with soy sauce and white pepper.*

Preparation time: 5 minutes
Cooking time: 15 minutes
Serves: 1, makes ½ cup (115 g) kaya

For the coconut jam (kaya):
· 2 eggs
· 2 egg yolks
· 1 cup (240 ml/8 fl oz) coconut milk
· 4 tablespoons brown sugar
· 4 tablespoons palm sugar
· 3 pandan leaves, knotted (optional)
· Pinch of salt

To assemble:
· 2 extra Soft-Boiled Eggs (page 14)
· 2 slices white bread, crusts removed
· ½ tablespoon (7 g) unsalted butter, at room temperature
· 1 tablespoon Kaya (coconut jam), for spreading
· Soy sauce, for serving
· Ground white pepper, for serving

Make the *kaya*:
In a medium bowl, beat the eggs and egg yolks until smooth.

Set up a double boiler. Fill a saucepan with 2 inches of water and bring to a simmer over medium heat. Place a large heatproof mixing bowl on top of the pot so that it rests on the rim without touching the water below. Add the coconut milk, brown sugar, palm sugar, and salt, stirring until the sugar is dissolved. Let the mixture come to a simmer, stirring occasionally, about 12 minutes.

Reduce the heat to low and remove the bowl from the heat, leaving the saucepot simmering, and adding more water if needed. Temper the eggs by pouring 1 tablespoon of the coconut mixture into the eggs, whisking vigorously to make sure they do not curd. Pour the eggs in a slow, steady stream into the coconut mixture, continuously stirring to temper.

Place back on the saucepot. Cook the mixture over low heat, stirring constantly (the water should be steaming with a small simmer) for 10 minutes, or until the mixture thickens to a thick paste. Remove from heat and reserve.

Assemble the *kaya* toast and eggs:
Set up a charcoal grill (barbecue) or heat a stovetop grill pan (griddle pan). Add the bread and grill on both sides until just toasted, 2 minutes per side. Spread both slices of toast with butter and *kaya*, sandwich together, and cut in half lengthwise.

Carefully crack the boiled eggs into a small bowl. The consistency should be runny with opaque whites. Season with soy sauce and white pepper. Serve kaya toast on the side and dip into the egg, if desired.

Toast with Coconut Jam and Soft-Boiled Eggs

MILK TOAST
UNITED STATES

Lauded American food writer M. F. K. Fisher referred to this dish as "a small modern miracle of gastronomy." Milk toast can be enjoyed many ways. Originating in New England, toasted sliced bread can be torn or left whole, but the toast is always doused in spice-infused warm milk. This dish was often prepared as a comforting remedy for convalescent children.

Preparation time: 5 minutes
Cooking time: 10 minutes
Serves: 1

· 2 slices white bread, toasted
· 1 tablespoon (15 g) unsalted butter, at room temperature
· ½ cup (120 ml/4 fl oz) full-fat milk
· 2 teaspoons sugar
· 1 teaspoon ground cinnamon

Butter the toast. In a small saucepan, bring the milk to a simmer over low heat, stirring to prevent scorching. Stir in 1 teaspoon of the sugar. In a small bowl, combine the remaining 1 teaspoon sugar and cinnamon and sprinkle the buttered toast with it. Chop the sugared toast into cubes and transfer to a cereal bowl. Pour the warmed milk over the bread. Allow the milk toast to soak for at least 1 minute before serving.

CRISPBREAD WITH SMOKED COD ROE SPREAD
SWEDEN

Kalles Kaviar is the brand of creamed smoked cod roe that comes in an iconic blue squeeze tube. It is commonly used to top knäckebröd (rye crispbread), bread rolls, and/or boiled eggs.

Preparation time: 5 minutes
Cooking time: 10 minutes
Serves: 4

· 8 knäckebröd, crispbreads, or rusks
· 4 Hard-Boiled Eggs (page 14), peeled and sliced
· 10 oz/300 g creamed smoked cod roe (such as Kalles Kaviar)

Serve the knäckebröd topped with slices of egg and the creamed smoked cod roe. Keep the roe on the table to serve more.

Crispbread with Smoked Cod Roe Spread

FRENCH BREAD ROLL WITH DULCE DE LECHE

BRAZIL

Dulce de leche, *known as* doce de leite *in Brazil, is a sweet condiment typically used for topping* torrada *(toast) or* pão frances *(French bread roll).*

Preparation time: 5 minutes
Cooking time: 5 minutes
Serves: 2

· 1 tablespoon Dulce de Leche (recipe follows)
· 1 tablespoon (15 g) unsalted butter, at room temperature
· 1 pão frances (French bread roll), halved

Butter the roll and toast on a hot griddle or frying pan, about 3 minutes. Spread toasted bread with *dulce de leche.*

DULCE DE LECHE

Cooking time: 3 hours

· 1 can (14 oz/397 g) sweetened condensed milk, preferably not a pop-top lid

Completely remove the label from the can. Place the can in a deep medium saucepan and fill with room-temperature water. The can should be completely submerged, covered by at least 2 inches (5 cm). Bring the water to a boil over medium-high heat and reduce to a simmer. Cook for 2 ½–3 hours to achieve a deeper caramel color. Make sure to keep the can covered with water at all times.

Using tongs, carefully remove the can from the water. Allow the can to cool completely before opening to avoid exploding dulce de leche. Spread on *pão frances* or store in the refrigerator for up to 3 weeks.

French Bread Roll with Dulce de Leche

ICHES

BREAKFAST
BURRITOS
UNITED STATES

Breakfast burritos are a common on-the-go meal in California and the American Southwest. They can have a variety of fillings, based on regional and personal preferences. The most classic is scrambled eggs, home fries, cheese, and sometimes bacon. In the Southwest, refried beans replace home fries. Serve with hot sauce. In Austin, Texas, variations of these ingredients (like migas, Scrambled Eggs with Crushed Tortilla Chips, page 36) are more often found in a smaller flour tortilla as a taco.

Preparation time: 20 minutes
Cooking time: 40 minutes
Serves: 1

· 1 flour tortilla (10 inches/25 cm)
· 2 slices (rashers) bacon (streaky)
· ¼ small onion, chopped
· 2 eggs
· Salt and freshly ground pepper
· ½ cup (100 g) Home Fries (page 16)
· 2 tablespoons shredded cheddar cheese
· ½ tablespoon canned green Hatch chilies or fresh jalapeño, chopped
· ½ avocado, pitted, peeled, and sliced
· Fresh salsa, for serving

Start with a cold cast-iron skillet or frying pan and place the bacon in flat. Slowly bring the heat to medium to let the fat render and result in crispy bacon. Cook on both sides until crispy, about 10 minutes. Transfer the bacon to paper towels to drain. Leave about 1 tablespoon of fat in the pan and discard the rest. Add the onion to the pan and cook until soft and translucent, about 5 minutes.

Meanwhile, in a small bowl, lightly beat the eggs.

Add the eggs to the pan, season with salt and pepper, and allow the egg to set over the cooked onion for 30 seconds. Add the home fries and pull the eggs in from the edge of the pan toward the center until curds begin to form. Continue to stir until the eggs are scrambled, about 30 seconds. Sprinkle the cheddar over the eggs, cover the pan, and cook for about 30 seconds to melt the cheese. Season with salt and pepper.

Lay the egg mixture down the center of the tortilla. Crumble the bacon on top of the eggs, sprinkle with the chilies, and top with the avocado. Fold one side of the tortilla to cover the contents of the burrito, tightly tucking in the eggs. Then fold both sides of the tortilla in, as though wrapping a present, and continue rolling up the burrito. Serve with salsa.

STEAMED TACOS

MEXICO

Tacos de canasta *are steamed and kept warm in a basket, also known as al vapor (steamed) or tacos sudados (sweaty tacos). Often found at street carts around Mexico City, the premade, portable nature of this dish makes it convenient for vendors and a no-wait breakfast for commuters on the way to work.*

Preparation time: 40 minutes
Cooking time: 1½ hours
Serves: 4

· 12 corn tortillas
· 2 tablespoons sunflower oil
· 1 lb (455 g) fresh chorizo, about 3 links, casings removed, crumbled
· 2 cups (520 g) refried beans
· ½ cup (120 ml/4 fl oz) Chili Oil (recipe follows)
· 1 medium white onion, chopped
· Salsa Verde (page 20), for serving

Line a small wicker picnic basket, a shoe box, or small shipping box with cloth, such as tea towels, leaving enough overhang to cover the top and a few extra to fill in any empty space. Line box with a plastic bag and add a layer of butcher paper on the bottom of the bag. The goal is to create an insulated environment to keep the tacos warm. Set aside.

Preheat the oven to 250°F (120°C/Gas Mark ½). Stack the tortillas and wrap in foil. Place in the oven to keep warm.

In a frying pan, heat the oil over medium heat. Add the chorizo and cook, stirring with a wooden spoon until browned, about 4 minutes. Transfer to paper towels to drain.

Remove the packet of tortillas from the oven. Working quickly, fill the tortillas with 2 tablespoons of refried beans, top with 2 tablespoons of chorizo, and fold over. Begin to fill the plastic bag by placing a row of 3 tacos on the butcher paper. Drizzle 2 tablespoons of the chili oil lightly over the row and sprinkle with chopped onion. Continue by stacking another row of 3 tacos, 2 tablespoons of chili oil, and onion. Continue twice more until the basket is filled. Cover the tacos with a layer of butcher paper and twist to close the plastic bag. Fill any empty space in the basket or box with tea towels to keep the tacos propped up and stacked. Allow the warm tortillas to steam, 1 hour. Serve with salsa verde and/or chili oil.

CHILI OIL

Preparation time: 10 minutes
Cooking time: 10 minutes
Makes: 1 cup (240 ml/8 fl oz)

· 1 medium white onion, chopped
· 3 cloves garlic, chopped
· 4 pasilla chilies, stemmed
· ½ cup (120 ml/4 fl oz) sunflower oil

Heat a dry frying pan over medium heat. Add 4 tablespoons of the oil and cook the onion, garlic, and chilies until the onion is soft and translucent and the chilies are soft and fragrant, about 8 minutes. Transfer everything to a blender. Add the remaining 4 tablespoons oil and blend until smooth. Reserve.

CITRUS-MARINATED PORK SANDWICH

MEXICO

*Torta de cochinita pibil is a sandwich (*torta*) filled with citrus marinated pork slow-roasted in banana leaves (*cochinita pibil*). Though this is not typically thought of as a breakfast food, street carts in the Yucatán Peninsula often sell out by mid-morning. It is commonly enjoyed in a* bolillo *roll with a soda. For the pickled onions, triple the recipe on page 24.*

Preparation time: 15 minutes, plus 6 hours marinating time
Cooking time: 3 ½ hours
Serves: 6

For the cochinita pibil:
· 3 lb (1.35 kg) boneless pork shoulder
· 2 teaspoons fine sea salt
· 1 tablespoon dried oregano
· 1 tablespoon black peppercorns
· 1 teaspoon cumin seeds
· ½ teaspoon whole cloves
· 1 teaspoon ground cinnamon
· 6 cloves garlic, chopped
· 3 tablespoons achiote paste
· Grated zest of 1 orange
· ½ cup (120 ml/4 fl oz) fresh orange juice (from 2 large oranges)
· 4 tablespoons fresh lime juice (from 2 limes)
· 2-3 banana leaves
· 1 large onion, cut into half-moons

For serving:
· 6 Bolillo rolls or hero rolls
· ¾ cup (115 g) pickled onions

Make the *cochinita pibil*:
Rub the pork with the salt.

With a mortar and pestle or in a food processor, grind the oregano, peppercorns, cumin seeds, cloves, and cinnamon into a powder. Add the garlic, achiote paste, orange zest, orange juice, and lime juice. Process the marinade until thoroughly combined.

Arrange the banana leaves side by side, slightly overlapping, on a baking sheet. Place the salted pork in the center, with enough banana leaf surrounding it for wrapping later. Pour the marinade over the pork, rubbing it in to make sure all sides are covered. Tightly fit the banana leaves and meat in a large, deep bowl. Add the sliced onions to the top and wrap the banana leaves tied with twine to secure the bundles. Refrigerate for at least 6 hours or up to overnight.

Remove the marinated pork from the refrigerator 1 hour before cooking. Preheat the oven to 300°F (150°C/Gas Mark 2).

In a roasting pan fitted with a rack, place the banana-leaf–wrapped meat, making sure it stays securely wrapped in the leaf. Bake until the meat is tender, about 4 hours, or until the internal temperature is around 180°F (82°C). When the pork is finished cooking, open the banana leaf and shred the meat inside. Transfer the shredded meat and the juices to a serving platter.

To serve:
Split open the *bolillo* rolls, add heaping spoonfuls of the pork, and top with pickled onions.

OMELET SANDWICH WITH KETCHUP

CUBA

Pan con tortilla *is simply a sandwich on an untoasted sweet roll with a very thin omelet, topped with ketchup. On a typical morning in Havana people might pick up a Cafecito (page 416) or Café con Leche (page 415), a guava-filled cookie, a* tostada *(toast) with butter, and even a frankfurter.*

Preparation time: 5 minutes
Cooking time: 15 minutes
Serves: 1

· 1 egg
· Salt and freshly ground pepper
· 1 tablespoon (15 g) unsalted butter
· 1 medianoche roll (sweet bread roll), split horizontally
· Ketchup, for serving

In a small bowl, beat the egg and season with salt and pepper.

In a medium frying pan, melt the butter over medium heat, swirling to coat the pan. Pour in the beaten egg, swirling to coat the pan with a thin layer of egg. Let the egg set for 30 seconds. Tilt the pan and use a spatula to fold the omelet in half. Let the omelet cook for 30 seconds more. Use a spatula to fold the omelet in half again, creating a soft triangular shape. Slide the omelet out of the pan and onto one half of the roll. Smear the egg with ketchup and top with the second half.

SPICED SCRAMBLED EGGS WITH VEGETABLES

INDIA

A popular version of scrambled eggs in Northern India, egg bhurji, *this spiced egg-and-vegetable mixture can be enjoyed on its own, with a side of toasted white bread rolls, or in a breakfast sandwich as a more portable option.*

Preparation time: 10 minutes
Cooking time: 10 minutes
Serves: 1

· 1 tablespoon ghee
· ½ small onion, diced
· 1 clove garlic, finely minced
· ½ small green chili, minced
· ½ medium tomato, diced
· 1½-inch (4 cm) piece fresh ginger, peeled and finely minced
· 3 eggs
· ¼ teaspoon ground turmeric
· ⅛ teaspoon cayenne pepper
· Salt and freshly ground black pepper
· 1 white bread roll, split and toasted, for serving
· Cilantro (coriander) leaves, for garnish (optional)

In a medium frying pan, heat the ghee over medium heat. Stir in the onion and cook until soft and translucent, about 5 minutes. Add the garlic, green chili, tomato, and ginger and cook until aromatic, about 3 minutes.

In a small bowl, whisk together the eggs, turmeric, cayenne, and salt and black pepper to taste. Pour the eggs into the pan. Allow them to set for a few seconds. With a wooden spoon, pull the edges of the eggs in toward the center until the egg begins to form curds. Continue to stir constantly until the eggs are scrambled, about 30 seconds. Transfer to a plate and top with cilantro (coriander), if using. Serve warm alongside the toasted roll.

STREET TOAST

SOUTH KOREA

This Korean breakfast sandwich, often sold on the street in the morning around bus stations and universities, is filled with a vegetable and ham omelet and topped with ketchup and brown sugar.

Preparation time: 15 minutes
Cooking time: 15 minutes
Serves: 1

· 2 eggs
· 2 tablespoons finely shredded cabbage
· 2 tablespoons carrot, grated or cut into julienne 1 inch (2.5 cm) long
· 2 scallions (spring onions), diced
· 1 slice deli ham, chopped
· Salt and freshly ground pepper
· 1 tablespoon olive oil
· 2 slices sandwich bread, toasted and buttered
· Brown sugar, for sprinkling
· 1 slice American cheese (optional)
· Ketchup, for serving

In a bowl, lightly beat the eggs. Add the shredded cabbage, carrot, scallions (spring onions), and ham and season with salt and pepper to taste.

In a small frying pan, heat the oil over medium heat. Pour the eggs into the pan and cook until golden brown, 1 minute per side. Use a spatula to fold the omelet in half. Sprinkle the buttered side of one piece of toast with brown sugar, top with the omelet, sprinkle with more sugar, top with the cheese (if using), add ketchup, and top with the second piece of toast. Cut in half and serve.

Street Toast

ROLLED FLATBREAD OMELET SANDWICH

UGANDA

A rolex is a thin vegetable omelet rolled up in a chapati *(flatbread) and served in newspaper. The name is said to come from street vendors calling out "rolled eggs" with a heavy Luganda (south Ugandan) accent and visitors hearing what sounded like "Rolex." The name stuck.*

Preparation time: 15 minutes, plus 30 minutes resting time
Cooking time: 20 minutes
Serves: 2

For the chapati:
· ½ cup (70 g) all-purpose (plain) flour
· Pinch of salt
· 4 tablespoons warm water
· Vegetable oil, for brushing

For the omelet:
· 4 eggs
· ½ cup (35 g) shredded green cabbage
· 4 tablespoons diced red onion
· ½ medium tomato, diced
· Salt and freshly ground pepper
· 2 tablespoons vegetable oil
· Chili sauce, for serving

Make the chapati:
In a medium bowl, combine the flour and salt. Slowly incorporate the warm water and stir with a wooden spoon until a shaggy dough forms. Transfer the dough to a floured work surface and knead with your hands until the dough is smooth, 10 minutes. If the dough is too wet, add a sprinkle more of flour. If it is too dry, add a touch more water and knead again until smooth. Cover with a tea towel and allow the dough to rest for 30 minutes.

Divide the dough in half and roll into individual balls. On a lightly floured work surface, use a rolling pin to roll out the balls into rounds, ¼ inch (6 mm) thick. Brush both sides of each chapati with some of the vegetable oil. Heat a frying pan or cast-iron skillet over medium heat. Cook one side of the chapati until it begins to brown and bubble, about 1 minute. Flip the chapati and cook for 30 seconds more or until brown spots appear and the bread is cooked through. Transfer to a tea towel and cover. Repeat for the second piece of dough. Set the frying pan aside for the omelet.

Make the omelet:
Crack the eggs into a bowl. Whisk in the cabbage, onion, and tomato. Season with salt and pepper.

In the reserved frying pan, heat 1 tablespoon of oil over medium heat. Pour half of the egg mixture into the pan and use a spatula to spread it out, but no larger than the diameter of the chapati. Allow the egg to cook and set on the bottom, about 30 seconds. Flip, using the spatula, and cook for 30 seconds more. Top the cooked egg pancake with a chapati. Flip the chapati and egg out of the pan egg-side up onto a plate. Roll it up into a wrap. Repeat with the remaining 1 tablespoon oil and remaining egg mixture to make a second omelet. Roll with the remaining chapati. Serve with chili sauce.

Rolled Flatbread Omelet Sandwich

STEWED BLACK-EYED PEA SANDWICH

SENEGAL

Ndambe *is a black-eyed pea and sweet potato stew that can be spread onto a sandwich. French occupation in Senegal until the 1960's imprinted an array of French-inspired dishes. Baguette stands on the streets of Dakar serve baguette sandwiches spread with butter or chocolate-hazelnut spread, or even filled with spaghetti,* Akara *(Black-Eyed Pea Fritters, page 291) with hot sauce, or eggs.*

Preparation time: 15 minutes, plus overnight soaking time
Cooking time: 1 hour
Serves: 2

· ½ cup (85 g) dried black-eyed peas (beans), soaked overnight
· ½ pound sweet potatoes (about 1 medium), diced
· 1 tablespoon olive oil
· ½ large yellow onion, chopped
· 1 clove garlic, minced
· 3 tablespoons tomato paste (purée)
· ½ tablespoon white wine vinegar
· ½ cup (120 ml/4 fl oz) chicken or vegetable stock
· ½ teaspoon chili powder
· ½ teaspoon fine sea salt
· ¼ teaspoon freshly ground black pepper
· 1 baguette, cut in half, and each piece split open (but not all the way through)
· 2 Hard-Boiled Eggs (optional; page 14), peeled and sliced

Drain the black-eyed peas (beans) and transfer to a medium saucepan. Add water to cover by 2 inches (5 cm). Bring to a boil over high heat, reduce to a simmer, cover, and cook until tender, about 30 minutes. Check for doneness by smashing a bean. Drain the beans and set aside.

In a medium saucepan, combine the potatoes with water to cover. Bring to a boil over medium-high heat and cook until the potatoes are tender, about 7 minutes. Drain the potatoes and allow them to cool.

Meanwhile, in a medium saucepan, heat the oil over medium heat. Add the onion and cook until soft and soft and translucent, 5 minutes. Add the garlic and cook until fragrant, about 1 minute. Stir in the tomato paste (purée) and ½ cup (120 ml/4 fl oz) water. Add the vinegar, stock, chili powder, salt, and black pepper. Stir together and bring to a simmer. Stir in the cooked peas and potatoes and simmer until the beans have absorbed the liquid, 15 minutes.

To serve, fill the baguette halves with the black-eyed pea filling and top with the sliced egg. Serve warm.

FRIED POTATO SANDWICH

INDIA

Vada pav is a fried potato sandwich and a typical street food in Mumbai. Fragrant from coriander seeds, it is topped with a combination of wet and dry chutneys (see Note) and is served in a soft bread roll (pav).

Preparation time: 10 minutes
Cooking time: 20 minutes
Makes: 2 small sandwiches (1 serving)

For the patties:
· 1 medium russet (baking) potato, peeled and cubed
· 2 teaspoons vegetable oil
· ¼ teaspoon coriander seeds
· 1 clove garlic, finely minced
· ¼ teaspoon ground turmeric
· Salt and freshly ground pepper

For the batter:
· 4 tablespoons all-purpose (plain) flour
· Pinch of salt

For frying:
· 4 tablespoons vegetable oil

For serving:
· 2 small bread rolls
· Chutney of choice, such as dry garlic chutney, dry peanut chutney, green coriander chutney, or sweet chutney

Make the patties:
In a small saucepan, combine the potato with water to just cover and bring to a boil over high heat. Reduce the heat to low, cover, and simmer until the potato is fork-tender, about 10 minutes.

Drain the potato and transfer to a bowl. Using a potato masher, mash the potato until no lumps remain. Allow the potatoes to cool slightly. Stir in the flour and salt with a wooden spoon to make a dough.

Meanwhile, in a small frying pan, heat the oil over medium-high heat. Add the coriander seeds and allow them to toast for about 1 minute. Add the garlic and sauté, stirring constantly, until aromatic, about 1 minute. Toss in the turmeric and salt and pepper to taste, mixing everything together until thoroughly combined.

Transfer the spice mixture to the mashed potato and mix well. Season with more salt, if needed. Form the mashed potato into 2 slightly flattened patties.

Make the batter:
In a shallow bowl, stir together the flour, 4 tablespoons water, and salt. The consistency should be runny, so add more water if needed.

Fry the patties:
In a frying pan, heat the oil over medium heat. Test for readiness by flicking a small piece of mashed potato into the oil. If it sizzles, it is ready. Dip all sides of the potato patty into the batter and carefully transfer to the pan. Fry the patties on each side until golden, 3 minutes per side. Transfer to paper towels to drain.

To serve:
Serve the patties warm in the rolls, with chutney slathered on either side of the roll.

Note: To use a dry chutney, heat 1 teaspoon of ghee over medium heat. Add 1 teaspoon of dry chutney. Remove from heat and spread on the warm roll.

See image on page 303

SANDWICHES

STEPHEN HARRIS
ENGLISH BREAKFAST

Stephen Harris is the chef and owner of the Michelin-starred restaurant The Sportsman, in Seasalter (Kent), in the UK. A member of a punk band, then a financial advisor, self-taught Harris began cooking professionally at age 34 and opened The Sportsman in his native town in 1998. Harris uses the best ingredients available in his seaside region, serving innovative regional cuisine that has transformed this former small-town pub into an internationally acclaimed restaurant.

I suppose one of the biggest problems with food in the UK is that we are so close to France. Just as the best way to look gorgeous is to hang out with some ugly friends, being next door to France has never helped our reputation. When it comes to food, we are the ugly friend.

Some people in Britain have even tried to big up our cooking reputation by saying we got the nickname "les rosbifs" (the roast beefs) for our spit-roasting skills rather than because the French think that is all we eat. I even remember being told by a fellow grape-picker of the Gallic variety that we earned that moniker because the color we turn in the sun is the same as perfectly cooked beef. Even French jokes have perfectly pink, medium-rare meat.

As a well brought-up middle-class Englishman, I long ago gave up on trying to justify our food and am instead a fully-fledged francophile. I have always lived very close to France. From my corner of the UK, I can even go shopping for my restaurant in France, through the Channel Tunnel, and I'm back by 2 pm.

On one trip in 1992, before gastro-tourism even had a name, I went with three friends to Dieppe, on the northern coast of France, for the weekend. This involved catching a four-hour ferry from Newhaven, in Sussex.

We stayed in a cheap hotel on the blustery sea front and watched the Ivory Coast win the African Nations cup on TV. In between, we went to restaurants. A highlight of the trip was a visit to a very prim and proper Michelin-starred place that could have been straight out of England. We can do the prim and proper bit—it's just the food we struggle with. I will always remember the langoustine with balsamic beurre blanc, a dish I have tried to replicate many times. The highlight of the time spent on the wrong side of the Channel was eating mussels in cider with chips on the quayside.

It soon became clear that our return journey would take place in a gale. The winds that funnel through the English Channel and have, in the past, protected us from foreign invaders, were going to be our fellow travelers. Within half an hour of leaving port, the sight on board was like one of those Hogarth paintings of the gin-palace-laden backstreets of eighteenth-century London.

A traumatized boatload of people arrived in Newhaven four hours later. We set off in the car for London. After a short time, we realized we were all starving. This rare combination of a delicate stomach and raging hunger called for a very British solution: the full English breakfast. Luckily this meal is available all day in most roadside greasy spoons and we stopped at the next available place.

Now, I have happily admitted our inferiority to the French in most matters relating to food, but I will not let them win on this one. Our trauma was so deep that our desire for a full English was visceral. It was no affectation or desire to impress anyone with our good taste—it was literally a gut reaction. The combination of salty bacon and spongy sausages, clashing with the creamy, bland egg yolks, all set off with the tang of brown sauce—ketchup is allowed—is also our nation's number-one hangover cure. The fried mushrooms are there to add something vegetable without resorting to anything green, and the thickly buttered toast will fill you up. This is all washed down with large mugs of tea. Bubble and squeak (fried leftover cabbage and potatoes) is optional.

Nothing else would do and everyone in the car was in total agreement. The French can keep their fancy langoustine, butter sauces, and harbor-side moules frites. Thanks to the winds of the Channel, our food won the day. This was a job for full English blandness and I don't think I have ever eaten a more welcome plate of food.

01. Full English PAGE 28   02. Pour-over Coffee PAGE 408   03. Eggs and Soldiers PAGE 50

ENGLISH BREAKFAST

BACON, EGG, AND CHEESE SANDWICH

UNITED STATES

This is the quintessential New York City breakfast. It is found in bodegas (corner stores) and street carts across the city. The 'BEC' is served on a kaiser roll (page 212).

Preparation time: 5 minutes
Cooking time: 15 minutes
Serves: 1

· 2 slices (rashers) bacon (streaky)
· ½ tablespoon (7 g) unsalted butter
· 2 eggs
· Salt and freshly ground pepper
· 2 slices American cheese
· 1 kaiser roll, store-bought or homemade (page 212), split open

Start with a cold cast-iron skillet or frying pan and place the bacon in flat. Slowly bring the heat to medium to let the fat render and result in crispy bacon. Cook on both sides until crispy, about 10 minutes. Transfer the bacon to paper towels to drain. Pour off some of the rendered bacon fat, leaving about ½ tablespoon in the pan.

Reduce the heat to medium and melt the butter. Crack in the eggs and season with salt and pepper. Cook for 1 minute and reduce the heat to low. Cook until the white is set and the edges are golden and crispy, about 1 minute 30 seconds more (or scramble by stirring constantly until just set, about 1 minute). Cover each of the eggs with a cheese slice and cover the pan for about 30 seconds to melt the cheese.

Use a spatula to stack one egg with cheese on top of the other, then transfer the eggs to the bottom half of the kaiser roll. Top with the bacon and top half of the roll. Slice in half and serve.

See image on page 128

STEAMED EGG, BACON, AND CHEESE SANDWICH

UNITED STATES

A departure from the traditional BEC (opposite): eggs are steamed, rather than fried, topped with breakfast meat and cheese, served on an English muffin (page 200). In Hawaii, Spam is common, but bacon (streaky), ham (Canadian bacon), or a sausage patty are all typical. This style of steaming eggs can be prepared ahead of time and kept warm or reheated, which is why it's a common technique in fast-food establishments.

Preparation time: 5 minutes
Cooking time: 15 minutes
Serves: 1

· 1½ tablespoons (25 g) butter, plus more for the mold
· 1 slice Canadian Bacon (page 323), a thin slice of ham or Spam cut in a round, or a sausage patty
· 1 egg
· Salt and freshly ground pepper
· 1 English muffin, store-bought or homemade (page 200), halved
· 1 slice American cheese

Butter a 4-inch (10 cm) round metal cookie cutter or a lid/ring from a wide-mouthed mason jar.

Heat a medium frying pan over medium heat. Add the meat and cook on both sides until browned. Transfer to paper towels to drain.

Place the cookie cutter or mason-jar ring (with the lip on the bottom) in the frying pan. Add 1 tablespoon butter to the center of the cookie cutter. Once the butter is melted, crack the egg into the center of the cookie cutter—it's okay if a little bit escapes through the bottom. Swirl the egg, breaking the yolk, and pour enough water into the pan to come up to just below the top rim of the cookie cutter (about 1 cup/240 ml). Cover to steam the egg until set, 5 minutes. Season with salt and pepper.

Meanwhile, toast the English muffin and spread with the remaining butter

Put the meat on one half of the English muffin. Top with the steamed egg and the American cheese. Close the sandwich with the remaining half of the English muffin. Let the heat from the egg and English muffin melt the cheese slightly before serving.

PORK ROLL, EGG, AND CHEESE ON A BAGEL
UNITED STATES

The sliced meat in this popular breakfast sandwich from New Jersey is called either Taylor ham or pork roll, depending on location—North Jersey considers the meat to be called Taylor Ham, while southern residents of the state refer to it as Pork Roll. In the 1800s, a man named Taylor began selling a processed pork product he called Taylor's Ham. Labeling laws eventually made the company change the product name to "pork roll," but fierce loyalists still call it Taylor ham. No matter how its ordered, the actual product is labeled pork roll, but both agree it is best when grilled and served on a bagel or Kaiser Roll (page 212) with eggs and cheese.

Preparation time: 5 minutes
Cooking time: 15 minutes
Serves: 1

· 2 slices Taylor pork roll
· 1 ½ tablespoons (30 g) unsalted butter
· 1 Everything Bagel (page 190), halved and toasted
· 2 eggs
· Salt and freshly ground pepper
· 2 slices sharp cheddar or American cheese

Make 4 small cuts evenly spaced around the pork-roll rounds to prevent them from curling up when cooked. Heat a cast-iron skillet over medium-high heat. Add the meat and cook until crisp and browned on both sides, about 6 minutes. Butter both sides of the bagel with ½ tablespoon of the butter and place the meat on the bottom half of the bagel.

Reduce the heat to medium and melt the remaining butter. Crack in the eggs and season with salt and pepper. Cook for 1 minute and reduce the heat to low. Cook until the white is set and the edges are golden and crispy, about 1 minute 30 seconds more (or scramble by stirring constantly until just set, about 1 minute). Cover each of the eggs with a cheese slice and cover the pan for about 30 seconds to melt the cheese.

Use a spatula to stack one egg with cheese on top of the other, then transfer the eggs to the bottom half of the bagel on top of the pork roll. Place the top half of the bagel on the sandwich, slice in half, and serve.

OPEN-FACE HAM, EGG, AND CHEESE SANDWICH
THE NETHERLANDS

Uitsmijter is an open-face sandwich with ham, cheese, and a fried egg. The Dutch name Uitsmijter *translates to "bouncer," as this dish was often served to bar patrons in the early hours of the morning before getting kicked out at closing time.*

Preparation time: 5 minutes
Cooking time: 5 minutes
Serves: 1

· 1 slice white bread
· 1 slice ham
· 2 thin slices aged Gouda cheese
· 1 Fried Egg (page 14)
· Salt and freshly ground pepper

On the slice of bread, lay the ham, cheese, and fried egg to create an open-face sandwich. Season with salt and pepper.

BANH MI
VIETNAM

This breakfast sandwich in Vietnam has varying regional fillings. The baguette used for a banh mi typically contains a little bit of rice flour to make it fluffier than its French counterpart. This version includes a two-egg omelet stuffed into a baguette spread with pâté and mayo and topped with pickled vegetables (Đô Chua).

Preparation time: 20 minutes, plus pickling time for the Pickled Vegetables (below)
Cooking time: 5 minutes
Serves: 1

· 1 Vietnamese banh mi roll or demi baguette, split lengthwise (but not all the way through)
· 1 tablespoon mayonnaise
· 1 slice goose or pork liver pâté, ¼ inch (6 mm) thick
· 2 eggs
· ¼ teaspoon fish sauce
· 1 tablespoon vegetable oil
· Salt and freshly ground pepper
· ¼ jalapeño chili, thinly sliced
· ¼ medium pickling cucumber, thinly sliced
· 3 tablespoons Pickled Vegetables (recipe follows)
· 2 sprigs cilantro (coriander), coarsely chopped
· Soy sauce, for drizzling

Spread the baguette on one side with the mayonnaise and pâté on the other.

In a small bowl, beat the eggs and fish sauce.

In a medium frying pan, heat the oil over medium heat, swirling to coat the pan. Pour in the beaten eggs, swirling to coat the pan with a thin layer of egg. Let the eggs set for 30 seconds. Tilt the pan and use a spatula to fold the omelet in half. Let the omelet cook for 30 seconds more. Slide the omelet out of the pan and onto the bottom half of the baguette.

Top the egg with as many slices of jalapeño and cucumber as desired. Top with 3-4 tablespoons of pickled vegetables and a sprinkle of cilantro (coriander) and drizzle with soy sauce over the top to taste. Close the sandwich and serve.

PICKLED VEGETABLES (DÔ CHUA)

Preparation time: 15 minutes, plus 1 hour pickling time
Makes: ½ cup (50 g)

· ¼ cup (60 ml/2 fl oz) rice vinegar
· ½ tablespoon sugar
· ¼ teaspoon fine sea salt
· ¼ lb (115 g) daikon radish (about ¼ medium), cut into matchsticks
· ½ medium-large carrot, cut into matchsticks

In a small bowl, combine the vinegar, ¼ cup (60 ml/2 fl oz) water, sugar, and salt and stir to dissolve the sugar and salt. Submerge the daikon and carrot in the mixture and stir well. Cover with a tea towel and let the mixture sit at room temperature for at least 1 hour.

BACON SANDWICH

UNITED KINGDOM

This "bacon butty" is assembled on buttered bread served with ketchup or brown sauce, a popular condiment in the UK with a sweet, peppery, and tart flavor. This sandwich is made with a heaping stack of back bacon, a cured (often smoked) pork, sliced thin, which includes the round of the loin and an extension of surrounding fat. Canadian bacon is made of only the round of the loin and American bacon (streaky bacon) is made of a much fattier cut from the belly.

Preparation time: 5 minutes
Cooking time: 10 minutes
Serves: 1

· 4 slices (rashers) back bacon or if not available, Canadian bacon (page 323)
· 2 slices white sandwich bread
· ½ tablespoon (7 g) unsalted butter, at room temperature
· Brown sauce or ketchup, for serving

Start with a cold cast-iron skillet or frying pan and place the bacon in flat. Slowly bring the heat to medium to let the fat render and result in crispy bacon. Cook on both sides until crispy, about 10 minutes. Transfer the bacon to paper towels to drain.

Over medium heat, add the bread to the pan and fry both sides in the rendered fat until golden, about 2 minutes. Lightly butter both pieces of the toasted bread. Sandwich the bacon between the slices and serve with brown sauce or ketchup.

PRINCESS SANDWICH

BULGARIA

This baked open-face sandwich made with egg and ground (minced) meat was popular in Bulgaria during the 1900s, as a way to stretch a small amount of ground meat into a more filling option.

Preparation time: 10 minutes
Cooking time: 15 minutes
Serves: 1–2

· ¼ lb (115 g) ground (minced) beef
· 1 egg
· ¼ small yellow onion, diced
· ½ teaspoon dried oregano or thyme
· ¼ teaspoon ground cumin
· Salt and freshly ground pepper
· 1 long slice country bread

Preheat the oven to 350°F (180°C/Gas Mark 4).

In a large bowl, combine the beef, egg, onion, oregano, cumin, and a pinch each of salt and pepper. Mix well with a wooden spoon or your hands until thoroughly combined. Place the bread on a baking sheet and spread with the meat mixture. Bake until the beef is cooked through, 15 minutes. Season with salt and pepper to taste.

Bacon Sandwich

SEMOLINA CRUST CHEESE SANDWICH

LEBANON

Akkawi, *a cheese similar to mozzarella, is baked with either a semolina crust or* kataifi *(shredded phyllo dough) crust to make a pastry called* knafeh. *The* knafeh *is cut into squares and placed in small purse-shaped bread pockets called* kaak *and drenched in* atyr, *a syrup made with orange blossom water.*

Preparation time: 10 minutes, plus 20 minutes soaking time
Cooking time: 30 minutes
Serves: 2–4

· 1 lb (450 g) akkawi cheese or mozzarella, sliced
· 1 cup (170 g) semolina flour
· 2 teaspoons sugar
· 6 tablespoons (85 g) unsalted butter, melted, plus more for greasing
· 6 tablespoons full-fat milk
· 2 kaak breads (see Note)
· Atyr Syrup (recipe follows), for serving

Preheat the oven to 450°F (230°C/Gas Mark 8).

In a bowl, mix the semolina with the sugar. Pour in the melted butter and milk and mix together with a wooden spoon to form a dough with the consistency of sandy putty. Lightly butter an 8-inch (20 cm) pie dish and press the mixture into it. Bake until golden, about 10 minutes. (Remove the dough, but leave the oven on.) Allow to cool slightly, then break the semolina up in a food processor or in a medium bowl with your hands until finely crumbled.

Grease the pie dish with butter and evenly press the semolina crumbs into the bottom of the plate. Top with the cheese and bake until the cheese has melted, about 20 minutes. Let the *knafeh* cool slightly and invert onto a plate, cheese-side down to show the crispy bottom. Drizzle with *atyr* syrup, slice, and stuff into *kaak* breads.

KNAFEH SANDWICH WITH KATAIFI CRUST

· 1 lb (450 g) akkawi cheese or mozzarella (see note), sliced
· ½ lb (225 g) kataifi (shredded phyllo dough)
· 1 stick (115 g) unsalted butter, melted, plus more for greasing
· 2 kaak flatbreads, split horizontally (see Note)
· Atyr Syrup (recipe follows), for drizzling

Preheat the oven to 450°F (230°C/Gas Mark 8).

Toss the *kataifi* with the melted butter, making sure the dough soaks up all of the butter. Grease an 8-inch (20 cm) pie plate and spread the *kataifi* mixture on it, pressing the layer down into the plate. Cover with a layer of the cheese slices. Bake until the pastry is golden, 20–25 minutes. Let the *knafeh* cool slightly and invert onto a plate, cheese-side down to show the crispy bottom. Drizzle with *atyr* syrup, slice, and stuff into *kaak* breads.

Notes: If *kaak* breads are not available, cut 1 pita in half. Brush with some oil and sprinkle with sesame seeds. Toast under the broiler until warmed and lightly toasted but not crisp.

If using salted *akkawi* or salted mozzarella, place the slices in a bowl with water and soak for 20 minutes. Drain and taste for saltiness. If it's too salty, cover the cheese with water again and let it soak for another 20 minutes.

If you can't find *kataifi*, buy regular phyllo dough and cut it into very thin shards that resemble shredded wheat.

See image on page 62

ATYR SYRUP

Preparation time: 5 minutes
Cooking time: 10 minutes
Makes: ¾ cup

· 1 cup (200 g) sugar
· 2 teaspoons lemon juice
· 1 teaspoon orange-blossom water

In a small saucepan, stir together the sugar and ½ cup (120 ml/4 fl oz) water and bring to a boil over high heat. Reduce the heat to medium and cook, stirring constantly, until the sugar is dissolved and the mixture is clear, 3 minutes. Remove the saucepan from the heat and stir in the lemon juice and orange-blossom water. Store in the refrigerator for up to 3 weeks.

ALMOND GRANITA
AND BRIOCHE
ITALY

Fresh brioche with a side of granita is a popular summer breakfast in Sicily. Dip the brioche in mandorla *(almond) granita.*

Preparation time: 15 minutes, plus 3½ hours soaking and freezing time
Cooking time: 5 minutes
Serves: 2

· 4 tablespoons slivered almonds, soaked for 1 hour
· 3½ oz (100 g) almond paste
· 2 brioche buns, homemade (page 214) or store-bought

Drain the almonds. In a food processor, coarsely grind and set aside.

In a small saucepan, bring 2 cups (475 ml/16 fl oz) water to a boil over medium-high heat. Remove from heat and allow the water to cool to 90°F (32°C). Whisk in the almond paste until dissolved. Pour the mixture into an 8-inch (20 cm) square baking pan. Add the ground almonds and stir to distribute evenly.

Transfer to the freezer and freeze for 1 hour. Using a fork, scrape and break apart any ice that has formed. Freeze again and repeat the process every 30 minutes another 4 times, for a total of 2½ hours. The granita should be frozen but appear creamy. If the mixture isn't frozen, return to the freezer for another 30 minutes.

Serve in a bowl alongside the brioche buns.

BRIOCHE
AND GELATO
ITALY

Rather than dipping a brioche in granita, as above, in this this popular Sicilian breakfast the gelato is sandwiched in the brioche, often with a dollop of whipped cream.

Preparation time: 5 minutes
Serves: 1

· 2 brioche buns, homemade (page 214) or store-bought
· 2 scoops gelato, any flavor
· Whipped cream, for serving (optional)

Top the bottom bun with gelato and whipped cream (if using) and sandwich with the other half of the bun.

Brioche and Gelato

TARTINE

FRANCE

The salt content in the butter is where this gets creative, as the French tend to have split preferences between unsalted, salted, and half-salted.

Preparation time: 5 minutes
Serves: 1

· 1 demi-baguette, sliced lengthwise, or 2 slices miche (sourdough)
· 1 tablespoon (15 g) unsalted, salted, or half-salted butter, at room temperature
· 2 tablespoons jam, any flavor

Spread the bread with butter and jam.

BREAD WITH BUTTER AND SWEET SPRINKLES

THE NETHERLANDS

The Dutch typically have a few slices of bread every morning, some sweet and some savory, never toasted. The savory version is spread with butter or margarine, then covered with cheese, liver pâté, or cold cuts. The sweet version also has butter or margarine, but then is generously covered with hagelslag *(sweet sprinkles). The sprinkles come in many colors but are mostly available in dark, milk, or white chocolate.*

Preparation time: 5 minutes
Serves: 1

· ½ tablespoon (7 g) unsalted butter, at room temperature
· 1 slice white or brown bread, or 2 zwieback, skorper, or rusks
· 2 tablespoons melk (milk) or puur (dark) chocolate hagelslag

Smear the butter across a slice of bread. Generously sprinkle with the *hagelslag* and serve.

Bread with Butter and Sweet Sprinkles

RYE BREAD WITH BUTTER

GERMANY

Butterbrot *is usually a slice of sourdough rye bread* (roggenbrot) *or a split roll* (Semmeln, *page 218) spread with butter or margarine and topped with one other ingredient, typically a generous serving of deli sliced cheese or jam.*

Preparation time: 5 minutes
Serves: 1

· 1 slice sourdough rye bread
· 1½–2 tablespoons (22–30 g) butter, at room temperature
· 2 slices cheese or 1 tablespoon jam

Generously slather the bread with the softened butter and top with cheese or jam.

BROWN CHEESE SANDWICH

NORWAY

Brunost *is a brown cheese with a rich flavor and hints of caramel. It is often found on a variety of breads or Norwegian waffles—a waffle molded into five connecting heart-shaped segments, each easily torn off and enjoyed as individual bites.*

Preparation time: 5 minutes
Serves: 1

· ½ tablespoon (7 g) unsalted butter, at room temperature
· 1 Norwegian waffle, lefse (potato-based flatbread), or bread or roll of choice
· 2 slices brunost cheese

Spread the waffle or bread with the softened butter and top with the cheese.

See image on page 372

GROUND MEAT STUFFED ROTI

SINGAPORE

Known as murtabak *or* martabak, *this roti-like pancakes originated in the Middle East but were adopted as a popular street food in Singapore and Malaysia. Often served with mutton or fish curry,* murtabak *are typically filled with egg, scallion (spring onion), and a choice of mixed meat. They are folded up and cut into rectangles, similar to a Chinese* jianbing *(Savory Stuffed Crepe, page 186).*

Preparation time: 20 minutes, plus 1 hour resting time
Cooking time: 30 minutes
Serves: 2

For the dough:
· 1½ cups (215 g) all-purpose (plain) flour
· ½ teaspoon fine sea salt
· 2 teaspoons ghee
· 1 egg
· 2 tablespoons vegetable oil, plus more for greasing

For the filling:
· 2 tablespoons vegetable oil
· 1 small yellow onion, diced
· 2 cloves garlic, minced
· 1 teaspoon grated fresh ginger
· 1 teaspoon ground turmeric
· 1 teaspoon garam masala
· ½ teaspoon chili powder
· ½ teaspoon fine sea salt
· ½ lb (225 g) ground (minced) mutton or chicken
· 2 eggs
· 1 tablespoon ghee, plus more if needed

Make the dough:
Whisk the flour and salt in a large bowl. Work in the ghee with your hands until evenly distributed. In a small bowl, whisk together 6 tablespoons water and eggs. Pour into the flour mixture and stir with a wooden spoon until a shaggy dough forms.

Turn the dough out onto a lightly oiled work surface and knead until smooth and elastic, about 10 minutes. Divide the dough into 4 equal parts and roll into balls. Spoon ½ tablespoon of the oil into each of 4 cups of a muffin tin. Add the dough balls to the cups and roll in the oil to cover all sides. Let the balls sit at room temperature, covered, for at least 1 hour but up to overnight.

Meanwhile, make the filling:
In a frying pan, heat the oil over medium heat. Add 4 tablespoons of the diced onion and cook until translucent, about 5 minutes. Add the garlic and cook until aromatic, about 1 minute. Stir in the ginger, turmeric, garam masala, chili powder, and salt. Stir in the meat, breaking it up as it cooks, until the meat is cooked through and browned, about 10 minutes. Transfer to a bowl and set aside to cool.

Cook the *murtabak*:
When the dough has rested, lightly oil a work surface. Take a ball of dough and roll it out with a rolling pin. Carefully stretch it out with your hands until it's almost thin enough to see through, but without holes, about 10 inches (25 cm) in diameter.

In a bowl, beat the eggs, then mix into the cooled mutton mixture. On a large griddle or a 12-inch (30 cm) cast-iron skillet, heat the ghee over medium heat. Working quickly, transfer one roti to the pan. Cover the center portion with half of the ground meat mixture and sprinkle with half of the remaining chopped onion. Cook until the bottom is golden, about 3 minutes. Fold the sides of the roti towards the center, enclosing the contents. Flip the *murtabak* and cook on the other side, adding more ghee if needed, until browned, about 1 minute. Repeat with the remaining roti dough, meat, and onion.

Cut in half and serve warm with an optional side of kari (curry) gravy, pickled carrots, and cucumbers.

SAVORY STUFFED CREPE

CHINA

Very popular in Beijing, jianbing *is a savory street-food crepe filled with an assortment of egg, fresh herbs, sauces, crispy wontons or* youtiao *(Chinese Cruller, page 306), and optional add-on proteins.*

Preparation time: 20 minutes, plus 1 hour resting time
Cooking time: 5 minutes
Serves: 2

· ½ cup (70 g) plus 2 tablespoons all-purpose (plain) flour
· ¼ teaspoon fine sea salt
· 5 tablespoons warm water
· 1 teaspoon vegetable oil, plus more for greasing
· 2 eggs
· 1 tablespoon sweet bean sauce
· Chili oil, to taste
· Chopped cilantro (coriander), for garnish
· 2 wonton wrappers, (store-bought) fried and chopped

In a small bowl, combine the flour and salt. Pour in the water and mix with a wooden spoon until a sticky dough forms, about 2 minutes. Brush the dough with the vegetable oil and set on a lightly oiled work surface. Cover with plastic wrap (cling film) and allow the dough to rest for at least 1–2 hours.

Divide the dough in half. Oil your hands to keep the dough from sticking. Carefully stretch one portion of dough with your hands until it's almost thin enough to see through, but without holes, about 10 inches (25 cm) in diameter.

Heat a large griddle or cast-iron skillet with a drizzle of vegetable oil over medium heat. Working quickly, transfer a *jianbing* to the griddle or frying pan. Crack an egg in the center of the *jianbing* and beat it carefully with a fork, taking care not to rip the dough. Cook until the egg begins to set, 2 minutes. Flip the *jianbing* and cook the egg side until browned, about 1 minute. Flip again to brown the other side, 1 minute.

To serve, transfer the *jianbing* to a plate and dress with ½ tablespoon sweet bean sauce, some chili oil, cilantro (coriander), and fried wonton wrappers. Fold the sides of the *jianbing* towards the center, enclosing the contents like an envelope. Flip over and cut in half. Repeat to make a second *jianbing*. Serve warm.

ROLLED SCALLION CREPE WITH EGG

TAIWAN

Dan bing, a Taiwanese-style scallion crepe with a scrambled egg melded to one side, is typically served with the addition of chopped scallions (spring onions). The pancake is rolled up and cut into bite-size pieces. It is then topped with a blend of soy and sweet chili sauces, but Sriracha or hoisin can also be used.

Preparation time: 10 minutes
Cooking time: 15 minutes
Serves: 2

For the crepes:
· 4 tablespoons all-purpose (plain) flour
· 1 tablespoon cornstarch (cornflour)

For the eggs:
· 2 eggs
· ¼ teaspoon toasted sesame oil
· ¼ teaspoon fine sea salt
· 1 scallion (spring onion), chopped
· 1 teaspoon vegetable oil

For the sauce:
· 2 tablespoons soy sauce
· 2 tablespoons sweet chili sauce

Make the crepes:
In a bowl, combine the flour, cornstarch (cornflour), and ½ cup (120 ml/4 fl oz) water. Mix until no dry spots remain. Let the batter rest for at least 5 minutes.

Meanwhile, prepare the eggs:
In a small bowl, beat together the eggs, sesame oil, and salt. In a medium frying pan, heat the vegetable oil over medium heat. Ladle half of the batter into the frying pan, swirling it around to coat the pan evenly. Cook until the rim starts to pull away from the sides of the pan, about 3 minutes. Flip the crepe and pour half of the egg mixture over it. Cook until the egg has begun to set, about 1 minute. Sprinkle the scallion (spring onion) evenly over the egg and cook for another minute. Flip and cook, egg-side down, until lightly browned, 30 seconds more. Repeat with the remaining batter and egg.

In a small bowl, combine the soy and sweet chili sauces and drizzle over the crepes. Roll up and slice into bite-size pieces. Serve warm.

BREADS

EVERYTHING BAGEL
UNITED STATES

After these boiled, then baked, rings of dough get split in half, they are usually toasted, and sandwiched with a "schmear" (generous spread) of store-bought or homemade Cream Cheese (page 75). Bagels are also made with different doughs such as egg, pumpernickel, and whole wheat. When toppings like coarse salt, sesame seeds, poppy seeds, "everything" seasoning (as in this recipe), or onion get thrown into the mix, ordering New York's most iconic breakfast becomes a highly personal experience, especially when topped with Lox (page 351).

Preparation time: 45 minutes, plus 1 hour rising time and overnight chilling time
Cooking time: 30 minutes
Makes: 6 bagels

For the dough:
· 2 teaspoons honey or barley malt syrup
· ¾ cup (175 ml/6 fl oz) plus 3 tablespoons warm water
· 1½ teaspoons active dry yeast
· 2¼ cups (305 g) bread flour (strong white flour)
· 1¼ teaspoons fine sea salt

For the "everything" topping:
· 2 tablespoons poppy seeds
· 2 tablespoons sesame seeds
· 1 tablespoon caraway seeds
· 1 tablespoon dried garlic (garlic powder)
· 1 tablespoon dried onion
· 2 teaspoons fine sea salt

For the poaching bath:
· 1 tablespoon honey or barley malt syrup
· 1 teaspoon baking soda (bicarbonate of soda)

In a small bowl, dissolve the honey in the water. Add the yeast and set the mixture aside until the yeast is frothy, about 10 minutes.

In a medium bowl, mix the flour with the salt. Add the yeast mixture and stir with a wooden spoon until a shaggy dough forms, pulling away from the sides of the bowl. Knead the dough until it's firm and elastic, 10 minutes. Place the dough in a lightly oiled bowl and cover with a tea towel. Let rest until it has doubled in size, 1 ½ hours.

Transfer the dough to a work surface and divide into 6 equal portions. Allow to rest for 5 minutes before rolling each portion of dough into a rope 8 inches (20 cm) long. Wrap around your four fingers with the two ends meeting under your hand. Roll the end pieces together to fuse. Place the shaped bagels on a lined baking sheet, cover tightly in plastic wrap (cling film), and refrigerate overnight, 8–12 hours.

Combine all topping ingredients in a small bowl.

Remove bagels from the refrigerator and allow to sit for 30 minutes. Fill a bowl with water. Throw in a bagel. If it floats, the bagels are ready to poach. If it doesn't, wait 10 minutes and try again.

Preheat the oven to 425°F (220°C/Gas Mark 7). Meanwhile, prepare the poaching bath. In a large saucepan, bring 2 quarts (1.9 liters) water to a boil. Reduce the heat to low and stir in the honey and baking soda (bicarb).

Poach the bagels: Using a slotted spoon, lower 3 bagels at a time into the liquid. Cook on one side for 1 minute. Flip the bagels over to poach the other side, 1 minute more. Using a slotted spoon, return to the lined baking sheet. Repeat with the remaining bagels. Sprinkle with the everything topping.

Reduce the oven temperature to 425°F (220°C/Gas Mark 7) and bake the bagels until golden, 18–20 minutes, rotating the sheet front to back halfway through baking. Store any leftover bagels in the freezer for up to 3 months.

Everything Bagels

MONTREAL-STYLE BAGELS

CANADA

Though this recipe is oven-baked, Montreal-style bagels are made in wood-fire ovens and come with toppings and accompaniments similar to those for an American bagel (see Everything Bagel, page 190). They tend to have a denser texture and a subtle sweetness, and a smaller center hole.

Preparation time: 45 minutes, plus 30 minutes rising time
Cooking time: 30 minutes
Makes: 6 small bagels

For the dough:
· 1¼ teaspoons active dry yeast
· 1 tablespoon sugar
· 2 tablespoons honey
· 1 egg
· 1 ½ tablespoons vegetable oil
· ½ teaspoon fine sea salt
· 2 ½ cups (340 g) bread flour (strong white flour), plus more as needed
· Sesame seeds, for topping (optional)

For the poaching bath:
· 2 tablespoons honey or barley malt syrup

Make the dough: In a large bowl, combine ¾ cup (175 ml/6 fl oz) warm water, yeast, and pinch of sugar. Set the mixture aside until the yeast is frothy, about 10 minutes. (If the yeast does not froth, check the expiration date. You may have to start over with fresher yeast.) Stir in the sugar, honey, egg, and oil. Stir in the salt and 1 cup (150 g) of the flour at a time until a shaggy dough forms, pulling away from the sides of the bowl.

On a work surface, knead the dough until firm and elastic, about 10 minutes. If the dough is very sticky, add up to 4 tablespoons more flour. Place the dough in a lightly oiled bowl and cover with a tea towel. Let the dough rest for 10–15 minutes.

Transfer the dough to a work surface and divide into 6 equal portions. Line a baking sheet with release foil or a Silpat to avoid sticking. To shape the bagels, roll each piece into a rope 8 inches (20 cm) long and connect the ends. Roll the ends together to seal, leaving a large hole in the center. Transfer the shaped bagels to the baking sheet and let them rest, covered, for 30 minutes.

Meanwhile, poach the bagels. Preheat the oven to 450°F (230°C/Gas Mark 8) and prepare the poaching bath. Bring a large saucepan of water to a boil. Reduce the heat to low and stir in the honey. Using a slotted spoon, lower 4 bagels at a time into the liquid. Cook on one side for 1 minute. Flip the bagels over to poach the other side, 1 minute more. Using a slotted spoon, transfer bagels to the baking sheet. Repeat with the remaining bagels. Sprinkle on sesame seeds, if using.

Bake the bagels until golden brown on all sides, 18–20 minutes. Serve warm or toasted. The bagels can be frozen for up to 3 months.

Montreal-Style Bagels

JERUSALEM-STYLE BAGELS

ISRAEL

These can be eaten plain or with any desired toppings, such as Labneh (page 74)—a great cream cheese replacement—and tomato. Jerusalem bagels are often coated in heaping amounts of sesame seeds and are a larger, thinner ring than an American bagel (see Everything Bagel, page 190). Their subtly sweet flavor is closer to a Montreal-Style Bagel (page 192).

Preparation time: 30 minutes, plus 50 minutes rising time
Cooking time: 20 minutes
Makes: 6 bagels

· 1¼ cups (295 ml/10 fl oz) warm water
· 2 ¼ teaspoons active dry yeast
· ¼ teaspoon sugar
· 4 tablespoons full-fat milk, warmed
· 4 tablespoons vegetable oil
· 3 tablespoons honey
· 1 teaspoon fine sea salt
· 5 cups (725 g) all-purpose (plain) flour, plus more as needed
· 1 egg
· ½ cup (70 g) sesame seeds

In a large bowl, combine the warm water, yeast, and sugar. Set the mixture aside until the yeast is frothy, about 10 minutes. (If the yeast doesn't froth, check the expiration date. You may have to start over with fresher yeast.) Stir in the milk, oil, and honey. Stir in the salt and 1 cup (145 g) of the flour flour at a time until a shaggy dough forms, pulling away from the sides of the bowl.

Turn the dough out onto a work surface and knead until firm and elastic, about 10 minutes. If the dough is very sticky and not elastic, add up to 4 tablespoons more flour. Place the dough in a lightly oiled bowl and cover with a tea towel. Let the dough rest until doubled in size, 25–30 minutes.

Line a baking sheet with release foil or a Silpat to avoid sticking. Lightly flour a work surface and punch down the dough to deflate the bubbles. Divide into 6 equal portions and roll into balls. Press a finger through the center of a ball, making a hole. Pick it up and gently stretch it out, squeezing the dough into an large oval, about 8 inches (20 cm) in diameter. Transfer the dough to the baking sheet. In a small bowl, lightly beat the egg. Brush the dough all over with the beaten egg. Sprinkle the top with a generous amount of sesame seeds. Cover with plastic wrap (cling film) or a tea towel and let the bagels rise for 20 minutes.

Meanwhile, preheat the oven to 350°F (180°C/Gas Mark 4).

Bake the bagels until golden brown on all sides, 20-25 minutes. Allow to cool on a rack. Serve warm or toasted.

BIALY

POLAND / UNITED STATES

This New York staple arrived in America by way of Poland. Whereas a bagel is boiled then baked, and has a hole in the center, bialys are baked and have an indentation in the center filled with diced onions that caramelize in the oven. Bialys are served with much of the same spreads as bagels, such as cream cheese or lox.

Preparation time: 30 minutes, plus 3 hours rising time
Cooking time: 30 minutes
Makes: 6 bialys

For the dough:
· ¾ cup (175 ml/6 fl oz) plus 3 tablespoons water
· ¾ teaspoon active dry yeast
· Pinch of sugar
· 2 ¼ cups (300 g) bread flour (strong white flour)
· 1 ¼ teaspoons fine sea salt
· Vegetable oil, to grease the bowl

For the filling:
· 2 teaspoons olive oil
· ¼ large yellow onion, finely diced
· ½ teaspoon poppy seeds
· Salt and freshly ground pepper
· Cornmeal, for sprinkling

Make the dough:
In a small bowl, combine the water, yeast, and sugar. Set the mixture aside until the yeast is frothy, about 10 minutes. (If the yeast doesn't froth, check the expiration date. You may have to start over with fresher yeast.)

In a large bowl, combine the bread flour and salt. With a wooden spoon, add the yeast mixture and stir until a shaggy dough forms. Turn the dough out onto a work surface and knead until firm and elastic, about 10 minutes. If the dough becomes too tough, run your hands quickly under water and continue to knead. Place the dough in a lightly oiled large bowl and cover with a tea towel. Let it rise until doubled in size, about 2 hours or up to overnight in the refrigerator.

Divide the dough into 6 equal portions and roll each into a ball. Set on a lightly floured baking sheet. Cover with plastic wrap (cling film) and let the rise until they double in size, 45 minutes to 1 hour.

Meanwhile, preheat the oven to 475°F (245°C/Gas Mark 9).

Make the filling:
In a medium frying pan, heat the olive oil over low heat. Add the onion and cook until caramelized, 15 minutes. Transfer the onion to a bowl and mix in the poppy seeds. Season with salt and pepper.

When ready to bake, sprinkle a large baking sheet with cornmeal. Gently stretch the pieces of dough into round about the size of a bagel, 4 ½ inches (11 cm) and press your thumb into the center to make an indentation for the filling. Place the shaped bialys on the baking sheet. Fill each bialy with about 1 teaspoon of the filling.

Bake the bialys until golden, 8–10 minutes. Allow to cool on a rack. Serve warm or toasted.

CLOTILDE DUSOULIER
FRENCH BREAKFAST

Clotilde Dusoulier is the author of the food blog and book Chocolate & Zucchini. *She lives in Paris with her husband and two sons.*

Picture two little children, both adorable and very blonde, waking up bright and early in the morning sunlight. Together they toddle into the garden carrying the makings of a perfect breakfast—white tablecloth, stacks of bowls, jars of homemade jam, fresh brioche and bread, a jug of juice—to surprise their delighted parents. The entire family sits down happily at the table, takes great big bites of slathered brioche, and drinks from the great big bowls, laughing all the while and looking at each other fondly. Oh, what a glorious day it's going to be!

Sounds cliché? Maybe because it's taken straight from a 1980's television ad promoting a French brand of instant coffee with chicory.

Advertisements both reflect and direct our collective imagination, and this one was immensely popular in France. Two generations of French men and women still know the song by heart, and I would argue it continues to shape what we perceive as the ideal breakfast—and what it means to us and our families.

It's probably why the French strive to recreate that bliss each morning. Of course, it looks different from region to region and from family to family, and according to whether it's a weekday or a weekend morning—whether we prioritize speed and convenience, or allow ourselves to linger longer, in the kitchen and at the table. But the intention is always the same: fresh and wholesome foods, pleasure and connection, a joyful start to the day.

Some of my very favorite and most memorable breakfasts were served to me at a *chambre d'hôte*, the French version of the bed and breakfast, in Burgundy some years ago. It did not involve adorable children—I didn't have any then—but was instead prepared by our hostess, who took due pride in waking up long before her guests to bake her own brioche, fry her own *merveilles* (fried strips of dough dusted in confectioners' sugar), and pop into the garden to pick berries for the fruit salad.

Every morning of our brief stay, my husband and I would roll out of bed and follow the smell of coffee down to the breakfast room, set up in a veranda full of greenery and flowers, eager to discover whatever delights our hostess had concocted for us that day. It was never anything showy or over-the-top, like you might get at a luxury hotel. These were time-tested, comforting preparations that seemed like they might be family recipes, honed and perfected over many years. Perhaps a cherry clafoutis with the stones in. Homemade bread with fresh butter from a nearby farm. A big puffy pancake. Scrambled eggs with local mushrooms.

It is those marvelous spreads that I think about to this day when I prepare a special-occasion breakfast for friends or family. Less is more, I remind myself. A hodgepodge of too many different things won't do. Instead, I prefer a few thoughtfully chosen elements that will surprise and delight—almost as if some imaginary little kids had assembled them for us.

01. Brioche PAGE 214   02. Almond Croissants PAGE 362   03. Croissants PAGE 358

04. Café au Lait **PAGE 415**   05. Pains au Chocolat **PAGE 360**   06. Tartine **PAGE 182**

ENGLISH MUFFIN
UNITED STATES

These "muffins" have airy crevices and are topped with butter and melted American cheese, or sometimes cream cheese or other toppings. Though not a typical breakfast food in England, English Muffins were invented by Victorian-era servants as a way to use leftover scraps of dough. They were often sold door to door, giving rise to the popular song, The Muffin Man. *English muffins as they are known in the United States were invented by Samuel Thomas Bath, a British immigrant living in New York City. He created what he called a split crumpet or "toaster crumpet," also known as the Thomas' Original English Muffins.*

Preparation time: 30 minutes, plus 2 hours rising time
Cooking time: 20 minutes
Makes: about 6 English muffins

· ¾ cup (175 ml/6 fl oz) full-fat milk, warmed
· ¾ teaspoon active dry yeast
· 1½ cups (215 g) all-purpose (plain) flour
· 1 teaspoon sugar
· 1¼ teaspoons fine sea salt
· 1 egg
· 2 tablespoons (30 g) unsalted butter, at room temperature
· Vegetable oil, to grease the bowl
· Cornmeal or semolina, for dusting

In a small bowl, combine the milk and yeast. Set the mixture aside until the yeast is frothy, about 10 minutes. (If the yeast doesn't froth, check the expiration date. You may have to start over with fresher yeast.)

In a large bowl, combine the flour, salt, sugar, egg, and butter. With a wooden spoon, add the yeast mixture and stir until a shaggy dough forms. In the bowl, knead until the dough is smooth, silky, and fairly sticky, about 5 minutes. Transfer the dough to a lightly oiled bowl. Cover the bowl with a tea towel and set aside to rise until doubled in size, about 2 hours.

Divide the dough into 6 equal portions. Roll each into a ball and flatten gently with your hands into a puck. Dust with cornmeal or semolina. Transfer the muffins to a baking sheet and set aside to rest for 15 minutes.

Meanwhile, heat a large cast-iron skillet over low heat and scatter a handful of the cornmeal or semolina into the skillet. Add the muffins, fitting 3 at a time, and cook until the bottoms are browned, about 8 minutes. Flip the muffins and cook until both sides are browned and the muffin is cooked through, about 8 minutes more (see Note).

To serve, let the English Muffins cool before puncturing each with the prongs of a fork poked around the perimeter. Carefully pull the halved apart. This "fork-splitting" gives the interior those definitive uneven nooks and crannies.

Note: If the inside of the muffin has not cooked all the way through, bake them in the oven at 350°F (180°C/Gas Mark 4) for an additional 8–10 minutes.

TATTIE SCONES
SCOTLAND

The "tattie" or potato scone is cut into triangles, and often enjoyed in a Scottish Fry Up (page 29). It is made with leftover potato from dinner the night before.

Preparation time: 15 minutes
Cooking time: 30 minutes
Serves: 4, makes 8 scones

· ½ lb (225 g) Yukon Gold potatoes (1 large), peeled and cubed
· 2 tablespoons (30 g) unsalted butter
· ½ cup (70 g) all-purpose (plain) flour, plus more for dusting
· ¼ teaspoon fine sea salt
· 1 teaspoon vegetable oil

In a medium saucepan, combine the potatoes with water to just cover and bring to a boil over high heat. Reduce the heat to low, cover, and simmer until the potatoes are fork-tender, about 10 minutes.

Drain the potatoes and transfer to a bowl. Using a potato masher, mash the potatoes with the butter until no lumps remain. Allow the potatoes to cool slightly. Stir in the flour and salt with a wooden spoon to make a dough.

Turn the dough out onto a lightly floured work surface.

Split the dough in half and roll each piece out to a round, ¼ inch (6 mm) thick, 6 inches (15 cm) in diameter. Cut the rounds into quarters to make wedges.

Lightly grease a cast-iron skillet with the oil and set over medium-high heat. Cook the scones until golden brown on both sides, about 3 minutes per side. Serve warm.

POTATO FARL
IRELAND

Farl is a potato flatbread or soda bread round cut into quadrants. Potato farl is also called "tattie bread," similar to Tattie Scones (above), but elevated with the addition of baking powder. The wedges are cooked in a skillet as an element of an Ulster Fry (Northern Irish Breakfast, page 29).

Preparation time: 15 minutes
Cooking time: 20 minutes
Serves: 4, makes 8 farls

· ½ lb (225 g) Yukon Gold potatoes (1 large), peeled and cubed
· 1 tablespoon (15 g) unsalted butter, plus more for cooking the bread
· ½ cup (70 g) all-purpose (plain) flour, plus more for dusting
· ¼ teaspoon fine sea salt
· ¼ teaspoon baking powder

In a medium saucepan, combine the potatoes with water to just cover and bring to a boil over high heat. Reduce the heat to low, cover, and simmer until the potatoes are fork-tender, about 10 minutes.

Drain the potatoes and transfer to a bowl. Using a potato masher, mash the potatoes with the butter until no lumps remain. Allow the potatoes to cool slightly. Stir in the flour, salt, and baking powder with a wooden spoon to make a dough.

Turn the dough out onto a lightly floured work surface. Split the dough in half and use a rolling pin to roll it out to a round ¼ inch (6 mm) thick. With a 6-inch (15 cm) round cookie cutter, cut out 1 round. Cut the round into 4 quarters.

In a medium frying pan, melt some butter over medium-high heat, swirling it around the pan to coat evenly. Cook the wedges until golden brown on both sides, about 3 minutes per side. Serve warm.

FLATBREAD WITH ZA'ATAR

LEBANON

A Man'oushe *(plural* Manakish*) is a Lebanese flatbread found on most street corners in Beirut. A local bakery* (fern*) will sell* manakish *with a variety of toppings, most commonly olive oil and za'atar (sumac, toasted sesame seeds, and thyme) or* keshek *(a dried goat yogurt and bulgur powder, opposite). Any* man'oushe *can be topped with stringy cheese by ordering it by the name "cocktail," for example: za'atar cocktail.*

Preparation time: 30 minutes , plus 1 hour rising time
Cooking time: 20 minutes
Makes: 8 flatbreads

· 1¼ cups (295 ml/10 fl oz) warm water
· 2 teaspoons active dry yeast
· A pinch plus 2 teaspoons sugar
· 3½ cups (505 g) all-purpose (plain) flour
· 1 teaspoon fine sea salt
· 2 tablespoons olive oil, plus more for bowl and brushing
· ½ cup (100g) za'atar

In a large bowl, combine the warm water, yeast, and pinch of sugar. Set the mixture aside until the yeast is frothy, about 10 minutes. (If the yeast doesn't froth, check the expiration date. You may have to start over with fresher yeast.)

In a large bowl, combine the flour, 2 teaspoons sugar, and salt. Pour in the yeast mixture and the olive oil. With a wooden spoon, stir until a shaggy dough forms and pulls away from the sides of the bowl. Turn out onto a work surface and knead until the dough is smooth, 10 minutes. Place the dough in a lightly oiled bowl and cover with a tea towel. Let the dough rest until doubled in size, about 1 hour.

Preheat the oven to 400°F (200°C/Gas Mark 6) with a baking sheet turned upside down on the middle rack.

Turn the dough out onto a lightly floured work surface and divide into 8 equal portions. Cover with a tea towel and let the dough rest for another 10 minutes. Flatten each portion and use a rolling pin to roll out to a very thin round, 10 inches (25 cm) in diameter. Brush with oil, leaving a ½-inch (1.25 cm) border around the rim, and sprinkle za'atar over the olive oil.

Carefully place 2 flatbreads on the heated baking sheet and bake until browned, 10–12 minutes. Wrap in a tea towel to keep warm, and repeat with the remaining dough. Serve warm.

FLATBREAD WITH KESHEK

LEBANON

A popular man'oushe *(Lebanese flatbread) topping,* keshek *is made from goat's milk yogurt and bulgur that has been dried and ground into a powder. This powder is mixed with tomato paste (purée) and baked on a* man'oushe.

Preparation time: 35 minutes, plus rising time for the dough
Cooking time: 20 minutes
Makes: 8 manakish

· Man'oushe dough (page 202)
· 2 small yellow onions, finely chopped
· ½ cup (115 g) keshek
· 2 teaspoon crushed chili flakes
· 6 tablespoons tomato paste (purée)
· 5 tablespoons sesame seeds
· Salt
· About ½ cup (120 ml/4 fl oz) olive oil, for brushing

Prepare the *man'oushe* dough as directed through the step of dividing into portions and letting rest for 10 minutes.

Preheat the oven to 400°F (200°C/Gas Mark 6) with a baking sheet turned upside down on the middle rack.

In a small bowl, combine the onions, *keshek*, chili flakes, tomato paste (purée), sesame seeds, and salt to taste. With a rolling pin, roll out the dough into a very thin round, 10 inches (25 cm) in diameter. Brush with oil, leaving a ½-inch (1.25 cm) border around the rim. Spread the *keshek* mixture over the breads, about 4 tablespoons each.

Carefully place 2 flatbreads on the heated baking sheet and bake until browned, 8–10 minutes. Transfer to a tea towel to keep warm, and repeat with the remaining dough. Serve warm.

FRIED FLATBREAD WITH HONEY

LIBYA

Sfinz *are North African donuts in the shape of a flatbread. The spongy texture makes them ideal drizzled with honey, especially popular as a breakfast before Jummah (Friday prayer) and Ramadan. A challenging savory variation is to crack an egg in the center of the* sfinz *while frying.*

Preparation time: 15 minutes, plus 3 hours rising time
Cooking time: 15 minutes
Makes: 6 flatbreads

· 1 cup (240 ml/8 fl oz) warm water
· ¾ teaspoon active dry yeast
· 1½ teaspoons sugar
· 2 cups (240 g) pastry flour (soft flour), plus more for dusting
· 1 teaspoon fine sea salt
· 1 teaspoon baking powder
· 2 tablespoons olive oil, plus more for kneading
· Vegetable oil, for deep-frying
· Honey, for serving

In a small bowl, stir the water, yeast, and a pinch of the sugar together. Set the mixture aside until the yeast is frothy, about 10 minutes. (If the yeast doesn't froth, check the expiration date. You may have to start over with fresher yeast.)

Whisk the flour in a large bowl. Stir in the salt, the remaining sugar, and baking powder. Pour in the yeast mixture and olive oil. Stir with a wooden spoon until a wet dough forms. Knead the dough in the bowl with lightly oiled hands until it comes together in a ball, about 1 minute. Cover the bowl with plastic wrap (cling film) and let the dough rest until doubled in size, about 3 hours.

Pour 2 inches (5 cm) vegetable oil into a wide, deep, heavy-bottomed pan and heat over medium-high heat. To test if the oil is ready to fry, carefully toss in a small piece of dough. If it sizzles, the oil is ready. Divide the dough into 6 pieces, about 1/3 cup (100 g) per portion. Form each portion into an even 6-inch round by stretching with your hands. Working in batches, slide the *sfinz* into the oil. Fry one side until golden brown and puffed up, 1 minute. Using a slotted spoon, turn over and fry until golden brown, 40 seconds more. Transfer the *sfinz* to paper towels to drain.

Repeat with the remaining dough. Allow the *sfinz* to cool slightly before serving warm with a drizzling of honey.

Fried Flatbread with Honey

CHEESE-FILLED FLATBREAD WITH EGG

GEORGIA

Khachapuri *is an eye- or boat-shaped bread that holds a generous amount of melted Sulguni (mildly salty, elastic white cheese), baked and topped with a raw egg, though in this recipe the egg is baked with a runny yolk. To eat, break up the egg and stir it into the cheese, then break off pieces of bread and dip into the egg mixture.* Khachapuri *varies based on region and though it is not so much a morning meal in Georgia, this version from Acharuli has recently gained popularity on a global scale as a weekend breakfast.*

Preparation time: 30 minutes, plus 1 hour rising time
Cooking time: 25 minutes
Makes: 2 flatbreads

For the dough:
· 4 tablespoons warm water
· ½ teaspoon active dry yeast
· ¼ teaspoon sugar
· ½ teaspoon fine sea salt
· ½ cup (70 g) all-purpose (plain) flour
· 1 tablespoon olive oil or vegetable oil, plus more for greasing

For the cheese filling:
· 1 cup (100 g) shredded Sulguni or mozzarella cheese
· ¾ cup (75 g) crumbled farmer cheese or fresh white cheese
· Salt and freshly ground pepper
· 3 eggs
· 2 tablespoons (30 g) salted butter, for serving

Make the dough:
In a large bowl, combine the water, yeast, and sugar. Set the mixture aside until the yeast is frothy, about 10 minutes. (If the yeast does not froth, check the expiration date. You may have to start over with fresher yeast.) Stir in the salt. Stir in the flour with a wooden spoon and mix until a shaggy dough forms and pulls away from the sides of the bowl. Pour in the olive oil and knead in the bowl until the oil is incorporated into the dough, about 1 minute. Turn out onto a lightly floured surface and continue to knead until the dough is smooth and elsatic, about 10 minutes. Place the dough in a lightly oiled bowl, cover, and let the dough rest until doubled in size, about 1 hour.

Make the cheese filling:
Combine the cheeses in a bowl and season with salt and pepper.

Bake the flatbreads:
Preheat the oven to 450°F (230°C/Gas Mark 8). Line a baking sheet with parchment paper.
    Turn the dough out onto a lightly floured surface and divide in half.
    With a rolling pin, roll one half into a 9-inch (23 cm) round. Roll up one side of the round about one-third of the way in toward the center. Repeat with the opposite side of the round to meet in the middle. Pinch the ends together on both sides to create a boat shape. Transfer to the baking sheet and repeat with the second round.
    Divide the filling equally between the openings of the "boats." In a small bowl, whisk 1 of the eggs. Brush the sides of the *khachapuri* with the beaten egg. Bake until golden brown, about 20 minutes.
    Create a well in the center of each boat with the back of a spoon and crack 1 egg into each well. Return the *khachapuri* to the oven and bake until the egg whites are just set, about 4 minutes. Allow the *khachapuri* to cool slightly before topping each with 1 tablespoon of butter and serving warm.

ROTI PRATA /
ROTI CANI

MALAYSIA / SINGAPORE

Called a roti prata *(or just* prata*) in Singapore and* roti cani *in Malaysia, this laminated flatbread (roti) is originally from India. It is typically served in Singapore and Malaysia with a small bowl of curry for dipping, and in Singapore, it can be ordered "plastered," with an egg fried on top or cooked inside.*

Preparation time: 45 minutes, plus 2 hours rising time
Cooking time: 20 minutes
Makes: 6 roti

· 1¾ cups (255 g) all-purpose (plain) flour, plus more for dusting
· 1 teaspoon sugar
· ½ teaspoon fine sea salt
· 4 tablespoons full-fat milk
· 2 tablespoons ghee, melted, plus 3 tablespoons
· ½ tablespoon vegetable oil, plus more as needed

In a large bowl, combine the flour, sugar, and salt. Pour in the milk, 4 tablespoons water, and melted ghee. Mix with a wooden spoon until a shaggy dough forms and pulls away from the sides of the bowl. Turn the dough out onto a lightly floured work surface and knead until the dough becomes smooth, elastic, and tacky, 5 minutes. Let the dough rest, about 15 minutes.

With greased hands, separate the dough into 6 equal portions. Roll the portions into balls, tucking the dough under itself to create domed balls no bigger than a golf ball.

Grease 6 cups of a muffin tin with vegetable oil and roll the ball around to cover it with oil. Cover the pan and let the dough rest in a warm place for 2 hours.

Working with one ball of dough at a time, grease your hands and a work surface with vegetable oil. Using a rolling pin, roll the dough out into a large, thin sheet. You should be able to almost see through it. If it rips a little, that's okay. Use your hands or the back of a spoon to coat the surface with ½ tablespoon of ghee and a light dusting of flour. Scrunch up the sheet lengthwise to form many small crimps, then coil it up like a snail shell. Let it rest and repeat with the remaining dough.

Flatten the coiled dough balls with your hands or a rolling pin to create a round about 10 inches (25 cm) in diameter. The *roti* should be very thin and almost translucent.

Heat a medium frying pan over medium heat with ½ tablespoon oil. Fry the *roti* on one side until it slightly puffs up and brown marks appear, 2 minutes. Flip and fry on the other side until golden brown, 2 minutes more. Repeat with the remaining dough, adding more oil as needed. Serve warm.

COCONUT ROTI

SRI LANKA

Called a pol roti *in Sinhalese and a* thengai rotti *in Tamil, this uniquely Sri Lankan* roti *is made with fresh coconut and is served for breakfast with a generous dollop of a dried fish condiment called* lunu miris, *fish curry, butter and shaved jaggery, or a sprinkle of sugar.*

Preparation time: 15 minutes, plus 30 minutes resting time
Cooking time: 10 minutes
Makes: 4 roti

· 1 cup (145 g) all-purpose (plain) flour, plus more as needed
· ½ cup (40 g) grated fresh coconut (see Note)
· ½ teaspoon fine sea salt
· 2 teaspoons coconut oil, plus more for greasing
· ¼ small onion, chopped
· 2 small green chilies, seeded and minced
· Lunu Miris (recipe follows), for serving

In a medium bowl, combine the flour, coconut, and salt. Rub the coconut oil into the mixture. Pour in 4 tablespoons of water and stir. Add 1 more tablespoon, 1 teaspoon at a time, to make a shaggy dough. Turn the dough out onto a lightly floured work surface and knead till a smooth dough forms, 5 minutes. If the dough is too dry, add more water, 1 teaspoon at a time. If it's too wet and sticky, add flour 1 tablespoon at a time. Knead in the onion and chilies, cover the dough with plastic wrap (cling film), and set aside to rest for 30 minutes.

Divide the dough into 4 equal portions and roll into balls. Grease each ball with a touch of coconut oil. With a rolling pin or using your hands, roll or stretch out each *roti* to a 5-inch (12.5 cm) round. The *roti* should be thin but have no rips.

Heat a cast-iron skillet over medium-high heat. Cook 1–2 *roti* at a time until browned on both sides, 2–3 minutes per side. Transfer to a tea towel to keep warm. Repeat with the remaining *roti*. Serve with *lunu miris*.

Note: Instead of freshly grated coconut you could use about 6 tablespoons (35 g) unsweetened shredded coconut (desiccated), soaked for 20 minutes in ½ cup (120 ml) coconut milk. Drain, keeping the coconut milk for another recipe, and use the coconut as fresh.

LUNU MIRIS

A condiment made with Maldive fish (a dried and cured fish, typically tuna), this staple ingredient in Sri Lankan cooking provides an umami flavor, much like Japanese katsuobushi *or dried anchovies in Southeast Asia. Either* katsuobushi *or dried anchovies can be substituted.*

Preparation time: 5 minutes
Makes: 1 cup (240 ml/8 fl oz)

· 5 dried red chilies, seeded and roughly chopped
· 1 tablespoon Maldive fish
· ¾ small onion, finely chopped
· 1 teaspoon lemon juice, or more as needed
· Salt

In a blender or with a mortar and pestle, pulse or pound the red chilies into small flakes. Add the Maldive fish and pulse or pound until combined. In a small bowl, stir together the chili flake/fish mixture, the onion, lemon juice, and salt to taste. Add more lemon juice if needed until the mixture holds together and the Maldive fish softens a little.

VEGETABLE ROTI

INDIA

Akki roti *is a rice-based flatbread from the state of Karnataka in southern India, with chopped vegetables and spices mixed into the dough.*

Preparation time: 20 minutes
Cooking time: 20 minutes
Makes: 4 *roti*

· 1 cup (160 g) rice flour
· ½ small onion, diced
· ½ carrot, grated
· ½ small green chili, chopped
· 2 tablespoons finely chopped cilantro (coriander) leaves
· ¼ teaspoon ground cumin
· 1 teaspoon fine sea salt
· Vegetable oil, as needed

In a medium bowl, combine the flour, onion, carrot, chili, cilantro (coriander), cumin, and salt, and mix until thoroughly incorporated. Add ½ cup (120 ml/4 fl oz) water, 1 tablespoon at a time, kneading as you go to hydrate the flour. Continue kneading in the bowl and adding water until the dough begins to hold together. Knead until a smooth dough forms, about 2 minutes.

Divide the dough into 4 equal portions. Oil a work surface and pat each portion of dough into a round about 6 inches (15 cm) in diameter, ⅛ inch (3 mm) thick. In a cast-iron skillet, heat 1 teaspoon oil over medium heat. Scrape an *akki roti* up from the work surface with a spatula and transfer to the pan. Cook the *roti* on both sides until browned, about 2 minutes per side. Transfer to a plate and repeat with the remaining dough, adding oil as needed. Serve warm.

SAVORY SPICED FLATBREAD WITH YOGURT

INDIA

Masala koki *are savory flatbreads eaten in northern India. They are mixed with aromatic spices, onions, and chilies, and served with yogurt.*

Preparation time: 20 minutes
Cooking time: 1 hour
Makes: 4 flatbreads

· 1 cup (120 g) whole wheat (wholemeal) flour, plus more for dusting
· 1 teaspoon fine sea salt
· 1 small onion, diced
· 1 small hot green chili, finely chopped
· ½ teaspoon ground cumin
· ½ teaspoon anardana (dried pomegranate seeds), ground or whole
· ½ teaspoon freshly ground black pepper
· 1 tablespoon white sesame seeds, toasted
· 5 tablespoons cilantro (coriander) leaves, finely chopped
· 1 tablespoon dried fenugreek leaves (optional)
· 3 tablespoons melted ghee, oil, or butter, plus more for pan-frying
· Yogurt, for serving

In a medium bowl, combine the flours, salt, onion, green chili, cumin, anardana, black pepper, cilantro (coriander), fenugreek leaves (if using), and ghee, butter, or oil. Knead until you get a crumbly dough, then gradually add 3–4 tablespoons water and stir until a firm dough comes together. Knead in the bowl until it comes together in a firm ball. Divide the dough into 4 equal portions, dust with flour, and roll into balls.

Heat a cast-iron skillet over medium heat. Flatten each ball slightly and shape it into a round about 6 inches (15 cm) in diameter and 1/8 inch (6 mm) thick. Place in the hot pan and cook on both sides until lightly browned, about 8 minutes. Make small slits into the *koki* throughout the cooking process to vent heat from the pan and help the *koki* cook all the way through. Brush both sides with ghee or oil and continue to cook until browned, about 5 minutes. Repeat with the remaining *koki*.

Transfer to a plate. Serve with yogurt.

Savory Spiced Flatbread with Yogurt

KAISER ROLL

UNITED STATES

This classic New York City breakfast roll is great on its own, spread only with butter, and is the bread of choice for a Bacon, Egg, and Cheese Sandwich (page 172), ordered from a bodega (corner store) or street cart. A special stamp used to score its top and a dusting of cornmeal make this roll distinctive.

Preparation time: 30 minutes, plus 1 hour 45 minutes rising time
Cooking time: 15 minutes
Makes: 4 rolls

- ½ cup (120 ml/4 fl oz) warm water
- 1 teaspoon active dry yeast
- A pinch, plus 2 teaspoons sugar
- 1 egg
- 1 tablespoon (15 g) unsalted butter, at room temperature
- 1¾ cups (260 g) bread flour (strong white flour)
- ½ teaspoon fine sea salt
- Cornmeal, for dusting

In a large bowl, combine the warm water, yeast, and pinch of sugar. Set the mixture aside until the yeast is frothy, about 10 minutes. (If the yeast doesn't froth, check the expiration date. You may have to start over with fresher yeast.)

Stir in the remaining 2 teaspoons sugar, egg, and butter until thoroughly combined. With a wooden spoon, stir in 1 cup (150 g) of the flour and the salt. Stir in the remaining flour until a shaggy dough forms and pulls away from the sides of the bowl. Turn out onto a lightly floured work surface and knead until it's smooth and elastic, 10 minutes. Place in a lightly oiled bowl, cover with plastic wrap (cling film), and let it rest until doubled in size, about 1 hour.

Turn the dough out onto the lightly floured surface and punch down. Divide the dough into 4 equal portions. Line a baking sheet with parchment paper and dust with cornmeal. Roll the portions into balls and flatten slightly into rounds. Press down gently with a kaiser-roll stamp or use a paring knife to create a pinwheel pattern with five arms. Place the rolls stamp-cut-side down and 2 inches (5 cm) apart on the baking sheet. Cover with plastic wrap (cling film) or a tea towel and let the rolls rest until they puff up, about 45 minutes.

Preheat the oven to 425°F (220°C/Gas Mark 7).

Flip the rolls back to stamp-side up. Bake until golden brown, 10–15 minutes. Allow the kaiser rolls to cool slightly before serving.

SCOTTISH MORNING ROLLS

UNITED KINGDOM

These soft bread rolls are enjoyed at all times of day but are particularly popular for breakfast sandwiches. While a typical Scottish Fry Up (page 28) would be enjoyed on a weekend, a morning roll filled with varying elements of a classic Scottish breakfast makes for the perfect on-the-go weekday breakfast.

Preparation time: 25 minutes, plus 1 hour 30 minutes rising time
Cooking time: 20 minutes
· Makes: 8 rolls

· ⅔ cup (150 ml/5 fl oz) full-fat milk, plus more for brushing
· ⅔ cup (150 ml/5 fl oz) warm water
· 2¼ teaspoons active dry yeast
· ½ teaspoon sugar
· 3 cups (450 g) bread flour (strong white flour), plus more for sprinkling
· 1 teaspoon fine sea salt
· Vegetable oil, for greasing

In a small bowl, combine the milk, water, yeast, and sugar. Set the mixture aside until the yeast is frothy, about 10 minutes. (If the yeast does not froth, check the expiration date. You may have to start over with fresher yeast.)

In a large bowl, combine the bread flour and salt. Create a well in the center of the flour and pour in the yeast mixture. Mix the dough with a wooden spoon until smooth. Knead in the bowl until it comes together, about 3 minutes, taking care not to overwork the dough. Place the dough in an oiled bowl and cover with a tea towel. Let the dough rise until doubled in size, 1–1½ hours.

Scoop the dough out onto a lightly floured surface and gently push down. Divide into 8 equal portions. Knead each portion for 1 minute, then shape into rolls. Lightly grease a baking sheet and place each ball on the sheet, placing 2 inches (5 cm) apart. Cover with a tea towel and allow the rolls to rise for 30 minutes more.

Preheat the oven to 400°F (200°C/Gas Mark 6).

Brush each roll with a bit of milk, covering all sides, and sprinkle with flour. Bake until golden brown, 16–20 minutes. Allow to cool on the pan before serving warm.

BRIOCHE
FRANCE

In France, warm brioche is accompanied by butter and jam and often a Café au Lait (page 415). In France, brioche comes in the form of rolls or a loaf.

Preparation time: 30 minutes, plus 2 hours rising time and overnight chilling time
Cooking time: 45 minutes
Makes: 1 loaf

· 3 tablespoons full-fat milk, slightly warmed
· 2 teaspoons active dry yeast
· 3 eggs
· 2 tablespoons sugar
· 1½ cups (215 g) plus 2 tablespoons all-purpose (plain) flour
· 1½ teaspoons fine sea salt
· 7 tablespoons (100 g) unsalted butter, cut into 1-inch (2.5 cm) pieces, at room temperature
· Vegetable oil, for greasing

In a small bowl, combine the milk, yeast, honey, and a pinch of sugar. Set the mixture aside until the yeast is frothy, about 10 minutes. (If the yeast doesn't froth, check the expiration date. You may have to start over with fresher yeast.)

Crack 2 of the eggs into the bowl of a stand mixer fitted with the paddle attachment. Beat on low speed until the eggs are frothy, 2 minutes. Add the remaining sugar and mix until dissolved, about 1 minute. Pour in the yeast mixture and continue to beat on low speed until combined, 20 seconds. Add the flour and salt and mix until the mixture comes together as a dough. Increase to medium and mix until the dough clings in one smooth mass, 4 minutes. Reduce the speed to low and add the butter, 1 tablespoon (15 g) at a time, beating on medium-low speed until fully incorporated before adding the next tablespoon. Transfer the dough to a lightly greased bowl and cover lightly with plastic wrap (cling film). Let the dough rest until doubled in size, about 2 hours. Turn the dough out onto an oiled plate or small baking sheet, press down into an even layer, and refrigerate, covered, at least 6 hours or overnight to firm it up.

Grease a 9 x 5 x 2½-inch (23 x 13 x 6.5 cm) loaf pan. The next morning, punch down the dough, transfer to a lightly floured work surface, and roll it into 8 x 12 inch (20 x 30 cm). Roll it from the down loosely from the 8 inch (20 cm) side. Seal the seam by gently pressing on it and place the dough seam-side down in the prepared loaf pan. Cover with plastic wrap and let the brioche rest until doubled in size, about 2 hours.

Preheat the oven to 400°F (200°C/Gas Mark 6).

In a small bowl, whisk the remaining egg. Brush the beaten egg over the surface of the brioche. Transfer to the oven and bake for 15 minutes, then reduce the heat to 350°F (180°C/Gas Mark 4) and continue baking until evenly golden brown, 25 minutes more. Cool in the pan for 10 minutes, then invert the brioche onto a cooling rack and allow it to cool before slicing and serving.

Brioche

PANDESAL

PHILIPPINES

These are small bread rolls that can be filled with a sunny-side up egg, Coconut Jam (page 150), peanut butter, kesong puti (cow's milk cheese), or Karne Norte (canned corned beef). Often accompanied by hot coffee or hot chocolate (Tablea, page 438).

Preparation time: 30 minutes, plus 2 hours rising time
Cooking time: 25 minutes
Makes: 6 large rolls

· ½ cup (120 ml/4 fl oz) plus 1 tablespoon full-fat milk, warmed
· 1½ teaspoons active dry yeast
· 2 tablespoons (30 g) unsalted butter, at room temperature
· 1 egg
· 4 tablespoons sugar
· ¼ teaspoon fine sea salt
· 1 cup (145 g) all-purpose (plain) flour, plus more for dusting
· ¾ cup (115 g) bread flour (strong white flour), plus more for dusting
· Vegetable oil, for greasing
· Breadcrumbs, for coating

In a small bowl, combine the warm milk and yeast. Set the mixture aside until the yeast is frothy, about 10 minutes. (If the yeast does not froth, check the expiration date. You may have to start over with fresher yeast.)

In a large bowl, combine the butter, egg, sugar, and salt until thoroughly incorporated. Stir in the all-purpose (plain) flour. Pour in the yeast mixture and stir in the bread flour (strong white flour). Stir until a wet, shaggy dough is formed and begins to pull away from the sides of the bowl. Turn out onto a lightly floured work surface and knead the dough until it is smooth and elastic, about 10 minutes. If the dough remains stubbornly sticky, dust the dough with bread flour. Place the dough in a lightly greased bowl, cover with plastic wrap (cling film), and let it rest until doubled in size, about 1 hour.

Line a baking sheet with parchment paper. Turn the dough out onto a lightly floured work surface. Divide into 6 equal portions. Roll each into a smooth ball and roll in breadcrumbs until coated. Place the *pandesal* on the baking sheet. Cover with a tea towel or plastic wrap and let them rest until they puff up, 45 minutes to 1 hour.

Meanwhile, preheat the oven to 350°F (180°C/Gas Mark 4).

Bake the *pandesal* until lightly golden, 20–25 minutes. Allow the rolls to cool on the pan before serving warm.

Pandesal

Preparation time: 25 minutes, plus 2 hours 15 minutes rising time
Cooking time: 20 minutes
Makes: 6 rolls

SEMMELN

AUSTRIA

An integral part of the Austrian breakfast table, semmeln, *along with other assorted breads and rolls, are enjoyed topped with a combination of butter, fresh cheese, jam, ham, or a Soft-Boiled Egg (page 14).*

· ½ cup (120 ml/4 fl oz) plus 2 tablespoons warm water
· 1½ teaspoons active dry yeast
· ½ teaspoon sugar
· 1¾ cups (255 g) all-purpose (plain) flour
· 1 teaspoon fine sea salt
· ½ tablespoon (7 g) unsalted butter, at room temperature
· 1 egg

In a small bowl, combine the water, yeast, and sugar. Set the mixture aside until the yeast is frothy, about 10 minutes. (If the yeast doesn't froth, check the expiration date. You may have to start over with fresher yeast.)

In a large bowl, combine the flour, salt, and butter. With a wooden spoon, stir in the yeast mixture. Stir until it forms a shaggy dough and starts to pull away from the sides of the bowl. Turn out onto a lightly floured work surface and knead until smooth and elastic, about 5 minutes. Place the dough in a lightly greased bowl, cover with plastic wrap (cling fillm) and let it rise until doubled, about 1½ hours.

Turn the dough out onto a lightly floured surface and punch down. Divide into 6 equal portions. Line a baking sheet with parchment paper. Roll the portions into rolls and place them on the lined baking sheet. Cover with plastic wrap or a tea towel and let them rest until puffed up, about 45 minutes.

Meanwhile, preheat the oven to 425°F (220°C/Gas Mark 7).

In a small bowl, whisk the egg. Brush the rolls with the beaten egg and score each *semmeln* with a sharp knife or bread scorer down the middle. Bake the *semmeln* for 15–20 minutes, until the rolls are golden brown. Allow the *semmeln* to cool on the pan before serving warm.

CURRANT BUNS

THE NETHERLANDS

A currant- or raisin-studded bun enjoyed with ham and Gouda cheese.

Preparation time: 25 minutes, plus 2 hours rising time
Cooking time: 20 minutes
Makes: 6 buns

· ½ cup (120 ml/4 fl oz) full-fat milk
· 1½ teaspoons active dry yeast
· 1¾ cups (255 g) plus 2 tablespoons all-purpose (plain) flour
· 3 tablespoons sugar
· ¼ teaspoon fine sea salt
· 2½ tablespoons (35 g) unsalted butter, at room temperature
· 1 egg
· ½ teaspoon ground cinnamon
· ½ cup (80 g) dried currants
· 1 tablespoon vegetable oil, for greasing

In a small bowl, combine the milk and yeast. Set the mixture aside until the yeast is frothy, about 10 minutes. (If the yeast does not froth, check the expiration date. You may have to start over with fresher yeast.)

In a large bowl, combine the flour, sugar, salt, and cinnamon. In a separate bowl, beat the butter and egg until combined. Pour the egg mixture into the flour, then slowly add the yeast mixture and stir with a wooden spoon until a wet, shaggy dough forms and starts to pull away from the sides of the bowl.

Turn the dough out onto a lightly floured work surface and knead until smooth, about 3 minutes. Knead in the currants. Place the dough in a lightly oiled bowl, cover with plastic wrap (cling film), and let it rest until doubled in size, 1–2 hours.

Line a baking sheet with parchment paper. Punch the dough down to deflate the bubbles and divide into 6 equal portions. Roll each portion into a smooth ball and place on the baking sheet. Cover the baking sheet with a tea towel or plastic wrap and let the dough rest until puffed, about 1 hour.

Meanwhile, preheat the oven to 400°F (200°C/Gas Mark 6).

Bake the currant buns until golden brown, rotating the sheet front to back halfway through baking, 15–20 minutes. Allow the currant buns to cool slightly on the pan before serving warm.

CINNAMON ROLLS
UNITED STATES

These enriched rolls got their start in Europe, after cinnamon brought over from Sri Lanka was introduced across the continent, inspiring varying versions of cinnamon-laced pastries. The Kanelbullar *from Sweden is most similar to the American cinnamon roll, minus the thick glaze. The Chelsea bun from England and the* Franzbrötchen *from Germany were brought to Philadelphia in the mid-1800s. These versions of the pastry were dubbed "sticky buns" or "honey buns." These now-iconic pastries doused in glaze are commonplace across the United States.*

Preparation time: 30 minutes, plus 3½ hours rising and chilling time
Cooking time: 30 minutes
Makes: 6 buns

For the dough:
· ½ cup (120 ml/4 fl oz) full-fat milk, warmed
· 1 teaspoon active dry yeast
· 2 tablespoons honey
· 2 cups (280 g) all-purpose (plain) flour
· ½ teaspoon fine sea salt
· 1 egg, beaten
· 3 tablespoons (45 g) unsalted butter, melted
· ½ teaspoon vanilla extract

For the filling:
· ¾ cup (145 g) light brown sugar
· 1 tablespoon granulated sugar
· 1 tablespoon ground cinnamon
· ½ teaspoon fine sea salt

For the rolls:
· 2 tablespoons (30 g) unsalted butter, melted
· Vegetable oil or butter, for the baking dish

For the icing:
· 1 cup (120 g) powdered (icing) sugar
· 3 tablespoons full-fat milk
· 1 teaspoon lemon juice

Make the dough:
In a small bowl, combine the warm milk, yeast, and honey. Set the mixture aside until the yeast is frothy, about 10 minutes.

In a large bowl, stir the flour and salt together. Pour in the yeast mixture and stir with a wooden spoon until the flour begins to hydrate. Beat the egg, then add to the dough along with the melted butter and vanilla and stir until a wet, shaggy dough forms. Knead on a lightly floured work surface until the dough turns into a smooth, elastic ball, 2–4 minutes. Place the dough in a lightly oiled bowl, cover with plastic wrap (cling film), and let it rest until doubled in size, about 2 hours.

Turn the dough out onto a lightly floured work surface and punch down. Cover in plastic wrap and chill in the refrigerator for at least 30 minutes and up to 1 hour so it becomes firmer and easier to work with.

To make the filling, stir together the brown sugar, granulated sugar, cinnamon, salt, and melted butter in a small bowl.

Make the rolls:
With a rolling pin, roll out the dough into a long rectangle 10 x 15 inches (25 x 38 cm), ¼ inch (6 mm) thick. Spread the melted butter over the dough, then sprinkle the filling. Starting with the long side of the dough closer to you, roll the dough away from you into a tight log. Slice crosswise into 6 equal pieces. Grease an 11 x 7-inch (18 x 28 cm) baking dish and arrange the rolls in the dish, cut-side down. Cover with plastic wrap and let the rolls rest until they puff up, about 1 hour.

Preheat the oven to 350°F (180°C/Gas Mark 4).

Bake the rolls until golden brown, rotating the sheet from front to back halfway through, about 30 minutes.

To make the icing, whisk together the powdered (icing) sugar, milk, and lemon juice in a small bowl until no lumps remain.

Allow the cinnamon rolls to cool slightly in the pan. Drizzle the icing on top. Serve warm.

PECAN
STICKY BUNS
UNITED STATES

Sticky buns use the same dough and technique as Cinnamon Rolls (page 220), with the addition of chopped nuts and a glaze baked in the pan with rolls resulting in a more "sticky" lacquered top. Originating in Germany, their versions of sticky buns are called Schnecken, *meaning "snails," or* Franzbrötchen *in Hamburg, most similar to the cinnamon roll.*

Preparation time: 30 minutes, plus 1 hour rising time and rising and chilling time for the Cinnamon Roll Dough
Cooking time: 35 minutes
Makes: 6 buns

· Dough from Cinnamon Rolls (page 220)

For the glaze:
· 6 tablespoons (85 g) unsalted butter, at room temperature
· ⅔ cup (130 g) dark brown sugar
· ½ cup (55 g) chopped pecans

For the filling:
· ½ cup (95 g) light brown sugar
· 1 ½ tablespoons ground cinnamon
· ½ cup (55 g) chopped pecans

For the buns:
· 3 tablespoons (45 g) unsalted butter, melted

Prepare the cinnamon bun dough through the first rise and 1-hour chilling time.

Meanwhile, make the glaze: In a small saucepan, melt the butter. Add the dark brown sugar and stir until dissolved and the sauce is gooey. Remove from the heat and stir in the pecans. Let cool.

To make the filling, stir together the light brown sugar, cinnamon, and pecans in a small bowl.

Make the buns:
Scrape the glaze into an 11 x 7-inch (28 x 18 cm) baking dish or 10-inch (25 cm) cast-iron skillet. With a rolling pin, roll out the dough into a long rectangle 10 x 15 inches (25 x 38 cm) and ¼ inch (6 mm) thick. Spread the melted butter over the dough, leaving a 1-inch (2.5 cm) border around the edges. Sprinkle the filling over the butter. Starting with the long side of the dough closer to you, roll the dough away from you into a tight log. Slice crosswise into 6 equal pieces. Place the buns cut-side down over the glaze in the baking dish. Cover with plastic wrap (cling film) and let the buns rest until they puff up, about 1 hour.

Preheat the oven to 350°F (180°C/Gas Mark 4).

Bake the buns until golden brown, rotating the sheet from front to back halfway through, about 30 minutes.

Allow the cinnamon rolls to cool slightly in the pan. Serve warm, glaze-side up.

CARDAMOM BUNS
SWEDEN

Kardemummabullar *in Sweden are similar to the American Cinnamon Roll (page 220) but are infused with ground cardamom and bare a lighter top glaze. These can be enjoyed in the morning or during Swedish* fika *(coffee break).*

Preparation time: 40 minutes, plus 2½ hours rising time
Cooking time: 30 minutes
Makes: 6 buns

For the dough:
· ½ cup (120 ml/4 fl oz) full-fat milk, warmed
· 1 teaspoon active dry yeast
· 2 tablespoons honey
· 2 cups (280 g) all-purpose (plain) flour
· ½ teaspoon ground cardamom
· ½ teaspoon fine sea salt
· 1 egg, beaten
· 2 tablespoons (28 g) unsalted butter, melted

For the filling:
· 4 tablespoons dark brown sugar
· 1 teaspoon ground cardamom
· 3 tablespoons (45 g) unsalted butter, at room temperature

For the glaze:
· 2 tablespoons light brown sugar
· ¼ teaspoon vanilla extract
· ½ teaspoon granulated sugar
· ¼ teaspoon ground cardamom

In a small bowl, combine the milk, yeast, and honey. Set aside until the yeast is frothy, about 10 minutes. In a large bowl, stir together the flour, ground cardamom, and salt. Add the yeast mixture and stir with a wooden spoon until the flour begins to hydrate. Beat the egg and add to the dough, along with the melted butter. Stir until a wet, shaggy dough forms. Turn the dough out onto a lightly floured work surface. Knead until the dough turns into a smooth, elastic ball, 4 minutes. It can be a bit sticky but shouldn't cling to your fingers. Place the dough in a lightly oiled bowl, cover with plastic wrap (cling film), and let it rest until doubled in size, about 2 hours.

To make the filling, combine the dark brown sugar, ground cardamom, and butter in a small bowl.

Preheat the oven to 350°F (180°C/Gas Mark 4).

Turn the dough out onto a lightly floured work surface and punch down. Roll the dough out into a rectangle, 6 x 14-inch (15 x 35 cm) and ¼ inch (6 mm) thick. Spread the filling mixture over the dough. With a short side facing you, fold the bottom one-third of the dough up, then fold the top one-third down over that. Cover and let rest for 10 minutes, then dust lightly with flour. With a rolling pin, gently roll out into a 6-inch (15 inch) square, ½ inch (1.25 cm) thick.

Cut 6 strands lengthwise 1 inch (2.5 cm) wide. Twist each strand by holding one end and gently stretching and twisting down to the other end. Coil the twisted strand to form a round bun shape, tucking the ends underneath. Place on a baking sheet lined with parchment paper and cover with plastic wrap (cling film). Let the buns rest until they puff up, about 40 minutes.

Bake until golden brown, rotating the sheet 180 degrees halfway through, 25–30 minutes.

Meanwhile make the glaze. In a small saucepan, combine 2 tablespoons water, brown sugar, and vanilla and bring the mixture to a boil over medium-high heat. Stir, then reduce the heat to low. Simmer until the sugar is dissolved and the mixture is clear, about 1 minute. Remove from the heat. Brush the buns immediately with the simple syrup and sprinkle with the sugar and ground cardamom.

Allow the buns to cool on the baking sheet before serving warm.

Cardamom Buns (left) and Danish (right, see page 368)

POPPY BUNS

CZECH REPUBLIC

Buchty are sweet, yeasted buns typically filled with plum spread (powidl), poppy seed spread, or a cottage cheese and raisin mix. These buns are intentionally baked close together so that they stick together. Choose from one of the three fillings; this recipe includes instructions to make the poppy-seed filling.

Preparation time: about 1 hour, plus rising and proofing
Cooking time: 20 minutes
Makes: 8 buns

For the dough:
· 4 tablespoons full-fat milk, warmed
· 1 teaspoon active dry or fresh yeast
· 2 tablespoons sugar
· 1¼ cups (180 g) all-purpose (plain) flour, plus extra for dusting
· ¼ teaspoon fine sea salt
· 1½ tablespoons (20 g) unsalted butter, melted and cooled
· 1 egg yolk
· Finely grated zest of 1 lemon
· ¼ teaspoon vanilla extract

For the poppy-seed filling:
· 6 tablespoons whole milk
· ¼ cup (35 g) ground or whole poppy seeds
· 2 tablespoons finely crushed butter cookies, such as shortbread
· 1 tablespoon dark rum
· ½ teaspoon vanilla extract
· ⅛ teaspoon ground cinnamon
· 4 tablespoons granulated sugar
· Pinch of grated lemon zest
· ½ cup (30 g) walnut halves (about 12 halves), finely chopped

For the buns:
· Vegetable oil, for greasing
· 2 tablespoons dark rum
· Powdered (icing) sugar

In a small bowl, combine the milk, yeast, and a pinch of the sugar. Set the mixture aside until the yeast is frothy, about 10 minutes.

Whisk the flour, sugar, and salt in a large bowl. Add the melted butter, egg yolk, lemon zest, and vanilla. With a wooden spoon, add the yeast mixture and stir until a shaggy dough forms. Knead the dough on a floured work surface until it is smooth and elastic, 5-8 minutes. Place it in a lightly greased bowl, cover with plastic wrap (cling film), and let it rest in a warm place until doubled in size, about 1 hour.

Meanwhile, make the poppy seed filling. If using whole poppy seeds, grind in small batches with mortar and pestle until they have changed from blueish to brown/purple and feel like wet sand. Heat the milk in a saucepan over medium heat until it steams. Add the ground poppy seeds and cook, stirring, until the milk has been absorbed, 1 minute. Stir in the crushed cookies, rum, vanilla, cinnamon, sugar, and lemon zest and leave to cool.

Preheat the oven to 350°F (180°C/Gas Mark 4). Lightly grease a small baking dish, or 11 x 7-inch (28 x 18 cm) loaf pan.

Turn the dough out onto a work surface and punch down. Do not knead. Pat it out to a rectangle, 4 x 8 inches (10 x 20 cm) and ½ inch (1.25 cm) thick. Slice the dough into eight squares. Press each out to 4 x 3 inches (10 x 8 cm). Dollop 1 tablespoon of filling into the center and top with 1 heaping teaspoon walnuts. Bring the sides up and over the filling and pinch to enclose the filling entirely. Roll gently to close the seams. Place the *buchty* seam-side down and side by side, touching, in the loaf pan. Cover with a tea towel and let prove in a warm place until puffed, about 15 minutes.

Bake until golden brown, about 20 minutes. Brush the tops with rum. Allow to cool slightly before sprinkling with powdered (icing) sugar. Serve warm.

Poppy Buns

Preparation time: 30 minutes, plus 2 ½ hours rising time
Cooking time: 35 minutes
Makes: 6 rolls

SWEET KOLACHE
CZECH REPUBLIC / UNITED STATES

Though kolaches are not always considered breakfast in the Czech Republic, Texas has adopted them into their morning culture. Sweet kolaches are sweet round buns, often open-faced, with fruit purees and cheese filling. The savory version (opposite) is more oblong in shape, with fillings enclosed such as sausage and cheese. Texas developed an affinity for kolache in the mid-1800s due to the Czech diaspora living in South and Central Texas, also known as "the Czech belt."

For the dough:
· ½ cup (120 ml/4 fl oz) full-fat milk, warmed
· 1 teaspoon active dry yeast
· 1¾ cups (255 g) all-purpose (plain) flour
· 1 tablespoon sugar
· ¼ teaspoon fine sea salt
· ½ teaspoon grated lemon zest
· 2 eggs
· 3 tablespoons (45 g) unsalted butter, melted
· Vegetable oil, for greasing

For the filling:
· ½ cup (75 g) blueberries
· 2 teaspoons lemon juice
· 1 tablespoon sugar
· ¼ teaspoon tapioca flour
· ¼ teaspoon ground ginger

Make the dough:
In a small bowl, combine the milk and yeast. Set the mixture aside until the yeast is frothy, about 10 minutes. (If the yeast doesn't froth, check the expiration date. You may have to start over with fresher yeast.)

In a large bowl, combine the flour, sugar, salt, and lemon zest. Stir in 1 of the eggs and the yeast mixture. Add the melted butter. Stir together until a shaggy dough forms and begins to pull away from the sides of the bowl.

Turn the dough out onto a lightly floured work surface and knead until the dough is smooth and elastic, about 5 minutes. It's okay if it's still a little sticky. Place the dough in a lightly oiled bowl, cover with plastic wrap (cling film), and let it rest in a warm place until it doubles in size, about 2 hours.

Preheat the oven to 350°F (180°C/Gas Mark 4). Line a baking sheet with parchment paper.

Turn the dough out onto a lightly floured work surface and punch it down. Divide the dough into 6 equal portions. With lightly greased hands, roll each portion into a ball and flatten slightly. Place on the baking sheet. Cover with plastic wrap or a tea towel and let the dough rest until puffed up, about 30 minutes.

Meanwhile, make the filling:
In a small saucepan, combine the blueberries, lemon juice, sugar, tapioca flour, and ginger and stir over medium-high heat until the blueberries are coated in the sugar. Cook until the blueberries begin to break down and form a thickened sauce, stirring occasionally, 8–10 minutes. Scrape the filling into a bowl and let it cool.

Press an indentation in the middle of each roll. Add a dollop of the blueberry filling. Whisk the remaining egg and brush it over the dough around the filling.

Bake until golden brown, about 25 minutes. Allow the *kolache* to cool slightly before serving warm.

Preparation time: 30 minutes, plus 2½ hours rising time
Cooking time: 35 minutes
Makes: 8 rolls

SAVORY KOLACHE
CZECH REPUBLIC / UNITED STATES

In the savory kolache, the filling is sealed inside the roll, while the sweet versions (opposite) have an exposed filling on top. Sausage and cheese are the filling of choice in South and Central Texas where these oblong-stuffed buns thrive as a morning meal.

For the dough:
· ½ cup (120 ml/4 fl oz) full-fat milk, warmed
· 1 teaspoon active dry yeast
· 2 eggs
· 3 tablespoons (45 g) unsalted butter, melted
· 1¾ cups (255 g) all-purpose (plain) flour
· ¼ teaspoon fine sea salt
· 1 tablespoon sugar
· Vegetable oil, for greasing

For the filling:
· 3 breakfast sausage links
· ½ cup (55 g) grated cheddar cheese

Make the dough:
In a small bowl, combine the milk and yeast. Set the mixture aside until the yeast is frothy, about 10 minutes. (If the yeast does not froth, check the expiration date. You may have to start over with fresher yeast.)

Stir 1 of the eggs and the melted butter into the yeast mixture. In a large bowl, combine the flour, salt, and sugar. Add the egg/milk mixture to the flour mixture and stir together until a shaggy dough forms and begins to pull away from the sides of the bowl.

Turn the dough out onto a lightly floured work surface and knead until the dough is smooth and elastic, about 5 minutes. It's okay if it's still a little sticky. Place the dough in a lightly oiled bowl, cover with plastic wrap (cling film), and let it rest until it doubles in size, about 2 hours.

Meanwhile, make the filling:
In a frying pan, cook the sausages over medium-high heat until golden brown on all sides, 8–10 minutes. Transfer to paper towels to drain.

Preheat the oven to 350°F (180°C/Gas Mark 4). Line a baking sheet with parchment paper.

Turn the dough onto a lightly floured work surface and punch it down. Divide the dough into 6 equal portions. With lightly greased hands, roll each portion into a ball and flatten slightly. Press an indentation in the middle of each piece of dough. Slice each sausage in half lengthwise. Press the sausage into the indentation and sprinkle with cheese. Tuck one side of the dough over the other to enclose the filling completely. Place on the lined baking sheet. Cover with plastic wrap or a tea towel and let the dough rest until puffed up, about 30 minutes.

Whisk the remaining egg and brush it over the rolls. Bake until golden brown, about 25 minutes. Allow the *kolache* to cool slightly before serving warm.

SESAME FLATBREAD

TAIWAN

A shaobing *is a round wheat bun covered in sesame seeds. The* bing *(flatbread) can be left plain or, when rectangular in shape, split in half and stuffed with an omelet, a* youtiao *(Chinese Cruller, page 307), or a variety of other fillings. It is often served with a glass of soy milk.*

Preparation time: 30 minutes, 1 hour 15 minutes rising and resting time
Cooking time: 20 minutes
Makes: 6 flatbreads

· ½ cup (120 ml/4 fl oz) plus 2 tablespoons warm water
· ¾ teaspoons active dry yeast
· ½ tablespoon sugar
· ½ cup (70 g) all-purpose (plain) flour
· ¼ teaspoon fine sea salt
· ½ teaspoon vegetable oil
· 4 tablespoons sesame seeds, toasted

In a small bowl, combine the water, yeast, and sugar. Set the mixture aside until the yeast is frothy, about 10 minutes. (If the yeast does not froth, check the expiration date. You may have to start over with fresher yeast.)

In a medium bowl, whisk together the flour and salt. Pour the yeast mixture into the flour followed by the oil, and mix with a wooden spoon until a firm dough comes together in a ball, about 3 minutes. Cover the bowl with a tea towel and allow the dough to rise until doubled in size, about 1 hour.

Preheat the oven to 350°F (Gas Mark 4). Line a baking sheet with parchment paper.

Turn the dough out onto a lightly floured work surface. With a rolling pin, roll the dough out into a rectangle, 10 x 12 inches (25 x 30.5 cm) and ¼ inch (6 mm) thick. Starting from a long side, roll up the dough into a tight log, pinching seam to seal. Cut crosswise into portions 2 inches (5 cm) wide. Roll each portion into a ball, gently push flat, and roll into a round 3 inches (7.5 cm) wide and ¼ inch (6 mm) thick. Let the dough rest for 15 minutes.

Brush the top of the dough with water and sprinkle with the sesame seeds. Place the buns seed-side down on the lined baking sheet and bake for 15 minutes. Flip the buns and bake for another 5 minutes, until both sides are browned.

Sesame Flatbread

PINEAPPLE BUNS

CHINA

The pineapple bun (bo lo bao) is a light-as-air sweet bread roll baked with a coating of crackled sugar and dry milk powder. Despite the name, this Chinese bakery staple does not contain pineapple but refers to the crackled top of the bun resembling the rigidity of a pineapple top. The technique is similar for making a Mexican concha (Sweet Roll with Crunchy Topping, page 232).

Preparation time: 40 minutes, plus 1 hour 45 minutes rising and resting time
Cooking time: 40 minutes
Makes: 8 buns

For the dough:
· ¾ cup (180 ml/6 fl oz) full-fat warm milk
· 2 teaspoons active dry yeast
· 4 tablespoons granulated sugar
· 1 large egg
· 2 ½ cups (350 g) bread flour
· 1 teaspoon fine sea salt
· 2 tablespoons unsalted butter, softened to room temperature, plus more for greasing

For the topping:
· 2 tablespoons dry milk powder
· ¾ cup (95 g) unbleached all-purpose flour
· ½ teaspoon baking powder
· ¼ (60 g) cup superfine sugar
· 2 tablespoons unsalted butter, softened to room temperature
· 2 egg yolks, separated
· 4 teaspoons milk

Make the dough:
In a small bowl, combine the milk, yeast, and a pinch of sugar. Set the mixture aside until the yeast is frothy, about 10 minutes. Add the egg and mix until thoroughly combined.

Combine the bread flour, remaining sugar, powdered milk, and salt. Stir the yeast mixture into the flour with a wooden spoon until a shaggy dough forms and pulls away from the sides of the bowls.

Turn the dough out onto a well-floured work surface and knead with floured hands. The dough will be sticky. Knead for 10 minutes until it comes together in a ball. Add the softened butter and continue to knead for another 10 minutes, until the ball is elastic and smooth. Place the dough in a lightly oiled bowl, cover with a tea towel, let rest until doubled in size, about 1½ hours.

Turn the dough out onto a well-floured work surface and punch it down. Do not knead. Separate into 8 equal portions. Roll the dough into round buns, cover with plastic wrap (cling film), and let rest for 45 minutes.

Make the topping:
In a small bowl, combine the milk powder, flour, baking powder, sugar, butter, and 1 of the egg yolks. Mix together with your hands, slowly adding the liquid milk until a smooth dough forms, about 5 minutes. Let the dough rest for 10 minutes.

Preheat the oven to 350°F (180°C/Gas Mark 4). Line a baking sheet with parchment paper.

Divide the topping into 8 equal portions. On a floured work surface, roll each portion into a ball and roll the balls into rounds, 3–4 inches (7.5–10 cm) across and about 1/8 inch (3 mm) thick. Place a sugar-dough round on top of each bun; it should drape about halfway down the sides. Transfer the buns to the lined baking sheet and brush with the remaining beaten egg yolk. Bake until the buns are golden and glossy, about 20–25 minutes. Allow them to cool slightly before serving.

Note: If you can't find superfine (caster) sugar, sometimes called bar sugar, grind granulated sugar in a food processor until the granules break down into finer grains, 5–8 seconds. Take care not to process too long.

STEAMED PORK BUNS

CHINA

Baozi *are typically enjoyed during dim sum, a Chinese-style morning meal also consisting of small steamed dishes and baked goods such as* jiaozi *(Pan Fried Dumplings, page 319),* luo buo gao *(Turnip Cake, page 403), Scallion Pancakes (page 136),* cheong fun *(Steamed Rice Rolls, page 285), Pineapple Buns (page 230), and more. They are always served with tea. In this recipe, the homemade pork filling can be omitted and replaced with ½ lb (225 g) store-bought char siu pork.*

Preparation time: 50 minutes, plus 1 hour rising time
Cooking time: 35 minutes
Makes: 6 buns

For the dough:
· ½ cup (120 ml/4 fl oz) lukewarm water
· 1⅛ teaspoons active dry yeast
· A pinch plus 1½ tablespoons sugar
· 1½ cups (215 g) all-purpose (plain) flour
· ¼ teaspoon fine sea salt
· ¼ teaspoon baking powder
· 1 tablespoon canola (rapeseed) oil, plus more for greasing

For the pork filling:
· ½ lb (225 g) ground (minced) pork
· 1 teaspoon grated fresh ginger
· 4 tablespoons chopped scallions (spring onions)
· 2 tablespoons soy sauce
· 1 tablespoon hoisin sauce
· 2 teaspoons toasted sesame oil

Make the dough:
In a small bowl, combine the water, yeast, and a pinch of sugar. Set the mixture aside until the yeast is frothy, about 10 minutes. (If the yeast doesn't froth, check the expiration date. You may have to start over with fresher yeast.)

In a medium bowl, whisk together the flour, salt, 1½ tablespoons sugar, and baking powder. Make a well in the center of the flour mixture and stir in the yeast mixture and oil. Stir together into a shaggy ball.

Turn dough out onto a lightly floured work surface and knead until the dough is smooth and elastic, about 10 minutes. Place the dough in a lightly oiled bowl, cover with a tea towel, and set aside until doubled in size, about 1 hour.

Make the filling:
In a small bowl, thoroughly mix the ground (minced) pork with the ginger, scallions (spring onions), soy sauce, hoisin, and sesame oil.

Turn the dough out onto a work surface and punch it down. Roll the dough into a long log and cut it into 6 equal pieces. With a rolling pin, flatten each piece into a round.

Cup your hand and drape a round of dough over it (this creates a well for the filling). Dollop 1 tablespoon of the filling into the center and then, with your free hand, pinch and pleat the dough closed over the filling, rotating the bun in your cupped hand as you do. Allow the buns to rest for 10 minutes.

Meanwhile, line a steamer basket with a round of parchment paper. Bring 2 inches (5 cm) water to a boil in the steamer.

Place 3–4 buns in the basket, cover, and steam for 15 minutes. Repeat with remaining buns. Serve warm.

SWEET BREAD ROLL WITH CRUNCHY TOPPING

MEXICO

Conchas, a popular Mexican pan dulce (sweet bread) with a crackled sugar coating, is often enjoyed with a Café de Olla (page 413).

Preparation time: 1 hr 20 minutes, plus rising and chilling time
Cooking time: 25–30 minutes
Makes: 6 very large rolls

For the dough:
· 3 tablespoons full-fat milk, warmed
· 2 teaspoons active dry yeast
· Pinch plus 2 tablespoons granulated sugar
· 4 eggs
· 2½ cups (360 g) all-purpose (plain) flour, plus more for dusting
· 1½ teaspoons fine sea salt
· 4 tablespoons (60 g) unsalted butter, cut into 1-inch (2.5 cm) cubes, at room temperature, plus more for your hands

For the sugar-dough topping:
· 4 tablespoons powdered (icing) sugar
· ½ cup (70 g) all-purpose (plain) flour
· ½ tablespoon unsweetened cocoa powder (optional)
· Pinch of ground Mexican canela or cinnamon (optional)
· 4 tablespoons (60 g) unsalted butter, at room temperature
· 1 egg yolk

Make the dough:
In a small bowl, combine the milk, 3 tablespoons water, yeast, and a pinch of the sugar. Set the mixture aside until the yeast is frothy, about 10 minutes. (If the yeast does not froth, check the expiration date. You may have to start over with fresher yeast.)

In the bowl of a stand mixer fitted with the dough hook, combine the yeast mixture with the eggs. Mix on medium-low until combined. Gradually add the flour. Beat in the sugar and salt. Continue to knead on medium-low speed until the dough becomes firmer, smooth and elastic, 5–7 minutes. Once it comes together, add the butter, one cube at a time, working it in completely before adding the next. Turn dough out into a lightly oiled bowl, cover with plastic wrap (cling film), and let it rise until doubled in size, about 1½ hours.

Place the dough in a bowl and punch it down. Do not knead. Cover in plastic wrap and refrigerate, 30 minutes to 1 hour. This will firm up the dough and make it easier to work with.

Line a baking sheet with parchment paper. Divide the dough into 6 equal portions. On a lightly floured surface, roll each portion into a round ball. Place the balls on the baking sheet. With buttered hands, gently pat the tops of the buns to coat them in butter. Cover with a tea towel and let it rise until almost doubled in size, about 30 minutes.

Make the topping:
In a medium bowl, whisk together the powdered (icing) sugar, flour, cocoa powder, and cinnamon. Add the butter and egg yolk and use a wooden spoon to stir to a cookie-dough consistency. Chill until firm.

Preheat the oven to 350°F (180°C/Gas Mark 4).

Bake the rolls:
Once the rolls have risen, divide the sugar dough into 6 equal balls and use a tortilla press or the bottom of a cast-iron pan to flatten into rounds, 3–4 inches (7.5–10 cm) in diameter and about ⅛ inch (3 mm) thick. Place a sugar-dough round on top of each bun; it should drape about halfway down the sides. Impress a design in the disk with a concha mold or use a knife to score it by mimicking the lines of a seashell, scoring about 5 lines.

Bake until the topping has crackled, and the bun is a golden color, rotating the sheet halfway through, 25–30 minutes. Serve warm.

Sweet Bread Roll with Crunchy Topping

CHALLAH

ISRAEL

In Israel, this beloved bread is practically on the table at every meal. At breakfast, it accompanies a combination of olives, cheese, eggs, and/or Israeli Shakshuka (page 66).

Preparation time: 35 minutes, plus 2½ hours rising time
Cooking time: 40 minutes
Makes: 1 loaf

- 2 ¼ teaspoons dry active yeast
- 4 tablespoons sugar or honey
- ¾ teaspoon fine sea salt
- 3 tablespoons (45 g) unsalted butter, melted and cooled
- 2 eggs
- 1 egg, yolk and whites separated
- 3 cups (435 g) all-purpose (plain) flour, plus more as needed
- 1 tablespoon oil or butter for greasing

In a large bowl, combine ½ cup (120 ml/4 fl oz) water, yeast, and 1 tablespoon of the sugar. Set the mixture aside until the yeast is frothy, about 10 minutes. (If the yeast does not froth, check the expiration date. You may have to start over with fresher yeast.)

Stir in the remaining sugar, the salt, melted butter, whole eggs, and egg yolk (reserve the egg white for brushing the dough). Stir in the flour 1 cup (145 g) at a time until a shaggy dough forms, pulling away from the sides of the bowl.

Turn the dough out onto a lightly floured work surface and knead the dough until it's smooth, about 10 minutes. If the dough is very sticky, add up to 4 tablespoons more flour, 1 tablespoon at a time. Knead until the dough no longer sticks to your hand and is firm. Place the dough in a lightly greased bowl, cover with a tea towel, and let the dough rise until doubled in size, about 2 hours.

Punch the dough down to deflate the bubbles and turn out onto a lightly floured work surface. Divide the dough into 3 equal portions. Roll the portions into ropes, 12 inches (30 cm) long. Line a baking sheet with parchment paper. Transfer dough to the sheet. Lay the ropes next to one another and pinch them together at one end. Braid (plait) the ropes together, tucking the ends under to seal. Cover with plastic wrap (cling film). Let the dough rise, about 30 minutes.

Meanwhile, preheat the oven to 350°F (180°C/Gas Mark 4).

Brush the challah with half of the egg white, making sure to get all of the sides and in the cracks of the braid. Lightly cover with the plastic wrap (cling film). Allow the dough to rise for 15 minutes.

Brush the bread a second time with the remaining egg white and allow it to rise for 15 minutes more.

Bake until golden on all sides, rotating the sheet from front to back halfway through, 35–40 minutes.

Allow the bread to cool before serving.

CHEESE BREAD

BRAZIL

Pão de queijo *are fluffy cheese rolls that have a definitive chewy texture from the use of tapioca flour. Traditionally, these rolls are made with Brazilian cheeses, such as queijo de Minas or queijo de Canastra, but parmesan or mozzarella can be used.*

Preparation time: 15 minutes
Cooking time: 30 minutes
Makes: 12 rolls

· ½ cup (120 ml/4 fl oz) full-fat milk
· 1 tablespoon vegetable oil
· 2 tablespoons (30 g) unsalted butter
· 1½ cups (180 g) tapioca flour, sour tapioca flour, or a 50/50 mix
· 1 egg
· ½ teaspoon fine sea salt
· ¾ cup (70 g) grated parmesan or mozzarella

Preheat the oven to 375°F (190°C/Gas Mark 5). Line a baking sheet with parchment paper.

In a small saucepan over medium-high heat, combine the milk, oil, and butter. Stir together and bring to a boil. When it begins to boil immediately remove the saucepan from the heat. Stir in the tapioca flour and mix constantly; it should quickly come together to form a dough, 1 minute. Stir in the egg and salt. Finally, stir in the cheese until everything is thoroughly incorporated. Set the dough aside and let it rest for 10 minutes.

Form 2 tablespoons of dough into balls. Flour your hands with tapioca flour if it makes it easier to handle the dough. Place the balls on the lined baking sheet.

Bake until golden and puffed up, 20–25 minutes.

Allow the rolls to cool before serving warm.

See image page 424.

SEMOLINA FLATBREAD

MOROCCO

Harsha, *a semolina bread, similar to a Colombian Arepa (page 314) in that it is pan-fried over low heat, is circular in shape, and uses a coarse flour to make the dough. Harsha is often enjoyed with cheese or a syrup made with honey and butter.*

Preparation time: 20 minutes
Cooking time: 15 minutes
Makes: 6 flatbreads

· 1¼ cups (210 g) semolina flour
· 2 tablespoons sugar
· ¼ teaspoon fine sea salt
· 1 teaspoon baking powder
· 5 tablespoons (75 g) unsalted butter, melted
· 4 tablespoons full-fat milk
· 1 tablespoon butter
· 1 tablespoon honey

In a medium bowl, combine the semolina, sugar, salt, and baking powder. Pour in the melted butter and stir with a wooden spoon until the flour begins to become hydrated. Add the milk and continue to stir until a soft dough begins to come together. Mix the dough with your hands until a soft dough forms. It should be able to hold the indent of your finger when pressed. Allow the dough to rest for 5–7 minutes so the semolina can absorb more of the milk and butter.

Divide the dough into 6 equal portions. Flatten between your palms into 3-inch (7.5 cm) patties ¼ inch (6 mm) thick.

Heat a cast-iron skillet over medium heat. Reduce the heat to low and cook 3 patties at a time, until browned on each side and cooked in the center, about 8 minutes per side. Transfer to a plate to cool.

To make the honey-butter syrup, in a small saucepan over medium heat, melt the butter and stir in the honey until combined. Slice the cooled *harsha* horizontally in half. Drizzle the syrup over the split *harsha* and serve.

MALAWAH

YEMEN

Malawah *is a laminated fried flatbread served with freshly grated or puréed tomato and Schug (page 26).*

Preparation time: 40 minutes, plus 30 minutes resting time and 15 minutes chilling time
Cooking time: 25 minutes
Makes: 4 flatbreads

· 1½ cups (215 g) all-purpose (plain) flour
· ½ cup (55 g) plus 2 tablespoons pastry flour (soft flour)
· 2 teaspoons sugar
· 1½ teaspoons fine sea salt
· 6 tablespoons (75 g) unsalted butter, cut into tablespoons, at room temperature, plus more as needed
· 1 medium overripe tomato, halved through the equator
· Schug, for serving (page 26)
· 4 Hard-Boiled Eggs, halved (page 14)

In a medium bowl, combine the flours, sugar, and salt. Make a well in the center and pour ½ cup (120 ml/4 fl oz) water in. Mix with your hands until a shaggy dough begins to form. Turn the dough out onto a lightly floured surface and knead until it comes together in a smooth dough, about 5 minutes. Place the dough in a lightly greased bowl, cover with a tea towel, and let it rest for 30 minutes.

Line a baking sheet with parchment paper and set aside. Grease a large cutting board with ½ tablespoon (7 g) of the butter. Turn out the dough onto the cutting board and divide it into 4 equal portions. Working with 1 portion at a time (keeping the other portions covered with a tea towel while you work), place the dough on the greased surface and place 1 tablespoon (15 g) of the softened butter on the dough. Spread the butter out with your hands in a circular motion, smearing the butter across the face of the dough, slowly stretching it out until it's nearly translucent. It's okay if there are a few rips. Roll the dough into a rope. Coil the rope into a spiral and transfer to the lined baking sheet. Repeat with the remaining portions, greasing the work surface as necessary.

Place the baking sheet of coils in the refrigerator for 15 minutes to firm up slightly.

Place 1 *malawah* between two sheets of parchment paper. With a rolling pin, roll out to a round, 8 ½ inches (2 cm) in diameter and ¼ inch (6 mm) thick. Repeat with the remaining coils.

Heat a cast-iron skillet over medium-high heat. Add 1 *malawah* and cook until browned on both sides, 2 minutes per side. Transfer to a plate and repeat with remaining *malawah*.

Grate the tomato using a cheese grater set over a flat plate or bowl and discard the skin.

Serve each *malawah* warm with a spoonful of grated tomato and Schug, and a hard-boiled egg.

BUTTERMILK BISCUITS
UNITED STATES

A common breakfast item in the Southern United States, biscuits are typically served with butter and honey, or gravy, or made into a sandwich with eggs bacon, or sausage. These are considered flaky biscuits "baking powder biscuits," while their cousins, Drop Biscuits (page 238), have a crumblier texture.

Preparation time: 15 minutes
Cooking time: 30 minutes
Makes: 6 biscuits

· 2 cups (290 g) all-purpose (plain) flour, plus more for dusting
· 1 tablespoon baking powder
· ½ teaspoon baking soda (bicarbonate of soda)
· 1 teaspoon fine sea salt
· 12 teaspoons sugar
· 10 tablespoons (140 g) very cold butter, cut into 1-inch (2.5 cm) pieces
· 1 cup (240 ml/8 fl oz) buttermilk, plus more for brushing

Preheat the oven to 400°F (200°C/Gas Mark 6). Line a baking sheet with parchment paper.

In a medium bowl, combine the flour, baking powder, baking soda (bicarb), salt, and sugar. Work the butter into the flour with a pastry (dough) blender or your hands until broken down to the size of peas. By hand, this can be achieved by rolling the flour-coated butter pieces across your fingers. Pour the buttermilk into the flour mixture and stir with a fork until the flour is hydrated, taking care not to overwork it.

Turn the dough out onto a lightly floured work surface and pat into a 6½-inch (16.5 cm) square 1 inch (2.5 cm) thick. With a 3-inch (7.5 cm) round biscuit cutter, cut out 4 biscuits. Gather up the scraps and pat out again to cut out another 2 biscuits. Place the biscuits on the lined baking sheet about ½ inch (1.25 cm) apart and brush with buttermilk.

Bake the biscuits until golden brown, 25–30 minutes. Serve warm.

DROP BISCUITS
UNITED STATES

A drop biscuit is made by spooning ("dropping") the biscuit dough directly onto a baking sheet, creating a more rustic look and crumbly texture than a cut-out Buttermilk Biscuits (above). Typically enjoyed with butter and honey or gravy or used as bread for a breakfast sandwich.

Preparation time: 10 minutes
Cooking time: 20 minutes
Makes: 4 large biscuits

· 1 cup (145 g) all-purpose (plain) flour
· 1½ teaspoons baking powder
· 1 teaspoon fine sea salt
· 2 teaspoon sugar
· 4 tablespoons (60 g) cold butter, cut into 1-inch (2.5 cm) pieces
· ½ cup (120 ml/4 fl oz) plus 2 tablespoons full-fat milk

Preheat the oven to 400°F (200°C/Gas Mark 6). Line a baking sheet with parchment paper.

In a medium bowl, combine the flour, baking powder, salt, and sugar. Work the butter into the flour with a pastry (dough) blender or your hands until broken down to the size of peas. By hand, this can be achieved by rolling the flour-coated butter pieces across your fingers. Pour the milk into the flour mixture and stir just until no dry spots remain, taking care not to overwork the dough. The mixture should look similar to paste.

Scoop up the dough by the ⅓ cup (100 ml/3 fl oz) and drop it onto the baking sheet. Bake until the biscuits are golden, 17–20 minutes. Allow them to cool on a rack before serving warm.

Drop Biscuits

D STEWS

TOASTED RICE AND FISH NOODLE SOUP

MYANMAR

Mohinga is a fish soup that has rice noodles that sit in a tangy lime and lemongrass broth thickened with toasted rice powder. It is one of the most beloved Burmese dishes and is typically sold as a street food.

Preparation time: 15 minutes
Cooking time: 1 hour 15 minutes
Serves: 4

For the toasted rice:
· 4 tablespoons long-grain white rice

For the soup:
· 2 tablespoons vegetable oil
· 2 cloves garlic, smashed
· ¼ red onion, thinly sliced
· 1-inch (2.5 cm) piece fresh ginger, peeled and finely chopped
· 2 stalks lemongrass, shredded or finely chopped
· 1 teaspoon ground turmeric
· 1½ teaspoons freshly ground pepper
· 1 teaspoon plus a pinch of salt
· 4 catfish fillets (about 6 oz/170 g each), picked for bones
· 4 tablespoons cooked chickpeas, crushed into a paste
· ¼ teaspoon chili powder

For serving:
· 8 oz (225 g) rice vermicelli noodles, softened per package directions
· Cilantro leaves, for garnish
· 2 snake beans (Chinese long beans), chopped
· 1 lime, quartered

Make the toasted rice:
Preheat the oven to 350°F (180°C/Gas Mark).

Spread the rice evenly on a baking sheet lined with parchment paper. Toast until the rice is golden, 25–30 minutes, stirring the rice around the sheet halfway through to avoid burning. Allow the toasted rice to cool, about 15 minutes. In a spice grinder/coffee mill, blend the rice to a powder.

Make the soup:
In a large saucepan, heat the oil over medium heat. Add the garlic, onion, ginger, lemongrass, turmeric, pepper, and salt. Fry the ingredients, stirring constantly, until the onion is soft and translucent, about 5 minutes. Add the catfish fillets to the mixture and cook until opaque and lightly browned, breaking up the fillets as they cook, about 7 minutes. Remove from the heat and set aside.

In a soup pot, bring 6 ½ cups (1.4 liters/48 fl oz) water to a boil. Add the chickpea paste and dissolve in the boiling water. Add the toasted rice flour and the fish mixture and stir to incorporate. Add a pinch of salt and the chili powder. Simmer over medium-low heat for 30 minutes.

To serve:
Divide the noodles into 4 bowls. Pour the soup over the noodles and serve topped with cilantro, snake beans, and a wedge of lime.

Toasted Rice and Fish Noodle Soup

TUNA AND YUCA STEW

ECUADOR

Encebollado is coastal breakfast in Ecuador. This fish stew is thickened with yuca (cassava) and topped with pickled onions, cilantro (coriander), and plantain chips, popcorn, or toasted corn nuts (giant corn).

Preparation time: 15 minutes, plus 1 hour pickling time
Cooking time: 40 minutes
Serves: 4

For the quick pickled onions:
· ½ tablespoon sugar
· ½ teaspoon fine sea salt
· ⅓ cup (75 ml/2.5 fl oz) rice vinegar or apple cider vinegar
· ½ small red onion, sliced into thin rings

For the soup:
· 1 tablespoon olive oil
· ½ lb (225 g) tuna
· ½ teaspoon cayenne pepper
· Salt and freshly ground black pepper
· 2 medium tomatoes, diced
· 1 medium yellow onion, diced
· 2 cloves garlic, minced
· 1 teaspoon ground cumin
· 5 sprigs cilantro (coriander), plus leaves for serving
· 1 lb (455 g) yuca (cassava), peeled and cubed
· Plantain chips, popcorn, or corn nuts (giant corn)

Make the quick pickled onions:
In a small bowl, dissolve the sugar and salt in ½ cup (120 ml/4 fl oz) water and the vinegar. Add the red onion, making sure each ring is coated. Cover with a tea towel or plastic wrap (cling film) and let the mixture sit at room temperature for at least 1 hour.

Make the soup:
In a heavy-bottomed saucepan, heat the oil over medium-high heat. Season both sides of the tuna with the cayenne and salt and black pepper to taste. Add the fish and cook on both sides until golden, about 8 minutes. Remove from the pan with a spatula and set aside.

Return the pan to medium heat and add the tomatoes, onion, and garlic. Sprinkle in the cumin and stir to coat the vegetables. Add 6 cups (1.4 liters/48 fl oz) water and the cilantro sprigs, then bring to a boil. With a slotted spoon, lower the cubed yuca (cassava) into the water and season with salt. Cook until tender, about 25 minutes.

Ladle the soup into bowls and flake the fish on top. Drain the red onion from the pickling liquid. Top each bowl with some pickled onion, cilantro leaves, and plantains chips, popcorn, or corn nuts.

HANGOVER SOUP

SOUTH KOREA

Haejang-guk is a typical breakfast in South Korea and includes soup (guk), fried rice, and banchan, small plates often consisting of various fermented vegetables (see page 270). There are many kinds of soups, depending on the region, family traditions, and available ingredients. Haejang-guk is a popular choice of soup, often considered a hangover cure for its generous inclusion of spicy chilies.

Preparation time: 15 minutes, plus 3 hours chilling time
Cooking time: 3 hours 20 minutes
Serves: 2-4

For the broth:
· 1 lb (455 g) ox bones, rinsed of blood (oxtail, cut crosswise in 2–3-inch pieces)

For the haejang-guk:
· ¼ head napa cabbage (Chinese leaf), about ½ lb (228 g)
· 4 cloves garlic, minced
· ½ cup (35 g) soybean sprouts
· 2 fresh shiitake mushrooms, stemmed and chopped
· 2 tablespoon gochugaru (ground Korean red pepper)
· 1 green Anaheim chili, chopped
· 1 scallion (spring onion), thinly sliced, white and green parts kept separate
· 2 teaspoons fish sauce

Make the broth:
In a medium stockpot cover the ox bones with water and bring to a boil over medium heat. Simmer the broth until cloudy, at least 3 hours (it should be opaque and cloudy). Strain through a fine-mesh sieve into a bowl (discard the bones). Cool completely and refrigerate the broth for at least 3 hours to chill. Skim off the fat from the surface and discard. Measure out 4 cups (950 ml/32 fl oz) broth and save the rest for another use.

Make the *haejang-guk*:
Fill a medium saucepan with water and bring to a boil. Add the cabbage and cook until slightly softened, about 8 minutes. Carefully drain the cabbage into a colander and run under cool water.

Slice the cabbage into thin shreds and transfer to a bowl. Add the garlic, sprouts, mushrooms, gochugaru, chili, scallion (gren onion) whites, and fish sauce. Toss and transfer to the reserved saucepan. Pour in the broth, bring to a boil, and cook for 5 minutes, stirring occasionally. Reduce the heat to low, cover, and simmer until the vegetables and mushrooms are tender, about 10 minutes longer. Serve warm topped with the scallion greens.

TOFU STEW

CHINA

This recipe for tofu nao *is for the savory version found in Northern China (in the South it tends to have a sweeter flavor profile).*

Preparation time: 5 minutes
Cooking time: 10 minutes
Serves: 2

· 1 tablespoon vegetable oil
· 4 tablespoons chopped scallions (spring onions)
· 1-inch (2.5 cm) piece fresh ginger, peeled and finely chopped
· 1 cup (80 g) chopped white mushrooms
· 2 tablespoons soy sauce
· 3 cups (710 ml/24 fl oz) chicken stock, homemade or store-bought
· 1 tablespoon potato starch
· 1 egg
· 1 container (10.5 oz/300 g) silken tofu, broken into pieces
· 1 teaspoon chili oil
· Salt and freshly ground white pepper

In a medium saucepan, heat the vegetable oil over medium-high heat. Add 2 tablespoons of the scallion (spring onion) and the ginger, stirring and cooking until soft, about 2 minutes. Add the mushrooms and cook until soft, about 3 minutes. Stir in the soy sauce and chicken stock and bring the mixture to a boil. Combine the potato starch with 2 tablespoons cold water and stir it into the boiling broth.

In a small bowl, lightly beat the egg. Return the saucepan to a boil. Stir in the beaten egg, then reduce the heat to medium-low. Add the silken tofu to the soup and simmer until heated through, 3–5 minutes. Remove the soup from the heat, stir in the chili oil, and season with salt and white pepper. Serve warm with the remaining 2 tablespoons scallions sprinkled on top.

MACARONI SOUP

CHINA

This Hong Kong soup is made with macaroni and a choice of cold cuts or luncheon meat, sometimes interspersed with corn, cubed carrots, and peas, and topped with a fried egg.

Preparation time: 5 minutes
Cooking time: 15 minutes
Serves: 2

· 3 cups (710 ml/24 fl oz) chicken stock
· 1 teaspoon soy sauce
· 1½ cups (85 g) elbow macaroni pasta
· 1 can (12 oz/340 g) Spam, cut into cubes; hot dogs, sliced; or deli ham
· 1 teaspoon vegetable or sesame oil
· 2 Fried Eggs (page 14)
· 4 tablespoons mix of cooked cubed carrots, corn, and peas (optional)

In a medium saucepan, bring the stock and soy sauce to a boil over medium-high heat. Stir in the macaroni and cook until al dente, stirring occasionally, about 7 minutes.

Meanwhile, in a medium frying pan, pan-fry the Spam, hot dogs, or deli ham over medium-high heat until crisped, about 4 minutes. Transfer to paper towels. To serve, divide the broth and noodles between two bowls. Add vegetables, if using, and top with Spam, hot dogs, or deli ham, and a fried egg.

CHICKEN PHỞ

VIETNAM

Phở is a clear broth made with chicken (gà) bones or pork (bò) bones and infused with anise and ginger, then topped with fresh herbs like basil, cilantro, and mint. In the North of Vietnam, which is influenced by Chinese food culture, phở is served hot, with a cleaner taste, and topped with lots of scallions (spring onions) and a vinegar and garlic sauce. In the South, which is more influenced by India, phở tends to be sweeter and served with fresh herbs like Thai basil, bean sprouts, and hoisin sauce (tương đen).

Preparation time: 10 minutes
Cooking time: 50 minutes
Serves: 2

For the soup:
· 1 boneless, skinless chicken breast
· 2 cloves garlic, smashed
· 2 star anise pods
· 3 whole cloves
· ½-inch piece fresh ginger, peeled and chopped
· 4 cups (950 ml/32 fl oz) chicken stock, homemade or store-bought
· 1 teaspoon fish sauce
· Salt
· 4 oz (115 g) rice vermicelli noodles, cooked per package directions

For serving:
· Cilantro (coriander), basil, and mint
· 1 scallion (spring onion), chopped
· ¼ red onion, sliced
· 1 small jalapeño, chopped

Place the chicken in a small saucepan and cover with water. Bring to a boil over medium-high heat and poach until the chicken is cooked through, 20–25 minutes. Transfer to a cutting board and when it is cool, cut into ½-inch (1.25 cm) pieces. Reserve the poaching liquid.

In a medium saucepan, toast the garlic, star anise, whole cloves, and ginger over medium heat until aromatic, about 2 minutes. Pour in the chicken stock and bring to a boil. Reduce the heat to a simmer. Stir in the fish sauce and salt to taste and simmer until the broth has reduced by ¼, about 20 minutes. Using a slotted spoon, discard the garlic, cloves, and star anise. Stir in the chicken pieces.

Cover the noodles with warm water and soak until pliable, about 10 minutes.

To serve:
Divide the noodles evenly between two bowls. Ladle the broth over the noodles and top with herbs, scallion, red onion, and jalapeño.

HAWAIIAN NOODLE SOUP
UNITED STATES

Inspired by Japanese, Chinese, and Filipino noodle dishes, saimin is a uniquely Hawaiian soup. Saimin noodles are wheat-based egg noodles that share similar qualities and can be substituted with soba noodles. The clean broth exudes a subtle sweetness and umami (harmonizing taste) from the dried shrimp and is topped with sliced Japanese fish cake (kamaboko).

Preparation time: 10 minutes
Cooking time: 1 hour 10 minutes
Serves: 2

· 4 tablespoons dried shrimp
· 4 dried shiitake mushrooms
· 1 small piece kombu (dried kelp)
· 1-inch (2.5 cm) piece fresh ginger, peeled and sliced
· 1 tablespoon soy sauce
· 4 oz (115 g) saimin noodles, cooked per package directions
· 2 eggs
· ½ tablespoon vegetable oil
· 1 scallion (spring onion), chopped
· 1 slice Spam, chopped
· 2 slices kamaboko (fish cake)

In a medium saucepan, bring 4 cups (950 ml/32 fl oz) water to a simmer over medium-high heat. Add the dried shrimp, dried shiitake mushrooms, kombu, ginger, and soy sauce. Reduce the heat to low and steep all the ingredients for at least 30 minutes and up to 1 hour. (The mixture should be hot but not simmering.) Strain the broth.

Whisk the eggs in a bowl. Heat the oil to a non-stick pan over medium heat. Add the eggs and cook for 30 seconds. Use a spatula to fold the omelet into thirds. Place on a plate and cut into thin slices.

To serve, divide the noodles between two bowls. Ladle the broth over the noodles and top with egg slices, scallion, Spam, and *kamaboko*.

MILK SOUP
COLOMBIA

Changua is a milk soup popular in the mountainous Central Andean region of Colombia. This dish dates back to the Muisca Tribe present before the Spanish conquest in the mid-1500s and the source of the legend of El Dorado.

Preparation time: 10 minutes
Cooking time: 20 minutes
Serves: 2

· 2 cups (475 ml/16 fl oz) full-fat milk
· 2 scallions (spring onions), chopped
· 2 sprigs cilantro (coriander), chopped, plus more for serving
· Salt and freshly ground pepper
· 2 eggs
· 2 slices (or 1 piece about 2 inches/5 cm thick) stale or extra-toasted bread, torn into pieces

In a medium saucepan, combine the milk and 2 cups (475 ml/16 fl oz) water and bring to a simmer over medium-high heat. Stir in scallions (spring onions) and chopped cilantro (coriander) and season with salt and pepper. Reduce the heat to medium and make a whirlpool with a spoon before carefully cracking the eggs, one at a time, into the soup. Poach until set, about 3 minutes, making sure the soup remains at a low simmer so the eggs do not fall apart.

Season the soup with salt and pepper. Divide the toasted bread between two bowls and pour the soup over the bread. Top with cilantro and serve.

Hawaiian Noodle Soup

CUT RICE NOODLE SOUP

CAMBODIA

Chinese in origin, kuy teav *refers to "cut rice noodles" and features a clear pork broth served with thin rice noodles and a variety of proteins. A bowl is accompanied by lime wedges, cilantro, pickled Thai chilies, crispy minced garlic, and soy sauce.*

Preparation time: 20 minutes
Cooking time: 3 hours 30 minutes
Serves: 2–4

For the soup:
· ¾ cup (60 g) dried shrimp
· 1 lb (455 g) pork neck bones
· ½ lb (225 g) pork tenderloin (fillet)
· 2 chicken drumsticks
· 1 bunch scallions (spring onions), trimmed and cut into 2-inch pieces
· ½ small white onion, chopped
· ½ small sweet potato, diced
· 1 carrot, chopped
· 1 small head bok choy, chopped
· ½ medium daikon, diced
· 1 head garlic, halved horizontally, plus 4 cloves garlic, chopped
· 1 tablespoon soy sauce, plus more for serving
· 1½ teaspoons fish sauce
· 1½ teaspoons sugar
· 4 tablespoons vegetable oil
· ½ lb (225 g) ground (minced) pork
· Salt and freshly ground pepper
· 6 oz (170 g) bean sprouts
· 8 large shrimp (prawns), peeled and deveined
· 8 oz (225 g) rice vermicelli, cooked per package directions
· 4 green lettuce leaves

For serving:
· Cilantro (coriander) leaves
· Pickled Thai chilles, thinly sliced
· Chili paste
· Lime wedges
· Scallions, thinly sliced

Make the soup:
In a small bowl, cover ½ cup (40 g) of the dried shrimp with water. Let stand for 30 minutes before draining.

In a soup pot, combine the soaked shrimp, pork bones, pork tenderloin (fillet), chicken drumsticks, scallions (spring onions), white onion, sweet potato, carrot, bok choy, daikon, garlic head halves, soy sauce, fish sauce, and sugar. Add 3 quarts (9.8 liters/96 fl oz) water and bring to a boil. Reduce to a simmer and cook about 30 minutes. A thermometer inserted in the thickest cut of the tenderloin should read 140°F (60°C). Transfer the tenderloin to a plate to cool, cover with plastic wrap (cling film), then refrigerate. Continue to simmer the broth until it reduces by half, about 2 hours 30 minutes more.

Meanwhile, in a small frying pan, heat 2 tablespoons of oil over medium heat. Add the chopped garlic and cook, stirring, until the garlic is browned and the oil is fragrant, about 6 minutes. Using a fine-mesh sieve, strain the oil into a small bowl and set the fried garlic aside.

Heat 1 tablespoon of oil over medium heat in a frying pan. Add the ground (minced) pork and season with salt and pepper. Cook, stirring occasionally, until the pork is browned, 10 minutes. Transfer to a bowl. In the same frying pan, heat 1 tablespoon oil. Add the remaining ¼ cup (20 g) dried shrimp and cook until fragrant, about 2 minutes.

Fill a large pot with water. Add the bean sprouts in a sieve and blanch them for 10 seconds. Transfer the bean sprouts to a bowl. Return the water to a boil and add the raw shrimp (prawns). Cook until they are pink, 3 minutes, then drain and transfer to a bowl.

Transfer chicken drumsticks from the soup pot to a bowl. Strain the broth through a fine-mesh sieve into another large pot, discarding the solids. Bring the broth back to a simmer and season with salt. Add the pork tenderloin and cook until warmed through, about 5 minutes.

Transfer the tenderloin to a carving board and thinly slice. Shred the chicken meat (discard the skin and bones).

Bring a medium pot of water to a boil over medium-high heat. Add the vermicelli noodles and cook until al dente, about 5 minutes. Drain the noodles and rinse under cold water. Pat them dry and return to the pot. Toss the noodles with the reserved garlic oil and fried garlic.

To serve:
Divide the lettuce leaves among 2 to 4 bowls. Cover the lettuce with noodles. Ladle in the broth and top with sliced tenderloin, shredded chicken, ground pork, cooked shrimp, and dried shrimp. Serve with the bean sprouts, cilantro (coriander), pickled chilies, chili paste, lime wedges, scallions (spring onions), and soy sauce.

See picture on the next page.

Cut Rice Noodle Soup (page 250–51)

SOUPS AND STEWS

PORK MEATBALL SOUP

VIETNAM

Originating in Moc village, Hanoi, bún moc *is a shiitake mushroom-infused broth with spiced meatballs made from pork paste. It is served over long rice noodles and topped with Vietnamese ham (*chả lụa*). This recipe includes a homemade version of pork paste made with ground pork, but it typically comes pre-seasoned and can be found at Asian grocery stores. If using store-bought pork paste, skip the first step in making the meatballs.*

Preparation time: 30 minutes
Cooking time: 3 hours
Serves: 2, makes 4 cups (950 ml/32 fl oz) broth and 12 meatballs

For the broth:
· 1½ lb (680 g) pork ribs
· 6 dried shiitake mushrooms, soaked in 1 cup (240 ml/8 fl oz) water for 20 minutes
· ¼ cup (7 g) dried wood ear mushrooms, soaked in ½ cup (120 ml/4 fl oz) water for 20 minutes, then chopped
· 1 teaspoon fish sauce
· ½ teaspoon fine sea salt

For the meatballs:
· ½ lb (225 g) ground pork
· 1 teaspoon baking powder
· 1½ teaspoons tapioca starch
· ¼ teaspoon fine sea salt
· ¼ teaspoon ground black pepper
· 3 teaspoons sugar
· 1 teaspoon fish sauce
· 2½ teaspoons vegetable oil

For serving:
· 8 oz (225 g) rice vermicelli noodles, cooked per package directions
· 4 tablespoons bean sprouts
· 1 scallion (spring onion), chopped
· Cilantro (coriander), chopped
· 4 slices chả lụa (Vietnamese ham)

Make the broth:
In a soup pot, cover the pork ribs in water and bring to a boil. Cook, covered for about 5 minutes. Foam should form on surface of the water. Remove from the heat, discard the water, and wash the pork ribs and pot from any leftover residue. Put the ribs back in the pot and cover with 8 cups (1.9 liters/2 qt) water. Bring to a boil over medium-high heat, then turn the heat to low and simmer until the broth reduces by half, about 2 hours 30 minutes longer.

Make the meatballs:
In 2 separate bowls, soak the shiitake mushrooms and the wood ear mushrooms in warm water for 20 minutes.

In a food processer, grind the ground meat with the baking powder, tapioca starch, salt and pepper, sugar, fish sauce, and vegetable oil.

In a small bowl, combine the pork paste and the drained wood ear mushrooms. With damp hands, mix the pork and mushrooms together to form 12 meatballs, 1 tablespoon each.

Remove the ribs from the broth and reserve for another use. Measure 4 cups (950 ml/32 fl oz) broth and bring to a boil over medium-high heat.

Use a slotted spoon to lower the pork balls into the broth. Boil until cooked through, about 5 minutes. Reduce to a simmer and add the shiitake mushrooms, along with their soaking water, and stir in the fish sauce and salt. Let simmer for 5 minutes more.

To serve:
Divide the noodles and pork balls between 2 serving bowls. Ladle the broth over the noodles and top with the bean sprouts, scallion, cilantro, and chả lụa.

HARUMI KURIHARA
JAPANESE BREAKFAST

Harumi Kurihara is one of the best-known food writers in Japan. She is the author of many cookbooks, including Harumi's Japanese Cooking.

My mother was a great cook. I was brought up to believe that it is natural to help with the cooking. Whenever she cooked, she would let me taste the dish, then asked, "How do you like it?" Even when I was little, I gave her my comments and suggestions: "Why don't you add a little salt and soy sauce?" Looking back, this may have been the starting point of my career in cooking.

Everything was in the Japanese style at home, with Japanese-style meals and the atmosphere of a Japanese-style house. I admired Western-style living, so when I got married, I was excited to have Western-style furniture, chairs in particular, and to cook Western-style meals such as scrambled eggs and coffee for breakfast, which I'd never had before. But I have not continued to cook Western-style meals, simply because I didn't want to force myself to cook unfamiliar dishes. I started thinking about cooking more Japanese meals.

I grew up watching my mother wake up early every morning to cook breakfast for my family. She taught me a great lesson: that it is very important to cook and eat breakfast. Today, that lesson is still in effect.

My favorite among my mother's breakfast dishes is a menu of freshly cooked rice, sesame miso soup, dried horse mackerel (caught and prepared in my hometown), natto with chopped spring onion and fish flakes, and homemade pickles in bran.

My mother never used instant stock in the broth of miso soup. First, she'd carefully make dashi with kelp and fish flakes. Then she roasted the sesame seeds slowly until they got sticky enough. She warmed the dashi and added miso paste. She'd poured this mixture into the pan and mix it with the sesame seeds, adding tofu she broke up with her hands. "Heat it, but do not boil it," she instructed.

Each year we celebrate the arrival of spring by putting a few Japan peppers into our sesame miso soup. The taste is beyond description, full-flavored, fragrant, wonderful—one I'll never forget.

01. Quick Pickled Vegetables PAGE 348   02. Miso Soup PAGE 260   03. Rice with Raw Eggs PAGE 68
04. Rice with Natto PAGE 274

05. Rolled Omelet PAGE 48   **06.** Toast with Sweet Red Bean Spread PAGE 149   **07.** Grilled Fish PAGE 348

WONTON SOUP

CHINA

Xiao huntun *is a Shanghainese wonton soup with two definitive elements: paper-thin wrappers that enclose the overstuffed dumplings, and a clean, no-frills broth.*

Preparation time: 30 minutes
Cooking time: 10 minutes
Serves: 2

For the broth:
· 4 cups (950 ml/32 fl oz) chicken stock
· ½-inch (1.25 cm) piece fresh ginger, peeled and chopped
· Salt

For the wontons:
· ¼ lb (115 g) ground (minced) pork
· ½-inch (1.25 cm) piece fresh ginger, peeled and minced
· 2 teaspoons rice wine
· 1 teaspoon soy sauce
· ¼ teaspoon ground white pepper
· ¼ teaspoon sugar
· ½ teaspoon fine sea salt
· 18 wonton wrappers, ⅛ inch (3 mm) thick

For serving:
· Sesame oil
· 1 scallion (spring onion), chopped
· Sesame oil
· Chili oil

Make the broth:
In a medium saucepan, combine the chicken stock, ginger, and salt to taste and bring to a boil over medium-high heat. Reduce the heat to low and keep at a simmer.

Meanwhile, make the wontons:
In a bowl, mix together the pork, ginger, rice wine, soy sauce, white pepper, sugar, and salt with a spoon or chopsticks. Stir until the mixture turns into a paste-like consistency.
    Dollop 1 teaspoon of filling into the center of a wonton wrapper. Dip your fingers in water and wet the perimeter of the wonton. (This will help the wonton seal properly.) Hold the wonton between your thumb and forefinger and gather the excess dough, pressing to seal just over the filling to create a purse.
    Bring a small saucepan of water to a boil over medium-high heat. Cook the wontons until they rise to the top, 3 minutes.

To serve:
With a slotted spoon, divide the wontons between 2 soup bowls. Pour warm broth over the wontons and top with scallion (spring onion) and a few drops of sesame and/or chili oil.

PORK AND WHITE PEPPER SOUP

SINGAPORE

Bak kut teh *translates to "meat bone tea." This reflects the pork rib steeping in the bowl when served as well as the delicate but pepper- and spice-infused broth. The soup is often served with youtiao (Chinese Cruller, page 306) to dip in the broth.*

Preparation time: 40 minutes, plus resting, tempering, and chilling time for the Chinese Cruller
Cooking time: 2 hours 30 minutes, plus cooking time for the Chinese Cruller
Serves: 2

For the spice mix:
· ¼ stick cinnamon
· 5 whole cloves
· 1 star anise
· 1 teaspoon white peppercorns
· 1 teaspoon coriander seeds

For the soup:
· 1 lb (455 g) pork ribs
· 4 dried shiitake mushrooms
· 1 small bulb garlic, rinsed, the top quarter cut off crosswise to reveal the cloves
· 3 tablespoons soy sauce
· 2 tablespoons fish sauce
· 2 teaspoons ground white pepper
· Chinese Cruller (page 306), for dipping in the soup

Make the spice mix:
Add all of the ingredients in the spice mix to a tea sachet and twist closed. A doubled piece of cheesecloth tied at the top can also be used.

Make the soup:
Add the pork ribs to a large stockpot. Cover just barely with water and bring to a boil, skimming off the fat as it rises to the surface. Reduce to a simmer and cook for 10 minutes. Use a slotted spoon to remove the ribs from the pot. Discard the water and clean the pot.

Return the ribs to the stockpot along with 6 cups (1.4 liters/48 fl oz) water, shiitake mushrooms, and garlic bulb. Bring to a simmer over medium-low heat. Add the spice sachet and simmer until the meat is tender and barely clinging to the bone, about 1 hour and 30 minutes.

Stir in the soy sauce, fish sauce, and white pepper. With a slotted spoon, transfer the ribs to a bowl. Allow the broth to simmer and reduce another 20 minutes. Remove the spice sachet.

Serve the broth in soup bowls with the whole ribs and accompanied by Chinese Crullers, for dipping.

MISO SOUP

JAPAN

Miso soup is always on the Japanese breakfast table. It's made from fermented soybean paste (miso) and dashi, a broth made from kombu (dried kelp) and katsuobushi (dried bonito flakes). The soup is often enjoyed in the morning with such other traditional Japanese breakfast items as tamagoyaki (Rolled Omelet, page 48), a bowl of rice or TKG (Rice with Raw Eggs, page 68), yakizakana (Grilled Fish, page 348), and asazuke (Quick Pickled Vegetables, page 348).

Preparation time: 5 minutes, plus time for making dashi
Cooking time: 10 minutes
Serves: 2

· 2 cups (475 ml/16 fl oz) Dashi (recipe follows)
· 3.5 oz (100 g) firm tofu, cut into ½-inch pieces
· 2½ tablespoons white miso, plus more as needed
· 3 scallions (spring onions), chopped
· ½ sheet nori, torn into pieces

In a small saucepan, bring the dashi to a boil over medium-high heat. Reduce the heat to medium-low, bring to a simmer, and add the tofu. Dilute the white miso with 1 teaspoon of hot dashi. Add the diluted miso to the soup and stir until combined. Stir in the scallions (spring onions) and nori and simmer for 3 more minutes. Remove the soup from the heat, taste, and add more miso for a stronger flavor, if desired. Serve warm.

See image on page 256

DASHI

Preparation time: 5 minutes, plus soaking time
Cooking time: 15 minutes
Makes: 2 cups (475 ml/16 fl oz)

· 0.7 oz (20 g) kombu (dried kelp)
· 2 cups (0.8 oz/25 g) katsuobushi (dried bonito flakes)

Gently clean the kombu with a damp cloth, leaving the white crystals intact, as that is where the umami flavor comes from. Soak the kombu in 3 cups (710 ml/24 fl oz) water for at least 3 hours or overnight.

In a saucepan, combine the kombu and soaking water and bring to a simmer, then remove the kombu. Add the katsuobushi and return to a simmer, about 30 seconds. Remove from the heat and let the katsuobushi steep for 10 minutes before straining dashi through a fine-mesh sieve or cheesecloth.

LENTIL STEW WITH CRUNCHY FRIED BREAD

INDIA

Dal pakwan *is a Sindhi dish (from an area in northern India that was previously part of the Sindh province of Pakistan) made with a spicy dal (split pea or lentil), topped with chutney—tamarind or* hari *(mint/cilantro)—and served with* pakwan *(crisp puffed flatbreads). A popular variation in the United States uses deep-fried flour tortilla quarters to replace the* pakwan.

Preparation time: 20 minutes, plus 3 hours soaking time
Cooking time: 45 minutes
Serves: 2

For the dal:
· ½ cup (85 g) chana dal, soaked in water for 3 hours, then rinsed well
· 3 tablespoons canola (rapeseed) or vegetable oil
· ½ teaspoon ground turmeric
· 1 jalapeño chili, chopped
· Salt
· 1 teaspoon amchur (dried mango powder)
· ½ teaspoon ground coriander
· ¼ teaspoon ground cumin
· Chili powder
· Finely chopped onion (optional)

For the pakwan:
· ½ cup (72 g) all-purpose (plain) flour
· 3 tablespoons whole wheat (wholemeal) flour
· ⅛ teaspoon fine sea salt
· ¼ teaspoon cracked black pepper
· ¼ teaspoon cumin seeds
· 1 tablespoon vegetable oil or ghee
· Vegetable oil, for frying

Make the *dal*:
In a saucepan (see Note), combine the chana dal and 2 cups (475 ml/16 fl oz) water and bring to a simmer over medium heat. Cook, covered, until the dal has the consistency of a thick soup (almost mushy, with few grains of the dal still visible), about 30 minutes.

In a separate pan, heat the oil over medium heat and add the turmeric, jalapeño, and salt to taste. Cook until the jalapeño is softened and fully coated with turmeric, about 5 minutes. Remove from the heat.

Pour the dal into a serving dish and sprinkle with the jalapeño mixture, amchur, coriander, cumin, chili powder to taste, and, if desired, chopped onion to taste.

Make the *pakwan*:
In a bowl, combine both flours, the salt, pepper, cumin seeds, and oil or ghee. Stir in about 4 tablespoons water, until a firm dough is formed. Divide the dough into 4 equal parts. Allow them to rest for 10 minutes. With a rolling pin, roll each piece of dough into a round. Prick the *pakwan* with a fork.

In a frying pan, heat about 4 tablespoons oil over medium heat. To test if the oil is ready for frying, add a small piece of *pakwan* dough. If it sizzles, the oil is ready. Carefully lower 2 *pakwan* at a time into the oil and fry until they are crisp and golden, about 1 minute per side. With a slotted spoon, transfer the *pakwan* to paper towels to drain. Repeat with the remaining *pakwan*. Serve alongside the dal.

Note: You can also cook the dal in a pressure cooker. Use only 1 cup (240 ml/8 fl oz) water and cook at medium-high pressure for 5 minutes, then let the pressure release naturally.

CHICKPEA AND TORN BREAD STEW

TUNISIA

Leblebi, a Tunisian breakfast staple, is a stew of chickpeas and stale bread (torn and nestled in the stew), served in a glazed clay bowl. It can be customized with garnishes, such as poached eggs, capers, raw onions, cilantro, parsley, tuna, and a drizzle of olive oil.

Preparation time: 10 minutes, plus 4 hours soaking time
Cooking time: 1 hour 10 minutes
Serves: 2–4

· 1 cup (200 g) dried chickpeas (see Note), soaked for at least 4 hours and drained
· Salt and freshly ground black pepper
· 1 tablespoon olive oil
· 1 small onion, chopped
· 3 cloves garlic, minced
· 1 teaspoon ground cumin
· 1 tablespoon harissa, or to taste
· 1 tablespoon lemon juice
· 2 cups (70 g) torn stale bread
· 2 Poached Eggs (page 15)

For serving (optional):
· Capers
· Chopped onions
· Cilantro (coriander) leaves
· Parsley leaves
· Canned tuna
· Olive oil, for drizzling

Make the stew:
In a medium saucepan, combine the chickpeas and 4 cups (950 ml/32 fl oz) water and bring to a boil over high heat. Season with salt to taste, reduce to a simmer, and cook the chickpeas until tender, about 1 hour. Drain, reserving 1 tablespoon liquid, and return the chickpeas to the saucepan.

In a medium frying pan, heat the oil over medium heat. Add the onion, season with salt, and cook until soft and translucent, about 5 minutes. Stir in the garlic, sprinkle the cumin over everything, and stir to coat. Season with more salt and pepper to taste. Add the reserved chickpea cooking liquid or 1 tablespoon water and cook, scraping up any browned bits.

Transfer the onion-garlic mixture to the saucepan of chickpeas. Stir in the harissa. Remove from the heat and stir in the lemon juice.

To serve:
Place torn bread in a bowl and pour the chickpea mixture on top to soak the bread. Top with the poached eggs. If desired, serve with an assortment of capers, raw onions, cilantro, parsley, tuna, and a drizzle of olive oil.

Note: You can make this with 1½ to 2 cups (245 to 330g) canned chickpeas, liquid reserved from the can. Omit the first step. Sauté the onion/garlic mixture as directed. Place the chickpeas in a saucepan and add the onion/garlic mixture and 2 cups (475 ml/16 fl oz) water. Simmer uncovered for 15–20 minutes to reduce the water by half. Stir in the harissa. Remove from the heat and stir in the lemon juice. Using canned chickpeas will cut the prep time by 4 hours and the cook time by 50 minutes.

Chickpea and Torn Bread Stew

CHICKPEA STEW WITH PUFFED FRIED BREAD

INDIA

Common in northern India, chole bhature *is a chickpea stew (*chole*) served with a puffy fried bread (*bhature*). In the United States, store-bought refrigerated biscuit dough is an easy way to achieve the light, flaky texture of* bhature.

Preparation time: 15 minutes, plus overnight soaking time
Cooking time: 2 hours
Serves: 2

For the *chole*:
· 1 cup (200 g) dried chickpeas, soaked overnight and drained
· 1 tablespoon vegetable oil
· 1 bay leaf
· 1 cinnamon stick
· ¾ teaspoon cumin seeds
· ½ teaspoon black peppercorns
· ½ small onion, chopped
· ½ teaspoon grated fresh ginger
· ½ teaspoon chopped garlic
· 1 medium tomato, diced
· ¾ teaspoon garam masala
· ¾ teaspoon ground coriander
· ½ teaspoon cayenne pepper
· ½ teaspoon ground cumin
· Salt

For the *bhature*:
· 1 cup (125 g) all-purpose (plain) flour
· ½ tablespoon semolina flour
· ½ teaspoon sugar
· ¼ teaspoon fine sea salt
· ¼ teaspoon baking powder
· pinch baking soda
· 1 teaspoon vegetable oil, plus more for greasing
· 2 tablespoons full-fat milk
· ¼ cup (70 g) yogurt

Make the *chole*:
Cover the soaked chickpeas with water in a medium saucepan and bring to a boil over medium-high heat. Reduce to a simmer and cook until the chickpeas are tender, about 45 minutes. Drain.

In a medium saucepan, heat the oil over medium heat. Add the bay leaf, cinnamon stick, cumin seeds, and peppercorns. Once the cumin seeds begin to crackle and the spices are aromatic, stir in the onion and cook until soft and translucent, 5 minutes. Stir in the ginger, garlic, and tomato. Add the garam masala, coriander, cayenne pepper, cumin, and salt and stir until everything is combined. Stir in the chickpeas. Add 1½ cups (355 ml/12 fl oz) water. Bring to a boil, then reduce to a simmer. Cover the *chole* and simmer until the water is absorbed and the chickpeas begin to break down, about 1 hour.

Meanwhile, make the *bhature*:
In a large mixing bowl, combine the flour, semolina, sugar, salt, and baking soda. Add the oil, yogurt, and milk and stir until a shaggy dough forms. Turn out onto a lightly floured work surface and knead the dough until smooth, about 10 minutes. Place the dough in a lightly oiled bowl, cover with plastic wrap (cling film), and let rest, 1 hour.

Turn the dough out and cut into 4 pieces. Roll each into a ball and let rest for 5 minutes. In a wok or deep frying pan, heat at least 4 inches (10 cm) of vegetable oil over medium heat.

Roll each ball of dough into a circle, 6 inches (15 cm) in diameter. Gently place the dough in the hot oil and use a ladle to press down on the dough, submerging it until it starts to puff up. Fry both sides until golden brown, about 45 seconds per side. Transfer to a paper towel to drain. Continue with the other dough rounds. Serve with *chole*.

SOUPS AND STEWS

KIDNEY BEAN STEW

YEMEN

Fasolia, Yemeni version of bean stew made with kidney beans and tomato paste, is found with variances around the Middle East. In Yemen this dish is made at home or found in markets, where it is sold alongside tea and bread.

Preparation time: 10 minutes
Cooking time: 35 minutes
Serves: 2–4

· 1 (15 oz/425 g) can kidney beans
· 1 tablespoon olive oil
· 1 small yellow onion, diced
· 1 clove garlic, finely minced
· ½ teaspoon cayenne pepper
· ¼ teaspoon ground cumin
· Salt and freshly ground black pepper
· ½ medium tomato, chopped
· 3 tablespoons tomato paste (purée)
· Cilantro (coriander) or parsley leaves, for serving

Drain the can of beans, reserving the liquid from the can. In a medium saucepan, heat the oil over medium heat. Stir in the onion and cook until soft and translucent, about 5 minutes. Add the garlic, cayenne, cumin, and salt and pepper to taste and toss to coat. Stir in the chopped tomato, tomato paste (purée), and 3 tablespoons of the reserved canned bean liquid. Bring to a simmer, then add the beans and 1 cup (240 ml/8 fl oz) water. Reduce the heat to low and simmer, stirring occasionally, until thickened, 20–25 minutes. Serve warm topped with cilantro (coriander) or parsley leaves.

MOROCCAN FAVA
BEAN STEW

MOROCCO

B'ssara is a hearty fava (broad) bean stew, commonly enjoyed in Northern Morocco. Spiked with cumin and rich with olive oil, this dish is often served with fresh khubz (Moroccan white bread).

Preparation time: 15 minutes, plus up to 8 hours soaking time
Cooking time: 1 hour 15 minutes
Serves: 2–4

· 1 tablespoon olive oil, plus more for drizzling
· 2 cups (340 g) dried fava (broad) beans, soaked for 4–8 hours, drained, and rinsed
· 3 cloves garlic, peeled
· Salt and freshly ground pepper
· Ground cumin and paprika, for serving

In a large saucepan, heat the oil over medium heat. Add the fava (broad) beans and garlic and cook, stirring constantly, until aromatic, about 5 minutes. Season with ½ teaspoon salt and pepper to taste. Add 3 cups (710 ml/24 fl oz) water and bring to a boil. Reduce the heat to medium, cover, and simmer until the beans are soft, about 1 hour. Working in batches if necessary, transfer the bean mixture to a blender. Puree the soup until smooth and season to taste with salt and pepper. Serve warm, sprinkled with cumin and paprika and a drizzle of olive oil.

EGYPTIAN FAVA BEAN STEW

EGYPT

Ful medames, "ful" or "foul" for short, is a stewed fava (broad) bean dish that originated in Egypt but is enjoyed all over the Middle East. It is often prepared in a large-batch cauldron called a qedra and served with a variety of toppings and sides, such as tahini, tomatoes, eggs, feta cheese, pickles, raw onions, baladi (Egyptian flatbread), and fresh parsley.

Preparation time: 10 minutes, plus overnight soaking time
Cooking time: 1 hour 50 minutes
Serves: 2

For the stew:
· 1 cup (340 g) dried fava (broad) beans, soaked for 4–8 hours, drained, and rinsed
· 2 tablespoons olive oil
· 3 cloves garlic, minced
· 1 teaspoon ground cumin
· ½ teaspoon crushed chili flakes
· 2 tablespoons lemon juice
· Salt and freshly ground pepper

For serving (optional)
· Tahini
· Chopped tomatoes
· Hard-boiled egg halves
· Feta cheese, cut into cubes
· Sliced pickles
· Thinly sliced onions
· Baladi (Egyptian flatbread)
· Chopped fresh parsley

Transfer the drained beans to a medium saucepan and add fresh water to cover the beans by about 2 inches (5 cm). Bring to a boil over medium-high heat, reduce the heat to low, and cook, covered, until the beans are very soft, about 1 hour 30 minutes. With a slotted spoon, transfer the cooked beans to a bowl and reserve the cooking liquid.

In a frying pan, heat the oil over medium heat. Stir in the garlic and cook until fragrant, about 2 minutes. Add the beans, cumin, and chili flakes, stirring to incorporate all the ingredients. Stir in the reserved bean cooking liquid and bring to a boil, cooking until the water has reduced by half, about 10 minutes.

Transfer the beans to a bowl and mash with the back of a fork until a chunky consistency is achieved. Stir in the lemon juice and season with salt and black pepper. Serve in bowls and top with tahini, chopped tomatoes, eggs, feta cheese, pickles, raw onions, *baladi*, and fresh parsley.

See image page 63.

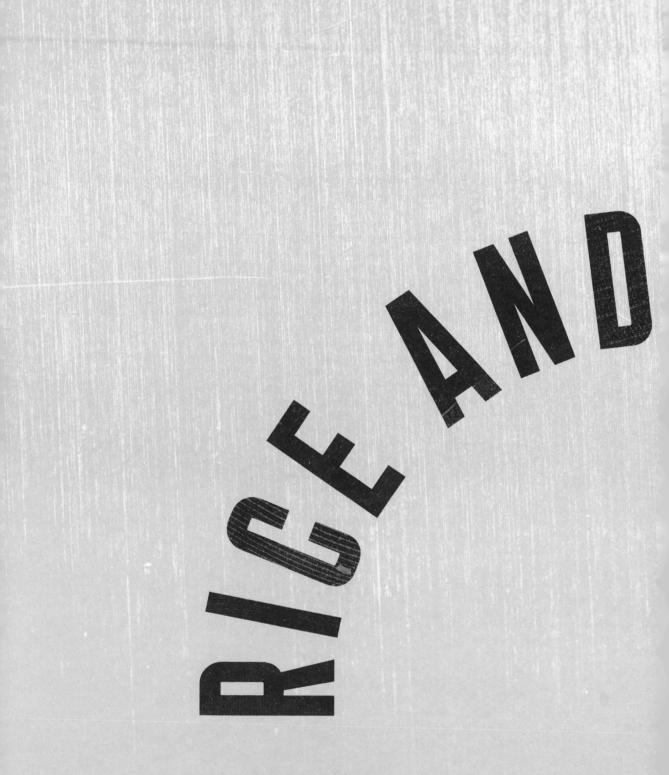

FRIED RICE WITH BANCHAN

SOUTH KOREA

Breakfast in South Korea is a parade of ingredients that have been repurposed from the night before, all served in bowls. Alongside soup such as Haejang-guk *(Hangover Soup, page 245), you'll find day-old rice crisped in a pan and cooked with eggs and leftover protein. No Korean meal is complete without* banchan, *side dishes such as Cabbage Kimchi and Spiced Cucumber.*

Preparation time: 30 minutes, plus soaking and fermenting time for the Cabbage Kimchi
Cooking time: 15 minutes
Serves: 2

· 2 teaspoons vegetable oil, plus more as needed
· ½ small onion, diced
· ½ cup (65 g) cubed carrots and/or peas, fresh or frozen
· 1 cup (160 g) day-old cooked white rice
· ¼ cup (70 g) leftover cooked protein (chicken, shrimp, beef, or pork)
· 1 egg
· 1 tablespoon soy sauce

For serving:
· 1 scallion (spring onion), green tops only, chopped
· Cabbage Kimchi (recipe follows)
· Spiced Cucumber (recipe follows)

In a medium skillet, heat the oil over medium heat. Add the onion and vegetables and sauté until the onion is translucent and the vegetables have softened, about 5 minutes. Stir in the rice and fry, tossing, for 1 minute. Stir in the protein and cook for 1 minute more. Push the rice to the side of the skillet, add more oil if needed, and crack the egg into the skillet. Break the yolk of the egg and stir to scramble, about 30 seconds. Stir into the rice. Stir in the soy sauce to combine. Taste and add more if needed.

To serve:
Serve fried rice in bowls and garnish with scallion greens. Serve *baechu kimchi* and *oi muchim* in small bowls on the side.

CABBAGE KIMCHI (BAECHU KIMCHI)

Preparation time: 20 minutes, plus 2 hours and 20 minutes soaking time and 2 days fermenting time
Makes: 2 cups (150 g)

·½ head napa cabbage (Chinese leaf), about 1 lb (455 g), stem trimmed, halved lengthwise, soaked in water for 20 minutes
· 4 tablespoons salt
· 1 tablespoon glutinous rice flour
· ½ tablespoon sugar
· 4 cloves garlic, smashed
· 1-inch piece fresh ginger, peeled and minced
· 1½ tablespoons fish sauce
· 4 tablespoons gochugaru (ground Korean red pepper)
· ¼ Korean radish, peeled and julienned
· 2 scallions (spring onions), chopped
· ½ large carrot, julienned

Drain the water from the napa cabbage (Chinese leaf) and rub the salt between all of the leaves, working from the outside in. Place the cabbage back into the bowl and let sit for 2 hours, gently turning every 30 minutes. The salt will extract water from the cabbage, while turning will help keep the mixture evenly salted.

In a saucepan over medium heat, combined 1 cup (230 ml/8 fl oz) water and the rice flour. Stirring occasionally, let the mixture simmer and thicken for about 5 minutes before adding the sugar. Stir to incorporate and remove from heat.

In a mortar and pestle (or in a food processor), combine the garlic, ginger, and fish sauce. Using the pestle, work the ingredients into a paste (or pulse in the food processor until finely chopped).

Transfer the garlic/ginger mixture to a bowl with the rice flour mixture. Add the gochugaru, radish, scallions (spring onions), and carrot and mix well with a wooden spoon. Take care if you use your hands for mixing; they might sting from the gochugaru.

Drain the cabbage and rinse under cold water. The cabbage should be pliable. Squeeze out any residual water from the leaves. Spread the vegetable paste between and around the leaves, working from the outside in. Fold the leaf (filled with the vegetable paste) in thirds from the stem to the tip and tuck neatly into an *onggi* (Korean earthenware pot) or a plastic container. Continue with the other quarters of the cabbage and let the container sit, covered, for 2 days at room temperature. Once the cabbage is fermented, it should produce bubbles and liquid when pushing down on it. Store the kimchi in the refrigerator, tightly covered, for up to 1 year.

SPICED CUCUMBER (OI MUCHIM)

Preparation time: 15 minutes
Makes: 1 cup (150 g)

· 1 English cucumber, chopped
· 1 clove garlic, minced
· 1 scallion (spring onion), chopped
· 1 tablespoon gochugaru (ground Korean red pepper)
· 1 tablespoon soy sauce
· 2 teaspoons toasted sesame oil
· 1 teaspoon sesame seeds

In a bowl, combine the cucumber, garlic, scallion (spring onion), gochugaru, soy sauce, sesame oil, and sesame seeds. Toss together until thoroughly combined.

SUGARED RICE
UNITED STATES

Common in the American South, this quick breakfast combines leftover rice, sugar, and butter. Using rice from the night before is a practical solution for leftovers, and a quick filling breakfast without having to cook rice from scratch.

Preparation time: 5 minutes
Cooking time: 10 minutes
Serves: 1

· 1 cup (150 g) leftover cooked rice
· ½ tablespoon salted butter or margarine
· 2 teaspoons sugar

Scrape the rice into a pan with a splash of water to avoid sticking. Cook over medium-high heat until warmed through, about 5 minutes. Stir in the butter until melted, then stir in the sugar. Serve warm.

PEANUT STICKY RICE
VIETNAM

Xôi is a bowl of sticky rice. Xôi đâu phộng is rice cooked with peanuts and topped with a sugar, sesame, and peanut mixture. There are many different toppings, depending on the region, including pâté (ground cooked meat that is mashed into a spreadable paste or formed into a log and sliced), pork floss (dried, shredded pork with the consistency of cotton candy), egg, corn, sliced chả lụa (a meat roll made of pork that has been pounded into a paste, then wrapped in a banana leaf and boiled).

Preparation time: 5 minutes, plus overnight soaking time
Cooking time: 50 minutes
Serves: 2

For the rice:
· 1 cup (185 g) glutinous (sticky) rice
· ½ cup (75 g) raw shelled peanuts, skins on
· Salt
· ½ cup (120 ml/4 fl oz) coconut milk

For the peanut topping:
· 2 tablespoons roasted peanuts
· 2 tablespoons toasted white sesame seeds
· ½ teaspoon sugar

Put the sticky rice in one bowl and the peanuts in a second bowl. Cover both with water and soak overnight.

Drain the water from the peanuts, transfer to a small saucepan, and cover with 2 inches (5 cm) fresh water and a sprinkling of salt. Bring the peanuts to a boil, reduce the heat to low and simmer, covered, until soft, about 40 minutes.

Meanwhile, drain the water from the rice. Stir the drained rice, ½ teaspoon salt, and the coconut milk into the simmering peanuts. Let the rice and peanuts cook, covered until the rice is soft and has soaked up the water and coconut milk, about 15 minutes.

Make the peanut topping: Pulse the roasted peanuts, sesame seeds, and sugar in a food processor. Serve the rice warm, topped with the peanut-sesame mixture.

SPROUTED PEAS WITH RICE AND FRIED ONIONS

MYANMAR

Pe pyot is a dish made with whole dried yellow peas (vatana), *often available at Indian food stores. They are sprouted and cooked with rice, topped with crispy onions, and served with naan or paratha, also called* Roti Prata *(page 207).*

Preparation time: 10 minutes, plus overnight soaking and sprouting time
Cooking time: 1 hour 15 minutes
Serves: 4

For the sprouted peas:
· 1 cup (145 g) dried whole yellow peas, soaked overnight
· ½ teaspoon fine sea salt, plus more to taste
· ¼ teaspoon baking soda (bicarbonate of soda)
· Freshly ground pepper

For the onions and rice:
· 3 tablespoons vegetable oil
· 1 small onion, halved and thinly sliced
· 4 cloves garlic, chopped
· 1 teaspoon ground turmeric
· 1 cup (135 g) cooked basmati rice
· Salt

Drain the soaked yellow peas and transfer to a large shallow bowl. Cover with a damp tea towel and allow the peas to sit for 36 hours. Rewet the towel as needed to keep a damp environment, until the peas begin to sprout.

Place the sprouted peas in a medium saucepan and cover with 3 cups (710 ml/24 fl oz) water. Stir in the salt and baking soda and bring the peas to a boil over high heat, then reduce the heat to low. Cover and cook, stirring occasionally, until the water is absorbed and the peas are tender, about 1 hour. Season with salt and pepper to taste.

Meanwhile, fry the onions. In a frying pan, heat the oil over medium-high heat. Working in batches, add the onion slices in a single layer, taking care not to crowd the pan. Fry until crispy and golden brown, about 20 seconds. Transfer to paper towels to drain and sprinkle with salt, to taste.

Drain almost all the oil from the pan, leaving enough to just coat the bottom. Lower the heat to medium and add the garlic. Cook, stirring constantly, until golden brown, 1 minute. Stir in the cooked peas and the turmeric until well coated. Stir in the rice. Let it all cook together for about 2 minutes, or until incorporated. Season to taste with salt.

Serve in bowls topped with the fried onion.

RICE WITH NATTO

JAPAN

Natto *is made of soybeans that have been fermented and broken down, taking on a slippery, glue-like texture. Found in Japanese markets in quick ready-to-eat packets,* natto *is classically served atop rice with a sprinkling of scallions. It can also be seasoned and topped with: a raw egg yolk, soy sauce,* katsuobushi *(dried bonito flakes), chopped scallions,* karashi *(spicy mustard),* kizami nori *(sliced dried and seasoned seaweed), herbs (*mitsuba *and* shiso*), and* gari *(pickled ginger).*

Preparation time: 5 minutes
Cooking time: 30 minutes
Serves: 2

· 1 cup (200 g) short-grain white rice, rinsed until water runs clear
· 3 oz (85g) natto (fermented soybeans) (about 2 packets)
· 1 scallion (spring onion), finely chopped
· Soy sauce

In a saucepan, combine the rice and 1¼ cups (295 ml/10 fl oz) water and bring to a boil. Reduce the heat to low, cover, and simmer until all the water is absorbed and the rice is tender, about 15 minutes. Remove from the heat, cover, and let the rice steam for 10 minutes, then fluff with a fork.

Divide the rice between 2 bowls. Top with natto and scallion and season with soy sauce to taste.

Rice with Natto

KEDGEREE

UNITED KINGDOM

Loosely inspired by the Indian dish khichri *(a dish of rice and dal), kedgeree has the addition of flaked smoked haddock and spices like curry powder (a British interpretation of Indian spices) to create a dish distinct to the United Kingdom. Popularized as a breakfast dish during the Victorian era, it is still commonly enjoyed today.*

Preparation time: 10 minutes
Cooking time: 30 minutes
Serves: 2–4

· 1 cup (200 g) long-grain white rice, such as basmati, rinsed until water runs clear
· 1 lb (455 g) smoked haddock, deboned
· ¾ cup (175 ml/6 fl oz) full-fat milk
· 2 bay leaves
· 1 teaspoon coriander seeds
· 1½ tablespoons (25 g) butter
· 1 medium onion, diced
· 1 clove garlic, minced
· 2 tablespoons curry powder
· 2 teaspoons ground turmeric
· Lemon juice
· Salt and freshly ground pepper
· 2 Hard-Boiled Eggs (page 14), peeled and halved
· Parsley leaves, for serving

In a medium saucepan, combine the rice and 2 cups (475 ml/16 fl oz) water and bring to a boil over medium-high heat. Cover, reduce the heat to low, and simmer until the grains are tender and water is absorbed, 15 minutes. Remove from the heat, fluff with a wooden spoon, and set aside. Leave covered for 10 minutes to steam, then fluff with a fork.

Meanwhile, in a separate saucepan, combine the haddock, milk, bay leaves, and coriander seeds. Bring to a simmer over medium heat and cook until the haddock is tender, about 7 minutes. Drain and discard the liquid. Transfer the haddock to a plate and flake with your hands or a fork.

In a frying pan, melt the butter over medium heat. Add the onion and garlic and cook until the onion is soft and translucent, about 5 minutes. Add the curry powder and turmeric and stir to combine with a wooden spoon. Cook and stir until the mixture is evenly coated with spices, 3 minutes. Reduce the heat to low. Add the rice to the curried vegetables and stir until combined. Remove from the heat and stir in the flaked fish. Stir in lemon juice, salt, and pepper to taste. Serve warm with halved hard-boiled eggs and parsley leaves.

RICE AND BEANS
COSTA RICA / NICARAGUA

Gallo pinto *is simply rice and beans fried together and often served with a side of eggs, fried plantains, avocado, and tortillas. In Costa Rica, this dish is made with black beans and topped with Salsa Lizano (the brand of a brown sauce condiment), while in Nicaragua, red beans are used.*

Preparation time: 10 minutes
Cooking time: 20 minutes
Serves: 2

- ½ cup (100 g) white rice
- ¾ cup (175 ml/6 fl oz) chicken stock
- 1 tablespoon vegetable oil
- ½ onion, diced
- ½ red bell pepper, diced
- 1 cup (175 g) canned black beans or red beans, bean liquid reserved
- 4 sprigs cilantro (coriander), chopped
- Salt and freshly ground pepper

For serving (optional):
- 4 eggs, fried (page 14) or scrambled (page 15)
- 1 plantain, sliced and pan-fried in oil until soft
- ½ avocado, pitted, peeled, and sliced
- 4 tortillas

In a medium saucepan, combine the rice and stock and bring to a boil over medium-high heat. Cover, reduce the heat to low, and simmer until the rice is fluffy and the liquid absorbed, 15 minutes. Leave covered for 10 minutes to steam, then fluff with a fork.

Meanwhile, in a medium frying pan, heat the oil over medium heat. Add the onion and bell pepper and cook, stirring occasionally, until the onion is soft and translucent and the pepper is soft, about 5 minutes. Stir in the beans and 2 tablespoons of the bean liquid. Simmer the mixture, stirring occasionally, until the rice has absorbed the liquid, about 2 minutes.

Fold the chopped cilantro (coriander) into the rice, then add to the beans and vegetables. Season with salt and pepper to taste. If desired, serve with eggs, fried plantains, avocado, and tortillas.

RICE WITH FRIED ANCHOVIES AND PEANUTS

MALAYSIA

Traditionally wrapped up in a banana leaf as a portable meal, nasi lemak *consists of a mound of fragrant rice cooked with coconut cream and pandan leaves, topped with fried anchovies, peanuts, sliced cucumber, a Boiled or Fried Egg (page 14), a slightly sweet spicy sauce called* sambal, *and sometimes chicken wings or other proteins.*

Preparation time: 1 hour 10 minutes
Cooking time: 30 minutes
Serves: 2

For the sambal:
· 3 dried red chilies
· 7 fresh red chilies, such as serranos or Thai chilis, seeded and chopped
· 4 shallots, cut into chunks
· 2 cloves garlic, peeled
· 5 tablespoons peanut (groundnut) oil
· 1 teaspoon anchovy paste
· 2 teaspoons sugar
· ½ small red onion, chopped
· Salt

For the rice:
· ½ cup (120 ml/4 fl oz) coconut cream
· 1 cup (200 g) basmati rice, rinsed, until the water runs clear
· 2 pandan leaves, knotted
· Salt

For topping:
· 3 tablespoons canola (rapeseed), peanut (groundnut), or vegetable oil
· 4 tablespoons raw shelled peanuts
· 1 cup (145 g) white anchovies (packed in water or oil), drained and patted dry
· 1 cucumber, sliced
· 1 Boiled or Fried Egg (page 14)

Make the sambal:
Soak the dried chilies in warm water until softened, 20 minutes. Drain, then remove stems. Remove the seeds for milder heat. Transfer to a food processor with the fresh chilis and blend to a paste. Set aside.

Clean the processor. Add the shallots and garlic and pulse until chopped, adding a touch of water to get the consistency of a paste.

In a wok or frying pan, heat the oil over low heat. Add the garlic/shallot mixture and anchovy paste. Sauté until the shallots are softened, about 3 minutes. Stir in the chili paste and cook for 5 minutes until the chilies are aromatic and the oil begins to separate. Stir in the sugar and onion, season to taste with salt, and cook for another 5 minutes, until the sugar is dissolved and the onion is soft and translucent. Remove the sambal from the heat and set aside.

Make the rice:
Stir the coconut cream into 1 cup (240 ml/8 fl oz) water in a medium saucepan. Add the rice and pandan leaves. Bring the mixture to a boil over medium-high heat. Stir, reduce the heat to low, cover, and simmer until the water is absorbed and the rice is tender, 15 minutes. Leave covered for 10 minutes to steam, then fluff with a fork, remove the pandan leaves, and stir in salt to taste. Keep warm.

Prepare the toppings:
In a frying pan, heat the oil over medium heat. Add the peanuts and fry until they're browned, about 3 minutes. Using a slotted spoon, transfer the peanuts to paper towels to drain. Stir in the anchovies and fry until they're golden, about 5 minutes. Using a slotted spoon, transfer the fried anchovies to paper towels to drain.

Lay a banana leaf on each plate. Dollop 1 cup (135 g) coconut rice onto the banana leaf. Top with fried anchovies and peanuts. Serve with the sambal, cucumber, and a hard-boiled or fried egg.

Rice with Fried Anchovies and Peanuts

RICE AND BEANS WITH TOMATO SAUCE
COLOMBIA

The most ideal use of leftovers comes in the form of Colombian calentao. A mix of day-old rice, beans, and any protein available is combined with an aromatic tomato sauce (hogao, a common topping for Arepas, pages 314–16, and Tamales, page 312). The calentao is then topped with a fried egg and served with an Arepa on the side.

Preparation time: 20 minutes
Cooking time: 40 minutes
Serves: 2

For the hogao:
· 2 tablespoons vegetable oil
· 3 scallions (spring onions), chopped
· 2 cloves garlic, minced
· ¼ small white or red onion, chopped
· 1 small tomato, chopped
· Salt and freshly ground pepper

For the calentao:
· 2 tablespoons vegetable oil
· ½ cup (80 g) day-old rice
· Salt and freshly ground pepper
· 1 cup (240 ml/8 fl oz) any combination of the following (ideally leftovers): cooked pinto beans, pasta, stewed pork, stewed vegetables, pulled chicken, chicharrón, sweet plantains, chorizo

For serving:
· 2 Fried Eggs (optional, page 15)
· 2 Arepas (page 314–16)

Make the *hogao*:
In a small saucepan, heat the oil over medium heat. Stir in the scallions (spring onions), garlic, and onion. Cook the onion until soft and translucent. Add the tomato and season with salt and pepper to taste. Stir and cook until the sauce is thickened, 10 minutes. Set aside.

Make the *calentao*:
In a small saucepan, heat the oil over medium heat. Add the rice and cook, stirring occasionally, until heated through and crispy, about 5 minutes. Season with salt and pepper to taste. Add the *hogao* and leftovers and stir to combine.

To serve:
Top with a fried egg, if desired, and serve with an arepa.

INSTANT NOODLES WITH FRIED EGG

NIGERIA

This dish consists of instant noodles, typically the popular Indomie brand, with fried eggs. It is served at mai shai *stalls, which also serve tea and other breakfast dishes like Nigerian Fried Eggs (page 31).*

Preparation time: 10 minutes
Cooking time: 20 minutes
Serves: 1

· 1 (3 oz/85 g) package Indomie instant noodles
· 2 teaspoons vegetable oil
· ¼ small red onion, diced
· ¼ red bell pepper, chopped
· 2 eggs
· Maggi liquid seasoning

Reserving the flavor packet, place the noodles in a heatproof bowl. Pour boiling water over the noodles and keep submerged until the noodles turn soft, 4 minutes. Drain the water and rinse the noodles under cold water to stop them from cooking any further.

In a small frying pan, heat the vegetable oil over medium heat. Add the red onion and bell pepper and cook until the vegetables are soft and the onion translucent, about 5 minutes. In a bowl, lightly beat the eggs. Pour into the pan and stir constantly until curds begin to form, about 30 seconds. Season with Maggi to taste. Add the noodles and contents of the flavor packet to the pan and toss together to combine. Cook the noodles until evenly coated, about 2 minutes more. Serve warm.

HAITIAN SPAGHETTI

HAITI

Italian-American pastas were introduced to Haiti by American troops, who influenced the culinary landscape with processed foods. This spaghetti dish is tossed with tomato paste (purée), garlic, onion, spices, and pork sausage or hot dog slices, then topped with Famosa (a brand of sweet ketchup from Haiti) and a pungent grated tête de maure *(French)/* tet de mò *(Creole) (can be substituted with Swiss cheese, aged Comté or Chällerhocker).*

Preparation time: 10 minutes
Cooking time: 20 minutes
Serves: 2–4

· 1 lb (455 g) spaghetti
· 2 tablespoons olive oil
· 2 spicy pork sausages or hot dogs, sliced into disks
· 1 clove garlic, minced
· ¼ white onion, diced
· 2 tablespoons tomato paste (purée)
· 2 sprigs thyme, leaves only
· 1 cube chicken bouillon (stock)
· Salt and freshly ground pepper
· Grated tête de maure or other pungent cheese
· Famosa (sweet ketchup) or regular ketchup

Bring a large pot of salted water to a boil over high heat. Cook the pasta according to package instructions. Reserve 2 tablespoons pasta water and drain.

Meanwhile, in a large frying pan, heat 1 tablespoon of the oil over medium heat. Add the sausages or hot dogs and cook until browned on both sides, about 6 minutes. Add the remaining 1 tablespoon oil and stir in the garlic, onion, tomato paste (purée), thyme, and bouillon (stock) cube. Cook, stirring often, until the onion is soft and translucent, about 5 minutes.

Add the cooked spaghetti to the frying pan along with the reserved pasta water. Toss to thoroughly coat the spaghetti in the sauce. Cook until the water has evaporated and the sauce is thick, about 3 minutes. Serve topped with the grated cheese and ketchup.

Haitian Spaghetti

STEAMED RICE ROLLS WITH PORK
VIETNAM

Bánh cuốn *are steamed rice flour rolls filled with seasoned ground pork, mushroom, and garlic. They are typically served with* Nước chấm, *a special dipping sauce made with fish sauce and lime.*

Preparation time: 15 minutes
Cooking time: 30 minutes
Serves: 2–4

For the batter:
· 1 cup (160 g) rice flour
· ¾ cup (90 g) tapioca flour
· ¼ teaspoon fine sea salt

For the filling:
· 1 tablespoon vegetable oil, plus more for greasing
· 1 shallot, sliced
· ½ cup (13 g) dried wood ear mushrooms, soaked in cold water for 30 minutes, drained, and chopped
· 1 clove garlic, minced
· ½ lb (225 g) ground (minced) pork
· 1 teaspoon fish sauce, plus more to taste
· Salt and freshly ground pepper

Make the batter:
In a bowl, mix together the rice flour, tapioca flour, and salt. Stir in 2 cups (475 ml/16 fl oz) water and mix until the batter is thoroughly combined and smooth.

Make the filling:
In a medium frying pan, heat the oil over medium heat. Add the shallot and wood ears and cook, stirring, until the shallot is soft, about 3 minutes. Mix the minced garlic and fish sauce into the pork and add it to the pan with the shallot. Season the meat with the fish sauce and salt and pepper to taste. Cook, stirring and breaking up the pork with a wooden spoon until the pork is browned, about 6 minutes. Transfer the filling to a bowl.

Set a medium nonstick frying pan over medium heat. Generously coat with oil and ladle in ¼ cup (60 ml) of the batter, swirling it around to coat evenly, about 1/8 inch (3 mm) thick. Cover with a lid and let the pancake cook for 1 minute. Carefully flip the pancake onto the plate. Fill the pancake with 2 tablespoons of the filling down the center and roll up the noodle. Continue with the rest of the batter and filling.

NƯỚC CHẤM

Preparation time: 10 minutes
Makes: ¼ cup (60 ml/2 fl oz)

· 1 tablespoon sugar
· 1 tablespoon fish sauce
· 2 teaspoons lime juice
· 1 clove garlic, finely chopped
· 2 fresh red chilies, finely chopped

In a small bowl, stir together the sugar, fish sauce, and 5 tablespoons water until the sugar is dissolved. Add the garlic, chilies, and lime juice.

STEAMED RICE ROLLS

CHINA

Cheong fun *(in Cantonese) are paper-thin rolls made of steamed rice flour, often filled with shrimp (prawns) or meat, and topped with soy sauce, scallions (spring onions), fried shallots, sesame seeds, and/or chili oil. They are made on special rectangular steam pans with vented holes perforated throughout. A steam-permeable cloth placed on top of the pan allows the steam to rise through and cook the rice batter. To achieve this at home, the recipes provides instructions for a double-boiler set-up. It won't have the traditional rectangular shape, but the concept is the same.*

Preparation time: 10 minutes
Cooking time: 10 minutes
Serves: 2

For the noodle roll:
· ½ cup (80 g) rice flour
· 1 teaspoon cornstarch (cornflour)
· ½ teaspoon tapioca flour
· ¼ teaspoon salt
· 1½ teaspoons vegetable oil, plus more for greasing
· 2 scallions (spring onions), finely chopped

For the sauce:
· 4 tablespoons soy sauce
· 2 teaspoons toasted sesame oil
· 1 tablespoon sugar

In a bowl, whisk together the rice flour, cornstarch (cornflour), tapioca flour, salt, oil, and 1½ cups (350 ml/12 fl oz) water until smooth. It should have the consistency of milk.

Set up a double boiler with an 8-inch (20 cm) round cake pan. Fill a large pot with 2 inches of water and bring to a simmer. Place a colander or vented steamer base in the pot. Generously grease the pan with oil. Stir the batter and pour half into the parn, swirling the pan to coat in an even layer as thin as possible, about 1/8 inch (3 mm) thick. Place on top of the steamer. Cover and steam for 2 minutes. Sprinkle half the scallions over the noodle sheet. Cover and steam for 2 minutes more. Repeat with the remaining batter and scallions to make a second sheet.

Remove the pan from the double boiler and let cool slightly. Roll into a log, remove from the pan and set aside. Take the tea towel from the steamer onto a flat work surface. Carefully peel off the towel while rolling into a log.

Repeat with the remaining batter and scallions, stirring the batter before pouring.

Meanwhile, make the sauce: In a small bowl, whisk together the soy sauce, sesame oil, and sugar until sugar is dissolved.

Cut each of the rolled noodles crosswise into 4 slices. Pour the sauce over the rice rolls and serve.

STUFFED RICE ROLLS WITH CHINESE CRULLER

TAIWAN

Fan tuan *are rice rolls are made by wrapping cooked rice around any number of ingredients including:* youtiao *(Chinese Cruller, page 306), egg, pickled vegetables, and pork or fish floss—dried shredded pork or fish with the consistency of cotton candy (candy floss). You can find pickled mustard greens in most Asian grocery stores. This dish is typically enjoyed with a glass of Soy Milk (page 440).*

Preparation time: 1 hour, plus 2 hours soaking time for the rice and resting, tempering, and chilling time for the Chinese Cruller
Cooking time: 5 minutes
Serves: 1

· 1 cup (185 g) glutinous (sticky) rice, rinsed until water runs clear and soaked for 2 hours
· 2 teaspoons vegetable oil
· 1 egg
· Salt and freshly ground pepper
· 1 tablespoon pickled mustard greens
· 1 teaspoon toasted sesame oil
· 3 tablespoons pork or fish floss
· 1 tablespoon chopped salted dried radish, soaked for 10 minutes to reduce saltiness and drained
· ½ tablespoon chopped scallion
· 1 Chinese Cruller (page 306)

Line the basket of a steamer or steamer insert with parchment paper. Spread the rice out evenly over the paper. In the steamer, bring 2 inches (5 cm) water to a boil. Steam the rice until tender, about 30 minutes. (Alternatively, use a rice cooker.)

Meanwhile, in a small bowl, lightly beat the egg. In a small frying pan, heat 1 teaspoon vegetable oil over low heat. Add the egg and season with salt and pepper. Let the egg set and brown slightly, about 2 minutes, flipping halfway through. Roll in the pan and remove from the heat. In the same pan, heat 1 teaspoon oil. Add the pickled mustard greens and cook for 3 minutes, until warmed through.

Lay a tea towel or napkin on the counter. Place plastic wrap (cling film) on top of the towel and brush with the sesame oil. Spread the warmed rice out into a rectangle in the center of the plastic wrap, long side closest to you. It should be just under ½ inch (2.5 cm) thick. If the rice is too cold, it will be difficult to roll. About 1 inch (2.5 cm) from the edge closest to you, add the rolled egg, pork or fish floss, salted radish, cilantro (coriander) or scallion, Chinese Cruller, and mustard greens. Lifting the plastic wrap at the edge closest to you, roll the rice over the filling to form a log, moving the plastic wrap out of the way. Squeeze gently to firm up the roll and discard the plastic wrap. Slice roll in half crosswise and serve.

Steamed Rice Rolls with Pork

AND FRIED

FALAFEL

EGYPT

Ta'meya *(falafel) are a mixture of crushed fava (broad) beans and spices, formed into balls and fried to a crisp, golden brown. Falafel are typically enjoyed with* baladi *(Egyptian flatbread), a drizzle of tahini, and a salad of fresh herbs.*

Preparation time: 20 minutes, plus overnight soaking time
Cooking time: 20 minutes
Serves 4–6, makes about 16 falafels

· ¾ cup (120 g) dried split fava (broad) beans, soaked overnight
· 4 cloves garlic, peeled
·½ medium yellow onion, quartered
·½ cup (10 g) cilantro (coriander) leaves
·½ cup (10 g) parsley leaves
· 2 tablespoons chopped fresh dill
· 1 teaspoon fine sea salt
· ¼ teaspoon chili powder
· ¼ teaspoon ground cumin
· ½ teaspoon cracked black pepper
·½ teaspoon baking soda (bicarbonate of soda)
· 1 egg
· Sesame seeds (optional)
· Vegetable oil, for deep-frying

Drain the beans and transfer to a food processor. Add the garlic and onion and pulse. Add the cilantro (coriander), parsley, and dill. Pulse until the mixture forms in a paste. Transfer to a bowl. Fold in the salt, chili powder, cumin, and pepper until thoroughly incorporated. (The mixture can be stored in freezer bags for up to 1 month.)

Line a baking sheet with parchment paper. Mix the baking soda (bicarbonate of soda) and egg into the bean paste with a wooden spoon or spatula until thoroughly combined. With your hands, scoop about 2 tablespoons of the mixture. Gently squeeze and flatten into a small puck, about 2 inches (5 cm) in diameter. Sprinkle with sesame seeds (if using) and place on the lined baking sheet. Repeat until all of the mixture is used.

Pour 2 inches (5 cm) oil into a wide, deep heavy-bottomed pan and heat over medium-high heat. Working in batches, fry the falafel on each side until browned, 3 minutes. Remove the falafel from the oil with a slotted spoon and drain well on a plate lined with paper towels. Serve warm.

BLACK-EYED PEA FRITTERS

NIGERIA

Akara *are black-eyed pea (black-eyed bean) fritters that accompany Nigerian Pap or South African Slap Pap (page 92), a fermented porridge. Black-eyes peas are soaked, meticulously peeled, then blended to create a smooth batter with an airy texture when fried.*

Preparation time: 35 minutes, plus 8 hours soaking time
Cooking time: 20 minutes
Serves 4, makes about 16 fritters

· ¾ cup (125 g) dried peeled black-eyed peas (beans), soaked for at least 8 hours
· ½ small onion, diced
· 1 habanero chili or other small chili, diced
· ¼ teaspoon sweet paprika
· Vegetable oil, for shallow-frying
· Salt and freshly ground pepper

Soak the peas (beans). Using your hands, rub the beans together to loosen their coats (skins). Skim the coats and continue the process until all the peas are skinned, about 20 minutes. Transfer to a food processor. Add the onion, chili, and paprika and puree. Set aside.

Pour 2 inches (5 cm) oil into a wide, deep heavy-bottomed pan and heat over medium heat. Check if the oil is ready by carefully adding a piece of pea mixture. If it sizzles, the oil is ready. Season to taste with salt and pepper. Spoon 1 heaping tablespoon of batter into the hot oil, fitting 4 in at a time. Fry, turning once, until golden brown on both sides, 3 minutes per side. Remove from the oil with a slotted spoon and drain well on a plate lined with paper towels. Serve hot.

SPICED FRITTERS

NEPAL

Called Gwaramari, *which translates to "round bread," these spiced, fried fritters are a popular breakfast in Kathmandu, typically enjoyed with milky tea or coffee.*

Preparation time: 10 minutes, plus up to overnight resting time
Cooking time: 20 minutes
Makes: 10 fritters

- ¾ cup (110 g) all-purpose (plain) flour
- ½ teaspoon baking powder
- ¼ teaspoon ground coriander
- ¼ teaspoon ground cumin
- ¼ teaspoon ground ginger
- ¼ teaspoon fine sea salt
- ⅛ teaspoon freshly ground black pepper
- Vegetable oil, for deep-frying

In a medium bowl, combine the flour, baking powder, coriander, cumin, ginger, salt, and pepper. Pour in ½ cup (120 ml/4 fl oz) water and stir until a shaggy dough forms, then knead until it comes together (it should be sticky) and pulls cleanly away from the sides of the bowl, 2 minutes. Cover with plastic wrap (cling film) and refrigerate for at least 3 hours.

Pour 2 inches (5 cm) vegetable oil into a wide, deep heavy-bottomed pan and heat over medium-high heat.

Working in batches so as not to crowd the pan, add the dough by the tablespoon and fry until the fritters are golden brown and have puffed to the top, 3–4 minutes. With a slotted spoon, transfer to paper towels to drain. Serve warm.

SPICED LENTIL FRITTER

INDIA

Medu vada *is a South Indian spiced lentil donut that is often seen on the table with* idli *(Fluffy Rice Cakes, page 401) and/or Dosa (page 130), and is served with various Chutneys and Sambar (pages 131–33).*

Preparation time: 50 minutes, plus 4 hours soaking time
Cooking time: 1 hour 10 minutes
Makes: 6–7 fritters

· ½ cup (70 g) dried split urad dal, washed and soaked for 4 hours
· 2 tablespoons rice flour
· ¼ teaspoon baking soda (bicarbonate of soda)
· ¼ teaspoon cumin seeds
· ¼ jalapeño or other green chili, finely chopped
· ½ teaspoon fine sea salt
· ¼ teaspoon freshly ground black pepper
· 3 fresh curry leaves, chopped
· Vegetable oil, for shallow frying
· Sambar (pages 133), for serving
· Tomato Chutney (page 132), Coconut Chutney (page 132), or Coriander Chutney (page 131), for serving

Drain the urad dal and transfer to a food processor. Add 3 tablespoons water and grind until soft and slightly fluffy, 2 minutes. Transfer to a bowl and whisk in the rice flour until the batter is light and fluffy. To test, drop a piece of the batter in a cup of water: if it floats, it's ready.

Add the baking soda (bicarbonate of soda), cumin seeds, jalapeño, salt, pepper, and curry leaves. Mix with your hands to combine.

Pour 1 inch (2.5 cm) vegetable oil into a wide, deep heavy-bottomed pan and heat over medium-high heat. To test if the oil is ready for frying, carefully add a piece of dough. If it sizzles, the oil is ready. With wet hands, scoop portions of dough the size of golf balls and form them into disks. Poke a hole through the center and smooth out on all sides. Repeat with the remaining dough. Working in batches, carefully lower the *medu vada* into the hot oil and fry until golden on one side, about 1 minute. Flip and fry for 1 minute more. Transfer to paper towels to drain.

Serve warm with sambar and coconut chutney.

See image on page 302

CORN FRITTERS WITH LOX AND POACHED EGGS

AUSTRALIA

A cross between a fritter and a pancake, these make a quick and easy savory base for lox and poached eggs.

Preparation time: 10 minutes
Cooking time: 20 minutes
Makes: 4 fritters

· 1 egg
· ½ cup (120 ml/4 fl oz) full-fat milk
· ⅔ cup (85 g) all-purpose (plain) flour
· ½ teaspoon baking powder
· 1 cup (145 g) corn kernels, fresh or drained canned
· Salt and freshly ground pepper
· 4 tablespoons vegetable oil
· 4 Poached Eggs (page 15) and 4 slices of Lox (page 351), for serving

In a medium bowl, whisk the egg and milk. Slowly add the flour and baking powder and whisk until smooth. Stir in the corn and season with salt and pepper.

Heat the oil in a cast-iron skillet over medium-high heat. Test if the oil is ready to fry by adding a small drop of batter into the oil. If it sizzles, it is ready. Spoon about ¼ cup (60 ml) of the batter into the oil to form a round, 2 fritters in at a time. Lightly fry on both sides until golden, about 2 minutes per side. Transfer to paper towels to drain. Repeat with the remaining batter.

Serve the corn fritters topped with lox and poached eggs.

STUFFED AND FRIED

Corn Fritters with Lox and Poached Eggs

FRY JACKS

BELIZE

Similar versions of this deep-fried dough are made elsewhere, such as Beignets (page 309) in New Orleans or sopapillas in the American Southwest and Mexico, but this savory recipe is specific to Belize.

Preparation time: 20 minutes, plus 20 minutes resting time
Cooking time: 10 minutes
Makes: 4 fry jacks (2 servings)

· 1 cup (145 g) all-purpose (plain) flour
· 1½ teaspoons baking powder
· Pinch of baking soda (bicarbonate of soda)
· ¼ teaspoon fine sea salt
· 1 tablespoon solid vegetable shortening
· Vegetable oil, for deep-frying

Whisk the flour, baking powder, baking soda, and salt into a large bowl. Cut the shortening into the flour, rolling it across your fingers until it is crumbled to the size of cornmeal. Create a well in the center of the flour and pour in 7 tablespoons water, one at a time. With your hands, mix into a shaggy dough. Knead until the dough is soft, about 2 minutes. Let the dough rest for 20 minutes. Turn the dough out onto a lightly floured work surface. Divide the dough into 2 equal portions. Roll each portion into a 6-inch (15) round, about ¼ inch (6 mm) thick. With a sharp knife, slice the round in half, then cut a 2-inch (2.5 cm) slit in the center of each half.

Pour 2 inches (5 cm) vegetable oil into a wide, deep heavy-bottomed pan and heat over medium-high heat. To test if the oil is ready for frying, carefully add a piece of dough. If it sizzles, it is ready. Carefully fry the dough on one side until golden brown and puffed up, 1-2 minutes. Flip and fry the other side, about 1 minute more. Transfer the fry jacks to paper towels to drain. Serve warm with cheese, refried beans, jam (guava or pineapple), or eggs.

Fry Jacks

Preparation time: 20 minutes
Cooking time: 5 minutes
Makes: 6 donuts

CAKE DONUTS

UNITED STATES

With a denser texture than a yeast-risen donut, simple cake donuts are commonly sprinkled with cinnamon sugar, but can have a whole range of toppings and glazes, as with Yeast Donuts (opposite). It is often enjoyed dunked in tea or coffee.

· 1½ cups (215 g) all-purpose (plain) flour, plus more as needed
· 1½ teaspoons baking powder
· 4 tablespoons sugar
· ¼ teaspoon ground cinnamon
· Pinch of fine sea salt
· 1½ tablespoons (20 g) unsalted butter, melted
· 4 tablespoons buttermilk
· 1 large egg
· Vegetable oil, for deep-frying

For the coating:
· 1 teaspoon ground cinnamon
· 4 tablespoons (52 g) sugar

In a large bowl, combine the flour, baking powder, sugar, cinnamon, and salt. In a small bowl, beat together the melted butter, buttermilk, and egg. Pour the buttermilk mixture into the flour mixture and stir with a wooden spoon until a shaggy dough forms. In the bowl, knead the dough a few times until smooth. Sprinkle with a bit more flour if the dough is too sticky to handle.

Turn the dough out onto a lightly floured work surface. Roll the dough out until it is about ½ inch (1.25 cm) thick. With a 2-inch (5 cm) round donut cutter, biscuit cutter, or the top of a mason jar, cut out 6 donuts. If you don't have a donut cutter (which will cut out a center hole), use a bottle cap or a knife to cut out the centers, 1 inch (2.5 cm) in diameter. Reserve the donut holes to fry (see Donut Holes, page 304).

Pour 2 inches (5 cm) vegetable oil into a wide, deep heavy-bottomed pan and heat over medium-high heat. To test if the oil is ready for frying, carefully add a piece of scrap dough into the oil. If it sizzles, it is ready. Working with 3 donuts at a time, carefully lower into the oil and fry on one side until golden brown, about 1 minute. Flip the donuts and fry the other side, 40 seconds more. Transfer the donuts to paper towels to drain.

In a wide, shallow bowl, mix the sugar and cinnamon, then roll the donuts in the mixture and serve warm.

YEAST DONUTS

UNITED STATES

The most popular donut found in the United States, the yeast donut has a variety of glazes, toppings, and fillings. This recipe is for a classic yeast-raised donut with either plain or chocolate glaze. Sprinkles can be added on top for extra color and crunch.

Preparation time: 1 hour, plus 2 hours 45 minutes rising time
Cooking time: 20 minutes
Makes: 8 donuts

For the donuts:
· ½ cup (120 ml/4 fl oz) full-fat milk, warmed
· 1 teaspoon active dry yeast
· 1 ½ cups (220 g) all-purpose (plain) flour, plus more as needed
· 2 tablespoons sugar
· ¼ teaspoon fine sea salt
· 1 egg
· ½ teaspoon vanilla extract
· 2 tablespoons (30 g) unsalted butter, melted and cooled
· Vegetable oil, for deep-frying

For the glaze:
· ½ cup (65 g) powdered (icing) sugar
· 1 tablespoon unsweetened cocoa powder (optional; for chocolate glaze)
· ½ teaspoon vanilla extract
· 1–2 tablespoons full-fat milk

In a large bowl, stir together the warm milk, yeast, and a pinch of sugar. Set the mixture aside until the yeast is frothy, about 10 minutes. (If the yeast does not froth, check the expiration date. You may have to start over with fresher yeast.) With a wooden spoon, stir in 1 cup (145 g) of the flour and the sugar. Stir in the salt, egg, vanilla, melted butter, and the remaining ½ cup (75 g) flour until a wet, shaggy dough forms and starts to pull away from the sides of the bowl.

Turn the dough out onto a lightly floured work surface. Knead the dough until it is smooth and elastic, about 5 minutes. It will still be a bit sticky, but that is okay. Place the dough in a lightly greased bowl, cover with plastic wrap (cling film), and let it rest until doubled in size, about 2 hours.

Turn the dough onto a lightly floured work surface and punch it down. Roll the dough out until it is ¼ inch (6 mm) thick. With a 3-inch (7.5 cm) round donut cutter, biscuit cutter, or the top of a mason jar, cut out 8 donuts. If you do not have a donut cutter (which will cut out a center hole), use an olive oil bottle cap or a knife to cut out the centers, 1 inch (2.5 cm) in diameter. Reserve the donut holes to fry later (see Donut Holes, page 304). Cover the donuts with plastic wrap or a tea towel and let the dough rest until it puffs up, about 45 minutes.

Pour 2 inches (5 cm) oil into a wide, deep heavy-bottomed pan and heat over medium-high heat. To test if the oil is ready for frying, carefully place a piece of scrap dough into the oil. If it sizzles, it is ready. Working with 3 donuts at a time, carefully lower the donuts into the oil and fry on one side until golden brown, 30–45 seconds. Flip the donuts and fry the other side, 20–30 seconds more. Transfer the donuts to paper towels to drain.

Meanwhile, make the glaze. Whisk the powdered (icing) sugar in small bowl. If making chocolate glaze, add the cocoa powder. Stir in the vanilla. Add the milk, a little bit at a time, until a pourable glaze is achieved.

Let the donuts cool slightly. Place them on a wire rack set in a rimmed baking sheet and pour the glaze evenly over each. Serve warm.

MEERA SODHA
INDIAN BREAKFAST

Meera Sodha was born in Lincolnshire, England, to Gujarati Indian parents. Her two cookbooks, Made in India *(2014) and* Fresh India *(2016), became instant bestsellers. She contributes a popular column about vegan cooking to* The Guardian.

Most of us start the day by eating with our hands. More than with any other meal, we feel compelled to touch our food in the morning. In India, this is of course the rule rather than the exception, especially when you eat dosa for breakfast. You have no choice but to break, tear, dip, and dunk one of the world's finest breakfast foods from plate to mouth.

The best I have ever found is from Mylari Dosa, a hole-in-the-wall shop in the city of Mysore. Here there is only masala dosa on the menu, served on a perfunctory steel tray.

The place is run by an old woman, her sari patterned and pressed, her skill specific and legendary. Over a lifetime, she has perfected the elements that make up this meal: a fermented and lace-edged rice pancake curled around soft mustard-seed and curry-leaf potatoes, the only accompaniment a pool of otherworldly coconut chutney. Now an octogenarian, she presides, owl-like, over two boys working in the narrow kitchen to fulfill the orders.

The boy who makes the dosas works with speed and precision, every small movement of his hands showing how many thousands he has made. He lifts a giant ladle of batter to aerate it several times: it looks likes liquid marshmallow, moving back and forth. In the same second, he spoons it onto a hot *tava* (frying pan) and smoothens it into concentric circles with a scraper. It is perfect. It is thick in the middle to create a soft pillow for the masala potatoes to nest in, and wafer-thin at the edges so it will shatter perfectly in the mouth.

As an onlooker, I fear he has left it too long—surely the face of it will stick and burn. But he barely watches as it cooks: in his bones he knows how long it needs, without needing to nurse it. The ghee is spooned on. And although ghee has just one name, endless variations exist. This one has the richness of butter with the flavor of dark roasted hazelnuts and a top-note of caramel. It is the ghee of Indian fairytales.

The second boy spoons and slops soft potatoes studded with citrus and smoke-flavored curry leaves, mustard seeds, cumin, and black pepper. They are all spices that grow within meters of the shop. Then he slops, quite unceremoniously, the world's best coconut chutney on the tray so that it spills over. These boys have felt the heat of twenty pairs of hungry eyes on them, but right now, it is my turn to eat.

I take a bite and look up to see if the woman is watching. She is, and we both know what I am thinking. In this moment, the traffic outside has subsided, the clatter of plates in the kitchen is no longer, the dogs are no longer yapping, and the clocks have stopped. Just now, there is me and this dosa, and it's going to be a good day.

01. Dosa with Aloo Masala PAGE 130-31   02. Coconut Chutney PAGE 132   03. Spiced Lentil Fritter PAGE 293
04. Sambar PAGE 133

05. Flattened Rice Porridge PAGE 98   **06.** Tomato Chutney PAGE 132   **07.** Chai Karak PAGE 429   **08.** Dosa PAGE 130

09. Coriander Chutney PAGE 131   **10.** Fried Potato Sandwich PAGE 167

DONUT HOLES

UNITED STATES

The small round cut-outs from the centers of a Cake Donut (page 298) or a Yeast Donut (page 299), donut holes can have the same glazes and toppings as full-size donuts.

Preparation time: 1 hour, plus 2 hours 45 minutes rising time for the Yeast Donuts
Cooking time: 5 minutes
Makes: 8 yeast or 6 cake donut holes

· Dough cut-outs from Cake Donuts (page 298) or Yeast Donuts (page 299)
· Glaze, from Yeast Donuts (page 299)

After making and frying the whole donuts, per the donut recipe, bring the frying oil back to temperature. Add the donut holes to the hot oil and fry on one side until golden brown, about 30 seconds. Flip the donut holes and fry on the other side, 30 seconds more. Transfer to paper towels to drain. Roll the donut holes in the glaze, allowing excess glaze to drip back into the bowl. Place the donut holes on a wire rack set in a rimmed baking sheet to cool slightly and allow the glaze to harden. Serve warm.

FRIED PLANTAIN DONUTS

VENEZUELA

Mandoca is a fried plantain and cornmeal donut from the Zulia (northwestern) state. They are served hot with grated queso blanco cheese.

Preparation time: 20 minutes
Cooking time: 30 minutes
Makes: 6 donuts

· ½ large yellow plantain, peeled
· 1 cup (130 g) finely ground cornmeal (masa harina)
· 4 tablespoons dark brown sugar
· ¾ cup (85 g) grated queso blanco or mozzarella, plus more for serving
· ¼ teaspoon fine sea salt
· 4 tablespoons hot water
· Vegetable oil, for deep-frying

In a small saucepan, combine the plantain with water to cover and bring to a boil. Reduce the heat to low and cook at a simmer until the plantain is tender, about 15 minutes. Drain.

In a medium bowl, mash the plantain until no lumps remain. (Alternatively, puree in a food processor or blender.) Stir in the cornmeal, brown sugar, cheese, and salt. Gradually add the hot water, stirring with a wooden spoon, until a dough forms. Knead in the bowl until a smooth dough forms, about 3 minutes. Let the *mandoca* dough rest for 10 minutes.

Pour 2 inches (5 cm) vegetable oil into a wide, deep heavy-bottomed pan and heat over medium-high heat. To test if the oil is ready for frying, carefully add a piece of dough. If it sizzles, it's ready. Separate the dough into 6 equal pieces. Roll each portion into a log 7 inches (18 cm) long. Bend each log to form a horseshoe shape and continue bending until the two ends meet. Press together to seal.

Working with 2 at a time, carefully lower each *mandoca* into the oil and fry on one side until golden brown, about 2 minutes. Using a slotted spoon, flip and fry the other side, about 2 minutes more. Transfer to paper towels to drain.

Serve sprinkled with more cheese.

SPANISH CHURROS

SPAIN

Churros, deep-fried sticks of batter, are typically served with Hot Chocolate (page 439). In Spain, churros are left bare, whereas in Mexico they receive a coating of cinnamon sugar. A churrera is a mechanism used to extrude the dough in the iconic star-like pattern, similar in shape to a youtiao (Chinese Cruller, page 306). A piping bag fitted with the star tip (nozzle) will suffice for home-use.

Preparation time: 15 minutes
Cooking time: 10 minutes
Serves: 2, makes 8 churros

· 2 tablespoons full-fat milk
· 2 tablespoons (30 g) unsalted butter
· ¼ teaspoon vanilla extract
· 2 teaspoons sugar
· Pinch of salt
· ½ cup (70 g) all-purpose (plain) flour
· 1 egg, beaten
· Vegetable oil, for deep-frying

In a medium saucepan, heat the milk, 2 tablespoons water, butter, vanilla extract, sugar, and salt over low heat, until the butter is melted. Bring to a simmer, then mix in the flour, stirring vigorously until the mixture comes together into a dough that pulls away from the sides of the pan, about 30 seconds. Transfer to a large bowl and let cool.

Using a wooden spoon or the paddle attachment on a stand mixer, add the beaten egg to the dough, a little at a time, slowly mixing until it comes together into a thick paste.

Pour 2 inches (5 cm) vegetable oil in a wide, deep heavy-bottomed pan and heat over medium-high heat. To test if the oil is ready for frying, carefully add a piece of batter. If it sizzles, it is ready. Fit a piping bag with a large star tip (nozzle) and spoon the batter into the bag. Pipe 4 straight lines of batter 4–6 inches (7.5–10 cm) long or one long coil shape into the oil, using about half of the batter. You may need to snip the batter with scissors to get it to leave the nozzle cleanly. Fry until golden on all sides, about 2 minutes per side, turning carefully with tongs. Use the tongs, to transfer the fried churros to paper towels to drain. Repeat with the rest of the batter.

Serve warm with hot chocolate.

CHINESE CRULLER

CHINA

Youtiao *are deep-fried dough in the shape of a stick, served hot with soy milk or torn into pieces as a topping for* Congee (page 99). *In Taiwan, they are often wrapped up in a rice roll filled with meat floss and pickled vegetables called* fan tuan (Stuffed Rice Rolls, page 284). *In Thailand a similar version, called* patanko, *is fried in an "X" shape and served with a sweet custard called* sangkaya.

Preparation time: 45 minutes, plus 2 hours resting and tempering time, and overnight chilling time
Cooking time: 10 minutes
Makes: 6 crullers

· 2½ cups (365 g) all-purpose (plain) flour
· 2 teaspoons baking powder
· 4 teaspoons sugar
· 1 cup (240 ml/8 fl oz) full-fat milk, warmed
· 2 eggs
· 2 teaspoons vegetable oil, plus more for deep-frying

In a medium bowl, combine the flour, baking powder, and sugar. With a wooden spoon, stir in the milk, egg, and vegetable oil until a shaggy dough comes together. Turn the dough out onto a generously floured work surface and knead until it is smooth, soft, and no longer sticky, about 10 minutes. Allow the dough to rest for 15 minutes. Shape the dough into a 6 x 3 inches (15 x 7.5 cm) rectangle and ¼ inch (6 mm) thick. Wrap in plastic wrap (cling film) and refrigerate for at least 8 hours or overnight. The next morning, let the dough come back to room temperature, 1 hour 30 minutes. It should feel very soft.

To shape the *youtiao*, cut the dough crosswise into strips 1 inch (2.5 cm) wide and 3 inches (7.5 cm) long. Layer one strip over another and press a lengthwise indentation into the top layer with a chopstick, sealing them both together. Pulling on both ends, slightly stretch the *youtiao* out into a 6-inch (15 cm) long shape. Repeat with the remaining slices.

Pour 4 inches (10 cm) vegetable oil into a wok or frying pan and heat over medium-high heat. To test if the oil is ready to fry, carefully add a small piece of *youtiao*. If it sizzles, it is ready. Working with 1 at a time, carefully lower the *youtiao* into the oil and fry, constantly turning until golden brown, about 1 minute. Flip to fry the other side, about 1 minute more. Using a slotted spoon, transfer to paper towels to drain. Serve warm.

STUFFED AND FRIED

Chinese Cruller

SWAHILI BUNS

KENYA

Mandazi *(nicknamed "Swahili buns") are fried, unsweetened, triangular-shaped donuts made with coconut milk and enjoyed in the African Great Lake region.*

Preparation time: 45 minutes, plus 2 hours rising time
Cooking time: 10 minutes
Makes: 6 buns

· 4 tablespoons warm water
· 1 teaspoon active dry yeast
· 3 tablespoons sugar
· 1½ cups (220 g) all-purpose flour
· ½ teaspoon fine sea salt
· 1 teaspoon ground cinnamon
· ½ teaspoon ground cardamom
· 4 tablespoons coconut milk
· 1 egg
· Vegetable oil, for deep-frying
· Powdered (icing) sugar, to sprinkle

In a small bowl, stir together the water, yeast, and a pinch of the sugar. Set the mixture aside until the yeast is frothy, about 10 minutes. (If the yeast does not froth, check the expiration date. You may have to start over with fresher yeast.)

In a large bowl, combine the flour, sugar, salt, cinnamon, and cardamom. With a wooden spoon, stir in the coconut milk, egg, and yeast mixture. Stir until a wet, shaggy dough forms and starts to pull away from the sides of the bowl.

Turn the dough onto a very lightly floured work surface and knead until smooth and elastic, 5 minutes. Use as little flour as possible, as it will affect the taste and texture of the *mandazi*. It will still be a bit sticky. Place the dough in a lightly oiled bowl, cover with plastic wrap (cling film), and let it rest until doubled in size, 2 hours.

Turn the dough out onto a lightly floured surface and punch down. Roll into a round, 1 inch (2.5 cm), thick and slice into 6 wedges.

Pour 2 inches (5 cm) vegetable oil into a wide, deep heavy-bottomed pan and heat over medium-high heat. To test if the oil is ready for frying, carefully add a piece of scrap dough. If it sizzles, it's ready. Working with 3 wedges at a time, carefully lower the dough into the oil and fry on one side until golden brown, about 30 seconds. Flip the *mandazi* and fry the other side, 30 seconds more. Using a slotted spoon, transfer the *mandazi* to a cooling rack lined with paper towels before showering with powdered (icing) sugar. Serve warm.

BEIGNETS
UNITED STATES

A staple dish of New Orleans, Louisiana in the South, this fried dough is coated in powdered sugar and served with Chicory Coffee (page 410).

Preparation time: 30 minutes, plus 2 hours rising time
Cooking time: 30 minutes
Makes: 34 beignets

· ¾ cup (175 ml/6 fl oz) plus 1 tablespoon warm water
· 1 teaspoon active dry yeast
· 4 tablespoons sugar
· ½ cup (120 ml/4 fl oz) evaporated milk
· 1 egg
· 2 tablespoons (30 g) butter, melted
· 3 cups (435 g) all-purpose (plain) flour, plus more for dusting
· ¼ teaspoon fine sea salt
· Vegetable oil, for greasing and deep-frying
· Powdered (icing) sugar, for sprinkling

In a small bowl, stir together the warm water, yeast, and a pinch of the sugar. Set the mixture aside until the yeast is frothy, 10 minutes. (If the yeast does not froth, check the expiration date. You may have to start over with fresher yeast.)

In a large bowl, use a fork to whisk together the evaporated milk, egg, melted butter, and the yeast mixture.

In a large bowl, add the flour, salt, and remaining sugar. Using a wooden spoon or the paddle attachment on a mixer, slowly pour in the wet mixture. It will make a very loose dough. Let it rest, covered, at room temperature for 20 minutes.

Turn the dough out onto a lightly floured work surface and knead until it is smooth and elastic, about 3 minutes. Use a little flour on the dough if needed. Place the dough in a lightly oiled bowl, cover with plastic wrap (cling film), and let it rise until doubled in size, about 2 hours, or up to overnight in the refrigerator.

Bring the dough back to room temperature. Turn the dough out onto a lightly floured surface and punch down. Roll it into a rectangle 12 x 18-in (30 x 45cm) and about ¼ inch (6 mm) thick. With a sharp knife or pastry cutter, cut the dough into 2½-inch (3.5 cm) squares.

Pour at least 1 inch (2.5 cm) vegetable oil into a wide, deep heavy-bottomed pan and heat over medium-high heat. To test if the oil is hot enough, carefully add a small piece of dough. If it sizzles, the oil is ready. Working with 4 at a time, carefully lower the beignets into the oil and fry on one side for 1 minute 30 seconds, then turn over and fry until puffed up and golden brown, about 1 minute. Transfer the beignets to a cooling rack lined with paper towels. Sprinkle with powdered (icing) sugar and serve warm.

TAMALES
MEXICO

In the morning in Mexico City, street corners are brimming with stands selling tamales *and* chilaquiles *(page 20) stands.* Tamales *are enjoyed throughout the country and in different variations all over Central and South America.*
A Mexican tamal *is often wrapped in a dried corn husk and uses nixtamalized (the process of soaking corn in an alkaline solution) masa.* Tamales *come with many filling options and can be topped with Salsa Verde or Salsa Roja (pages 20–21). In the morning,* tamales *are often served in a* bolillo *(bread roll) to create a* guajolote/torta de tamal— *basically a* tamale *sandwich.*

Preparation time: 30 minutes
Cooking time: 1 hour 40 minutes
Makes: 10 tamales

For the chicken:
· ½ lb (225 g) boneless, skinless chicken breasts
· ½ lb (225 g) boneless, skinless chicken thighs
· 4 cloves garlic, smashed with the side of a knife
· 1 teaspoon black peppercorns
· 1 teaspoon fine sea salt

For the masa:
· 8 tablespoons (100 g) lard or solid vegetable shortening
· 1½ cups (180 g) finely ground cornmeal (masa harina)
· ¾ teaspoon baking powder
· 1 teaspoon fine sea salt

For the filling
· 3 tablespoons vegetable oil
· 3 tablespoons all-purpose (plain) flour
· ¾ cup (175 ml/6 fl oz) Salsa Verde (page 20)
· Salt, to taste

For wrapping:
· 15 dried corn husks, soaked in water for 1 hour

In a pot, combine the chicken breasts, thighs, garlic, peppercorns, salt, and 4 cups (950 ml/32 oz) water. Bring to a boil and cook until the chicken is cooked through, about 20 minutes. Using a slotted spoon, transfer the chicken to a plate. Strain the broth of the peppercorns and put the broth back in the pot. When the chicken is cool enough, shred it. Return the chicken broth to the heat and simmer for 15 minutes more. Remove from the heat and set the broth aside.

In a stand mixer (or in a large bowl with a hand mixer), beat the lard with 2 tablespoons of the reserved chicken broth until fluffy. Gradually add the cornmeal, baking powder, and salt, continuing to beat the mixture. Add 1 cup (240 ml/8 fl oz) of broth, a little at a time, until a dough forms. Switch to the paddle attachment or knead with your hands until the mixture is smooth.

In a medium saucepan, heat the oil over medium heat. Stir in the flour and cook until lightly browned, about 3 minutes. Stir in the salsa verde and cook until it has thickened, about 2 minutes. Stir in the salt and shredded chicken to coat and set aside.

Lay out the soaked corn husks with the narrow end of the husk pointing toward you. Scoop 3 tablespoons of the masa onto the wide end of the corn husk and spread it until it's about ¼ inch (6 mm) thick, leaving a border of husk around the masa. Add 2 tablespoons filling down the center of the masa. Wrap the two sides of the husk following its natural shape, then fold the tip of the husk up towards the wide end. Tie the tamale with a strip of husk. Repeat with remaining husks.

In a steamer or a large saucepan fitted with a steamer insert, bring about 2 inches (5 cm) chicken broth to a boil, adding water if needed. Place an inverted small bowl in the center of the steamer insert and prop up the tamales around the bowl with the open end facing up. Reduce the heat to medium-low. Steam until cooked (the dough should easily pull away from the husks), 45 minutes, keeping in mind that they will firm up a little more after cooling. Let cool for 5 minutes and serve warm topped with salsa verde.

Tamales

FRESH CORN TAMALES

ECUADOR

Humitas *are the Ecuadorian version of Tamales (page 310), made with fresh corn instead of masa (a dough of nixtamalized corn flour and water) and wrapped in fresh corn husks to steam.*

Preparation time: 20 minutes
Cooking time: 1 hour 15 minutes
Makes: 10 tamales

· 2 ears corn, with husks
· 1 cup (115 g) shredded mozzarella cheese
· 1 egg
· 1 teaspoons sugar
· ¼ cup (35 g) cornmeal
· 1 tablespoon heavy (whipping) cream
· ¼ teaspoon fine sea salt

Bring a saucepan of water to a boil. Remove the husks from the corn and soak in the boiling water until pliable, about 3 minutes. Transfer to a cooling rack lined with paper towels and let the husks cool.

Meanwhile, slice the kernels off of the cobs and transfer to a blender. Add the mozzarella, egg, sugar, cornmeal, cream, and salt. Blend until combined into a thick paste. If it's not thick enough, add up to 2 more tablespoons cornmeal.

Use one husk to make strips for tying. Lay out the soaked corn husks with the narrow end of the husk pointing toward you. Overlap 2 husks to create a larger surface area for the filling. Scoop 3 tablespoons of the corn filling onto the wide end of the corn husk and spread it on the husk until it's about ¼ inch (6 mm) thick, leaving a border of husk around the masa. Fold the tails of the corn husks to encase the batter like an envelope, then fold the left and right sides over like a letter. Make sure the batter is evenly distributed, filling about ¾ of the way up the husks. Tie the *humitas* with a strip of husk. Set aside, propped up slightly to keep the batter in place, and repeat with the remaining husks and batter.

In a steamer or a large saucepan with a steamer insert, bring 2 inches (5 cm) water to a boil. Steam the *humitas* until the tamale easily pulls away from the husks, 45 minutes to 1 hour. Serve warm.

STUFFED POTATO FLATBREAD

INDIA

Aloo paratha *is a North Indian unleavened, whole wheat flatbread. Though not always stuffed, this version is filled with* aloo *(spiced potatoes) and served with yogurt and lime pickle.*

Preparation time: 30 minutes, plus 2 hours resting time
Cooking time: 40 minutes
Makes: 4 flatbreads

For the dough:
· 1 cup (145 g) whole wheat flour
· ¼ teaspoon canola (rapeseed) oil
· ¼ teaspoon fine sea salt

For the filling:
· 2 medium white potatoes, peeled and quartered
· ½ teaspoon fine sea salt
· ¼ teaspoon sweet paprika
· ½ teaspoon crushed fennel seeds
· ¼ teaspoon garam masala
· 2 tablespoons cilantro (coriander) leaves

For cooking:
· Vegetable oil or ghee, for pan-frying

Make the dough:
In a medium bowl, mix together the flour, 4 tablespoons water, oil, and salt and knead until it's smooth. Cover with a wet paper towel and set aside for 2 hours.

Meanwhile, make the filling:
In a medium pot, combine the potatoes with water to cover by 2 inches (5 cm). Bring to a boil and cook until tender and soft enough to easily mash, about 15 minutes. Drain and return to the pot. Mash the potatoes with the salt, spices, and cilantro (coriander).

Divide the filling into 4 portions and divide the dough into 4 equal balls. Lightly flour the dough balls and roll into rounds, 4 inches (10 cm) in diameter. Put a portion of filling in the center of each and enclose the filling with the dough. Roll the ball with a rolling pin into an 8-inch (20 cm) round.

Cook the flatbreads:
Place a frying pan over medium-high heat. Place a paratha in the frying pan and cook for 2 minutes, then flip the paratha and brush the top of the paratha with 1½ teaspoons of oil and cook for 2 minutes. Flip and brush the top with 1½ teaspoons of oil. Flip and continue to cook until golden brown, 1 minute more. Transfer to a plate. Repeat with the remaining paratha. Serve warm.

AREPAS
COLOMBIA

Arepas are one of the most staple dishes in Colombia and Venezuela. Versions of the dish drastically vary based on region and personal preferences. This recipe is for griddled or stovetop arepas, but they can also be deep-fried, sometimes with an egg nestled inside (page 316). Arepas are eaten daily topped or stuffed with cheese (Cheese Arepas, below) and an assortment of other toppings and/or fillings based on the time of day.

(page 316)

Preparation time: 10 minutes
Cooking time: 15 minutes
Makes: 4 arepas

- · 1 cup (200 g) precooked white or yellow cornmeal
- · ½ teaspoon fine sea salt
- · 1 tablespoon vegetable oil
- · 1 cup (240 ml/8 fl oz) warm water
- · 1 tablespoon (15 g) unsalted butter

In a bowl, combine the cornmeal, salt, oil, and warm water. Stir with a wooden spoon or spatula until no dry spots remain. Leave the dough to stand and firm up, about 5 minutes. Knead the dough with your hands until the dough reaches the consistency of putty. If needed, add up to 2 more tablespoons warm water. Divide the dough into 4 balls. Sandwich between two sheets of plastic wrap (cling film) and use the bottom of a pan to flatten the balls to a ¼-inch (6 mm) thickness.

Heat a plancha, griddle, arepa pan, or frying pan to low heat. Add the butter and let it melt before adding the arepas. Cook until both sides are golden brown and have formed a crisped crust, about 8 minutes per side. Serve warm topped with butter.

CHEESE AREPAS
COLOMBIA

Arepas de queso are made with grated cheese mixed into the cornmeal, creating an extra layer of flavor and helping to bind the arepa in the frying process. Arepas de queso can also be split open after cooking and filled with more cheese or enjoyed topped with butter and grated cheese.

Preparation time: 15 minutes
Cooking time: 5 minutes
Makes: 4 arepas

- · 1 cup (200 g) precooked white or yellow cornmeal
- · ½ cup (55 g) grated mozzarella cheese, plus 2 tablespoons for serving
- · ¼ teaspoon fine sea salt
- · 1 cup (240 ml/8 fl oz) warm water
- · 2 tablespoons (30 g) unsalted butter, at room temperature, plus more for serving

In a bowl, combine the cornmeal, mozzarella, and salt. Pour in the warm water and 1 tablespoon of the butter. Leave the mixture to stand for about 5 minutes to firm up a bit. Knead everything together with your hands until the dough reaches the consistency of putty. If needed, add up to 2 more tablespoons warm water.

Divide the dough into 4 balls. Sandwich between two sheets of plastic wrap (cling film) and use the bottom of a pan to flatten the balls to a ¼-inch (6 mm) thickness.

Heat a plancha, griddle, arepa pan, or frying pan to low heat. Add 1 tablespoon of butter and let it melt before adding the arepas. Cook until both sides are golden brown and have formed a crisped crust, about 8 minutes per side. Serve warm topped with butter. Smother with butter and add 2 tablespoons of mozzarella cheese to the top of each arepa. Once the cheese is melted, about 2 minutes, remove from the pan and serve, topped with more cheese.

Cheese Arepas

STUFFED AND FRIED

FRIED EGG
AREPAS

COLOMBIA

Arepas de huevo *are a traditional arepa dish from the Caribbean coast of Colombia. The arepa is deep-fried with an egg hidden inside.*

Preparation time: 15 minutes
Cooking time: 20 minutes
Makes: 4 arepas

· Vegetable oil, for deep-frying
· 4 uncooked arepas (above)
· 4 eggs
· Salt and freshly ground pepper
· Suero (sour cream), for serving

Pour 4 inches (10 cm) oil into a wide, deep heavy-bottomed pan and heat over medium-high heat. Test to see if the oil is ready by carefully adding a piece of arepa. If it sizzles, it's ready. Add the arepas and cook until both sides are browned and have a crisp crust, about 4 minutes.

Let the arepas cool slightly before making a slit into the side with a paring knife to create a pocket, being careful not to slice all the way through. Crack an egg into a small bowl or teacup. Season with salt and pepper. Pour an egg into the slit of an arepa. Carefully lower the arepa into the frying oil using tongs, holding steady with the tongs until the egg starts to set, 30 seconds. Fry the arepa until the egg is cooked, about 3 minutes more. Repeat with remaining eggs and arepas. Serve warm with *suero* (sour cream).

STUFFED AND FRIED

GREEN PLANTAIN BALLS WITH CHEESE

ECUADOR

Bolón de verde, *or green plantain dumplings, are filled with cheese, chorizo, or chicharrón, and fried until crispy. They are accompanied by coffee and hot sauce. Bolón are similar to Peruvian tacacho, which is also made with green plantains, but instead of being filled, chorizo is mixed into the plantain mash and served with* cecina *(cured meat).*

Preparation time: 15 minutes
Cooking time: 30 minutes
Makes: 4 plantain balls

· 2 tablespoons (30 g) unsalted butter
· 2 green plantains, peeled and sliced into thick chunks
· ¼ teaspoon ground cumin
· Salt
· ½ cup (60 g) crumbled queso fresco
· Vegetable oil, for deep-frying

In a medium frying pan, melt the butter over medium-high heat, swirling to evenly coat the pan. Add the plantain slices and cook until they are soft and golden brown on both sides, 15 minutes.

Transfer the plantains to a bowl and mash to a paste. Stir in the cumin and salt to taste until combined. With your hands, form the mashed plantain into 4 palm-size balls. Push your thumb into a ball to indent it. Fill it with 1 tablespoon of cheese and shape it back into a ball. Repeat with the remaining plantain balls and cheese.

Wipe out the frying pan. Add 2 inches (5 cm) oil to the pan and return it to medium-high heat. To test if the oil is ready, add a piece of the plantain dough. If it sizzles, it is ready. Using tongs, carefully lower the dumplings into the hot oil. Fry until the dumplings are browned on each side, about 3 minutes. Transfer to paper towels to drain. Serve warm.

FRIED PLANTAINS WITH CHEESE

ECUADOR

This comfort dish is enjoyed in South America and parts of the Caribbean. In its most basic form, whole ripe plantains are fried and stuffed with cheese. Other fillings can include guava jam, onions, or ground meat.

Preparation time: 10 minutes
Cooking time: 10 minutes
Serves: 2

· 2 ripe yellow plantains, peeled
· 1½ tablespoons (25 g) butter
· 1 cup (115 g) shredded mozzarella cheese (or a mixture of half mozzarella and half queso fresco)

Trim the two ends off the plantains. Using a paring knife, make a slit from one end of the plantain to the other, taking care not to slice all the way through to the other side, and stopping short of the ends.

In a small frying pan, melt the butter over medium heat, swirling it around the pan to coat evenly. Fry the plantains, cooking until each side is golden, about 5 minutes. Carefully stuff them with the shredded mozzarella and sprinkle the rest on top. Reduce the heat to low and cover the frying pan, allowing the cheese to melt, 1–2 minutes. Serve warm.

PAN FRIED DUMPLINGS

CHINA

Jiaozi are pan-fried, boiled, or steamed pork dumplings typically served alongside xiaolongbao *(soup dumplings), turnip cake (page 403), and other dim sum. Store-bought dumpling wrappers are typically used, but this is a recipe to make them from scratch.*

Preparation time: 1 hour, plus 1 hour resting time
Cooking time: 15 minutes
Makes: 4 dumplings

For the wrapper dough:
· 2 cups (290 g) all-purpose (plain) flour

For the filling:
· ½ lb (225 g) ground (minced) pork
· 1 cup (90 g) finely chopped napa cabbage (Chinese leaf)
· ½ cup (50 g) chopped scallions (spring onions)
· 4 tablespoons chopped garlic chives
· 2 teaspoons minced peeled fresh ginger
· 2 tablespoons soy sauce
· 1 teaspoon toasted sesame oil
· 1 teaspoon Shaoxing cooking wine
· 1 teaspoon sugar
· Salt and freshly ground pepper

For the dipping sauce:
· 4 tablespoons soy sauce
· 1 tablespoon rice vinegar
· 1 teaspoon toasted sesame oil
· ¼ teaspoon chili oil

Place the flour in a medium bowl. Add just enough cool water (about ¾ cup/175 ml/6 fl oz), a little at a time, to form a shaggy dough. Turn the dough out onto a work surface and knead with your hands until the dough comes together, 5 minutes. If the dough is too dry and the flour is loose, add a touch more water and knead until the dough is smooth. Let the dough rest, covered with a dish towel, for 1 hour.

Meanwhile, prepare the filling. In a large bowl, combine the pork with the cabbage, scallions (spring onions), garlic chives, ginger, soy sauce, sesame oil, wine, and sugar. Season with salt and pepper and stir.

Once the dough has rested, knead once more on a work surface. It should be elastic and smooth to the touch. Divide the dough in half and roll each piece into a long rope. Cut the rope into ½–1 inch (1.25–2.5 cm) pieces. Keep the dough that's not being used covered with a tea towel or plastic wrap (cling film). Flatten the pieces with your hands and with a lightly floured rolling pin, roll each piece into a round, 3 inches (7.5 cm) in diameter and 1/8 inch (3 mm) thick.

Using your fingers, wet the perimeter of the dough. Pull the dough up around the filling, pinching together at the top to seal and continuing around until the dumpling is sealed. Use your fingers to make small pleats along the sealed edge. Line the dumplings on a floured baking sheet and keep covered with a tea towel until ready to cook. At this stage, the dumplings can also be frozen for later use.

When ready to cook, bring a pot of water to a boil. Fill the pot with as many dumplings as can fit. When they rise to the surface, add 1 cup (240 ml/8 fl oz) cold water. When the pot returns to a boil, transfer the cooked dumplings to a serving platter using a slotted spoon. (If using frozen dumplings, repeat the boiling to cold water process three times to make sure the dumplings are cooked through.)

In a small bowl, combine the soy sauce, rice vinegar, sesame oil, and chili oil. Serve alongside warm dumplings.

BACON

UNITED STATES

Bacon is a quintessential breakfast protein in the United States, and a common accompaniment to eggs and buttered toast in The Diner Breakfast (page 16). Pork belly is used in this recipe to give the bacon its definitive streaks of fat. In the United Kingdom this is called "streaky bacon." Canadian Bacon (opposite) is made from the leaner loin and sliced into rounds. Also cut from the loin, bacon in the United Kingdom serves as the titular element of a bacon butty (Bacon Sandwich, page 176) and is often included in a Full English (page 28).

Preparation time: 20 minutes, plus 8 days curing time
Cooking time: 2 hours
Make: 1 pound (455 g)

· 1 lb (455 g) pork belly, about 1½ inches (4 cm) thick, skin removed
· 4 tablespoons dark brown sugar
· 2 tablespoons pure maple syrup
· 2 tablespoons strong coffee
· 1 tablespoon apple cider vinegar
· 1 tablespoon fine sea salt
· 2 teaspoons freshly ground pepper

Rinse the pork belly thoroughly. In a gallon-size zipseal plastic bag, combine the brown sugar, maple syrup, coffee, vinegar, salt, and pepper. Add the pork belly and massage the cure mixture into all sides of the pork belly using your hands. Seal all air out of the bag and store it on a baking dish in the refrigerator for 7 days, massaging the meat to work in the cure and flipping the bag daily. Rinse the cured pork belly and discard the solids. Pat dry with a towel and place on a baking rack in the refrigerator for a minimum of 6 hours (overnight is best).

Preheat the oven to 225°F (110°C/Gas Mark ¼).

Place the pork belly, fat-side up, directly on the rack of the oven and place a large roasting pan directly underneath it. Roast the meat until a thermometer inserted in the thickest part of the meat, making sure to penetrate the fat into the flesh, reads 150°F (66°C), about 2 hours. Let the pork belly cool, then cut into slices as thin or as thick as desired. To store the bacon, wrap it tightly in plastic wrap (cling film) and then overwrap with foil. Store in the refrigerator for up to 1 week, or in the freezer for 3 weeks.

To cook the sliced bacon in a pan: Start with a cold cast-iron skillet or frying pan and place 2 slices (rashers) bacon in flat. Slowly bring the heat to medium to let the fat render and result in crispy bacon. Cook on both sides until crispy, about 10 minutes. Transfer the bacon to paper towels to drain.

To cook bacon in the oven, place the bacon strips on a sheet pan and place in an unheated oven. Set the temperature to 400°F (200°C/Gas Mark 6) and let the oven slowly come to temperature. Cook the bacon for about 20 minutes total, or until the fat has rendered and the bacon is crispy. Drain before serving.

CANADIAN BACON

CANADA

Canadian breakfasts are similar to those in the United States, except when it comes to the bacon. Canadian bacon comes from the loin (the area between the shoulders and the back legs of the pig), while American Bacon (opposite) comes from the belly. It is cured and sometimes smoked. Canadian bacon can be served with eggs, waffles, pancakes, and most traditional diner staples, most popularly with Eggs Benedict (page 58). Peameal bacon, a form of Canadian bacon, used to be rolled in crushed yellow peas (peameal), but now cornmeal is the more popular option.

Preparation time: 15 minutes, plus 4 days curing time
Cooking time: 15 minutes
Makes: 1 pound (455 g)

· 1 lb (455 g) boneless pork loin
· ½ cup (120 ml/4 fl oz) pure maple syrup
· 1 tablespoon fine sea salt
· ½ teaspoon whole black peppercorns
· 1 tablespoon mustard seeds
· 1 tablespoon vegetable oil

In a bowl, combine 1 cup (240 ml/8 fl oz) water, maple syrup, salt, peppercorns, and mustard seeds. Pour the liquid into a large zipseal plastic bag and add the pork loin. Squeeze all the air out of the bag. Place on a plate in the refrigerator for 4 days.

Once cured, remove the bacon and pat it dry, discarding the marinade. Allow the bacon to rest, uncovered, in the refrigerator overnight and up to 24 hours. Cut the bacon crosswise into slices about ¼ inch (6 mm) thick. Store, wrapped in plastic wrap (cling film) in the refrigerator for up to 1 week.

To cook the bacon, start with a cold cast-iron skillet or frying pan and add the oil. Place the bacon in flat. Slowly bring the heat to medium to let the fat render and result in crispy bacon. Cook on both sides until browned, about 10 minutes. Repeat with remaining bacon slices (rashers). Serve warm.

COUNTRY HAM WITH RED-EYE GRAVY AND GRITS

UNITED STATES

Preparation time: 10 minutes
Cooking time: 30 minutes
Serves: 2

- ½ cup (70 g) corn grits
- 4 tablespoons full-fat milk
- ½ tablespoon (7 g) unsalted butter
- Salt and freshly ground black pepper
- 1 teaspoon vegetable oil
- 2 slices country ham, cut in half
- 4 tablespoons brewed black coffee
- ½ cup (120 ml/4 fl oz) chicken stock
- ¼ teaspoon sugar

Part of a typical hearty breakfast in the American South, country ham is dry-cured before being smoked. The ham is sliced, grilled, and topped with "red-eye" coffee-infused gravy, served with a side of grits (a "red-eye" is a black coffee with a shot of espresso). The term "red-eye gravy" or "birds-eye gravy" is also a reference to the appearance of the red ham slices peeking through the gravy on the plate, resembling a bloodshot eye. Grits (page 83) soak up the gravy.

In a medium saucepan, bring 2 cups (475 ml/16 fl oz) water to a boil over medium-high heat. Stir in the grits, reduce the heat, and cook at a steady simmer, stirring constantly until thickened, 30 minutes. Add the milk and butter, and season with salt and pepper. Return to a simmer and stir to avoid burning. Season to taste with salt and remove from the heat.

In a frying pan, heat the oil over medium heat. Place the country ham slices in the pan and cook until browned on both sides, flipping once, about 10 minutes. Transfer to paper towels to drain. Reduce the heat to medium and stir in the coffee with a wooden spoon, scraping up any ham bits. Stir in the chicken stock and sugar. Simmer until thickened, about 3 minutes.

Scrve the grits topped with country ham, gravy, and a generous seasoning of salt and pepper.

Country Ham with Red-Eye Gravy and Grits

CHICKEN-FRIED STEAK WITH SAUSAGE GRAVY

UNITED STATES

Another specialty of the American South, this hearty breakfast features tenderized steak, breaded and fried like chicken, then smothered in sausage gravy. Biscuits and Fried Eggs (page 14) round out the meal.

Preparation time: 30 minutes
Cooking time: 30 minutes
Serves: 2

For the steaks:
· ½ cup (70 g) all-purpose (plain) flour
· 4 tablespoons buttermilk
· 1 egg
· ½ teaspoon fine sea salt
· ¼ teaspoon freshly ground pepper
· ⅛ teaspoon sweet paprika
· ¼ teaspoon garlic powder
· ⅓ cup (75 ml/2.5 fl oz) vegetable oil
· 2 cube steaks (minute steaks), 6 oz (170 g) each

For the sausage gravy:
· ¼ lb (115 g) bulk pork sausage or pork breakfast sausage
· 1 tablespoon all-purpose (plain) flour
· ½ cup (120 ml/4 fl oz) full-fat milk
· ⅛ teaspoon cayenne pepper
· Salt and freshly ground black pepper
· 2 Fried Eggs (page 14), for serving
· 2 Buttermilk Biscuits (page 238), for serving

Prepare the steaks:
Place the flour in a shallow bowl. In another shallow bowl, whisk together the buttermilk, egg salt, pepper, paprika, and garlic powder.

In a frying pan or cast-iron skillet, heat the vegetable oil over medium-high heat until hot enough to fry. Test if it is ready for frying by adding a small piece of the steak. If it sizzles, it is ready. Dredge both sides of the steaks in the spiced buttermilk, then dip in the flour, tapping off the excess. Carefully add to the frying pan with tongs. Cook, flipping once, until cooked through, 2–3 minutes per side. Transfer to a baking dish and cover with foil to keep warm.

Meanwhile, make the sausage gravy:
In a medium saucepan, cook the sausage over medium heat, breaking it up with a wooden spoon, until browned, about 10 minutes. Remove and reserve the sausage from the pan, leaving the rendered fat. Stir in 1 tablespoon flour to make a roux (a smooth mixture of fat and flour that helps thicken sauces). Cook, stirring with a wooden spoon to create a smooth paste, making sure there are no lumps and cooking off the flour taste, 2 minutes. Stir in the milk and bring to a simmer. Whisk constantly until thickened, 2 minutes. Add the sausage back in the pan and season with the cayenne and salt and pepper, to taste. Stir to combine and let simmer on low heat for 1 minute more.

Serve each fried steak with a helping of the sausage gravy, a fried egg, and a biscuit.

SAUSAGE WITH EGGS
TURKEY

Sucuk *(Turkish sausage) is made with ground beef, salt, garlic, and a variety of spices like sumac and cumin. Sucuklu yumurta is served fried in a pan, either alone or with eggs. This would be served in a Turkish breakfast spread alongside the same accompaniments as* menemen *(Scrambled Eggs with Tomato and Peppers, page 46).*

Preparation time: 5 minutes
Cooking time: 10 minutes
Serves: 2

· ½ tablespoon olive oil or butter
· 8 slices of sucuk (Turkish dried sausage) about ¼ inch (6 mm) thick
· 2 eggs
· Salt and freshly ground pepper
· Crushed chili flakes (optional)

In a medium nonstick skillet, heat the oil or butter over medium heat. Add the sausage and begin to brown but not crisp on one side, about 2 minutes. Flip and brown the other side, about 2 minutes more. Push the sausage to the sides of the pan.

Crack in the eggs and season with salt. Cook for 1 minute and reduce the heat to low. Cook until the white is set and the edges are golden and crispy, about 2 minutes more. In the last 30 seconds of cooking, use a spoon to baste the egg white with hot butter or oil, helping to finish cooking the white. Use a thin spatula to transfer the sausage slices and eggs onto two plates. Serve sprinkled with pepper and/or chili flakes.

LORNE SAUSAGE
SCOTLAND

Unique to Scotland, this spiced pork and beef sausage comes in square slices. It is fried and served as part of a classic Scottish Fry Up (page 29) or served on a Breakfast Roll (page 29).

Preparation time: 15 minutes, plus 2 hours freezing time
Cooking time: 15 minutes
Serves: 6, makes 2 pounds (910 g)

· 1 lb (450 g) ground (minced) beef
· 1 lb (450 g) ground (minced) pork
· 1 cup (150 g) fine dried breadcrumbs
· 2 teaspoons fine sea salt
· 1 teaspoon freshly ground pepper
· 1 teaspoon ground coriander
· ¼ teaspoon ground nutmeg
· 1 teaspoon olive oil for frying, plus more for greasing

In a large bowl, and using your hands, mix together the beef, pork, breadcrumbs, salt, pepper, coriander, and nutmeg until thoroughly combined. Add ½ cup (120 ml/4 fl oz) water and mix well until combined.

Lightly grease a 9 x 5-inch (23 x 12.5 cm x 7cm) loaf pan, then line with plastic wrap (cling film), allowing plenty of overhang. Press the meat into the loaf pan and cover with the overhanging plastic wrap. Place in the freezer until hard enough to slice, about 2 hours.

Remove the loaf from the pan and plastic wrap and cut into slices ½ inch (1.25 cm) thick. In a medium frying pan, heat the oil over medium heat. Add half of the slices and fry the sausage on both sides until cooked through and browned, about 10 minutes. Spoon away some of the residual fat in the pan, then cook the rest of the sausage. Serve hot.

ALVIN CAILAN
FILIPINO BREAKFAST

A graduate of the Oregon Culinary Institute, Chef Alvin Cailan began learning to cook at a very young age. He worked for many fine establishments such as Castagna, Olympic Provisions, Bouchon, French Laundry, and MB Post, before opening his first food truck, Eggslut, in 2011 in his hometown of Los Angeles. Eggslut now has locations throughout the city and one in Las Vegas. He also opened Amboy, a Filipino take-out restaurant in LA's Chinatown focused on Inihaw-style lunches of grilled meats. In 2018, Cailan opened The Usual, an American comfort-food diner, in New York.

Being woken up by the smell of garlic is normal, right? Well, it was for me. As a child I lived a pretty eventful life. I was often exhausted from studying, hustling to be an awesome baseball and basketball player, and juggling between good and evil. So waking up in the morning and having breakfast was a big deal for me and my overbearing parents. Both of them worked, which means they were up at 5 am, when my caffeinated father would whistle a tune to wake me up. That whistle haunts me to this day. But it also meant, "Wake up! Breakfast is ready." So I would get up, make my bed, shower, and head to the kitchen to fix myself a plate of delicious goodness, then get on with my day.

Breakfast in the Cailan household was usually the same every day. Our garage freezer was always full of *pandesal* from Valerio's Bakery. Defrosted and reheated, it was dipped in coffee, spread with peanut butter, and used to clean the egg yolk of our plates. *Longanisa* was our go-to breakfast meat option; if we didn't have it, we would substitute with spam or canned corned beef. Our pantry contained dozens of each. To round off our breakfast, my dad (the cook of the family) would prepare a plate with a dozen fried eggs on it. Little did I know that eggs would eventually define my career as a chef. Weekend breakfast was a treat: we had *pandesal*, *Longanisa*, eggs, and garlic fried rice—my absolute favorite thing in the world. Our meals revolved around rice. When we had leftovers from the previous day's dinner, it was made into garlic fried rice in the morning. Yes—my breath had a kick. Yes—as I burped throughout the day I'd be reminded of my pungent breakfast. And honestly, I didn't care.

Breakfast for my family was so important. It was a way for my father to show his love for his family before long days, working late to establish his business and make sure we were financially secure. We always knew that he would make us breakfast, and to my brother and me it was everything.

Generally speaking, breakfast for Filipinos is arguably the most important meal of the day. Though regionally it may consist of different ingredients, one style of breakfast is the most popular: "Silog," a portmanteau for Siningag (fried rice) and Itlog (egg). The combination of the two with an added meat or fish has defined the Filipino breakfast in both the Philippines and America. There are very popular restaurants that only serve silog. Ask any Pinoy about breakfast and I will guarantee that they will not only talk about silog, but passionately describe how much they love that dish.

As Filipino food grows in popularity here in America, I know for sure that our breakfast traditions will make waves and really become a part of the American breakfast culture.

01. Spanish Bacon with Garlic Fried Rice and Fried Eggs PAGE 340   02. Spicy Vinegar PAGE 337
03. Cured Beef with Garlic Fried Rice and Fried Eggs PAGE 339

04. Chocolate Rice Porridge PAGE 102   05. Coconut Jam PAGE 150   06. Pandesal PAGE 216

HAMBURGER WITH RICE AND GRAVY

UNITED STATES

Loco moco is a Hawaiian comfort food, said to have been invented by teenagers looking for an Asian-American hybrid breakfast. A mound of white rice is crowned with a hamburger patty slathered in gravy and topped with a fried egg.

Preparation time: 20 minutes
Cooking time: 40 minutes
Serves: 2

For the gravy:
· 2 tablespoons olive oil
· ½ cup (45 g) finely chopped cremini (chestnut) mushrooms
· ½ small shallot, diced
· 1 sprig thyme
· Salt and freshly ground pepper
· 1 tablespoon all-purpose (plain) flour
· 2 cups (475 ml/16 fl oz) vegetable, chicken, or beef stock

For the burgers:
· ½ lb (225 g) ground (minced) beef
· ½ medium onion, diced
· ¼ teaspoon fine sea salt
· ¼ teaspoon freshly ground pepper
· 1 teaspoon Worcestershire sauce (optional)
· 1 egg
· 1 tablespoon olive oil

For serving:
· 1 cup (185 g) cooked short-grain white rice
· 2 Fried Eggs (page 14)
· 1 scallion (spring onion), chopped
· Hot sauce and/or ketchup (optional)

Make the gravy:
In a medium saucepan, heat the oil over medium heat, swirling to coat the pan. Add the mushrooms, shallot, and thyme, and season with salt and pepper. Cook, stirring occasionally to avoid burning, until mushrooms are soft and browned, about 5 minutes. Discard the sprig of thyme. Stir in 1 tablespoon of flour to make a roux (a smooth mixture of fat and flour that helps thicken sauces). Cook, stirring with a wooden spoon to create a smooth paste, making sure there are no lumps and cooking off the flour taste, 2 minutes. Stir in the stock, 1 cup (240 ml/8 fl oz) at a time, and bring to a simmer. Whisk constantly until thickened, 3 minutes. Season with salt and pepper, to taste. Pour the gravy into a heatproof bowl, cover to keep warm, and set aside.

Make the burgers:
In a large bowl, mix together the beef, onion, salt, pepper, Worcestershire (if using), and egg with a spatula or wooden spoon until just incorporated; take care not to overwork the meat. Using your hands, shape the mixture into 2 patties, indenting the center of each patty. Season on both sides with salt and pepper.
 In a large frying pan, heat the oil over medium heat. Add the hamburger patties and cook until browned, about 5 minutes. Flip the patties, cover, and cook until cooked through, about 5 minutes. Remove from the heat.

To serve:
Heap the rice onto 2 plates. Top with a hamburger patty, gravy, fried egg, and scallion (spring onion). Serve with hot sauce or ketchup.

HAWAIIAN BREAKFAST PLATE

UNITED STATES

Portuguese sausage (longanisa), scrambled or fried eggs, white rice and/or macaroni salad, and grilled Spam make up a Hawaiian breakfast plate.

Preparation time: 15 minutes
Cooking time: 30 minutes
Serves: 2

· 2 tablespoons olive oil
· 4 longanisa (Portuguese sausage) links, homemade (see Sausage with Garlic Fried Rice and Fried Eggs, page 336) or store bought
· 2 slices Spam
· 2 slices or rings fresh pineapple
· 4 eggs, scrambled (page 15) or fried (page 14)
· ½ cup (100 g) white rice, cooked according to package instructions
· 1 cup (185 g) Macaroni Salad (recipe follows)

In a medium frying pan, heat 1 tablespoon of the oil over medium heat. Add the sliced sausage and cook until browned on both sides, about 8 minutes. Transfer to paper towels to drain.

Add the remaining 1 tablespoon oil to the pan. Cook the Spam over medium heat until browned, about 6 minutes.

To serve, on each of 2 plates, arrange a slice of Spam, a slice or ring of pineapple, a scoop of macaroni salad, a scoop of white rice, and 2 eggs. Divide the cooked sausage between the two plates. Serve warm.

MACARONI SALAD

Preparation time: 5 minutes
Cooking time: 10 minutes
Makes: 2 cups (450 g)

· 1 cup (115 g) elbow macaroni, cooked according to package instructions
· 1 tablespoon apple cider vinegar
· ⅓ cup (75 g) mayonnaise
· 4 tablespoons full-fat milk
· ½ teaspoon sugar
· 2 tablespoons shredded carrot
· Salt and freshly ground pepper

In a medium bowl, add the pasta and vinegar and stir to coat the pasta. Add the mayonnaise, milk, sugar, and carrot. Season to taste with salt and pepper. Make sure the pasta is thoroughly coated and the carrot is evenly distributed. Chill, covered with plastic wrap (cling film), in the refrigerator for 2 hours.

MARINATED PORK CHOPS WITH BROKEN RICE

VIETNAM

Cơm tấm sườn nướng *is a Southern Vietnamese breakfast consisting of a thin, marinated pork chop served with broken rice and a fried egg. Broken rice is just regular rice broken into fragments. It is commonly used in Vietnamese cooking as it yields a drier texture that soaks up flavors more easily.*

Preparation time: 15 minutes, plus 2 hours marinating time
Cooking time: 30 minutes
Serves: 2

For the pork chops:
· 2 cloves garlic, minced
· 3 tablespoons grated lemon zest or 1 stalk lemongrass, finely chopped
· 3 scallions (spring onion), chopped
· 1 tablespoon sugar
· 1 tablespoon peanut (groundnut) oil, or any neutral cooking oil
· 1 tablespoon soy sauce
· ½ tablespoon fish sauce
· ½ teaspoon freshly ground pepper
· 2 bone-in pork chops, pounded to about ¼ inch (6 mm)

For serving:
· 2 cups (160 g) cooked broken jasmine rice
· 2 Fried Eggs (page 14)
· ½ cucumber, sliced
· ½ tomato, sliced

In a food processor, combine the garlic, lemon zest, scallion (spring onion), sugar, peanut oil, soy sauce, fish sauce, and pepper. Pulse until smooth.

Place the pork in a 9 x 13-inch (23 x 33 cm) baking dish. Pour the marinade over the pork evenly. Cover the dish with plastic wrap (cling film) and marinate for at least 2 hours or up to overnight in the refrigerator.

Heat a cast-iron skillet or grill pan (griddle pan) over medium-high heat. Add the pork to the pan. Cook the pork, flipping once, until cooked through, about 3 minutes per side.

Place each pork chop on a plate and serve accompanied by cooked broken rice, a fried egg, and cucumber and tomato slices.

COCONUT MARINATED PORK WITH BROKEN RICE

CAMBODIA

Bai sach chrouk is a dish of coconut-marinated grilled pork over broken rice, topped with a Fried Egg (page 14) and served with pickled cucumber and radish. Broken rice is a popular ingredient in Southeast Asian cooking, as whole grain rice is typically exported and can be a more expensive option for locals. Broken rice is also preferred for its stickier texture and quick cooking time.

Preparation time: 20 minutes, plus 3 hours marinating time
Cooking time: 20 minutes
Serves: 2

For the pork:
· 1 clove garlic, minced
· 1 tablespoon palm sugar, dark brown sugar, or honey
· 2 tablespoons soy sauce
· ½ tablespoon fish sauce
· ½ cup (120 ml/4 fl oz) coconut milk
· Juice of ½ lime
· ¾ lb (340 g) boneless pork shoulder or blade end roast, cut into slices ½ inch (1.25 cm) thick

For the quick-pickled vegetables:
· ½ cup (120 ml/4 fl oz) rice vinegar
· 1 tablespoon sugar
· ½ teaspoon fine sea salt
· 1 daikon radish, julienned
· ½ cucumber, julienned
· 2–3-inch (5–8 cm) piece fresh ginger, peeled and thinly sliced
· 2 cloves garlic, peeled
· 2 fresh bird's eye chilies, coarsely chopped

For assembly:
· 1 tablespoon vegetable oil
· 2 cups (270 g) cooked jasmine rice, broken rice if available
· Cilantro (coriander) leaves, for serving

Marinate the pork:
In a bowl, combine the garlic, palm sugar, soy sauce, fish sauce, coconut milk, and lime juice and stir to combine. Add the pork to the bowl and coat with the marinade. Cover with plastic wrap (cling film) and refrigerate for 3 hours or up to overnight.

Meanwhile, make the quick-pickled vegetables:
In a small bowl, combine the vinegar and ½ cup (120 ml/4 fl oz) water. Add the sugar and salt and stir to dissolve. Add the daikon, cucumber, ginger, garlic, and chilies and make sure all are coated. Cover with a tea towel and let the mixture sit at room temperature for at least 1 hour.

Assemble the dish:
In a cast-iron skillet, heat the oil over medium-high heat. Remove the pork from the marinade, letting excess drip off. Add the pork to the pan, flipping once, until cooked through, about 5 minutes per side.

Remove the vegetables from the pickling liquid. Serve the pork over cooked rice garnished with cilantro (coriander) and pickled vegetables on the side.

SAUSAGE WITH GARLIC FRIED RICE AND FRIED EGGS
PHILIPPINES

A "silog set," such as longsilog, *is the perfect example of how much fun Filipino people have with abbreviations and nicknames, especially at breakfast. Each of these plates is customizable and given a nickname based on what is on the plate (protein) along with* sinangag *(garlic fried rice) and* itlog *(egg). The protein is abbreviated and* silog *is added to the end to identify it as a set. Choose a protein—* Longganisa, Tapa, Tocino, *or Spam are the most popular—then pair with* sinangag *(Garlic Fried Rice, below), a Fried Egg (page 14), and* sinamak *(Spicy Vinegar, below).*

Longganisa is a Filipino sausage; the dish served with rice and a fried egg is called Longsilog. *This sausage is also found in the Hawaiian Breakfast Plate (page 333), there spelled* longanisa.

Preparation time: 20 minutes, plus overnight marinating time, 1 hour chilling time, and pickling time for the Spicy Vinegar
Cooking time: 30 minutes
Serves: 2

For the sausage:
· 2 cloves garlic, finely minced
· 1 tablespoon sugar
· 1 tablespoon vinegar
· 1¼ teaspoons sweet paprika
· 1 teaspoon fine sea salt
· ½ teaspoon soy sauce
· ¼ teaspoon freshly ground pepper
· ½ lb (225 g) ground (minced) pork
· ½ tablespoon vegetable or olive oil

For serving:
· Garlic Fried Rice (recipe follows)
· Spicy Vinegar (recipe follows)
· 2 Fried Eggs (page 14)

Make the sausage:
Mix together the garlic, sugar, vinegar, paprika, salt, soy sauce, and pepper until thoroughly combined. Using your hands, mix the meat into the marinade until evenly combined. Cover with plastic wrap (cling film) and refrigerate overnight, but no longer than 12 hours.

Shape the sausage into 4 links by rolling 2 tablespoons of the meat mixture in individual sheets of wax (greaseproof) paper, each about 2 inches (5 cm) long and 1 inch (2.5 cm) thick. Set the links in the refrigerator for about 1 hour or until firm and set.

When ready to cook, in a medium frying pan, heat the oil over medium heat. Fry the sausage links until browned on all sides and cooked through, about 10 minutes.

To serve:
Divide the sausage, fried eggs, and Garlic Fried Rice between 2 plates. Serve with Spicy Vinegar.

GARLIC FRIED RICE (SINANGAG)

Preparation time: 5 minutes
Cooking time: 15 minutes
Makes: 2 cups (400 g)

· 1 tablespoon vegetable, peanut (groundnut), or olive oil
· 4 cloves garlic, minced
· 2 cups (320 g) cooked white rice
· ½ teaspoon toasted sesame oil
· Salt
· 1 scallion (spring onion), sliced

In a medium frying pan, heat the oil over medium heat. Add the garlic and cook until browned and crispy, about 1 minute. Add the cooked rice and stir to combine with the garlic. Stir in the sesame oil, salt, and scallion (spring onion) and cook until the rice is heated through, about 5 minutes.

SPICY VINEGAR (SINAMAK)

Preparation time: 10 minutes, plus 2 days pickling time
Makes: 2 cups (500 ml/15 fl oz)

· 10 fresh bird's eye or Thai chilies
· 5 cloves garlic, peeled
· 1½-inch (4 cm) piece fresh ginger, peeled and thinly sliced
· ½ small white onion
· 2 teaspoons black peppercorns
· 2 cups (475 ml/16 fl oz) distilled white or coconut vinegar

In a mason jar, combine the chilies, garlic, ginger, white onion, and peppercorns. Pour in the vinegar and seal the jar tightly. Store at room temperature for at least 2 days to allow the spices and vinegar to blend.

Cured Beef with Garlic Fried Rice and Fried Eggs

CURED BEEF WITH GARLIC FRIED RICE AND FRIED EGGS

PHILIPPINES

Tapa *is cured beef. When paired with* sinangag *(Garlic Fried Rice, page 337), a Fried Egg (page 14), and* sinamak *(Spicy Vinegar, page 337), you get a combo plate called* Tapsilog.

Preparation time: 20 minutes, plus overnight marinating time and pickling time for the Spicy Vinegar
Cooking time: 30 minutes
Serves: 2

For the cured beef:
· 2 tablespoons soy sauce
· 2 cloves garlic, finely minced
· 1 tablespoon sugar
· ¼ teaspoon fine sea salt
· ⅛ teaspoon freshly ground pepper
· ½ lb (225 g) beef sirloin, thinly sliced and cut into strips
· 2 tablespoons vegetable oil

For serving:
· 2 Fried Eggs (page 14)
· Garlic Fried Rice (page 337)
· Spicy Vinegar (page 337)

Make the cured beef:
In a medium bowl, combine the soy sauce, garlic, sugar, salt, and pepper. Massage the thinly sliced sirloin into the mixture. Cover with plastic wrap (cling film) and refrigerate overnight.

When ready to cook, in a medium frying pan, heat the oil over medium-high heat. Cook the meat until browned, about 8 minutes.

For serving:
Divide the cured beef, fried eggs, and Garlic Fried Rice between two plates. Serve with Spicy Vinegar.

SPANISH BACON WITH GARLIC FRIED RICE AND FRIED EGGS
PHILIPPINES

Tocino *is the Spanish version of bacon that can be either boiled or fried. When paired with* sinangag *(Garlic Fried Rice, page 337), a Fried Egg (page 14), and* sinamak *(Spicy Vinegar, page 337), you get a combo plate called* Tocilog.

Preparation time: 30 minutes, plus 2 days marinating and pickling time for the Spicy Vinegar
Cooking time: 30 minutes
Serves: 2

For the Spanish bacon:
· ½ lb (225 g) pork shoulder, thinly sliced
· 1 teaspoon fine sea salt
· 3 tablespoons sugar
· 2 cloves garlic, finely minced
· 2 tablespoons pineapple juice
· 1 teaspoon soy sauce
· ½ teaspoon sweet paprika
· ½ teaspoon freshly ground pepper
· 2 tablespoons vegetable oil

For serving:
· 2 Fried Eggs (page 14)
· Garlic Fried Rice (page 337)
· Spicy Vinegar (page 337)

Make the Spanish bacon:
In a medium bowl, combine the salt, sugar, garlic, pineapple juice, soy sauce, paprika, and pepper stirring until the sugar has dissolved. Add the pork shoulder and massage with the marinade. Cover with plastic wrap (cling film) and refrigerate for 2 days to cure.
     When ready to cook, drain off the marinade. In a medium frying pan, heat the vegetable oil over medium heat. Cook the meat until browned on both sides, about 6 minutes.

For serving:
Divide the Spanish bacon, fried eggs, and Garlic Fried Rice between two plates. Serve with Spicy Vinegar.

SPAM WITH GARLIC FRIED RICE AND FRIED EGGS
PHILIPPINES

Spam is a canned pork product popular in the Philippines, Japan, and Hawaii. When paired with sinangag *(Garlic Fried Rice, page 337), a Fried Egg (page 14), and* sinamak *(Spicy Vinegar, page 337), you get a combination plate called* Spamsilog.

Preparation time: 20 minutes, plus pickling time for the sinamak
Cooking time: 25 minutes
Serves: 2

For the Spam:
· 1 tablespoon vegetable oil
· 4 slices Spam, ¼-inch (6 mm) thick

For serving:
· 2 Fried Eggs (page 14)
· Garlic Fried Rice (page 337)
· Spicy Vinegar (page 337)

Prepare the Spam:
In a cast-iron skillet or frying pan over medium-high heat, add the oil. Fry the Spam on both sides until browned and crispy, about 3 minutes.

To serve:
Divide the Spam, fried eggs, and Garlic Fried Rice between two plates. Serve with Spicy Vinegar.

Spanish Bacon with Garlic Fried Rice and Fried Eggs

BUBBLE AND SQUEAK

ENGLAND

Traditionally made with leftovers from a roast dinner, bubble and squeak is a large potato cake mixed with cabbage and other cooked meat and vegetables. It is fried in a pan, then sliced for a weekend breakfast, often served with an egg on top. The name was given to the dish by 18th Century author, Thomas Bridges in his book A Burlesque Translation of Homer: *"We therefore cook'd him up a dish of lean bull-beef with cabbage fry'd and a full pot of beer beside; bubble they call this dish, and squeak; our taylors dine on't thrice a week."*

Preparation time: 15 minutes
Cooking time: 45 minutes
Serves 4–6

· 4 tablespoons (60 g) unsalted butter, plus more if needed
· ¼ medium onion, diced
· 1½ cups (100 g) thinly sliced cabbage
· ½ cup (70 g) chopped cooked meat (bacon, sausage, black pudding)
· 1 cup (135 g) finely chopped cooked vegetables (carrots, peas, Brussels sprouts)
· 3 medium russet (baking) or Yukon Gold potatoes (about 4 oz/115 g each), boiled and mashed, or ¾ lb (340 g) leftover mashed potatoes
· Salt and freshly ground pepper
· 4–6 Fried Eggs (page 14)

In a frying pan, melt the butter over medium heat, taking care that the butter doesn't brown. Add the onion and cook until soft and translucent, about 5 minutes. Stir in the cabbage and cook until it's colored, about 4 minutes. Add the cooked meat and vegetables. Mix in the mashed potatoes and incorporate with the contents of the pan. Season to taste with salt and pepper.

Use a flexible spatula to shape the potato mixture into a cake, evenly filling the bottom of the pan. Cook until browned, about 7 minutes. Flip the cake, adding 1 tablespoon more of butter if the pan is dry, and brown on the other side, 5 minutes more.

To serve, slice the cake into wedges and serve each portion topped with a fried egg.

CORNED BEEF HASH

UNITED STATES

Corned beef and potatoes are chopped into bits, cooked on a griddle or a cast-iron skillet, and served with toast. Though hash made with fresh corned beef is now the most common version in the United States, canned corned beef became a popular option in the 1940's during wartime rationing—and it is still a popular version in the Philippines. A hash is the perfect way to use leftovers. Similar to Bubble and Squeak (opposite), an English potato cake, hash can be any combination of meat and vegetables, but it always has potatoes.

Preparation time: 15 minutes
Cooking time: 20 minutes
Serves: 2

· 1 cup (150 g) diced peeled russet (baking) potatoes
· 1 tablespoon (15 g) unsalted butter
· ½ medium yellow onion, diced
· 1 clove garlic, minced
· Pinch of cayenne pepper
· Salt and freshly ground black pepper
· 1 cup (165 g) coarsely chopped cooked corned beef

In a saucepan, combine the potatoes with water to cover. Bring to a boil over medium-high heat and cook until the potato is fork-tender, about 5 minutes. The potatoes shouldn't be too mushy in the center. Drain the potato and allow it to cool.

Meanwhile, in a cast-iron skillet or frying pan, heat butter over medium heat. Add the corned beef and cook until browned, about 2 minutes. Add the onion and cook until soft and translucent, about 5 minutes. Add the garlic, cayenne, and salt and black pepper to taste, and stir to combined. Add the potato mixture and stir to combine. Allow the hash to cook until crisp and crusted on the bottom, about 5 minutes. Flip and cook until crisped and browned on the other side and the potato is tender, 3 minutes more. Remove from the heat and serve.

HAM CROQUETAS

UNITED STATES

Croquetas de jamón *are a popular morning meal at Cuban cafes in Miami. Croquetas are whipped potatoes and ham that are rolled into two-bite logs, covered in breadcrumbs, and deep-fried. A good* croqueta *has a light-as-air texture in the center and a thin, crispy outer layer. Saltine crackers are always served alongside in order to sandwich the* croquetas *between crackers for extra crunch, and to avoid greasy fingers. Enjoy with a Cafecito (page 416).*

Preparation time: 20 minutes, plus overnight chilling time
Cooking time: 15 minutes
Serves: 3; makes 12 croquetas

- ½ lb (225 g) ham, cut into chunks
- ½ cup (70 g) all-purpose (plain) flour
- ¼ teaspoon ground nutmeg
- ¼ teaspoon garlic powder
- Salt and freshly ground pepper
- 2 tablespoon (15 g) unsalted butter
- 1 tablespoon finely chopped yellow onion
- ¾ cup (175 ml/6 fl oz) full-fat milk
- 3 eggs
- 2 cups (225 g) fine dried breadcrumbs
- Vegetable oil, for deep-frying
- Saltine crackers, for serving

In a food processor, pulse the ham until coarsely ground. In a shallow bow, mix together the flour, nutmeg, garlic powder, ¼ teaspoon salt, and 1/8 teaspoon pepper.

In a medium frying pan, melt the butter over medium heat. Add the onion and cook until soft and translucent, about 5 minutes. Add the ground ham and stir in the flour mixture and milk. Cook, folding together with a spatula, until a paste forms. Remove the paste from the heat, transfer to a bowl, and refrigerate, covered, overnight.

The next day, roll the paste between your palms into elongated ovals, roughly 2 inches (5 cm) long. In a shallow bowl, beat the eggs and season with salt and pepper. Spread out the breadcrumbs in a second shallow bowl.

In a deep 12-inch (30 cm) frying pan or cast-iron skillet, heat 2 inches (5 cm) oil over medium-high heat. Test the oil by adding a small piece of *croqueta* mixture. If it sizzles, it is ready. Dip the *croquetas* in the egg, allowing excess to drip off. Roll in the breadcrumbs, covering entirely. Working in batches (do not crowd the pan), lower the croquettes into the hot oil with tongs and fry until golden brown, about 2 minutes. Let drain on paper towels.

Serve with saltine crackers.

Ham Croquetas

GOETTA
UNITED STATES

Goetta is a breakfast patty made with ground meat, grains, and spices typically found in the American Midwest. It can be enjoyed with eggs on the side or made into a sandwich.

Preparation time: 15 minutes, plus overnight chilling time
Cooking time: 2 hours 20 minutes
Makes: one 9 x 5-inch (23 x 12.5 cm x 7cm) loaf (8 servings)

· 1 cup (175 g) steel-cut oats
· 1½ teaspoons fine sea salt
· ½ lb (225 g) ground (minced) beef
· ½ lb (225 g) bulk pork sausage
· 1 tablespoon onion powder
· 1 teaspoon freshly ground pepper
· 2 bay leaves
· 2 tablespoons vegetable oil, plus more for greasing
· 4 slices white bread
· 1 clove garlic, peeled and halved
· Fried Eggs (page 14)

In a large saucepan, bring 3 cups (710 l/24 fl oz) water to a boil over high heat. Add the oats and salt and reduce the heat to a very low simmer. Cover and cook, stirring often, until the oats are tender and the water is absorbed, about 1 hour. Mix in the beef, sausage, onion powder, pepper, and bay leaves. Use a wooden spoon to break up the meat, until evenly incorporated. Cover and cook for 1 hour more.

Remove the bay leaves and let the mixture cool slightly.

Meanwhile, lightly grease a 9 x 5-inch (23 x 12.5 cm x 7cm) loaf pan and line with plastic wrap (cling film), allowing plenty of overhang. Pour the mixture into the loaf pan and cover with the overhanging plastic wrap. Refrigerate for at least 5 hours and up to overnight.

Turn the goetta out of the loaf pan and cut into ½-inch (1.25 cm) slices. In a frying pan, heat 1 tablespoon vegetable oil over medium heat and cook the slices until browned on both sides, about 8 minutes. Meanwhile, toast the bread and rub with the cut garlic. Repeat with more oil and the remaining slices of goetta or store in the refrigerator for up to 1 week.

Serve the goetta topped with a fried egg and a slice of toast on the side.

SCRAPPLE
UNITED STATES

Scrapple is a mid-Atlantic breakfast staple made by slow-cooking pork scraps, often offal (organs and entrails), with cornmeal and flour to make a loaf. This is an entry-level scrapple recipe, as the mixture is typically described as including "everything but the oink." It is sliced, grilled, and served with eggs or turned into a breakfast sandwich with white bread and cheese.

Preparation time: 30 minutes, plus 3 hours chilling time
Cooking time: 2 hours 40 minutes
Makes: one 9 x 5-inch (23 x 12.5 x 7 cm) loaf (8 servings)

For the scrapple:
· 1¼ lb (565 g) boneless pork shoulder
· ¾ lb (340 g) ham hock (skinned)
· 2 medium yellow or white onions, halved
· 4 cloves garlic, peeled
· 1 medium stalk celery, roughly chopped
· 4 bay leaves
· 1 tablespoon whole black peppercorns
· 2 tablespoons ground sage
· ½ teaspoon cayenne pepper
· Salt
· 1 cup (130 g) yellow cornmeal

For serving:
· 1 tablespoon vegetable oil
· 2 slices white bread, toasted
· 1 Fried Egg (page 14)

In a large pot, combine the pork shoulder, ham hock, onion halves, garlic, celery, bay leaves, and peppercorns with just enough water to submerge the contents by 2 inches (5 cm). Bring to a boil over high heat, skimming off any fat that rises to the surface. Reduce the heat, cover, and simmer until the meat is very tender and easily slips off of the bone, about 2 hours 15 minutes. With a slotted spoon, transfer the meat to a bowl to cool. Strain the broth into a separate bowl and discard solids. Rinse out the pot and set aside.

When cool enough to handle, pull all the meat from the bones, making sure to remove any smaller bones. Transfer the meat to a food processor and pulse slowly to coarsely chop (alternatively, finely chop with a sharp knife).

Measure out 4 cups (950 ml) of the broth into the cleaned pot (save the rest for another use). Add the chopped meat, sage, cayenne, and salt to taste. Bring to a gentle boil over medium-high heat, then reduce to a simmer. Whisking constantly, slowly stream in the cornmeal and cook, whisking to avoid lumps, until the mixture thickens, 15 minutes.

Lightly grease a 9 x 5-inch (23 x 12.5 cm x 7cm) loaf pan, lined with plastic wrap (cling film), allowing plenty of overhang. Pour the mixture into the loaf pan and cover with the overhanging plastic wrap. Refrigerate for at least 5 hours and up to overnight.

Turn the scrapple out of the pan and use a serrated knife to cut into slices ½ inch (1.5 cm) thick, 2 per person. In a medium frying pan, heat the oil over medium heat. Add 2 scrapple slices and cook until browned and crispy, about 5 minutes. Using a spatula, carefully flip the scrapple and cook on the other side until browned and crispy, about 5 minutes more. Repeat with more oil and the remaining slices of scrapple or store in the refrigerator for up to 1 week.

Serve scrapple slices with a fried egg and toast on the side or make it into a sandwich (see below).

Scrapple Sandwich: To make scrapple into a sandwich, add a slice of American cheese to each of 2 scrapple slices while they are still in the pan. Let the cheese melt for 30 seconds before stacking the two slices on top of each other. Place the scrapple stack on a piece of toast, top with a fried egg and a second piece of toast. Serve with ketchup.

GRILLED FISH

JAPAN

Grilled fish, yakizakana *in Japanese, is one of several traditional breakfast options, which include:* tamagoyaki *(Rolled Omelet, page 48), a bowl of rice, Miso Soup (page 260), and* asazuke *(Quick Pickled Vegetables, below). In this recipe, a grill pan is used but in Japan, tiny drawer-broilers (grills) are common in most kitchens to make quick work of cooking a small piece of fish—typically: salmon, smelt, or dried horse mackerel (*aji*).*

Preparation time: 30 minutes, plus pickling time for the Quick Pickled Vegetables
Cooking time: 40 minutes
Serves: 2

· 2 salmon fillets (3–5 oz/85–140 g each), rinsed
· 1 teaspoon vegetable oil
· Salt

For serving:
· Soy sauce
· Rolled Omelet (page 48)
· Cooked white rice
· Miso Soup (page 260)
· Quick Pickled Vegetables (recipe follows)

Set a grill pan (griddle pan) over medium-high heat, brush the oil onto the pan. Salt both sides of the fish. Add the fish, skin-side down, and cook until the flesh becomes opaque about halfway through, about 5 minutes. Flip and cook until the flesh becomes opaque, another 5 minutes more (see Note).

To serve:
Serve the fish on a small plate, with a side of soy sauce for dipping. Serve *tamagoyaki*, white rice, miso soup, and *asazuke* in separate small bowls.

Note: For crisper skin on the salmon, position a rack in the top third of the oven and preheat the broiler (grill). Cook the fish as above, but do not flip; transfer the salmon skin-side up to a foil-lined baking sheet and broil (grill) 3–5 minutes to crisp the skin and the flesh becomes opaque. Be careful to watch that the skin doesn't burn.

See image on page 257

QUICK PICKLED VEGETABLES (ASAZUKE)

Preparation time: 15 minutes, plus 1 hour pickling time
Makes: 1 cup (135 g)

· 4 tablespoons diced eggplant (aubergine)
· ½ cup (70 g) napa cabbage (Chinese leaf), chopped into 1-inch pieces
· ½ cup (70 g) cucumber, sliced into thin ribbons
· 1 teaspoon fine sea salt
· ½ teaspoon sugar

Put all the vegetables in a zipseal plastic bag with the salt and sugar. Seal the bag and use your hands to move the ingredients around, making sure to coat them in the salt and sugar. Place in a shallow baking dish to catch any liquid that might escape and weight the bag down with a heavy pot or pan. Let sit for at least 1 hour, so the salt has a chance to pull out the liquids, then squeeze the remaining water out of the mixture and serve.

Quick Pickled Vegetables

PORK SKEWERS

THAILAND

Muu ping *are a popular Thai breakfast enjoyed on the go. These grilled pork skewers are served with a bag of sticky rice. The rice is used to grab a piece of pork and pull off the skewer, so that your hands stay clean. It's typically accompanied by* jaew, *a sweet but mildly spicy chili sauce used for dipping.*

Preparation time: 20 minutes, plus 2 hours marinating time
Cooking time: 25 minutes
Serves: 2

- ½ tablespoon minced cilantro (coriander) stems
- 1 clove garlic, peeled
- ½ teaspoon white peppercorns or ¼ teaspoon ground white pepper
- ½ teaspoon coconut palm sugar
- ½ tablespoon fish sauce
- 2 teaspoons Thai soy sauce (or regular soy sauce)
- 1½ teaspoons oyster sauce
- ½ lb (225 g) pork loin, cut against the grain into ½-inch (1.25 cm) pieces
- 2 tablespoons coconut milk, for basting
- Jaew chili sauce, for serving
- ½ cup (125 g) cooked sticky rice, for serving

With a mortar and pestle or in a food processor, combine the cilantro (coriander) stems, garlic, and white peppercorns or ground white pepper. Blend together until thoroughly combined.

In a large bowl, combine the cilantro mixture with the palm sugar, fish sauce, soy sauce, and oyster sauce. Mix well until combined. Stir in the pork and coat in the marinade. Cover the bowl with plastic wrap (cling film) and refrigerate for 2 hours. Meanwhile, soak 4 bamboo skewers in water for 1 hour.

Thread 6 pieces of marinated pork onto each skewer. Set up a charcoal grill (barbecue) for medium-low heat or heat a grill pan (griddle pan) over medium heat. Place the skewers on the grill and baste with coconut milk. Cook the skewers, turning every so often, until cooked through and charred, 10 minutes. Serve the skewers with sticky rice and *jaew* chili sauce.

LOX

UNITED STATES

Lox and smoked salmon are enjoyed for breakfast around the world, from a side on the Israeli Breakfast Plate (page 26) to Norway, where it is eaten with scrambled eggs, to New York, where every morning street carts and delis add it to a bagel with cream cheese and optional tomato, onion, and capers. This recipe is for a simple cured salmon, lox. The many nomenclatures for lox and/or smoked salmon can be confusing, so here's a quick guide: lox or "belly lox" is cured and sometimes cold-smoked; gravlax originates in Scandinavia and is cured with salt, sugar, and dill, sometimes cold-smoked; Nova lox is cured or brined then cold-smoked; and "kippered" salmon is hot-smoked and cooked all the way through. "Smoked salmon" can refer to any of these.

Preparation time: 20 minutes, plus 2 days curing time
Serves: 4–6

· 1 lb (455 g) wild salmon belly, rinsed, skin on, pin bones removed
· 3 tablespoons light brown sugar
· 3 tablespoons granulated sugar
· ½ cup (65 g) fine sea salt
· 1 tablespoon grated lemon zest

In a small bowl, combine the brown sugar, granulated sugar, salt and pepper until thoroughly combined. Cover both sides of the salmon pieces with the sugar-salt mixture in a shallow bowl or dish. Sprinkle the lemon zest on the flesh side. Fold the salmon in half widthwise, flesh sides together, and wrap in plastic wrap (cling film). Place the wrapped salmon in a baking dish or shallow glass bowl. Weight the fish down with significant weight (about 3 lb/1.4 kg), using another baking dish and cans of beans, plates, or bottles of wine. Refrigerate the weighted down salmon.

After 12 hours, remove and discard any of the liquid that's accumulated. Flip the wrapped fish and reapply the weights, and return to the refrigerator for another 12 hours. Discard the liquid, and flip the wrapped fish again, reapply the weights, and return the salmon to the refrigerator. Allow the salmon to continue to cure, draining the liquid at the end of each day, for a total of 2–5 days, depending how concentrated you want the flavor.

When ready to serve, rinse the fish, pat dry, and slice very thin at a 15-degree angle.

SHRIMP AND GRITS

UNITED STATES

The southern United States is known for its love of grits, a thick, coarsely ground cornmeal porridge. There are plain grits with butter, sometimes cheese (page 83), Country Ham with Red-Eye Gravy and Grits (page 324), and shrimp and grits often topped with bits of andouille sausage or bacon. Native American tribes in the region would make dishes from corn ground into a coarse, gritty texture on a stone mill. Grits were then adopted by settlers and turned into one of the South's most beloved foods. Creole cooks adapted the idea and added shrimp (prawns), a common local ingredient due to their close proximity to the Gulf of Mexico.

Preparation time: 15 minutes
Cooking time: 40 minutes
Serves: 2

· 2 tablespoons (30 g) unsalted butter
· ½ medium yellow onion, diced
· 1 clove garlic, minced
· ½ teaspoon fresh thyme leaves
· 1 tablespoon all-purpose (plain) flour
· ½ cup (120ml/4 fl oz) fish or chicken stock
· ½ lb (225 g) shrimp (prawns), peeled and deveined
· 1 teaspoon lemon juice, plus more for serving
· ½ teaspoon Worcestershire sauce
· ⅛ teaspoon cayenne pepper
· Salt and freshly ground black pepper
· Grits (page 83)
· Parsley, for serving

In a deep-frying pan or shallow saucepan, melt the butter over medium heat. Add the onion and garlic and cook until the onions are soft and translucent, and the garlic is aromatic, 5 minutes. Stir in the flour to make a roux (a smooth mixture of fat and flour that helps thicken sauces). Cook, stirring with a wooden spoon to create a smooth paste, making sure there are no lumps and cooking off the flour taste, 2 minutes. Stir in the fish stock and bring to a light simmer, stirring occasionally to avoid any clumps. Add the shrimp (prawns) to the liquid and poach until the shrimp are pink and cooked through, about 3 minutes. Stir in the lemon juice, Worcestershire sauce, cayenne, and salt and black pepper to taste. The gravy should be smooth and thickened.

Divide grits between 2 bowls, with a helping of shrimp and gravy. Garnish with parsley, and season with salt and pepper to taste, and an extra squeeze of lemon, if you prefer.

LAVERBREAD
AND COCKLES

WALES

A mix of seaweed and cockles, cooked in bacon fat, laverbread has nothing to do with "bread." It is a boiled puréed seaweed often mixed with oatmeal before being fried in a pan and/or along with cockles, served in a Welsh Fry Up (page 29).

Preparation time: 10 minutes, plus 2 hours soaking time if using fresh cockles
Cooking time: about 12 minutes
Serves: 2

· 1 cup (115 g) frozen cooked cockle meat, cooked drained cockle meat from a jar or can in brine, or about 1lb 2oz (500g) fresh cockles in shells
· 4 slices (rashers) bacon (streaky)
· ½ cup (85 g) prepared laverbread from a can or jar, or 4 sheets of nori (approx. 8 x 7 inches (20cm x 18 cm), total weight about ½ oz (15g)
· 2 tablespoons (30 g) unsalted butter
· Salt and freshly ground pepper
· 2 slices white bread, toasted, for serving

If using frozen cooked cockles, defrost under cold water for 10 minutes, using two changes of water, then drain well. If using fresh cockles, soak or 'purge' the cockles in salted water before cooking.

Put the cockles into a deep bowl of heavily salted cold water (it should be like seawater) and leave in refrigerator for 2 hours, after which they may have expelled sand and grit. Rather than draining, lift out all the cockles from the water and discard any open shells that do not close when tapped.

Heat a medium frying pan over medium heat. Add the cockles and a splash of water (or wine or cider), cover, and cook over a high heat for 3–4 minutes or until the shells are open. Discard any that have not opened. When cool enough, pick out the meat.

Start with a cold cast-iron skillet or frying pan and place the bacon in flat. Slowly bring the heat to medium to let the fat render and result in crispy bacon. Cook on both sides until crispy, about 10 minutes. Transfer the bacon to paper towels to drain, and reserve bacon for a Welsh Fry Up (page 29)

Add the cockles to the bacon fat and stir until warmed, about 1 minute. Stir in 1 tablespoon of the butter. Season to taste with salt and pepper and stir until the butter has melted. Move the cockles to one side of the pan and add the prepared laverbread or soaked nori and the remaining 1 tablespoon butter to the other. Cook until the butter has melted and the laverbread has formed a creamed spinach consistency, about 30 seconds. Slide onto 2 plates and serve with the bacon, toast, and other elements of a Welsh Fry Up.

See image on page 171.

ACKEE AND SALTFISH
JAMAICA

Ackee is a buttery tropical fruit with a slight tang. It pairs perfectly with salted fish and Caribbean Johnny Cakes (page 296).

Preparation time: 15 minutes
Cooking time: 1 hour 20 minutes
Serves: 4

- ¼ lb (115 g) salt cod
- 3 tablespoons coconut oil
- 3 cloves garlic, minced
- 1 medium yellow onion, diced
- 1 small tomato, diced
- 2 scallions (spring onions), sliced
- ½ small green chili, seeded and diced
- ½ small red bell pepper, sliced
- ½ small orange bell pepper, sliced
- ½ tablespoon chopped fresh parsley
- 1 cup drained canned ackee fruit (about half a 19 oz/538 g can)
- ½ teaspoon freshly ground black pepper
- Salt

To de-salt the cod, place it in a saucepan, cover with water, and bring to a boil over medium-high heat. Drain the water from the pot, re-fill it, and bring to a boil again. Repeat once more. (Alternatively, soak the cod overnight in a bowl of water.) Flake the de-salted cod and set aside.

In a medium frying pan, heat the oil over medium heat. Add the garlic, yellow onion, tomato, scallions (spring onions), chili, and bell peppers and stir together with a wooden spoon. Sauté until the onion is soft and translucent, 5 minutes. Stir in the cod and parsley and cook for 3 minutes more. Gently stir in the ackee and cook for 5 minutes. Season with the black pepper and salt to taste.

TUNA WITH GRATED COCONUT
MALDIVES

Mas Huni is a dish of fresh, grated coconut, Maldive fish, and onions. Maldivian fish is a cured tuna commonly used in local and Sri Lankan cooking. In this dish, canned tuna is a common substitute. Enjoy it with a laminated flatbread called, roti.

Preparation time: 15 minutes
Serves: 2

- ½ cup (80 g) diced red onion (about 1 small onion)
- 1 small green banana pepper or mild green chili, diced
- Grated zest of 1 lime
- 3 tablespoons lime juice
- Salt and freshly ground black pepper
- 1 can (5 oz/140 g) tuna packed in olive oil, drained and flaked
- 1 cup (80 g) grated fresh or frozen coconut
- Roti, for serving (see Roti Prata on page 207)

In a bowl, stir together the onion, banana pepper, lime zest and juice, and salt and black pepper to taste. Stir in the tuna. Mix in the coconut until thoroughly incorporated. Serve with *roshi* (*roti*).

Tuna with Grated Coconut

PIES AND

PASTRIES

CROISSANTS
FRANCE

In 1683, bakers in the city of Vienna were the only ones awake during a planned underground invasion by the Ottomans. The bakers heard suspicious noises and were able to warn the city and stop the attack. To celebrate the victory over the Turks, the bakers created Kipferl *(meaning crescent, in German) inspired by the crescent shape on the enemy flag. Today the* kipferl *is more commonly known as a croissant. The Viennese tradition of rich pastries has influenced baked goods around the world. The French refer to this style as* viennoiserie *and include the croissant, Brioche (page 214), Pain au Chocolat (page 360), Almond Croissant (page 362), and many more. In France, the croissant is typically enjoyed as a special weekend breakfast; in Austria, the Kipferl is an everyday pastry. Croissants are a prime example of a laminated pastry, a technique that produces many thin layers by repeatedly folding and rolling out butter in the dough to achieve airy, flaky layers after baking.*

Preparation time: 1 hour 15 minutes, plus 15 hours chilling and rising time
Cooking time: 25 minutes
Makes: 8–10 croissants

For the dough:
· 1¼ cups (307 g / 10.75 fl oz) full-fat milk, warmed
· 2¼ teaspoons active dry yeast
· 4 tablespoons sugar
· 1 tablespoon (15 g) unsalted butter, melted
· 3 cups (435 g) plus 2 tablespoons all-purpose (plain) flour, plus more for dusting
· 1 teaspoon fine sea salt

For the butter package:
· 2 sticks (225 g / ½ lb.) unsalted butter, at room temperature

For the egg wash:
· 1 egg
· 1 tablespoon full-fat milk

Make the dough:
Combine the milk, yeast, and a pinch of sugar. Set the mixture aside until the yeast is frothy, about 10 minutes. (If the yeast doesn't froth, check the expiration date. You may have to start over with fresher yeast.)

In the bowl of a stand mixer fitted with the dough hook, stir together the yeast mixture, remaining sugar, and melted butter. With the mixer on low, add the flour and salt. Increase the speed to medium and knead the dough until it's elastic and smooth, 3 minutes. Turn the dough out onto a lightly floured work surface and roll the dough into a 6-inch (15 cm) square, making sure the dough remains 1 inch (2.5 cm) thick. Cover tightly with plastic wrap (cling film) and refrigerate for 8 hours or overnight.

Prepare the butter package:
Place the sticks of softened butter in the center of a 12 x 16 inch (30 x 40 cm) sheet of parchment paper. Fold one half of the parchment paper over the butter, lining up the crease of the paper with the edge of the butter so that there's no space between the butter and crease. Use a rolling pin to lightly pound the butter to flatten it. Fold the parchment paper to make a 6-inch (15 cm) square. With the rolling pin, pound the butter until it fills all corners of the parchment paper square. Place in the refrigerator until firm but still pliable, 20 minutes.

Laminate the dough:
10 minutes before laminating the dough, remove the butter package from the refrigerator. Turn the dough out onto a lightly floured surface. Roll it into a 10-inch (25 cm) square. Set the butter in the center of the dough square like a diamond. Enclose the butter in the dough by pulling each side in over the butter to meet in the middle. Flip the dough package over and lightly flour the work surface. Roll the dough into a rectangle, 8 x 20 inches (20 x 50 cm). Brush off any excess flour. With a short side facing you, fold the bottom one-third of the dough up, then fold the top one-third down over that, like folding a business letter. Cover with plastic wrap (cling film) and place in the refrigerator for at least 30 minutes.

On a lightly floured surface, place the dough with the spine of the letter fold to your left, like a book. Roll the dough into a rectangle, 8 x 20 inches (20 x 50 cm). Brush off excess flour. With a short side facing you, repeat the fold. Wrap in plastic wrap (cling film) and place back into the refrigerator until firm, about 30 minutes more.

Repeat the fold and refrigeration three more times. These folds create the flaky layers croissants are famous for. After the last fold, wrap the dough and refrigerate at least 8 hours or overnight.

Shape the croissants:
The next day, turn the rested dough out onto a lightly floured surface. With the open seam sides on the right and left, roll the dough into a rectangle, 8 x 20 inches (20 x 50 cm). It should be about ¼ inch (6 mm) thick. Line a large baking sheet with parchment paper. Rotate the strip of dough so that the long side is facing you. Starting from the bottom corner of the rectangle and using a sharp knife, cut a diagonal to create a long triangle shape. Continue cutting triangles with the remaining dough, 8–10 total. Holding the base of the triangle, stretch the dough out gently. Starting at the base of the triangle, roll the croissant towards the acute tip of the triangle. Press gently on the tip so that it remains tucked underneath the base and does not pop up and unravel during proofing and baking. Place the croissants on the baking sheet, placing the pastries at least 2 inches (5 cm) apart. Cover with plastic wrap (cling film) and allow the croissants to puff up, about 1½ hours.

Meanwhile, preheat the oven to 400°F (200°C/Gas Mark 6).

Bake the croissants:
In a small bowl, make the egg wash by whisking together the egg and the milk.

Check the croissants: They should look well-risen and slowly spring back but leave a small dimple when pushed lightly with a finger. This means they're perfectly proofed. When ready, brush each croissant with the egg wash. Bake until beginning to brown (about 15 minutes), rotate the pans, and reduce the heat to 350°F (180°C/Gas Mark 4). Continue baking the croissants until they are deeply golden brown but not burnt, 5–10 minutes more. If using 2 baking sheets at the same time, rotate them halfway through cooking. Allow the croissants to cool before serving.

....

See images on pages 198 and 361

....

PAIN AU CHOCOLAT

FRANCE

Made with the same enriched dough as a croissant, this pastry is in the shape of a fist and has a dark chocolate stick (specifically made for Pain au Chocolat) buried in the center.

Preparation time: 1 hour 15 minutes, plus 15 hours chilling and rising time
Cooking time: 25 minutes
Makes: 10–12

· Dough from Croissants (page 358)
· 20–24 pain au chocolat sticks (3 x½ x ¼ inch /7.5 x 1.25 x 0.6 cm), or dark chocolate, cut to size
· Egg wash: 1 egg beaten with 1 tablespoon milk

Roll, fold, and chill the dough per the instructions for making croissants, up to the point of shaping the pastries.

Roll the dough into a rectangle, 12 x 16 inch (30 x 40 cm) and about ¼ inch (6 mm) thick, with the long side facing you. Cut the dough in half lengthwise. Line 2 large baking sheets with parchment paper. Using the chocolate stick for scale, cut the dough into 3 x 5½ inch (7.5 x 14 cm) rectangles. Place 2 chocolate sticks side by side, aligned with the end of the large side of the rectangle and roll it up. Tuck the seam underneath and place it seam side down on a baking sheet. Repeat with the remaining rectangles and chocolate sticks. Place the pastries at least 2 inches (5 cm) apart. Cover with plastic wrap (cling film) and allow the pastries to puff up, about 1½ hours. Repeat with the second half of the dough.

Meanwhile, preheat the oven to 400°F (200°C/Gas Mark 6).

Check the pastries: They should look well-risen and slowly spring back but leave a small dimple when pushed lightly with a finger. This means they're perfectly proofed. When ready, brush each pastry with the egg wash. Bake for 15 minutes. Reduce the heat to 350°F (180°C/Gas Mark 4) and bake until deeply golden brown but not burnt, about 5–10 minutes more. If using baking two sheets at the same time, rotate them half way through cooking. Allow to cool before serving.

Croissants (page 358–59), Pains au Chocolat, Almond Croissants (page 362)

ALMOND CROISSANTS
FRANCE

For croissants aux amandes, *a classic croissant shape is filled with almond crème and topped with slivered almonds.*

Preparation time: 20 minutes, plus chilling and rising time
Cooking time: 40 minutes
Makes: 6 croissants

· 6 Croissants (page 358)
· 1 stick (115 g) unsalted butter, at room temperature
· 4 tablespoons granulated sugar
· 2 eggs
· ¾ cup (75 g) almond flour
· 2 teaspoons all-purpose (plain) flour
· Sliced almonds
· Powdered (icing) sugar

Make 6 croissants.

Preheat the oven to 350°F (180°C/Gas Mark 4). Line a baking sheet with parchment paper.

In the bowl of a stand mixer (or in a large bowl with a hand mixer), cream the butter and granulated sugar together until fluffy. Add the eggs and beat on a low speed until combined and fluffy, about 1 minute. Gradually beat in the almond flour and all-purpose (plain) flour, until the almond cream is the consistency of cake batter.

Slice the croissants horizontally in half. Place them on the lined baking sheet. With an offset (icing) spatula, spread a tablespoon or two of the almond cream on the bottom half of each croissant. Replace the croissant tops. Spread 1 tablespoon of almond cream on the outside of the croissant and sprinkle with sliced almonds.

Bake the croissants until the cream is set and golden brown, about 12 minutes. Allow the croissants to cool before sprinkling with powdered (icing) sugar and serving.

See images on pages 198 and 361

CRESCENT ROLLS
ARGENTINA

Similar to Croissants *(page 358),* medialunas *are crescent-shaped* facturas *(pastries) sometimes sweetened with a glaze (*almíbar*). They can be enjoyed split in half, filled with slices of ham and cheese or with* Dulce de Leche *(page 154), and put under the broiler (grill) to melt the cheese. The rolls are typically served with* Café con Leche *(page 415) and a shot glass of sparkling water.*

Preparation time: 1 hour 20 minutes, plus 2 hours 40 minutes rising, chilling, and proofing time
Cooking time: 20–25 minutes
Makes: 14 rolls

For the dough:
· 1¼ cups (300 ml/10 fl oz) full-fat milk, warmed
· 2 teaspoons active dry yeast
· 1 tablespoon sugar
· 3½ cup (505 g) all-purpose (plain) flour, plus more for dusting
· ½ teaspoon fine sea salt
· 1 egg, beaten
· Vegetable oil, for greasing

For the butter package:
· 2 sticks (225 g) unsalted butter, at room temperature
· 1 egg yolk, for the egg wash
· 4 tablespoons sugar, for the glaze

Make the dough:
In a small bowl, combine the milk, yeast, and a pinch of sugar. Set the mixture aside until the yeast is frothy, about 10 minutes. (If the yeast doesn't froth, check the expiration date. You may have to start over with fresher yeast.)

In a large bowl, combine the flour, salt, and remaining sugar. Make a well in the center of the flour. Pour in the yeast mixture and egg.

Stir with a wooden spoon until a shaggy dough forms and starts to pull away from the sides of the bowl. Turn the dough out onto a lightly floured work surface. Knead until the dough becomes smooth and elastic, about 10 minutes. Place in a lightly greased bowl, cover with plastic wrap (cling film), and let it rise until it doubles in size, about 45 minutes.

Meanwhile, prepare the butter package:
Prepare the butter package according to the directions in Croissants (page 358).

Turn the dough out onto a lightly floured surface and punch down. With a rolling pin, roll into a rectangle, about ½ inch (1.25 cm) thick and 16 x 9-inches (40 x 23 cm). Place the butter package on one end, fold the other half of the dough up and over the butter to seal it in. Roll the dough into a rectangle again, about ½ inch (1.25 cm) thick and 16 x 9-inches (40 x 23 cm). With a short side facing you, fold the bottom one-third of the dough up, then fold the top one-third down over that, like folding a business letter. Cover loosely with plastic wrap (cling film) and place in the refrigerator for 30 minutes.

Turn the cold, rested, and slightly risen dough out onto a lightly floured surface. Roll into a rectangle, about ¼ inch (6 mm) thick and about 12 x 17-inches (30 x 42cm). Line 2 large baking sheets with parchment paper. Trim the edges of the rectangle (this lets the layers rise fully) and rotate the strip of dough so that the long side faces you. Starting from the bottom corner of the rectangle and using a sharp knife, cut a diagonal to create a long triangle shape. Continue cutting triangles with the remaining dough, making 14 total. Holding the base of the triangle, stretch the dough out gently. Starting at the base of the triangle roll the *medialuna* towards the acute tip of the triangle. Press gently on the tip so that it remains tucked underneath the base and doesn't pop up and unravel during proofing and baking. Place the *medialunas* on the baking sheets, placing the pastries at least 2 inches (5 cm) apart. Cover with plastic wrap (cling film) and allow the croissants to puff up, about 1 hour 30 minutes.

Meanwhile, preheat the oven to 400°F (200°C/Gas Mark 6).

Bake the rolls:
Preheat the oven to 400°F (200°C/Gas Mark 6).

In a small bowl, whisk together the egg yolk and 1 teaspoon water.

Check the *medialunas*: They should look well-risen and slowly spring back but leave a small dimple when pushed lightly with a finger. This means they're perfectly proofed. Brush each with the egg wash. Bake for 15 minutes. Reduce the heat to 350°F (18°C/Gas Mark 4) and bake until deeply golden brown but not burnt, about 5–10 minutes more. If using baking 2 sheets at the same time, rotate them halfway through cooking. Let cool on a rack with a backing sheet underneath.

Meanwhile, make the glaze. In a small saucepan, combine ½ cup (120 ml/4 fl oz) water and sugar and stir over medium-high heat until the sugar dissolves, 1 minute. Remove the syrup from the heat.

Once the *medialunas* have cooled, drizzle with the glaze, allowing the excess to fall onto the baking sheet below. Serve warm.

CORNETTI
ITALY

A smaller, less buttery version of a croissant, a cornetto *(plural:* cornetti*) can be served* vuoto *(empty) or filled with orange marmalade, pastry cream, sweet ricotta, pistachios, or Nutella. It is often enjoyed with a Cappuccino (page 419).*

Preparation time: 1 hour 30 minutes, plus 7 hours rising and chilling time
Cooking time: 20 minutes
Makes: 10 cornetti

For the dough:
· 4 tablespoons full-fat milk, warmed
· 4 tablespoons warm water
· 2¼ teaspoons instant (fast-acting) yeast
· 4 tablespoons sugar
· 1 tablespoon grated orange zest
· 1 tablespoon (15 g) unsalted butter, melted
· 2 eggs
· 2 cups (290 g) plus 2 tablespoons all-purpose (plain) flour
· ¼ teaspoon fine sea salt
· Vegetable oil, for greasing

For the butter package:
· 2 sticks (225 g) unsalted butter, at room temperature

For the topping:
· 1 egg yolk
· 1 tablespoon full-fat milk
· Raw sugar, for sprinkling

For serving:
· Apricot jam

Make the dough:
In the bowl of a stand mixer fitted with the dough hook, combine the milk, warm water, yeast, sugar, and orange zest. Mix on low speed until just combined. Add the melted butter. Add the eggs, one at a time, beating well after each addition. Gradually add the flour and salt and mix on medium speed until a smooth, sticky dough forms, 5 minutes. Place the dough into a lightly oiled bowl, cover with plastic wrap (cling film), and allow it to rise until doubled in size, about 2 hours.

Make the *cornetti*:
Meanwhile, prepare the butter package according to the directions in Croissants (page 358)

Turn the dough out onto a lightly floured surface. Roll it out into a 10 x 6-inch (25 x 15 cm) rectangle. Set the butter in the center of the dough square like a diamond. Enclose the butter in the dough by pulling each side in over the butter to meet in the middle. Cover tightly with plastic wrap (cling film) and refrigerate for 30 minutes.

Turn the dough package onto a lightly floured surface. Roll the dough into a 10 x 6-inch (25 x 15 cm) rectangle about ¼ inch (6 mm) thick. Brush off any excess flour. With a short side facing you, fold the bottom one-third of the dough up, then fold the top one-third down over that, like folding a business letter. Cover with plastic wrap and refrigerate for at least 30 minutes.

On a lightly floured surface, place the dough with the spine of the letterfold to your left, like a book. Roll the dough out into a rectangle again, 10 x 6-inch (25 x 15 cm). Brush off excess flour. With a short side facing you, fold the bottom one-third of the dough up, then fold the top one-third down over that, like folding a business letter. Wrap in plastic wrap and place back into the refrigerator, about 30 minutes. Turn the dough out onto a lightly floured surface and roll the dough back into a 10 x 6-inch (25 x 15 cm) rectangle. Brush off excess flour. With a short side facing you, fold the bottom one-third of the dough up, then fold the top one-third down over that, like folding a business letter. Repeat the fold and refrigeration two more times. These folds

PIES AND PASTRIES

create the flaky layers. On the last fold, keep the wrapped dough refrigerated for 1 hour.

Turn the rested dough out onto a lightly floured surface. Roll into a rectangle, 8 x 20 inches (20 x 50 cm). The rectangle should be just about ¼ inch (6 mm) thick. Line 2 baking sheets with parchment paper. Starting from the bottom corner, slice 10 triangles with a sharp knife. Starting at the base of the triangle, roll the cornetto toward the tip of the triangle. The triangle should tuck underneath the base a little so that it doesn't pop up and unravel during proofing and baking. Place the *cornetto* on a baking sheet. Repeat with the remaining cornetti, placing 2 inches (5 cm) apart. Cover with plastic wrap and allow the *cornetti* to puff up, about 1½ hours.

Bake the *cornetti:*
Preheat the oven to 400°F (200°C/Gas Mark 6).Check the *cornetti:* They should look well-risen and slowly spring back but leave a small dimple when pushed lightly with a finger. This means they're perfectly proofed.

In a small bowl, whisk together the egg yolk and milk to make an egg wash. Once the cornettos have risen, brush each with the glaze wash. Sprinkle with raw sugar.

Bake for 15 minutes. Reduce the heat to 350°F (180°C/Gas Mark 4) and bake until deeply golden brown but not burnt, about 5–10 minutes more. If using 2 baking sheets at a time, rotate them halfway through cooking. Allow the cornetti to cool before serving.

EGG TARTS
PORTUGAL

Breakfast in Portugal typically consists of a slice of bread with cheese, a pastel de nata *(egg tart), or a sweet pastry. When Portuguese settlers reached Macau, China, they brought along this sweet egg custard puff pastry. Now, egg tarts are enjoyed in China—mostly in Hong Kong (where they are a little sweeter) and Macau (a little more savory)—as a breakfast treat. This recipe is for the original Portuguese version.*

Preparation time: 30 minutes, plus 40 minutes chilling and cooling
Cooking time: 15 minutes
Makes: 18 tarts

- 1 10 x 15 inch (25 x 38 cm) sheet all-butter puff pastry, store-bought or homemade (page 384)
- Butter, for greasing
- All purpose flour, for rolling
- ¾ cup (175 ml/6 fl oz) full-fat milk, warmed
- ½ cup (105 g) sugar
- 1 cinnamon stick
- ¼ teaspoon vanilla extract
- 5 egg yolks
- Ground cinnamon, for dusting

Preheat the oven to 500°F (260°C/Gas Mark 10) with the rack in the top third of the oven.

Roll the puff pastry sheet to a 10 x 15 inch (25 x 38 cm) rectangle, ¼ inch (6 mm) thick. Roll it up from the short side into a tight log 10 inches (25 cm) long. Wrap tightly with plastic wrap (cling film) and let it firm up in the refrigerator, about 25 minutes.

Trim the uneven ends of the log and slice the log crosswise into ½-inch (1.25 cm) thick disks. You should have about 18 disks. Roll each disk to about 4 inches (10 cm) in diameter. Grease 18 muffin tins or 18 egg-tart tins with butter (or coat with cooking spray). Fit the dough rounds into the muffin cups and use your fingertips to work the pastry around the edges, just shy of the rim. Prick the dough a few times with a fork. Refrigerate the dough while you prepare the custard filling.

In a small saucepan, combine 4 tablespoons water, sugar, and cinnamon stick. Bring to a boil over medium-high heat, stirring until the sugar is dissolved, about 1 minute. Remove the simple syrup from the heat. Scoop out and discard the cinnamon stick and stir in the vanilla extract. In a separate bowl, whisk the egg yolks and, whisking constantly, add the warm milk in a steady stream. Whisking constantly, drizzle in the simple syrup. Return the mixture to the small saucepan and place over low heat. Cook, using a spatula to stir and scrape the bottom of the pot constantly, until thickened to the consistency of heavy cream, about 4 minutes. Transfer to a liquid measuring cup with a spout.

Ladle the custard mixture into the tins, filling the cups about three-quarters of the way. Place the tins on a baking sheet to protect the bottoms of the pastries from burning. Bake for 10 minutes, until the custard is golden brown. Turn on the broiler (grill) to high and cook until the custard has caramelized and blackened in spots, 3–5 minutes. Allow the tarts to cool in the muffin tin for 5 minutes before transferring to a cooling rack. Cool for 10 minutes more before removing tarts from their tins. Dust with cinnamon and serve warm.

Egg Tarts

DANISH

DENMARK / UNITED STATES

Spandauer is a vanilla crème and fruit jam-filled danish, topped with icing for a sweet weekend morning bite in Denmark. Also known as a Danish in American English, this pastry comes in many forms. In this recipe, the vanilla crème is made the American way, with cream cheese. In Denmark, wienerbrød *refers to any number of enriched pastries like this one including:* tebirkes, chokoladebolle, kanelgiffel, frøsnapper, *and more.*

Preparation time: 45 minutes, plus 4 hours chilling and rising time
Cooking time: 25 minutes
Makes: 9 pastries

For the pastry dough:
· ¼ cup (60 ml/2 fl oz) plus 2 tablespoons full-fat milk
· 1½ teaspoon active dry yeast
· 2 tablespoons sugar
· 2 eggs, divided
· 1¾ cups (225 g) unbleached all-purpose flour
· ¼ teaspoon fine sea salt
· ¾ cups (12 tablespoons or 1½ sticks); 165 g unsalted butter

For the filling:
· 4 oz (115 g) cream cheese, at room temperature
· 1 teaspoon full-fat milk
· 1 large egg yolk
· 4 tablespoons powdered (icing) sugar
· Pinch of salt
· ¼ teaspoon vanilla extract
· ½ tablespoon sugar
· 3 tablespoons raspberry or strawberry preserves

For assembly and icing:
· Egg wash: 1 egg whisked with a touch of water
· ¾ cup (90 g) powdered (icing) sugar
· 2 tablespoons full-fat milk, plus more as needed
· ¼ teaspoon vanilla extract

Combine the milk, yeast, and a pinch of sugar. Set aside until the yeast is frothy, about 10 minutes. Stir in 1 egg until combined. In a separate bowl, combine the flour, remaining sugar, and salt. Add the butter cut into cubes; flatten and roll across your fingers until they are pea-size. Stir in the milk/yeast mixture until you have a shaggy, sticky dough. Turn out onto a piece of plastic wrap (cling film), pat into a square, and wrap tightly. Refrigerate for at least 2 hours or up to overnight.

Turn the chilled dough out onto a lightly floured surface. Roll the dough into a rectangle, about 8 x 20 inches (20 x 50 cm) and ¼ inch (6 mm) thick. With a short side facing you, fold the bottom one-third up and the top one-third over that, like folding a business letter. Wrap the dough and let it chill in the refrigerator for 15 minutes.

Turn the dough so that the spine of the dough is to your left, like a book. Roll the dough into an 8 x 20 inches (20 x 50 cm) rectangle about ¼ inch (6 mm) thick and repeat the letter fold. Chill for 15 minutes. Repeat the folding, rolling, and chilling three more times. Cover tightly in plastic wrap and chill in the refrigerator for at least 1 hour.

Preheat the oven to 350°F (180°C/Gas Mark 4). In a medium bowl, whisk together all of the filling ingredients (minus the preserves) until smooth and set aside.

Roll the chilled dough on a lightly floured surface into a 12-inch (30 cm) square. Cut into 9 4-inch (10 cm) squares. Fold the corners in toward the center. Dollop 2 teaspoons of filling topped with 1 teaspoon of jam in the center of each danish. Seal. Cover with a tea towel and let rest until they puff up slightly, about 30 minutes.

Transfer the pastries to a parchment-lined baking sheet. Brush with egg wash. Bake until golden brown, 22–25 minutes. Meanwhile, whisk the powdered (icing) sugar, the milk, and vanilla until no lumps remain. Drizzle the icing over the still-warm pastries. Serve warm.

See image on page 223.

SUGAR-SOAKED PUFF PASTRY WITH CLOTTED CREAM

IRAQ

Kahi, *a puff pastry soaked in simple syrup, is topped with* geymar, *a clotted cream made from buffalo milk, similar to* kaymak *(page 78). Geymar is also enjoyed spread over* khubz *(flatbread).*

Preparation time: 10 minutes, plus overnight setting time
Cooking time: 30 minutes
Serves: 2

For the *geymar*:
· 2 teaspoons cornstarch (cornflour)
· 1 cup (240 ml/8 fl oz) heavy (whipping) cream

For the *kahi*:
· ¼ sheet store-bought puff pastry, thawed if frozen (14 oz. / 397 g) or homemade (page 384)
· 1 tablespoon (15 g) unsalted butter or ghee, melted
· ¾ cup (150 g) sugar

Make the *geymar*:
Make this the day before serving. In a small bowl, combine the cornstarch (cornflour) with a touch of the cream and stir until smooth. No lumps should remain. Pour the remaining cream into a small saucepan and stir, slowly bringing to a steady simmer over medium heat. Stir in the cornstarch paste and cook, stirring, until the cream thickens, about 20 minutes. Pour the thickened cream into an 8-inch (20 cm) square baking dish, 2¾ inches (7 cm) deep, and let it cool completely. Cover with plastic wrap (cling film), and refrigerate for 24 hours, allowing the cream to set.

Prepare the *kahi*:
Preheat the oven to 375°F (190°C/Gas Mark 5). Line a baking sheet with parchment paper.
    Lay the puff pastry sheet on the lined baking sheet and bake until the pastry is puffed and golden, about 15 minutes.
    Meanwhile, in a small saucepan, combine ¾ cup (175 ml/6 fl oz) water and sugar and bring the mixture to a boil over medium-high heat. Stir, then reduce the heat to low. Allow the syrup to simmer until the sugar is dissolved and the mixture is clear, about 1 minute. Remove from the heat.
    When the puff pastry is cool to the touch, slice into 4 separate pieces. Slice the *geymar* into 4 rectangular pieces and remove from the dish using a spatula. If the geymar is too soft to slice, use 2 tablespoons for each piece of *kahi*. Drizzle the sugar syrup over each puff pastry piece and top with a slice of *geymar*.

FREDRIK BERSELIUS
NORDIC BREAKFAST

Originally from Sweden, Fredrik Berselius has spent most of his culinary career in New York. He opened Aska in its original Brooklyn location in 2012 and was soon recognized for bridging the culinary heritage of his upbringing with his immediate environs. Within less than a year, Berselius earned his first Michelin star and Aska was named one of the 10 Best New Restaurants in America by Bon Appétit. *In 2016, soon after Berselius reopened Aska in a new location, his restaurant was awarded two Michelin stars.*

Crispy flatbread broken into bite-size pieces over a bowl of fermented milk, sweetened with a sprinkle of white caster sugar. As a child, I loved the crunchy texture and sweet-and-sour flavor of this classic breakfast; I still love its simplicity. A quite common use of everyday household staples, it was the perfect go-to breakfast treat, especially on a sunny summer morning in Stockholm. A large round blue and brown parchment paper package of knäckebröd was always stored in a cupboard above the refrigerator. Filmjölk, poured from the classic Tetra Pak box, was refreshing with its typical sour notes of lactic acid developed by the fermentation of the milk. The sweetness from the sugar balanced everything out and helped turn two very common pantry items into a light and delicious breakfast.

Growing up in Sweden, what I ate for breakfast changed regularly, according to the day of the week and the time of year. The first meal of the day was considered as important as lunch and dinner. It was often more elaborate than knäckebröd and filmjölk, but was in a similar spirit. Hot oatmeal with homemade fruit compote, cinnamon, and milk. Toasted hearty bread, butter, jam, and cheese. Bread with fish roe and a boiled, sliced egg with a sprig of dill. A cup of dark roasted coffee, or black tea with honey and milk. Everyday breakfast staples often included grains, in the form of hearty breads and porridges; dairy, including butter, cheese, and milk; cured or preserved ingredients, like smoked fish, fish roe, pickled herring, or ham; and baked goods and pastries topped with berry jams and served with fruit.

People made time for breakfast: sitting down at the breakfast table to enjoy a meal together was a way to ease into the day. On warm, sunny summer days, we would share a light meal at a table in the backyard, and on dark, cold winter mornings, with freezing temperatures and perhaps snow on the ground, we would sit down around the table in a cozy, warm, candlelit kitchen.

I still consider breakfast as important as any meal of the day and take the time to prepare and sit down for it daily. What I make for breakfast changes with the seasons but I always keep it rooted in my Scandinavian heritage.

01. Brown Cheese Sandwich PAGE 184   02. Filmjölk PAGE 76   03. Ymer with Ymerdrys PAGE 77   04. Ymerdrys PAGE 77

05. Danish PAGE 368 and Cardamom Buns PAGE 222   06. Crispbread with Smoked Cod Roe Spread PAGE 152

RYE CRUST PASTRIES STUFFED WITH RICE

FINLAND

Finns eat an assortment of rye and sourdough breads accompanied by cheeses, charcuterie, and smoked salmon or overnight baked oat porridge. In the northeastern region of Finland, bordering Russia, Karjalanpiirakka, *rye crust pastries, can be found at gas stations, canteens, and cafes, filled with an assortment of ingredients, most popularly oat porridge, mashed potato, or, as in the following recipe, rice with egg butter.*

Preparation time: 1 hour 20 minutes
Cooking time: 15-20 minutes
Makes: 9 pastries

For the filling:
· ½ cup (100 g) short-grain rice
· 2 cups (475 ml/16 fl oz) full-fat milk, plus more for brushing
· Salt

For the dough:
· ½ cup (60 g) rye flour, dark rye if possible
· 3 tablespoons all-purpose (plain) flour
· ¼ teaspoon fine sea salt
· Vegetable oil, for greasing
· Milk, for brushing

For the egg butter:
· 1 Hard-Boiled Egg (page 14), peeled and chopped
· 3 tablespoons unsalted butter, at room temperature
· Salt and freshly ground pepper

Make the filling:
In a small saucepan, bring 1 cup (240 ml/8 fl oz) water to a boil. Add the rice and a pinch of salt and return to a boil. Reduce the heat to low, stir, then cover. Cook the rice at a simmer until the water is all absorbed, about 15 minutes. Stir in the milk and cook the rice at a simmer, uncovered, until it reaches the consistency of rice porridge, about 35 minutes. Scrape the thickened, creamy rice into a wide bowl of baking dish and allow it to cool completely and become thick.

Preheat the oven to 450°F (245°C/Gas Mark 9). Line a baking sheet with parchment paper.

Meanwhile, make the dough:
In a medium bowl, combine both flours and salt. Pour in 4 tablespoons water and stir with a wooden spoon until a shaggy dough forms. Knead for about 2 minutes until it forms a smooth dough.

Shape the pastries:
Turn the dough out on a lightly floured work surface. Roll the dough into a rope about 9 inches (23 cm) long and slice into 9 portions, each 1 inch long. Roll into balls. With a rolling pin, roll out each portion into a nearly paper-thin round about 4 ½ inches (11 cm) across. Dollop 2–3 tablespoons of filling into the center of each round and spread around, leaving a border of about ¾ an inch (1.5 cm). Fold one border slightly over the filling without stretching the round. Repeat with the opposite side. Pinch the ends together to form eye-shaped boats, with the rice filling mostly uncovered. Crimp the borders by pinching the dough to create a scalloped edge around the filling.

Place the pastries on the lined baking sheet. Brush the dough with milk. Bake the *karjalanpiirakka* until the rice is bubbling and browned, 15–20 minutes.

Meanwhile, prepare the egg butter:
Put the chopped hard-boiled eggs in a small bowl and fold in the butter. Season with salt and pepper.

Serve the *karjalanpiirakka* warm, topped with the egg butter.

Preparation time: 30 minutes
Cooking time: 1 hour
Serves: 4

SPINACH PIE

GREECE

Spanakopita *is a spinach pie of crispy phyllo dough filled with spinach and cheese. Greeks typically have an espresso first thing in the morning. It is more common to enjoy a pie around 10 am or to stop at a bakery on the way to work.*

· 4 cups (4 oz/115 g) raw spinach
· 4 tablespoons grated Parmesan cheese
· ½ cup (75 g) crumbled feta cheese
· ½ teaspoon fine sea salt
· ¼ teaspoon freshly ground pepper
· ½ cup (25 g) chopped fresh parsley or dill
· Olive oil, for brushing the phyllo
· 3 sheets store-bought phyllo dough, halved
· 1 egg

Preheat the oven to 325°F (160°C/Gas Mark 3).

Bring a small saucepan of water to a boil. Lower the spinach into the boiling water and blanch for 30 seconds. Transfer with a slotted spoon to a tea towel and squeeze the liquid out of the spinach. (If the spinach is wet it will make the pie soggy.) Roughly chop the spinach.

In a bowl, combine the spinach, Parmesan, feta, salt and pepper, and parsley or dill. Brush an 8-inch (20 cm) square baking dish with olive oil. Place 1 phyllo half-sheet in the dish, letting the edges hang over the sides. Brush with olive oil and set another half-sheet over, brushing with olive oil. Repeat once more. There should be 3 layers on the bottom of the pan. Spread the filling evenly over the sheets. Place a half-sheet over the filling, brush with olive oil. Repeat with the remaining 2 half-sheets, brushing with olive oil. Fold any extra edges toward the center and brush with olive oil.

Bake until the phyllo is crisped, about 1 hour. Increase the oven temperature to 375°F (190°C/Gas Mark 5) and bake until golden, about 5 minutes more. Allow the spanakopita to cool slightly before slicing and serving.

CHEESE PIE
GREECE

Tiropita *is a cheese pie of crispy phyllo dough stuffed with cheese and egg.*

Preparation time: 25 minutes
Cooking time: 1 hour
Serves: 4

· 1 cup (150 g) crumbled feta cheese
· ½ cup (125 g) ricotta cheese
· ½ cup (45 g) grated Parmesan cheese
· 2 eggs
· ½ teaspoon fine sea salt
· ¼ teaspoon freshly ground pepper
· Olive oil, for brushing the phyllo
· 3 sheets store-bought phyllo dough, halved

Preheat the oven to 325°F (160°F/Gas Mark 3).

In a small bowl, combine the feta, ricotta, parmesan, eggs, salt, and pepper. Stir until thoroughly combined.

Brush an 8-inch (20 cm) square baking dish with olive oil. Place 1 phyllo half-sheet in the dish, letting the edges hang over the sides. Brush with olive oil and set another half-sheet over, brushing with olive oil. Repeat once more. There should be 3 layers on the bottom of the dish. Spread the filling evenly over the sheets. Place a half-sheet over the filling and brush with olive oil. Repeat with the 2 remaining half-sheets, brushing with olive oil. Fold any extra edges toward the center and brush with olive oil.

Bake until the phyllo is crisped, about 1 hour. Increase the oven temperature to 375°F (190°C/Gas Mark 5) and bake until lightly golden, about 5 minutes more. Allow the *tiropita* to cool slightly before slicing and serving.

Cheese Pie

CHEESE-STUFFED PUFF PASTRY

ISRAEL

Originally from Turkey, bourekas *are pockets of puff pastry stuffed with cheese and found across the Middle East and North Africa. In the* shuks *(open-air markets) in Israel, larger versions of* bourekas *are served as breakfast sandwiches, filled with slices of hard-boiled egg, pickles, tahini, and grated tomato.*

Preparation time: 30 minutes
Cooking time: 40 minutes
Makes: 9 pastries

· ½ cup (75 g) crumbled feta cheese
· ½ tablespoon ricotta cheese
· 2 eggs
· Salt and freshly ground pepper
· All-purpose (plain) flour, for dusting
· 1 sheet puff pastry, store-bought or homemade (page 384)
· 1 tablespoon sesame seeds, for topping

In a medium bowl, combine the feta, ricotta, and 1 of the eggs. Season with salt and pepper. Fold together with a spatula until combined.

Preheat the oven to 375°F (190°C/Gas Mark 5). Line a baking sheet with parchment paper.

In a small bowl, whisk the remaining egg and set aside. On a lightly floured work surface, roll the puff pastry sheet into a 12-inch (30 cm) square. Cut the pastry into 9 squares. Dollop 1 tablespoon of the filling into the center of each square. Brush the borders of the squares with the whisked egg (this will help the dough to adhere easily) and fold one corner of the square over the filling to form a triangle, pressing lightly around the perimeter to seal the edges.

Arrange the sealed pastries on the baking sheet and brush with the whisked egg, then sprinkle with sesame seeds. Bake until the pastry has puffed up and is golden, 35–40 minutes. Allow the *bourekas* to cool slightly before serving warm.

Cheese-Stuffed Puff Pastry

CHEESE EMPANADAS

BOLIVIA

Popular all over South America, empanadas de queso *are pockets of fried dough stuffed with cheese and dusted with powdered (icing) sugar. This version from Bolivia is sometimes enjoyed with* api morado, *a thick, purple corn beverage, similar to Mexican* Atole *(page 436). Countries across South America have their own ways of making empanadas. Fillings, dough, and technique can vary depending on the country, region, or family. This recipe features a classic empanada dough that can be filled with anything you'd like.*

Preparation time: 30 minutes, plus 30 minutes chilling time for the Basic Empanada Dough
Cooking time: 10 minutes
Makes: 6 empanadas

· Basic Empanada Dough (below)
· 2 cups (250 g) crumbled queso fresco or grated mozzarella cheese
· Powdered (icing) sugar, for sprinkling

Make the dough and cut out 6 empanada rounds as directed.

Place about 2 tablespoons of cheese in the center of each dough round. Dab your finger in water and wet the border of the dough (this will help the empanadas better adhere), fold one half over the filling to make half-moons, and press the edges together to seal. Crimp the perimeter with a fork, dipped in water to help the seal. Place the empanadas on a baking sheet. Cover the baking sheet with plastic wrap (cling film) and refrigerate for 30 minutes.

Pour 2 inches (5 cm) oil into a wide, deep heavy-bottomed pan and heat over medium-high heat. To test if the oil is ready for frying, carefully add a piece of scrap dough. If it sizzles, it's ready. Carefully two empanadas at a time into the oil. Fry on one side until browned, about 45 seconds. Flip and fry the other side until browned, about 45 seconds more. Transfer to paper towels to drain. Repeat with remaining empanadas. Sprinkle with powdered (icing) sugar. Allow the empanadas to cool slightly before serving.

BASIC EMPANADA DOUGH

Preparation time: 20 minutes, plus 30 minutes chilling time
Makes: enough for 6 empanadas

· 1½ cups (215 g) all-purpose (plain) flour
· ½ teaspoon fine sea salt
· 4 tablespoons (60 g) unsalted butter, cut into 1-inch (2.5 cm) pieces
· 1 egg yolk

In a medium bowl, whisk the flour and salt. Toss the butter in the flour. Flatten and crumble the butter cubes with your fingertips until the butter is broken down to the size of peas. In a small bowl, stir together the egg yolk and 4 tablespoons water. Gradually pour the egg mixture into the flour, tossing and kneading the dough until it comes together. If the dough crumbles when squeezed together, add more water, one teaspoon at a time, until it comes together. Knead until the dough is smooth. Form into a ball, cover with plastic wrap (cling film) and place in the refrigerator until firm, 30 minutes to 1 hour.

Turn the chilled dough out onto a lightly floured work surface. Roll the dough to a thickness of 1/8 inch (3 mm). With a 5-inch (12.5 cm) round biscuit cutter or a paring knife and a small plate as a template, cut out 6 rounds of dough.

Cheese Empanadas

GUAVA AND CHEESE EMPANADAS
UNITED STATES

With roots in Cuba, this pastry is more commonly found in Miami. Empanadas de queso y guayaba *come stuffed with a filling of guava jam and cream cheese. This filling is also popular in* pastelitos, *an enriched pastry similar to a* boureka *(Cheese-Stuffed Puff Pastry, page 378).*

Preparation time: 30 minutes, plus 30 minutes resting and chilling time for the Basic Empanada Dough
Cooking time: 10 minutes
Makes: 6 empanadas

· Basic Empanada Dough (page 380)
· 6 oz (170 g) cream cheese, sliced into tablespoons
· 6 oz (170 g) guava paste, cut into six ½-inch (1.25 cm) slices
· Vegetable oil, for deep-frying
· Sugar, for sprinkling

Make the dough and cut out the empanada rounds as directed.
  For each empanada, place 1 tablespoon/slice of cream cheese and guava paste next to each other in the center of a round of dough. Dab your finger in water and wet the border of the dough, fold one half over the filling to make half-moons, and press the edges together to seal. Crimp the perimeter with a fork dipped in water. Place the empanadas on a baking sheet. Cover with plastic wrap (cling film) and place the empanadas in the refrigerator to rest for 30 minutes.
  Pour 2 inches (5 cm) oil into a wide, deep heavy-bottomed pan and heat over medium-high heat. To test if the oil is ready for frying, carefully add a piece of scrap dough. If it sizzles, it's ready. Carefully place 2 empanadas at a time into the oil. Fry on one side until browned, about 45 seconds. Flip with a slotted spoon and fry the other side until browned, about 45 seconds more. Transfer to paper towels to drain. Repeat with remaining empanadas. Sprinkle with sugar. Allow the empanadas to cool slightl before serving.

GREEN PLANTAIN EMPANADAS
ECUADOR

Known as empanadas de verde, *this naturally gluten-free empanada dough is bound together by the starch in green plantains. The mixture is rolled out just as a typical flour-based empanada dough. They are filled with cheese and often enjoyed with a* Cafecito *(page 416).*

Preparation time: 30 minutes
Cooking time: 40 minutes
Makes: 4 empanadas

· 3 large green plantains, peeled and cut into thirds
· 2 tablespoons (30 g) unsalted butter, at room temperature
· Salt
· ½ cup (60 g) crumbled queso fresco or grated mozzarella cheese
· All-purpose (plain) flour, for dusting
· Vegetable oil, for frying

In a medium saucepan, cover the chopped plantains with water. Bring to a boil. Reduce the heat to low and simmer, covered, until the plantains are tender, 20 minutes. Reserving the cooking liquid, transfer the plantains to a large bowl. Mash the plantains with the butter and salt, adding up to ½ cup (120 ml/4 fl oz) of cooking liquid to achieve a paste-like consistency. Cover the dough with plastic wrap (cling film) and let rest at room temperature, about 15 minutes.
  Lightly flour a work surface. Divide the plantain mixture into quarters and roll each into a ball. Flatten into disks and sprinkle 2 tablespoons of cheese in the center of each. Fold the dough over the cheese to create a half-moon and pinch and seal the open edge.
  Pour 2 inches (5 cm) oil into a wide, deep heavy-bottomed pan and heat over medium-high heat. Test if the oil is ready for frying, then submerge each empanada with tongs and fry until browned, about 1 minute.
  Allow the empanadas to cool slightly before serving warm.

SCONES
UNITED STATES

A popular baked good at coffee shops around the United States, scones can have fillings that vary from sweet, like blueberry or dried fruits, to savory, like bacon and cheddar cheese. They are often served with butter. In the UK, scones are made with less butter and are more typical for afternoon tea, served with clotted cream and jam.

Preparation time: 20 minutes
Cooking time: 20 minutes
Makes: 6 scones

· 2 cups (290 g) all-purpose (plain) flour
· 2 tablespoons granulated sugar
· ½ tablespoon baking powder
· ¼ teaspoon fine sea salt
· 5 tablespoons (70 g) cold unsalted butter, cubed
· ½ cup (100 g) of any combination of dried currants, chocolate chips, chopped dried fruit, or crumbled bacon, shredded cheese, and chopped chives
· ½ cup (120 ml/4 fl oz) full-fat milk or heavy (whipping) cream
· 2 tablespoons heavy (whipping) cream, plus more for brushing
· Raw sugar, for sprinkling (optional)

Preheat the oven to 400°F (200°C/Gas Mark 6).
　In a large bowl, combine the flour, sugar, baking powder, salt, and butter. Coat the butter in flour and crumble with your fingers to the size of peas. Add the currants. Make a well in the center of the dough and pour in the milk and cream. Stir with a wooden spoon until the ingredients are hydrated and the dough sticks together.
　Turn the dough out onto a piece of parchment paper and pat into a round 1 inch (2.5 cm) thick. With a sharp knife, slice into 8 wedges. Pull the wedges slightly away from each other. Brush lightly with heavy cream and sprinkle with raw sugar (if using).
　Bake until golden, 18–20 minutes. Cool slightly before serving.

JOHNNY CAKES
JAMAICA

Johnny cakes are biscuits found in the Bahamas, Jamaica, US Virgin Islands and Belize. They are often served with butter, jams, cheese, or refried beans, and pair well with Ackee and Saltfish (page 354). Originally called "journey cakes" for their durability on long trips, the name eventually evolved to "Johnny." In the Northeastern United States, especially in Rhode Island, Johnny Cakes (page 118) are pancakes made with cornmeal.

Preparation time: 30 minutes
Cooking time: 15 minutes
Makes: 8 Johnny cakes

· 2 cups (290 g) all-purpose (plain) flour, plus more for dusting
· 2 teaspoons baking powder
· 1 tablespoon sugar
· 2 tablespoons (30 g) vegetable shortening, plus more for greasing
· ½ cup (120 ml/4 fl oz) coconut milk

Preheat the oven to 400°F (200°C/Gas Mark 6) and grease a baking sheet with vegetable shortening.
In a medium bowl, combine the flour, baking powder, and sugar. Add the shortening and roll the pieces with your fingertips to crumble until they are broken down to the size of peas. Pour in the coconut milk and stir with a wooden spoon until a sticky, shaggy dough forms. Knead on a floured work surface until a stiff dough forms, about 2 minutes.
　Divide the dough into 8 equal portions. Roll into 2-inch (5 cm) balls. Cover and let rest for 15 minutes. Assemble the balls on the baking sheet, pressing down on each to flatten. Pierce the tops with a fork and bake for 18 minutes or until golden brown. Serve warm.

ROLLED CHEESE PIE

BULGARIA

Similar to the Greek Tiropita *(Cheese Pie, page 376),* banitsa *is filled with a mixture of eggs and fresh cheese, then baked until golden brown. The stuffed phyllo is coiled into a baking dish, sealing the cheesy contents inside.*

Preparation time: 30 minutes
Cooking time: 40 minutes
Serves 4–6, makes one 9-inch (23 cm) pie

· 1 cup (225 g) Bulgarian plain (natural) yogurt
· ¾ cup (180 g) crumbled fresh farmer cheese or fresh white cheese
· 3 eggs
· 3 tablespoons (45 g) unsalted butter, melted
· 5 sheets puff pastry dough

Preheat the oven to 350°F (180°C/Gas Mark 3).

In a small bowl, combine the yogurt, cheese, and eggs. Stir to combine well. Brush a 9-inch (23 cm) pie plate with some of the melted butter. Brush one sheet of phyllo dough lightly with more melted butter. Spread some of the filling across the sheet and roll up lengthwise into a log. Curve it along the wall of the pie plate. Continue with the remaining phyllo, melted butter, and filling, rolling them up and coiling them snugly into the pie dish. Brush the top of the *banitsa* with melted butter.

Bake until the *banitsa* is golden brown, 35–40 minutes. Increase the oven temperature to 375°F (190°C/Gas Mark 5) and bake about 5 more minutes. Allow the *banitsa* to cool slightly before slicing and serving.

PUFF PASTRY DOUGH

This "rough" or quick puff pastry dough can be used for the Egg Tarts (page 366), Cheese-Stuffed Puff Pastry (page 378), and Sugar-Soaked Puff Pastry with Clotted Cream (page 369).

Preparation time: 45 minutes, plus 2 hours chilling time
Makes: 1 sheet 10 x 15 inch (25 x 38 cm)

· 2 cups (290 g) all-purpose (plain) flour
· 1/2 teaspoon fine sea salt
· 2 sticks (225 g) plus 1 tablespoon (15 g) butter, cold, cut into 1-inch (2.5 cm) pieces

Whisk the flour and salt into a medium bowl. Toss the butter into the flour and flatten with your fingertips. Roll the butter to crumble until it's very small. Pour in 6 tablespoons ice water, 2 tablespoons at a time, tossing with your hands until the flour is hydrated. Mix the dough until it comes together. Add more ice water if the dough is too dry. Be careful not to overwork the dough or it might become too tough. Knead the dough until it comes together, about 1 minute. The dough is ready when it doesn't crumble when squeezed. Form the dough into a square, wrap in plastic wrap (cling film) and refrigerate for 20 minutes.

On a lightly floured work surface, roll the dough into a rectangle, 10 x 15 inch (25 x 38 cm). With a short side facing you, fold the bottom one-third of the dough up, then fold the top one-third down over that, like folding a business letter. Turn the dough so that the spine of the dough is to your left, like a book. Roll the dough into a rectangle, 10 x 15 inch (25 x 38 cm) and repeat the letter fold. Cover with plastic wrap and refrigerate until firm, 30 minutes. Repeat this process of folding, rolling, and refrigerating two more times.

QUICHE LORRAINE

FRANCE

This egg pie studded with bacon and laced with cheese is a common breakfast item in the United States, but its origins lie in France. Often enjoyed for lunch or at picnics, quiche Lorraine in France is made with lardons (small, fatty bits of pork that are salt-cured and not smoked) and tends to be a thinner layer of egg custard than the deep-dish American version.

Preparation time: 1 hour, plus chilling if making own crust
Cooking time: 25 minutes
Makes: one 9-inch (23 cm) quiche (8 servings)

· Homemade Pie Dough/Shortcrust Pastry (page 386) or one 9-inch (23 cm) store-bought frozen crust
· Butter, for greasing
· 3 slices (rashers) thick-cut bacon (streaky)
· 3 eggs
· Pinch of ground nutmeg
· ½ teaspoon fine sea salt
· Pinch of freshly ground pepper
· 1¼ cups (300 ml/10 fl oz) heavy (whipping) cream
· ½ cup (55 g) finely grated Swiss cheese, such as Emmental

Preheat the oven to 350°F (180°C/Gas Mark 4). Butter a 9-inch (23 cm) 2 inch (5 cm deep) glass plate or quiche pan.

Roll the dough out to a round, 12 inches (30 cm) in diameter and 1/8 inch (3 mm) thick, and fit it into the pie plate, using your fingers to fill in the bottom round and edges smoothly with the dough. Trim the overhanging dough, then crimp the perimiter by pinching the edge about ¼ inch (6 mm) to form a border. Prick the base of the quiche with a fork and chill in the refrigerator for 5 minutes or until firm.

Butter a sheet of foil and gently press it, buttered-side down, into the pie dish, completely covering the dough. Pour in dried beans, rice, or pie weights. Blind-bake until the pastry is set and feels dry, 15–20 minutes. Remove the weights, then return to the oven for another 10–15 minutes until pale golden. Leave the oven on.

Start with a cold cast-iron skillet or frying pan and place the bacon in flat. Slowly bring the heat to medium to let the fat render and result in crispy bacon. Cook on both sides until crispy, about 10 minutes. Transfer the bacon to paper towels to drain.

In a medium bowl, whisk together the eggs, nutmeg, salt, and pepper. Whisk in the cream until thoroughly combined. Sprinkle the crumbled bacon into the blind-baked crust. Sprinkle in the Swiss cheese. Pour the egg mixture over everything.

Bake until the custard is just set, with a gentle wobble in the center, about 25 minutes. Allow the quiche to cool for 1 hour before serving, as it will continue to set out of the oven. Slice and serve warm.

HAND PIES
UNITED STATES

Popularized in the United States as an on-the-go breakfast item, hand pies are personal-size pies filled with various flavored jams and topped with icing or sprinkles, also commonly known by the brand name Pop-Tarts. They are warmed in a toaster.

Preparation time: 30 minutes, plus chilling time for the Pie Dough
Cooking time: 20 minutes
Makes: 6 hand pies

For the hand pies:
· Pie Dough/Shortcrust Pastry (below)
· 6 tablespoons raspberry jam, or desired flavor
· 2 teaspoons tapioca flour
· 1 egg

For the glaze:
· 4 tablespoons raspberries
· ½ cup (60 g) powdered (icing) sugar
· Sprinkles (optional)

Preheat the oven to 350°F (180°C/Gas Mark 3).
  Prepare the dough as directed. On a lightly floured work surface, roll the dough out into a round ¼ inch (6 mm) thick. Slice off the round ends to make an 8-inch (20 cm) square. With a sharp knife, cut the square into three equal strips (about 2½ inches/6.5 cm wide). Cut each strip crosswise in half to make a total of 6 rectangles.
  In a small bowl, combine the jam and tapioca flour. Dollop 1 tablespoon of the filling on one end of each dough rectangle. Dab your finger in water and wet the border of the dough (this will help the hand pies better adhere), fold one half of the rectangle over the filling to make a smaller rectangle, and press the edges together to seal. Crimp the perimeter with a fork dipped in water and poke holes in the tops. Transfer the pies to a baking sheet lined with parchment paper. In a small bowl, beat the egg. Brush the pies with the egg. Bake until golden brown, 16–18 minutes. Allow the pies to cool slightly.
  Puree the raspberries in a small food processor or blender and strain the puree through a fine-mesh sieve set over a bowl. Whisk the powdered (icing) sugar in a small bowl. Pour the raspberry puree into the powdered sugar and whisk until smooth. Pour the glaze over the pies and shower with sprinkles, if desired.

PIE DOUGH / SHORTCRUST PASTRY

Preparation time: 10 minutes, plus chilling
Makes: about 1lb/ 450g of dough, enough for 6 Hand Pies or a 9-inch (23 cm) Quiche Lorraine (page 384)

· 2 cups (290 g) all-purpose (plain) flour
· 1 tablespoon sugar (hand pies or sweet crust only)
· ½ teaspoon fine sea salt
· 10 tablespoons (140 g) cold unsalted butter, cut into small cubes

In a large bowl, whisk the flour, salt, and sugar (if using). Add the butter. Flatten and crumble the cubes with your hands and fingers until the butter is broken down to the size of peas. Add 2 tablespoons of ice water and toss frequently from the bottom up. Continue adding water, 1 teaspoon at a time, until the dough comes together. Flatten to a round, 1-inch (2.5 cm) thick. Smooth the edges and wrap tightly in plastic wrap (cling film). Refrigerate for at least 1 hour before rolling out. It should be cold but not solid.

Hand Pies

CAKES

BANANA BREAD

AUSTRALIA

Also commonly enjoyed in the United States, this loaf cake is made with overripe bananas and can be enjoyed sliced fresh or toasted with butter.

Preparation time: 15 minutes
Cooking time: 1 hour
Makes: 1 loaf (12 servings)

· 1 stick (115 g) unsalted butter, at room temperature, plus more for greasing
· ½ cup (100 g) granulated sugar
· ½ cup (95 g) light brown sugar
· 2 eggs
· 3 overripe bananas, mashed
· ½ teaspoon fine sea salt
· 1 teaspoon vanilla extract
· 1 teaspoon ground cinnamon (optional)
· 2 cups (290 g) all-purpose (plain) flour
· 1 teaspoon baking powder
· ½ teaspoon baking soda (bicarbonate of soda)
· ½ cup (50 g) chopped walnuts
· 4 tablespoons semisweet chocolate chunks (optional)

Preheat the oven to 375°F (190°C/Gas Mark 5). Butter a 9 x 5-inch (23 x 12.5 cm) loaf pan. Fit parchment paper into the pan, allowing two sides to fold over. This will help remove the banana bread from the pan easily. Coat the parchment paper with butter.

In the bowl of a stand mixer (or a large bowl with a hand mixer), cream the butter, granulated sugar, and brown sugar until fluffy. Whisk in the eggs until combined. Using a wooden spoon, stir in the bananas, salt, vanilla, and cinnamon (if using). In a small bowl, combine the flour, baking powder, and baking soda (bicarbonate of soda). Stir the flour mixture into the banana mixture and mix until no dry spots remain. Fold in the walnuts and chocolate (if using).

Pour the batter into the loaf pan and smooth the top. Bake until the bread has domed and browned and a skewer inserted into the center of the bread should come out clean, 55–60 minutes. Allow the bread to cool in the pan for 10 minutes. Remove the loaf from the pan and let it cool on a rack, about 25 minutes or longer. Slice and serve.

Banana Bread

ORANGE POUND CAKE
BRAZIL / PORTUGAL

Bolo de Laranja, *as known in Brazil and Portugal, is an unfrosted orange pound cake often kept on the counter at home for a quick morning meal.*

Preparation time: 15 minutes
Cooking time: 45 minutes
Makes: 1 cake, 18–20 slices

· 2 cups (290 g) all-purpose (plain) flour
· 1¾ cups (350 g) granulated sugar
· Grated zest of 1 orange
· Juice of 3 oranges (about 1¼ cups [300 ml])
· 3 eggs
· 4 tablespoons vegetable oil
· 2 teaspoons baking powder
· ¼ teaspoon fine sea salt

Preheat the oven to 350°F (180°C/Gas Mark 4). Grease a 10 x 2½ inch (25 by 6.5 cm) Bundt pan with oil and dust with flour, tapping out the excess.

In a large bowl, add the flour, sugar, baking powder, and salt. Whisk to combine and aerate, then make a well in the middle. Whisk together the orange zest, orange juice, eggs and oil in a medium bowl. Pour into the flour mixture, then whisk until no dry spots remain.

Pour the batter into the prepared Bundt pan. Bake until risen and golden and a skewer inserted into the middle of the cake comes out clean, 40–45 minutes. Allow the cake to cool in the pan for 20 minutes before inverting it onto a cooling rack. You may need to use a palette knife to loosen the edges of the cake. Allow the cake to cool completely before slicing and serving.

LEMON MUFFINS
SPAIN

Magdalenas *are lemon-infused muffin typically enjoyed with Café con Leche (page 415).*

Preparation time: 10 minutes
Cooking time: 20 minutes
Makes: 6 muffins

· 4 tablespoons sugar
· 2 teaspoons grated lemon zest
· 4 tablespoons (60 g) unsalted butter, at room temperature, plus more for greasing
· 2 eggs
· 2 teaspoons full-fat milk
· ¾ cup (110 g) plus 1 tablespoon all-purpose (plain) flour
· 1 teaspoon baking powder

Preheat the oven to 375°F (190°C/Gas Mark 5). Generously coat 6 cups of a muffin tin with butter.

In a large bowl, combine the sugar and lemon zest. Rub the lemon zest into the sugar to release its oils, about 1 minute. Add the butter and, with an electric mixer or by hand, cream the butter and sugar together until fluffy. Whisk in the eggs until the mixture is frothy. Whisk in the milk. Using a wooden spoon, gradually stir in the flour and baking powder until a thick batter forms.

Fill the muffin cups halfway. Bake until golden brown, about 20 minutes. Allow the muffins to cool in the tin for 5 minutes before transferring them to a cooling rack.

Orange Pound Cake

BLUEBERRY MUFFINS

UNITED STATES

The blueberry muffin is a classic breakfast baked good. This version is studded with blueberries, but other popular varieties include chocolate chip, banana nut, Bran Muffins (page 395), and Morning Glory Muffins (page 398).

Preparation time: 15 minutes
Cooking time: 30 minutes
Makes: 6 muffins

- ½ cup (100 g) sugar
- 1 teaspoon grated lemon zest
- 4 tablespoons (60 g) unsalted butter, at room temperature, plus more for greasing
- 1 egg
- ½ teaspoon vanilla extract
- 1 cup (145 g) all-purpose (plain) flour
- 1 teaspoon baking powder
- ¼ teaspoon fine sea salt
- 6 tablespoons full-fat milk
- 1 cup (150 g) blueberries
- Sugar (granulated or turbinato), for sprinkling

Preheat the oven to 375°F. Generously grease 6 cups of a muffin tin with or butter.

In a large bowl, combine the sugar and lemon zest. Rub the lemon zest into the sugar, allowing it to release its oils, about 1 minute. Add the butter and, with an electric mixer or by hand, cream the butter and sugar together until fluffy. Whisk in the egg and vanilla. In a bowl, combine the flour, baking powder, and salt. With the mixer running, alternate adding the flour mixture and the milk, beginning and ending with the flour, mixing just until incorporated. Fold in the blueberries.

Divide the batter evenly among the muffin cups. Sprinkle the tops with sugar. Bake until the muffins have domed and are golden, about 30 minutes. Allow the muffins to cool in the tin for 5 minutes before transferring them to a cooling rack.

BRAN MUFFINS
UNITED STATES

These muffins boast caramelized notes from the brown sugar and bursts of sweetness from the raisins. They have high fiber content from the bran— the light outer layer of the grain husk separated from the flour after the milling process.

Preparation time: 15 minutes
Cooking time: 20 minutes
Makes: 6 muffins

- ¾ cup (45 g) wheat bran
- ½ cup (70 g) all-purpose (plain) flour
- ¾ teaspoon baking powder
- ½ teaspoon baking soda (bicarbonate of soda)
- ¼ teaspoon fine sea salt
- ½ cup (120 ml/4 fl oz) buttermilk
- 3 tablespoons vegetable oil, plus more for greasing
- 1 egg
- ½ teaspoon vanilla extract
- 1 tablespoon dark brown sugar
- 4 tablespoons raisins

Preheat the oven to 375°F (190°C/Gas Mark 5). Generously coat 6 cups of a muffin tin with oil.

In a large bowl, combine the wheat bran, flour, baking powder, baking soda (bicarbonate of soda), and salt. In a small bowl, whisk together the buttermilk, oil, egg, vanilla, and brown sugar. Pour the liquid mixture over the flour and stir with a wooden spoon to combine until a batter forms. Fold in the raisins. Divide batter evenly among the muffin cups. Bake until the muffins have domed and are golden, about 20 minutes. Allow the muffins to cool in the tin for 5 minutes before transferring them to a cooling rack.

SPICED BREAKFAST CAKE

THE NETHERLANDS

This spiced rye cake is called ontbijtkoek (breakfast cake). The spice blend is similar to gingerbread and its dense interior makes for a perfect bread replacement. It is always topped with a generous serving of butter. This bread is also popular at children's birthday parties for a game called koehappen. The cake is sliced and strung on a string, just out of reach of the blindfolded children below. Adults raise and lower the string of cake for the kids, who hope to snag a bite.

Preparation time: 15 minutes
Cooking time: 1 hour 10 minutes
Makes: 1 loaf (12 servings)

· 1¼ cups (170 g) all-purpose (plain) flour
· ¾ cup (110 g) rye flour
· 4 tablespoons (60 g) dark brown sugar
· 2½ teaspoons baking powder
· 1½ teaspoons ground cinnamon
· 1 teaspoon ground cardamom
· ½ teaspoon ground cloves
· ½ teaspoon ground ginger
· ¼ teaspoon ground nutmeg
· ⅛ teaspoon fine sea salt
· 1 cup (225 ml/8 fl oz) full-fat milk
· ½ cup (180 g) honey
· 2 tablespoons molasses (dark treacle)
· ½ teaspoon vanilla extract
· Softened butter, for greasing and serving

Preheat the oven to 350°F (180°C/Gas Mark 4). Grease a 9 x 5 x 2½ inch (23 x 12.5 x 6 cm) loaf pan.

In a large bowl, stir together both flours, brown sugar, baking powder, ground spices, and salt. In a separate bowl, stir the milk, honey, molasses (treacle), and vanilla together. Add the milk mixture to the flour mixture and stir into a smooth batter.

Pour the batter into the prepared loaf pan. Bake until a skewer inserted in the center comes out with only a few crumbs attached, about 50 minutes. Allow the ontbijtkoek to cool in the pan for 15 minutes before inverting onto a cooling rack to cool completely before slicing and serving with butter.

Spiced Breakfast Cake

Preparation time: 15 minutes
Cooking time: 20 minutes
Makes: 6 muffins

MORNING GLORY MUFFINS

UNITED STATES

Popularized by a Nantucket café of the same name, the morning glory muffin dates to the back-to-the-land health movement of the 1970's. The muffin is filled with carrots, apple, and raisins.

· ¾ cup (110 g) all-purpose (plain) flour
· 4 tablespoons whole wheat (wholemeal) flour
· ½ teaspoon baking powder
· ¼ teaspoon baking soda (bicarbonate of soda)
· ¾ teaspoon ground cinnamon
· ¼ teaspoon ground ginger
· ¼ teaspoon fine sea salt
· ⅓ cup (35 g) shredded carrot
· ⅓ cup (35 g) shredded green apple
· ⅓ cup (50 g) raisins
· 4 tablespoons chopped walnuts
· 2 tablespoons flaxseeds (linseeds)
· ½ cup (95 g) dark brown sugar
· 1 egg
· 6 tablespoons coconut milk
· 4 tablespoons vegetable or coconut oil, plus more for greasing
· ¼ teaspoon vanilla extract

Preheat the oven to 375°F (190°C/Gas Mark 5). Generously coat 6 cups of a muffin tin with oil.

In a medium bowl, combine the flours, baking powder, baking soda (bicarbonate of soda), cinnamon, ginger, salt, carrot, apple, raisins, walnuts, and flaxseeds (linseeds). In a large bowl, stir together the brown sugar, egg, coconut milk, oil, and vanilla. Pour the flour mixture into the liquid and stir with a wooden spoon to form a batter.

Divide the batter among the muffin cups. Bake until the muffins have domed and are golden, about 25 minutes. Allow the muffins to cool in the tin for 5 minutes before transferring them to a cooling rack.

Morning Glory Muffins

COFFEE CAKE
UNITED STATES

Coffee cake, which also goes by the name "crumb cake," because of its crumbled sugar (streusel) topping. It's a cake named not because it contains coffee, but because it goes best with coffee.

Preparation time: 20 minutes
Cooking time: 40 minutes
Makes: 1 cake (12 servings)

For the streusel:
· 1 cup (145 g) all-purpose (plain) flour
· ¾ cup (145 g) light brown sugar
· 2 tablespoons granulated sugar
· ¼ teaspoon fine sea salt
· 6 tablespoons (85 g) unsalted butter, melted

For the cake:
· 2 cups (275 g) unbleached cake (soft) flour
· 1½ teaspoons baking powder
· 1 teaspoon ground cinnamon
· ½ teaspoon fine sea salt
· 1 stick (115 g) unsalted butter, at room temperature, plus more for greasing
· 1 cup (200 g) granulated sugar
· ½ cup (95 g) light brown sugar
· 1 teaspoon vanilla extract
· 1 tablespoon grated lemon zest
· 2 eggs
· ½ cup (120 ml/4 fl oz) full-fat milk

Preheat the oven to 350°F (180°C/Gas Mark 4). Butter a 13 x 9-inch (33 x 23 cm) baking pan.

Make the streusel topping:
In a small bowl, mix together the flour, both sugars, and salt. Pour in the melted butter and stir with a wooden spoon until crumbles form. Set aside.

Make the cake:
In a medium bowl, combine the flour, baking powder, cinnamon, and salt. In a stand mixer fitted with the whisk attachment (or in a large bowl with a hand mixer), cream the butter and both sugars until fluffy. Fold in the vanilla and lemon zest. Add the eggs, 1 egg at a time, beating well after each addition. Alternate between slowly adding the flour mixture and milk, beating well after each and whisking until no dry spots remain.

Pour the batter into the pan. Sprinkle the streusel evenly over top. Bake until a skewer inserted in the center comes out with only a few crumbs attached, 40–45 minutes. Allow the coffee cake to cool in the pan for 10–15 minutes before slicing into squares and serving.

FLUFFY RICE CAKES

INDIA

Idli are fluffy rice cakes made with a fermented batter similar to dosas and served with sambar and chutney in southern India. Idli are steamed in specialty metal trays which have shallow, round indentations and small holes to let the steam get through to the idli batter within.

Preparation time: 20 minutes, plus 6 hours soaking and 12 hours fermenting time
Cooking time: 10 minutes, per batch
Makes: 15-17 rice cakes

· 4 tablespoons urad dal
· 1 teaspoon fenugreek seeds
· 1 cup (185 g) parboiled (converted) or "easy cook" rice
· 1 teaspoon fine sea salt
· Vegetable oil, for greasing
· Sambar (page 131), Coconut Chutney (page 133), and Tomato Chutney (page 132), for serving

In a small bowl, combine the urad dal and fenugreek. Add ¾ cup (175 ml/6 fl oz) water, cover, and let soak for 4 hours. In a separate small bowl, let the rice soak in 1½ cups (1. 4liters/48 fl oz) water for 4 hours.

Drain the urad dal and rice. Transfer the urad dal (and fenugreek) to a food processor or blender and grind with ½ cup (120 ml/4 fl oz) of fresh water until a smooth paste forms, scraping down the sides as needed. Scrape the dal batter into a bowl and process the soaked rice in two batches, using 6 tablespoons fresh water and half of the rice in each, until a smooth paste forms. Combine the rice batter with the urad-dal batter and stir well. Cover with plastic wrap (cling film) and allow the batter to ferment at room temperature for at least 9 hours or up to 12 hours. Stir the salt into the batter.

In an idli pan or a pot that can hold an idli rack, bring 2 inches (5 cm) water to a boil. Lightly grease the idli molds with a little oil. Working in batches, fill the idli molds with 2 tablespoons of the batter in each well. Steam for 8–10 minutes until well risen and firm. If you find the idli hard to remove from the molds, let them sit for 10 minutes to settle. They can be reheated easily by steaming for a few moments, or a few seconds in the microwave. Serve hot with sambar and the chutneys.

STEAMED RICE CAKES

PHILIPPINES

Putong puti are rice cakes topped with cheese or salted egg and accompanied with Tablea (page 438), the local version of hot chocolate.

Preparation time: 10 minutes, plus 30 minutes resting time
Cooking time: 45 minutes
Makes: 12 rice cakes

· 2 cups (315 g) rice flour
· ½ cup (100 g) plus 2 tablespoons sugar
· 2½ teaspoons baking powder
· ¼ teaspoon fine sea salt
· ¾ cup (175 ml/6 fl oz) coconut milk

In a medium bowl, combine the rice flour, sugar, baking powder, and salt. Pour in 1 cup (240 ml/8 fl oz) water and the coconut milk. Whisk together until no dry spots or lumps remain.

Fill a large saucepan with 2 inches (5 cm) water. Fit a steamer basket in the saucepan. Bring the water to a boil. Working in batches, ladle about ⅓ cup (80ml) of batter into 4 individual tins/molds (similar to small cupcake tins/molds), filling them three-quarters of the way up with the batter. Steam the *putong puti* until a skewer inserted into the center of one comes out clean, about 15 minutes. Allow the *puti* to cool in the tins/molds for 10 minutes before transferring to a serving plate. Repeat with the remaining batter.

TURNIP CAKE

CHINA

Though called turnip cake (luobo gao in Chinese and lo bak go in Cantonese), this cake is actually made with daikon radish. The shredded radish is steamed into a cake and enjoyed at dim sum (a meal of small plates) along with Scallion Pancakes (page 136), cheong fun (Steamed Rice Rolls, page 285), Pineapple Buns (page 230), and more. Luobo gao is also the main ingredient in Singaporean chai tow kway (Carrot Cake, page 52).

Preparation time: 50 minutes, plus 25 minutes cooling time
Cooking time: 1 hour
Makes: 1 cake

· 1 large daikon radish (about 1 lb/455 g), peeled and grated
· 1 tablespoon vegetable oil
· 3 oz (85 g) Chinese-style bacon, chopped
· 3 dried shiitake mushrooms, soaked for 30 minutes, stemmed, and diced
· 2 tablespoons dried shrimp, rinsed, soaked for 30 minutes, and chopped
· 1 teaspoon sugar
· 1 cup (160 g) rice flour
· ½ teaspoon fine sea salt
· 3 tablespoons vegetable oil

In a medium saucepan, combine the grated daikon and pour in enough water to just submerge the radish. Bring to a boil over medium-high heat, reduce the heat to low, and simmer, uncovered, until most of the water has been absorbed and the radish begins to look like porridge, about 30 minutes. Remove from heat.

Meanwhile, in a frying pan, heat the oil over medium heat. Add the bacon and mushrooms and cook until slightly browned, 5 minutes. Add the shrimp and stir-fry until cooked through, about 2 minutes. Add the bacon mixture to the radish and stir until combined.

In a large bowl, combine the rice flour and salt. Put the pot with the radish and bacon mixture on a low heat. Add the rice batter and stir until combined. The batter should quickly thicken, about 1 minute. Remove from heat.

Meanwhile, in a steamer or a large saucepan fitted with a steamer insert, bring 2 inches (5 cm) water to a boil.

Pour the batter into an 8-inch (20 cm) square baking dish and place it in the steamer. Cover and steam until set and firm, about 30 minutes. Remove from the steamer and allow to completely before inverting it onto a plate.

Cut into 4-inch (10 cm) square slices 1 inch (2.5 cm) thick. In a frying pan, heat the oil over medium heat and fry the cake on both sides until golden brown and crispy bits begin to form, about 3 minutes per side. Serve warm or room temperature.

STEAMED RICE CAKES WITH PRESERVED RADISH

SINGAPORE

Hawker centers are open-air food courts popular in Singapore for all-day dining. In the morning, vendors serve chwee kueh, *a steamed rice cake medallion made in a small metal mold, similar to an egg-tart mold with smooth sides. The cakes are topped with diced preserved daikon radish (*chye poh*).*

Preparation time: 10 minutes
Cooking time: 1 hour
Serves/Makes: 2 / 10 cakes

For the rice cakes:
· ¾ cup (120 g) rice flour
· 2 tablespoons tapioca flour
· Pinch of salt
· ¾ cup (175 ml/6 fl oz) boiling water
· Vegetable oil, for greasing

For the topping:
· 4 tablespoons diced chye poh (preserved salted daikon), well rinsed to remove excess salt
· 1 clove garlic, minced
· 2 tablespoons diced shallot
· 1 teaspoon soy sauce
· 2 tablespoons vegetable oil
· ½ teaspoon sugar

Make the rice cakes:
In a heatproof bowl, combine the rice flour, tapioca flour, and salt. Stir in ¼ cup (60 ml) cold water. Stirring constantly, gradually add the boiling water, until the batter is the consistency of a thick pancake batter.

In a steamer or a large saucepan fitted with a steamer insert, bring 2 inches (5 cm) of water to a boil. Working in batches if needed, place the empty, greased *chwee kueh* or egg-tart molds on the wire rack and cover to heat the molds for about 2 minutes. Uncover and carefully pour the batter into each of the molds, leaving ¼ inch (6 mm) at the top. Cover and steam for 50 minutes, adding more water as needed. Remove the molds from the steamer and allow the cakes to set for 10 minutes.

Meanwhile, prepare the topping:
Drain the *chye poh* well and transfer to a small bowl. Mix in the garlic, shallot, and soy sauce. In a wok or medium frying pan, heat the oil over medium heat. Add the *chye poh* mixture and cook, stirring constantly, until browned, about 5 minutes. Remove from the heat and stir in the sugar.

To serve, remove the cakes from their molds. Dollop the filling on top and serve warm.

Steamed Rice Cakes with Preserved Radish

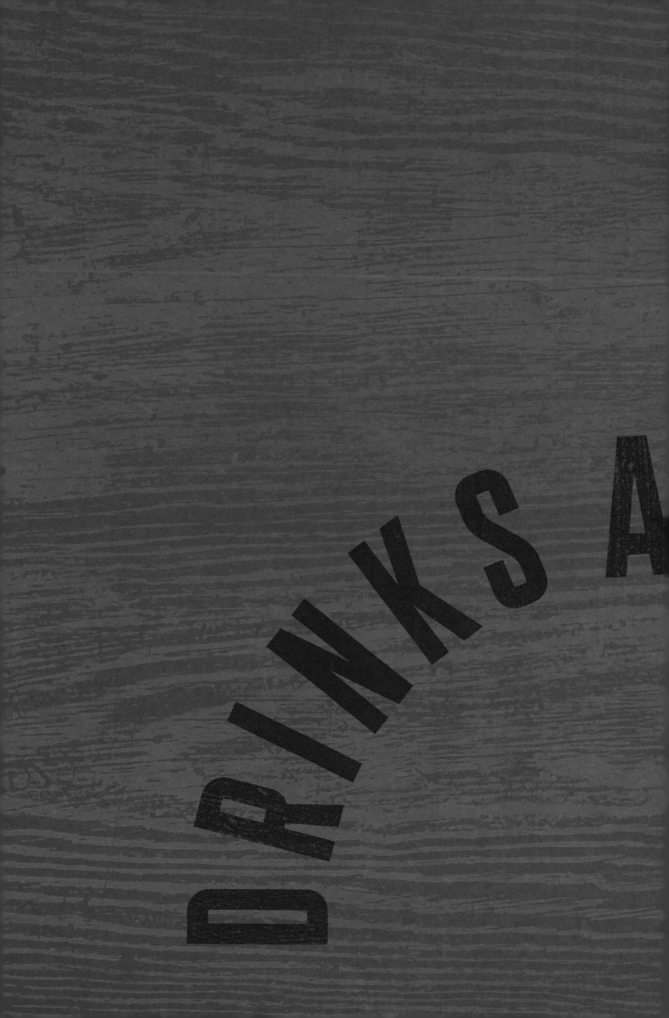

POUR-OVER COFFEE

UNITED STATES / GLOBAL

In this classic coffee-brewing technique, water is slowly hand-poured over coffee grounds though a filter and into a cup. Filter vessels can come in individual cup size or larger sizes like a Chemex.

Preparation time: 5 minutes
Cooking time: 5 minutes

· 3 tablespoons (30 grams) freshly ground coffee beans, dark or medium roast, to taste
· 2½ cups (590 ml/20 fl oz) boiling water

If grinding your own beans, they should be ground to the size of coarse salt. Place a paper filter into the pour-over carafe and wet it by pouring a touch of hot water into it to wash out the papery aroma that could end up infusing the coffee. Dump out the water from the carafe. Place the ground coffee in the filter and pour some of the hot water over the coffee, moving from around the edges into the center, about 5 seconds. You should use just enough water to hydrate the coffee. Allow the water to drip, about 20 seconds. Pour a bit more water over in a stream that lasts about 10 seconds. Let the coffee drip into the carafe. Continue to do this 2 more times until there is no more water and the coffee has brewed, about 3 minutes total.

 *See image on page 128.*

VIETNAMESE ICED COFFEE

VIETNAM

Caphe sua da is a classic way to take coffee in Vietnam and has become a popular sweet coffee option around the world. The differentiating factors of Vietnamese coffee are the use of a phin filter (a single-cup metal pour-over mechanism where the ground coffee is kept in a chamber as it steeps in hot water) and the addition of sweetened condensed milk in lieu of granulated sugar.

Preparation time: 10 minutes
Cooking time: 5 minutes
Serves: 1

· 3 tablespoons sweetened condensed milk
· 3 tablespoons (70 g) dark-roast ground coffee
· About 1 cup (250 ml/8 fl oz) boiling water
· Ice

Pour the sweetened condensed milk into a heat-safe glass or cup. Fit a Vietnamese *phin* filter over the glass/cup. Fill the center chamber with the ground coffee. Cover it with the perforated metal filter (which comes with the *phin*). Pour a touch of water over the filter to hydrate the coffee. Once wet, fill the *phin* with the boiling water. Allow the coffee to drip over the condensed milk, about 6 minutes. Stir together the coffee and milk. Fill a separate drinking glass with ice. Pour the coffee over the ice and serve immediately.

Vietnamese Iced Coffee

STOVETOP ESPRESSO

GLOBAL

A coffee shop espresso requires a machine with nine bars of atmospheric air pressure and controlled water temperature of 190–200°F (88–93°C) to "pull" (extract) the coffee into a 1-ounce (30 ml) shot with perfect crema *(fine foam that forms on top on an espresso indicating good pressure). To best achieve this at home, a stovetop espresso machine can be used. Moka and Brikka (Bialetti) models are popular throughout Europe and Latin America. They use a bottom chamber of water to create steam, which rises through the middle chamber of grinds, then collects in the top chamber to as a concentrated distillation of coffee.*

Preparation time: 5 minutes
Cooking time: 5 minutes
Serves: 3

· 3 tablespoons finely ground coffee

In a small 3-cup stovetop espresso maker, fill the bottom chamber with water up to the safety valve, then spoon the coffee into the filter chamber. Screw the espresso maker together and place over medium heat. (The flames of the stove should not surround the espresso maker, but be directly under.) Once the espresso begins to gurgle and filter through to the top, reduce the heat to low. When the espresso maker has stopped gurgling, the espresso is ready. Divide among espresso cups. Serve hot.

    VG VT 15 5

CHICORY COFFEE

UNITED STATES

Coffee with ground chicory root (a plant often used as a coffee replacement or natural flavor enhancer for its woody notes and buttery mouthfeel) is often enjoyed with Beignets (page 309) in New Orleans, Louisiana.

Preparation time: 5 minutes
Cooking time: 5 minutes
Serves: 2

· 2 tablespoons freshly ground coffee, dark or medium roast, to taste
· 1 tablespoon ground chicory root
· 2½ cups (590 ml/20 fl oz) boiling water

If grinding your own beans, they should be ground to the size of coarse salt. Place a paper filter into the pour-over carafe and wet it by pouring a touch of hot water into it to wash out the papery aroma that could end up infusing the coffee. Dump out the water from the carafe. Place the ground coffee and chicory root in the filter and pour some of the hot water over the coffee, moving from around the edges into the center, about 5 seconds. You should use just enough water to hydrate the coffee. Allow the water to drip, about 20 seconds. Pour a bit more water over in a stream that lasts about 10 seconds. Let the coffee drip into the carafe. Continue to do this 2 more times until there is no more water and the coffee has brewed, about 3 minutes total. Serve hot.

    VG VT 15 5

Stovetop Espresso
....

INSTANT COFFEE
GLOBAL

Instant coffee is a freeze-dried coffee intended to be hydrated before use. One of the most commonly enjoyed brands across the world is Nescafé. In Lebanon, Nescafé is enjoyed with powdered milk called Nido, a coffee ritual leftover from wartime, when fresh milk was sparse.

Preparation time: 5 minutes
Cooking time: 5 minutes
Serves: 1

· 2 teaspoons instant coffee
· 1 cup (250 ml/6 fl oz)
· Powdered milk, to taste

Bring water to a near boil in a tea kettle. Pour the instant coffee into a large mug. Pour the boiling water over the coffee. Stir in the powdered milk and serve hot.

FRAPPE
GREECE

A strong blended iced beverage made with instant coffee.

Preparation time: 5 minutes
Makes: 1

· 2 teaspoons instant coffee
· 1 teaspoon sugar
· Ice cubes, for serving
· Milk, for serving

In a tall drinking glass, combine the coffee and sugar. Pour 1 tablespoon of water over the coffee. Whip with a frother or stir vigorously with a spoon until the coffee forms a thick foam and doubles in the cup (or shake in a shaker with ice). Drop in ice cubes as desired and top off with 2 tablespoons water or cold milk. Serve immediately.

CAFÉ DE OLLA

MEXICO

A spiced coffee enjoyed with a Sweet Bread Roll with Crunchy Topping (page 232) or other Mexican breads or pastries. It is served hot in an earthen olla *(clay pot) or mug.*

Preparation time: 10 minutes
Cooking time: 5 minutes
Serves: 2

· 1 tablespoon dark brown sugar or panela (unrefined cane sugar)
· ½ cinnamon stick, preferably Mexican
· 2 tablespoons medium- to coarse-ground Mexican coffee, dark or medium roast (to taste)

In a small saucepan, combine 2 cups (475 ml/16 fl oz) water, brown sugar, and cinnamon stick. Bring to a boil over medium-high heat, stirring once or twice, until the sugar is dissolved, about 1 minute. Stir in the coffee and remove the saucepan from the heat. Allow the coffee to steep, about 5 minutes, before removing the cinnamon stick and serving hot.

CAFÉ TOUBA

SENEGAL

Coffee that's roasted, ground, and brewed with whole Selim pepper (also known as guinar pepper), this brew is said to have medicinal stomach-settling qualities from the spice, as well as a floral, peppery bite. Sometimes cloves are included. It is served with a generous amount of sugar, but no milk.

Preparation time: 5 minutes
Cooking time: 5 minutes
Serves: 2

· 3 tablespoons dark-roast coffee beans
· 2 teaspoons whole Guinea pepper (grains of paradise)
· 2½ cups (590 ml/20 fl oz) boiling water
· Sugar

In a small frying pan over medium heat, toast the coffee beans and Guinea pepper until aromatic, about 4 minutes. Be careful not to burn them. Once toasted, grind the beans and pepper together in a coffee grinder or with a mortar and pestle until they are about the size of coarse salt. Place a paper filter into the pour-over carafe and pour a touch of boiling water into it to wash out the papery aroma that could infuse the coffee. Dump out the water. Pour the ground coffee/pepper into the filter and pour some of the hot water over the coffee, moving from the edges into the center, about 5 seconds. You should use just enough water to hydrate the coffee. Allow the water to drip, about 20 seconds. Pour a bit more water over in a stream that lasts about 10 seconds. Let the coffee drip into the carafe. Continue to do this two more times until there is no more water and the coffee has brewed, about 3 minutes total. Stir in sugar to taste and serve hot.

ARABIC COFFEE
UNITED ARAB EMIRATES

Served hot and in small cups featuring an ornamental design, gahuwa arabia (Arabic Coffee) is infused with cardamom (and sometimes saffron) and made with lightly roasted beans.

Preparation time: 10 minutes
Cooking time: 15 minutes
Serves: 2

· 2 tablespoons ground arabica coffee
· 2 teaspoons ground cardamom
· Pinch of saffron (optional)

In a Turkish coffee pot (*cezve*) or a small saucepan, bring 2 cups (475 ml/16 fl oz) water to a boil over medium heat. Reduce the heat to low and let the boil come to a simmer, in order to avoid burning the coffee. Add the coffee but do not stir. When foam begins to form, about 10 minutes, remove the pot from the stove. Allow the foam to settle and then stir in the ground cardamom. Return the coffee to the stovetop and heat again on low heat until foam begins to reappear but does not come to a boil, about 30 seconds. Remove the pot from the heat and allow the coffee to stand until the coffee grounds fall to the bottom, about 2 minutes. Add the saffron (if using). Serve hot.

MILKY COFFEE
INDIA

This common morning beverage of coffee with warm milk is sometimes sprinkled with ground cinnamon or cocoa powder.

Preparation time: 5 minutes
Cooking time: 5 minutes
Serves: 2

· 4 teaspoons instant coffee
· 2 tablespoons sugar
· 2 cups (475 ml/16 fl oz) full-fat milk, warmed
· Ground cinnamon or cocoa powder, for serving

Divide the instant coffee, sugar, and 2 teaspoons water between two tall mugs. Whisk until the mixture becomes thick like a paste and the sugar has dissolved. Divide the warm milk between the mugs and mix with a spoon until no lumps remain. Serve hot with a dusting of ground cinnamon or cocoa.

CAFÉ CON LECHE
SPAIN

Popular around the world, this hot coffee and scalded milk drink originated in Spain. Café con leche is most commonly by Latin Americans around the world.

Preparation time: 5 minutes
Cooking time: 5 minutes
Serves: 1

· ½ cup (120 ml/4 fl oz) full-fat milk
· ½ cup (120 ml/4 fl oz) freshly brewed coffee
· Sugar (optional)

In a small saucepan, bring the milk to a simmer. It shouldn't boil, but instead begin to steam, about 180°F (82°C). When the milk is steaming, remove it from the heat. Pour the coffee into a coffee cup and pour the steamed milk over. Stir to combine. Stir in sugar to taste, if desired. Serve hot.

CAFÉ AU LAIT
FRANCE

Coffee with hot milk, typically served in a bowl.

Preparation time: 5 minutes
Cooking time: 5 minutes
Serves: 1

· ¾ cup (175 ml/6 fl oz) full-fat milk
· 1 cup (240 ml/8 fl oz) freshly brewed coffee

In a small saucepan, bring the milk to a simmer. It shouldn't boil, but instead begin to steam, about 180°F (82°C). When the milk is steaming, remove it from the heat. Whisk until it becomes just frothy. Pour the coffee into a mug or a bowl. Pour in the steamed milk. Serve hot.

See image on page 199.

TURMERIC LATTE
UNITED STATES

This latte was popularized in the United States, mostly in southern California as a health-oriented alternative to caffeinated beverages.

Preparation time: 5 minutes
Cooking time: 5 minutes
Serves: 1

· ¾ cup (175 ml/6 fl oz) almond milk (page 440) or coconut milk
· 1 teaspoon sugar or sweetener of choice
· 2 teaspoons grated fresh turmeric (¾ inch/2 cm)
· 1 teaspoon ground cinnamon, plus more for serving
· ½ teaspoon ground ginger

In a small saucepan, whisk together the milk, sugar, turmeric, cinnamon, and ginger. Heat over medium heat, but do not bring to a boil. Once the mixture begins to steam, remove the pan from the heat. Whisk until frothy. Strain through a fine-mesh sieve into a mug, pressing against the solids with a wooden spoon. Serve hot with a dusting of cinnamon, if desired.

TURKISH COFFEE
TURKEY

A popular drink in Turkey (and throughout the Middle East), this strong coffee is served in small cups. The word for breakfast in Turkish is kahvalti, *which translates to "before coffee."*

Preparation time: 5 minutes
Cooking time: 5 minutes
Serves: 2

· 1½ tablespoons finely ground Turkish coffee
· Sugar (optional)

In a Turkish coffee pot (*cezve*), combine 2 cups (475 ml/16 fl oz) water, ground coffee, and sugar to taste (if using), but do not stir much to combine. Set over medium heat and allow the contents to mostly mix together when they come to a boil. Right before the coffee boils, a ring of foam will form on the top. Divide this foam between two espresso cups. Return the coffee to a boil, about 30 seconds. Fill each cup halfway with coffee. Return the coffee to a boil again, about 15 seconds. Top off each cup with the remaining coffee. Let the coffee grinds settle to the bottom (about 30 seconds) before serving hot.

CAFECITO
CUBA / UNITED STATES

In Miami and Cuba, coffee is made strong, balanced by copious amounts of sugar, and topped with frothy espuma *(foam). A* colada *is a Cuban coffee that comes in one large cup and smaller thimble-size cups on the side, meant to share with friends.*

Preparation time: 5 minutes
Cooking time: 5 minutes
Serves: 3

· 2 tablespoons demerara sugar
· 3 oz Stovetop Espresso, brewed with Cuban coffee (page 410)

Spoon the sugar into a small heatproof pitcher. Prepare the espresso as per directions. As the espresso begins to brew in the stovetop maker, pour about 1 teaspoon of the espresso over the sugar and then return the espresso maker to the stovetop to finish brewing. Whisk the coffee and sugar together until the sugar dissolves and a thin layer of espuma forms on the top. Pour 1 oz of the coffee into each 3 espresso cups. Serve hot.

Turkish Coffee

FREDDO ESPRESSO

GREECE

The very hot summers in Greece result in a preference for cold drinks. This double shot of espresso is iced and frothy.

Preparation time: 10 minutes
Cooking time: 5 minutes
Serves: 1

· 2 shots (30 ml/1 fl oz each) Stovetop Espresso (page 410)
· 4 ice cubes, plus more for serving

Prepare the espresso as per directions. Place 4 ice cubes in a drinking glass. Pour the hot espresso over the ice cubes and froth with a frother (or shake in a shaker) until the ice cubes have melted and the espresso has foamed. Fill a drinking glass with more ice cubes. Pour the frothed espresso over the ice and serve immediately.

LATTE

ITALY/ UNITED STATES

Called a caffè latte in Italy, this drink has a higher ratio of steamed milk to coffee than a cappuccino (opposite). In the United States, it is popular to order a latte with nondairy milk (such as nut, oat, or soy), or even without coffee, such as a Turmeric Latte (page 415) or a Matcha Latte (page 428).

Preparation time: 5 minutes
Cooking time: 5 minutes
Serves: 1

· 1 shot (30 ml/1 fl oz) Stovetop Espresso (page 410)
· 1¼ cups (295 ml/10 fl oz) full-fat milk, nut, oat, or soy milk

Prepare the espresso as per directions. In a small saucepan, bring the milk to a simmer. It shouldn't boil, but instead begin to steam, about 180°F (82°C). When the milk is steaming, remove it from the heat. Froth the milk until it has doubled in volume and foamed. If you do not have a frother, pour the milk into a jar, cover, and shake until it froths and doubles in volume. Pour the espresso into a wide coffee cup. Holding back the foam, pour the milk into the latte first. Top the latte with the foam and serve immediately.

CAPPUCCINO

ITALY

A cappuccino is equal parts espresso, steamed milk, and milk foam. In Italy, cappuccini are enjoyed until lunchtime, accompanied by fette biscottate *(a rusk or small, sweetened, twice-baked bread slice) topped with butter and jam or Nutella, or a pastry.*

Preparation time: 5 minutes
Cooking time: 5 minutes
Serves: 1

· 1 shot (30 ml/1 fl oz) Stovetop Espresso (page 410)
· ¾ cup (175 ml/6 fl oz) milk, dairy (whole or fat-free/skimmed), almond, or oat

Prepare the espresso as per directions. In a small saucepan, bring the milk to a simmer. It shouldn't boil, but instead begin to steam, about 180°F (82°C). When the milk is steaming, remove it from the heat. Pour the milk into a chilled pitcher. Froth the milk until it foams. Pour the espresso into a cappuccino cup. Pour the milk over the espresso, moving back and forth to distribute it evenly around the espresso. Finish with the foam on top and serve immediately.

FREDDO CAPPUCCINO

GREECE

Freddo cappuccino is essentially a Freddo Espresso (opposite) topped with thick, frothy milk. Chilled coffee beverages are an important part of Greek café culture.

Preparation time: 5 minutes
Cooking time: 5 minutes
Serves: 1

· 2 shots (30 ml/1 fl oz each) Stovetop Espresso (page 410)
· 2 teaspoons sugar (optional)
· Ice cubes
· ⅓ cup (75 ml/2.5 fl oz) chilled full-fat milk

Prepare the espresso as per directions. Stir in sugar to taste (if using). Fill a tall drinking glass with ice cubes and pour the espresso over the ice. Froth the milk with a frother until it foams. If you do not have a frother, pour the milk into a jar, cover, and shake until it froths and doubles in volume. Pour the milk and foam over the espresso. Serve immediately.

FLAT WHITE
AUSTRALIA

A flat white is similar to a Latte (page 418) but has a higher ratio of coffee to milk. This drink originated in Australia but is enjoyed globally.

Preparation time: 5 minutes
Cooking time: 5 minutes
Serves: 1

· 1 shot (30 ml/1 fl oz) Stovetop Espresso (page 410)
· ¾ cup (175 ml/6 fl oz) full-fat milk

Make the espresso as per directions. In a small saucepan, bring the milk to a simmer. It shouldn't boil, but instead begin to steam, about 180°F (82°C). When the milk is steaming, remove it from the heat and whisk ferociously (or froth it with a frother) until it doubles in volume. With a spoon, mix the top froth to the bottom of the mixture for a smooth texture. Pour the shot of espresso into a coffee cup and pour the milk over. Serve immediately.

ESPRESSO MACCHIATO
ITALY

Called a caffè macchiato in Italy, this drink is made with one shot of espresso "stained" or "spotted" (macchiato) with just a drop of frothy milk.

Preparation time: 5 minutes
Cooking time: 5 minutes
Serves: 1

· 1 shot (15 ml/0.5 fl oz each) Stovetop Espresso (page 410)
· Sugar (optional)
· 1 tablespoon full-fat milk

Prepare the espresso per directions. Pour the espresso into a small coffee cup. Add sugar to taste, if desired. Froth the milk with a frother and pour over the espresso. Serve immediately.

See image on page 86.

CORTADO
SPAIN

In Spain, a cortado translates from the verb cortar *(to cut) and refers to a single shot of espresso "cut" with an equal amount of steamed milk. The addition of sugar would make this a Cuban* cortadito *or* café cubano. *If adding sugar, follow the instructions from the Cafecito (page 417) as the sugar process is the same.*

Preparation time: 5 minutes
Cooking time: 5 minutes
Serves: 1

· 1 shot (15 ml/1 fl oz) Stovetop Espresso (page 410)
· Sugar (optional)
· 2 tablespoons full-fat milk

Prepare the espresso per directions. Pour the espresso into a small coffee cup. Add sugar to taste, if desired. In a small saucepan, bring the milk to a simmer. It shouldn't boil, but instead begin to steam, about 180°F (82°C). When the milk is steaming, remove it from the heat and pour over the espresso. Serve immediately.

VIETNAMESE EGG COFFEE
VIETNAM

Cà phê trứng is a special coffee topped with a frothy, sweetened egg yolk mixture, creating a rich depth of flavor.

Preparation time: 15 minutes
Cooking time: 5 minutes
Serves: 1

· 3 tablespoons dark-roast ground coffee
· About 1 cup (250 ml/8 fl oz) boiling water
· 1 egg yolk
· ¼ teaspoon vanilla extract
· 2 tablespoons sweetened condensed milk
· Sugar

Fit a Vietnamese *phin* filter over a glass. Fill the center chamber with the ground coffee. Cover it with the perforated metal filter (which comes with the *phin*). Pour a touch of water over the filter to hydrate the coffee. Once wet, fill the *phin* with the boiling water. Allow the coffee to drip over the condensed milk, about 6 minutes.

While the coffee is brewing, prepare the egg cream. In a small bowl, whisk together the egg yolk and vanilla until the egg yolk is frothy, about 1 minute. Whisk in the condensed milk, 1 tablespoon at a time, until the mixture is thick and creamy. Fill two-thirds of a cup with coffee. Pour the egg mixture on top and serve immediately. Stir in sugar to taste, if desired and serve.

MANOELLA BUFFARA
BRAZILIAN BREAKFAST

Originally trained as a journalist, Manoella Buffara spent the early years of her cooking career working at prestigious restaurants, including Noma in Copenhagen and Alinea in Chicago. She opened Restaurant Manu, which focuses on regional Brazilian cooking and the use of local produce, in her hometown of Cutiriba in 2011, and is now considered one of the most successful chefs in Latin American gastronomy.

Our summer vacation has arrived. My brother and I can't wait to get to the farm, in the small community of Cruzeiro do Sul, where my father has corn and sugarcane fields and raises cows and other animals. We go there each July; in Cruzeiro there's always sun and heat.

The car packed, we depart at 6 am, anxious to arrive. It's a little cloudy; we can barely see anything but an immense whiteness. Nothing can diminish the joy of being in Daddy's old pickup truck, on the red dirt roads.

We go past several places where warm *pastel* (meat pie) is sold on the side of the road, with delicious *garapa* (freshly squeezed sugarcane juice with a few drops of lemon).

We reach the old town. First, we go to the marketplace to buy flour from a neighbor, eggs from Mr. Nakamura, and fresh butter made in the dairy-seller's house.

The first morning, we wake up when the cock crows. We go to the dairy cows with our cups to get milk. We smell bread baking in the wood stove, yams with cane syrup, homemade pumpkin jam, and Mrs. Antonia's fresh cheese. Everything on that breakfast table created memories that are with me to this day.

Here in Brazil, the country is as big as the richness of flavors. Incomes vary a great deal in the various regions of Brazil. The characteristics of the menu of each Brazilian region or state come from the cultural heritage of the settlers, modified according to the availability of local ingredients.

As a result, the diversity of breakfasts is enormous. I was amazed when I first ate the typical breakfast of the northeastern Pernambuco region, which includes goat *buchada* (stuffed goat stomach), yucca, and more. In Sao Paulo, the typical breakfast consists of bread with butter and a *pingado* (milk and coffee); in Minas Canastra cheese or cheese bread is almost mandatory. Breakfast in the coastal Paraná, where I'm from, consists of bread with an egg and *chineque* (a type of sweet bread); there, it is common to eat yams instead of bread. In southern Brazil, where international influences combine, breakfast seems to be quite varied. It is possible to find several types of sausages, cheeses, and honey.

In the northern part of the country, consumption of *pupunha* (palm heart) is widespread. Peach palm fruits are usually consumed after being boiled in water and salt, or in the form of flour. They can also be used to manufacture jams and jellies. The consumption of *cupuaçu* cakes (made with the fruit of a tropical rainforest tree, related to cocoa) is also common, along with *macaxeira* (a local name for cassava), fried banana, *bacuri* jelly (made from the fruit of another local tree), cassava porridge, and the famous açaí juice. Wet tapioca with chestnut milk is also common.

Despite the continental dimensions of Brazil, one food is considered the most important throughout the country: cassava. The tuber, which guarantees satiety and is gluten-free, has several names in the country. Baked or fried, it is part of breakfast—and many other meals—in several regions.

Bananas are also common in the Northeast and in the South. Couscous (sweet or salty), curd cheese, and butter cheese spread on bread are also eaten at breakfast.

Breakfast is particularly important in rural parts of the country: the first meal of the day helps sustain laborers as they work hard from sunrise to sunset.

The traditional recipes of the Midwest are typical of the *cerrado*, the Brazilian savanna. There, you can find the bread, rice cake, *pequi* nut cake, meatloaf with *guariroba*, and the famous juice of *cajazinho* (all typical fruits of the *cerrado*). In the southeast, in Minas Gerais, we enjoy *biju*, a flatbread made with cassava flour, roasted, and topped with butter or fresh cheese; in the countryside of São Paulo, it's fried eggs with bacon and *cuscuz paulista* (a local variation on couscous). The list goes on and on . . . and every breakfast is accompanied by great Brazilian coffee.

01. Orange Pound Cake PAGE 392 02. Avocado Smoothie PAGE 436 03. Cheese Bread PAGE 235

04. Stoveto Espresso PAGE 410   05. Açaí Bowl PAGE 445   06. Tapioca-Flour Crepes PAGE 120

MOROCCAN MINT TEA

MOROCCO

Fresh mint leaves steeped in hot water, sometimes combined with gunpowder green tea and sugar.

Preparation time: 5 minutes
Cooking time: 5 minutes
Serves: 1

· 1 tablespoon green tea leaves (optional)
· 6 fresh mint leaves
· 1 cup (140 ml/8 fl oz) boiled water
· Sugar (optional)

If using green tea leaves, place them in a tea ball or bag, then in a heatproof cup or mug. Add the fresh mint leaves loose in the mug. Pour the hot water over the leaves and let steep for 3 minutes before removing the green tea leaves. The mint will typically stay steeping in the cup. Enjoy hot, sweetened with sugar if desired.

KINKÉLIBA LEAF TEA

BURKINA FASO / MALI / SENEGAL

The kinkéliba leaf is steeped to make a traditional tonic drink in tropical savannah countries such as Senegal, Mali, and Burkina Faso. It is believed to be an aid to weight loss and have detoxifying properties. Instant coffee is often added to the brew.

Preparation time: 5 minutes
Cooking time: 5 minutes
Serves: 1

· 1 tablespoon dried kinkéliba leaves
· 1 teaspoon instant coffee (optional)
· 1 cup (240 ml/8 fl oz) just-boiled water

Place the loose leaves in a tea ball or bag, then in a heatproof cup or mug. Add the instant coffee, if using. Pour the hot water over the leaves and stir to dissolve the instant coffee. Let steep for 3 minutes before removing the tea leaves. Enjoy hot.

ROSE TEA

IRAN

*Dried rose petals are an essential tea ingredient in Persian culture. Instead of loose cane sugar, the tea is sweetened with rock candy (crystal sugar) swizzle sticks (*nabat*).*

Preparation time: 5 minutes
Cooking time: 5 minutes
Serves: 4

· ¾ cup (.5 oz/12 g) dried rosebuds
· 4 cups (950 ml/32 fl oz) just-boiled water
· Rock candy (crystal sugar) swizzle sticks (nabat), for serving

Place the rosebuds in a heatproof cup or mug. Pour the hot water over them and cover with a linen or tea towel. Let steep for 5 minutes and serve hot with *nabat*.

QISHR

YEMEN

A more economical version of coffee is this brew using cascara—*dried coffee cherries (the fruit that surrounds the coffee bean)—mixed with ginger and cinnamon. Since this is made with the husk rather than the coffee bean itself, this is considered a tea and not a coffee.*

Preparation time: 5 minutes
Cooking time: 20 minutes
Serves: 4

· 1 cup (140 ml/8 fl oz) cascara (dried coffee cherries)
· ½ teaspoon ground cinnamon
· 1 teaspoon grated fresh ginger
· Sugar

In a medium saucepan, combine 4 cups (950 ml/32 fl oz) water, cascara, cinnamon, ginger, and sugar to taste. Bring to a boil over medium heat, then reduce the heat to low. Simmer the *cascara* until the water is stained red, 10 minutes. Transfer the tea to a teapot and serve hot.

MATCHA
UNITED STATES

Matcha is a finely ground green tea that is whisked with the water, rather than steeped, to create a cloudy green drink. The tea powder is frothed with a special bamboo whisk (an electric frother can also be used). Though matcha originated in Japan, it is not served there with breakfast (when the tea of choice is sencha green tea), but more typically enjoyed in the afternoon. In the US, matcha has become a more common morning beverage. Enjoy matcha on its own or as a replacement for coffee, such as with Matcha Latte (below).

Preparation time: 5 minutes
Cooking time: 5 minutes
Serves: 1

· 1 teaspoon green matcha powder

In a small saucepan, bring 1 cup (240 ml/8 fl oz) water to a simmer. It should be hot but not boiling. Remove from the heat. Sift the green matcha powder into a large teacup and mix with 1 teaspoon hot water until combined. Pour in the remaining water and whisk in an "M" formation with a bamboo whisk or frother, until just frothy, 10–15 seconds. Serve hot.

MATCHA LATTE
UNITED STATES

A Latte (page 418) made with Matcha (above) replacing the espresso. Often times matcha lattes are prepared with an alternative milk to dairy, such as nut, oat, or soy. This beverage is considered to be a healthier option than the traditional dairy and coffee drink.

Preparation time: 5 minutes
Cooking time: 5 minutes
Serves: 1

· ½ teaspoon green matcha powder
· ½ teaspoon honey or agave
· ½ cup (120 ml/4 fl oz) full-fat milk, nut, oat, or soy milk

In a small saucepan, bring 1 teaspoon water to a simmer. It should be hot but not boiling. Remove from the heat. Sift the green matcha powder into a large teacup and mix with 1 teaspoon hot water until combined.

In a small saucepan, bring the milk to a simmer. It should be hot but not boiling. Remove from heat and add the honey. Stir to combine. Slowly pour in milk and honey or agave into the matcha and whisk in an "M" formation with a bamboo whisk or frother, until just frothy, 10–15 seconds. Serve immediately.

MASALA CHAI

INDIA

Often shortened to "chai," this spiced black tea is infused with aromatic spices and typically served with milk. In the United States, chai is sometimes used as a replacement in coffee-based drinks, most commonly in a Latte (page 418), or Dirty Chai (chai latte with a shot of espresso).

Preparation time: 10 minutes
Cooking time: 10 minutes
Serves: 2

· 4 green cardamom pods
· 4 black peppercorns
· ½ cinnamon stick
· 1 teaspoon grated fresh ginger
· ½ cup (120 ml/4 fl oz) full-fat milk
· 1 tablespoon loose black tea leaves
· Sugar

In a small saucepan, combine the cardamom pods, peppercorns, and cinnamon stick and toast over medium heat until aromatic, about 2 minutes. Pour 1½ cups (355 ml/12 fl oz) water and milk over the spices and bring to a simmer. Add the ginger, then reduce the heat to low and simmer for 5 minutes. Add the tea leaves and remove from the heat. Allow the tea to steep for 4–5 minutes. Stir in sugar, to taste. Strain the chai through a fine-mesh sieve into a teapot. Discard the spices and tea leaves. Serve hot.

CHAI KARAK

QATAR / UNITED ARAB EMIRATES

Originally from India and Pakistan, this cardamom-infused milk tea has become a popular morning ritual in the United Arab Emirates and Qatar.

Preparation time: 10 minutes
Cooking time: 5 minutes
Serves: 4

· 1 tablespoon whole black tea leaves
· 10 cardamom pods, crushed
· ½ cup (120 ml/4 fl oz) sweetened condensed milk (optional)
· Sugar (optional)

In a small saucepan, combine the tea, cardamom, and 1½ cups (355 ml/12 fl oz) water and bring to a simmer over medium heat. Remove from heat and let steep for 5 minutes. Add the sweetended condensed milk and sugar, if desired. Pour the milk tea through a fine-mesh sieve into a teapot and serve hot.

MATE

ARGENTINA

*Also known as yerba mate, mate is made by steeping almost an entire cup with loose tea leaves in small amounts of water. It is sipped through a metal straw (*bombilla*) with a filter at the end to catch all the loose leaves. This helps keep the liquid hot and manage its high caffeine levels. This tea goes perfectly with* facturas, *Argentine pastries such as* medialunas *(Crescent Rolls, page 362).*

Preparation time: 5 minutes
Cooking time: 5 minutes
Makes: 1 cup

· 3 tablespoons yerba mate

In a small saucepan, bring ¼ cup (60 ml) water to a boil over high heat. Pour the loose yerba mate into a large teacup or mug. Place a *bombilla* or metal straw into the cup and pour half of the water over the mate, just shy of submerging the leaves fully. Serve with a twist of orange peel on the rim of the glass. Sip the tea through the *bombilla* and keep adding water to refill as needed.

PULLED TEA

MALAYSIA

Teh tarik is a pulled tea found in kopitiam *(local coffee shops), hawker centers (in Singapore), and at street stalls in Malaysia, Singapore, and Indonesia. The sweet black tea is ribboned or "pulled" back and forth between two cups while mixing and frothing sweetened and condensed milk.*

Preparation time: 5 minutes
Cooking time: 8 minutes
Serves: 4

· 8 black tea bags
· 2 tablespoons sweetened condensed milk

In a small saucepan, bring 4 cups (950 ml/32 fl oz) water to a boil over high heat. Add the tea bags, then remove from the heat, letting the tea steep for 8 minutes. Stir in the sweetened condensed milk. Pour the tea into a large cup. Pour the tea in a steady stream back into the saucepan, raising the cup so that the tea pours like a waterfall into the saucepan. Repeat three more times. This helps the tea become frothy. Distribute the tea into 4 mugs or heat-safe cups and serve hot.

Mate

MANGO JUICE
COLOMBIA

This can be made with any available fruits, including guava, passion fruit, or papaya, or even more exotic fruits like soursop, curuba, or mamey.

Preparation time: 10 minutes
Serves: 2–4

· 4 cups (11/2 lb/660 g) chopped mango
· 3 cups (710 ml/24 fl oz) milk or water
· 1½ tablespoons sugar

In a blender, combine the mango, milk, and sugar and blend until smooth. Serve over ice.

ORANGE JUICE
GLOBAL

The most lauded of all morning juices, orange juice is found on breakfast tables around the world, either freshly squeezed or made from frozen orange concentrate.

Preparation time: 10 minutes
Serves: 1

· 4 large oranges, halved

Press the oranges through a citrus press. If a juicer is not available, peel the oranges and combine them in a blender. Blend until smooth. For blender method only: use a wooden spoon, press the juice through a fine-mesh sieve (for no pulp) or a colander (for some pulp) into a medium jar or pitcher. Serve immediately or refrigerate to chill.

This recipe can also be made with grapefruit for a more pungent citrus beverage. For grapefruit juice, use 1 large grapefruit, halved.

See image on page 128.

MORIR SOÑANDO
DOMINICAN REPUBLIC

Freshly squeezed orange juice, milk, and sugar are vigorously stirred with chipped ice until frothy. This drink has quite a romantic name, Morir Soñando or "to die dreaming."

Preparation time: 5 minutes
Serves: 2

· Ice cubes, chipped or crushed
· 1½ cups (355 ml/12 fl oz) evaporated milk, chilled
· 4 tablespoons sugar
· ¼ teaspoon vanilla extract
· 1 cup (240 ml/8 fl oz) orange juice, preferably homemade (above), chilled

Fill a small pitcher the crushed or chipped ice cubes. Add the evaporated milk, sugar, and vanilla and stir until well combined. Add the orange juice and stir vigeoursly until frothy. Serve immediately.

Morir Soñando

POMEGRANATE JUICE

ISRAEL

Popular in Israeli shuks *(open-air markets), fresh pomegranate juice is manually squeezed and enjoyed throughout the day.*

Preparation time: 10 minutes
Serves: 2

· 4 pomegranates, halved

Juice each half of the pomegranate in a manual citrus press. Serve right away or refrigerate to chill.

See image page 63.

PAPAYA JUICE

BRAZIL

Brazilians enjoy breakfast at cafés with over forty different types of fruit to choose from. The fruit (most popularly, papaya) is tossed in a blender with water, orange juice, or milk.

Preparation time: 10 minutes
Serves: 1

· ½ papaya, peeled, seeded, and coarsely chopped
· 1 cup (240 ml/8 fl oz) orange juice, store-bought or homemade (page 432)
· 2 teaspoons lemon juice
· 1 teaspoon honey or sugar (optional)

In a blender, combine the papaya, orange juice, lemon juice, and honey or sugar and blend until smooth. Serve immediately or refrigerate to chill.

POG

UNITED STATES

A blend of pineapple or passionfruit, orange, and guava is a popular juice enjoyed in Hawaii. Though this beverage is enjoyed throughout the day, a fresh POG features a more lively alternative to the classic orange juice (page 432).

Preparation time: 10 minutes
Serves: 1-2

· 2 cups (10 oz/300 g) chopped fresh pineapple or 1 passionfruit
· ½ cup (120 ml/4 fl oz) orange juice, store-bought or homemade (page 432)
· 3 guavas, top and bottom trimmed off, seeds removed
· 1 tablespoon honey or sugar (optional)

In a blender, combine the pineapple or passion fruit (inside flesh and seeds), orange juice, guavas, 2 tablespoons water, and honey and blend until smooth. Pour the juice through a fine-mesh sieve into a medium jar. With a wooden spoon, press the juice through until only seeds and pulp remain in the sieve. Serve immediately or refrigerate to chill.

PRESSED JUICE
AUSTRALIA / UNITED STATES

Highly popular in Australia and warmer American cities like Los Angeles, pressed juice is a healthy drink option enjoyed with an array of fruit and vegetable combinations. A juicer liquefies fruits and vegetables and separates the juice from the pulp, rinds, and seeds. If you do not have a juicer, you can use a blender—though it won't technically be a "pressed juice." The flavor profile will remain the same but the texture will be less smooth.

GINGER-TURMERIC JUICE

Preparation time: 10 minutes
Serves: 2

· 1 green apple, cored and halved
· 3 large carrots (375 g)
· 1 lemon, peeled and halved
· ½-inch (1.25 cm) piece fresh ginger, peeled
· ½ teaspoon ground turmeric or 1-inch (2.5 cm) turmeric root

Process all ingredients through a juicer. (Alternatively, blend everything in a high-powered blender with 4 tablespoons water until smooth. Pour the juice through a fine-mesh sieve into a medium jar. With a wooden spoon, press the juice through until only seeds and pulp remain in the sieve.) Serve immediately.

See image on page 86

GREEN JUICE

Preparation time: 10 minutes
Serves: 2

· 3 leaves Tuscan kale (cavolo nero)
· 1/2 cucumber, cut in half lengthwise
· 1 green apple, cored and halved
· 1 celery stalk
· 1 lime, peeled and halved
· ½-inch (1.25 cm) piece fresh ginger, peeled

Process all ingredients through a juicer. (Alternatively, in a high-powered blender, blend the ingredients with ½ cup (120 ml/4 fl oz) water until smooth. Pour the juice through a fine-mesh sieve into a medium jar. With a wooden spoon, press the juice through until only seeds and pulp remain in the sieve.) Serve immediately.

See image on page 86

AVOCADO SMOOTHIE
BRAZIL

Brazilians enjoy fruit beverages regularly and vitamina *is one version where avocado is blended into a smoothie with milk and sugar.*

Preparation time: 10 minutes
Serves: 1

· ½ large avocado, pitted, peeled, and chopped
· 1 tablespoon honey
· ½ cup (120 ml/4 fl oz) full-fat milk
· 4 ice cubes

In a blender, combine the avocado, honey, milk, and ice cubes and blend until smooth. Serve immediately.

See image on page 424.

ATOLE
MEXICO

Atole is a ground corn–based drink often found at Mexican street carts accompanying Tamales (page 310) or Chilaquiles (page 20). There are other versions of this across Central and South America. In Mexico, you can find champurrado *(a chocolate* atole*) and in Bolivia there is* api, *a version made with white or purple corn (*api morado*). Nicaragua has a toasted-corn version called Pinolillo (page 438).*

Preparation time: 5 minutes
Cooking time: 15 minutes
Serves: 2

· 4 tablespoons finely ground cornmeal (masa harina)
· 4 tablespoons full-fat milk
· 1 cinnamon stick
· 2 tablespoons light brown sugar
· Ground cinnamon, for dusting

Place the masa harina in a small saucepan. Slowly pour in 1½ cups (355 ml/12 fl oz) water, whisking constantly to avoid lumps. Bring the mixture to a simmer over medium heat. Whisk in the milk, cinnamon stick, and brown sugar. Reduce the heat to low and whisk constantly to avoid clumps forming. Once the *atole* begins to thicken, 5–10 minutes, discard the cinnamon stick. If it's too thick, add more water. Pour into coffee cups. Serve hot with a dusting of ground cinnamon.

CHAMPURRADO

Prepare as directed for the *atole*, adding ⅓ cup (75 g) roughly chopped dark chocolate along with the milk, cinnamon, and sugar.

Atole

PINOLILLO
COSTA RICA / NICARAGUA

A toasted-cornmeal and cocoa spiced drink similar to a Mexican Champurrado (see Atole, page 436), but more often served chilled.

Preparation time: 10 minutes
Cooking time: 5 minutes
Serves: 2

· 2 tablespoons cornmeal
· 1¾ cups (415 ml/14 fl oz) full-fat, dairy, or coconut milk
· 2 tablespoons unsweetened cocoa powder
· 1½ teaspoons sugar, plus more to taste
· ¼ teaspoon ground cinnamon

In a small frying pan, toast the cornmeal over medium heat until lightly browned, 3 minutes. Transfer the cornmeal to a spice grinder or mortar and pestle and grind into a fine powder. Transfer the toasted cornmeal to a blender and add the milk, ½ cup (120 ml/4 fl oz) water, cocoa powder, sugar, and cinnamon. Blend until thoroughly combined. Taste and add more sugar if desired. Serve chilled or over ice. Pinolillo can also be heated in a small saucepan over medium heat and served as a hot beverage.

TABLEA
PHILIPPINES

This hot chocolate is made from melted disks of whole cacao beans, whisked with milk. The nickname Tablea comes from tsokolate tablea, *chocolate tablets. Typically, it is paired with* Pandesal *(page 216) and white cheese.*

Preparation time: 5 minutes
Cooking time: 10 minutes
Serves: 2

· 6 tablea (chocolate disks)
· ½ cup (120 ml/4 fl oz) full-fat milk
· 1 tablespoon sugar

In a small saucepan, bring 1½ cups (355 ml/12 fl oz) water to a boil. Add the *tablea* and stir until melted. Continue cooking, stirring constantly with a wooden spoon, until the mixture is thickened, about 3 minutes. Reduce the heat to low and whisk in the milk and sugar until the hot chocolate becomes frothy. Serve hot.

SUBMARINO
ARGENTINA

In this Argentinian drink, a small bar of bitter chocolate is dropped into a glass of hot steamed milk (sinking to the bottom, like a submarine) and stirred until melted.

Preparation time: 5 minutes
Cooking time: 5 minutes
Serves: 1

· 1 cup (240 ml/8 fl oz) full-fat milk
· 1 bar (2 oz/57 g) dark chocolate
· Sugar (optional)

In a small saucepan, heat the milk over medium heat until it begins to steam, about 2 minutes. Fill a glass with the steaming-hot milk. Add the chocolate bar and stir with a spoon until the chocolate has melted. Add sugar to taste, if desired.

HOT CHOCOLATE

SPAIN

Hot chocolate in Spain is a different preparation than in other parts of the world. The addition of cornstarch helps thicken the drink to dip Churros (page 308), deep-fried sticks of dough.

Preparation time: 5 minutes
Cooking time: 10 minutes
Serves: 2

- 2 cups (475 ml/16 fl oz) full-fat milk
- 2 teaspoons cornstarch (cornflour)
- ½ cup (115 g) coarsely chopped dark chocolate
- 4 tablespoons sugar

In a small saucepan, combine the milk and cornstarch (cornflour). Whisk together until the cornstarch dissolves and the milk begins to steam, about 2 minutes. Reduce the heat to low and whisk in the chopped dark chocolate. Whisk in the sugar and return the heat to medium. Whisk constantly until the hot chocolate is heated and thickened, 3–5 minutes. Pour into 2 mugs. Serve hot.

SPICED HOT CHOCOLATE

MEXICO

Most Spanish-speaking countries have their version of hot chocolate. In the Mexican hot chocolate ritual, special wooden whisks called molinillos *are used to froth the chocolate in a* chocolatero *(clay pitcher). Similar to Tablea (opposite) in the Philipines, Mexican chocolate comes in tablets but Aztec (Mexican chocolate) often comes spiked with cinnamon, dried chilies, and added sugar.*

Preparation time: 5 minutes
Cooking time: 10 minutes
Serves: 2

- 2 segments of a tablet, Mexican chocolate (6 oz/180 g)
- 2 cup (475 ml/16 fl oz) full-fat milk

In a small saucepan, bring the milk to a simmer. Add the chocolate and stir with a *molinillo* or whisk until melted. Continue cooking, stirring constantly, until the mixture is frothy, about 3 minutes. Serve hot.

FRESH SOY MILK

CHINA

*Soy milk (*doujiang*) is a common accompaniment to most breakfast dishes in China and Southeast Asian countries. It can be used to dip long donuts,* youtiao *(Chinese Cruller, page 306) or just as a refreshing drink in the morning. The solids leftover from making the milk are called* okara *and can be used as a protein replacement in a variety of recipes.*

Preparation time: 25 minutes, plus overnight soaking time
Cooking time: 10 minutes
Makes: 4 cups (950 ml/32 fl oz)

· ½ cup (95 g) dried soybeans

Soak the soybeans in 2 cups (475 ml/16 fl oz) water overnight.

Drain the soybeans and peel (discard the skins). Transfer to a blender with 4 cups (945 ml/32 fl oz) water. Blend until thoroughly combined and no bits of the soybean remain.

Line a fine-mesh sieve with a double layer of cheesecloth (or use a nut bag) and set over a small saucepan. Strain the liquid into the pan (save the solids for another use). Heat the soy milk over medium heat (do not let boil), stirring and discarding any foam or skin that may form on top, about 10 minutes. Remove the milk from the heat. Allow it to cool before storing in an airtight container in the refrigerator for up to 3 days.

ALMOND MILK

UNITED STATES

An alternative to dairy milk, almond milk is often used as a replacement in coffee drinks, with cereal, or in a glass on its own.

Preparation time: 10 minutes, plus 6 hours soaking time
Cooking time: 10 minutes
Makes: 4 cups (950 ml/32 fl oz)

· 1 cup (145 g) skin-on almonds
· 2 pitted dates
· Pinch of salt

Soak the almonds in water to cover for at least 6 hours or up to overnight. At the same time, soak the dates in ¼ cup (60 ml/2 fl oz) water.

Drain the almonds and add them to a blender with 4 cups (950 ml/32 fl oz) water. Add the dates and their soaking liquid and salt. Blend until the liquid is milky and creamy.

Line a fine-mesh sieve with a double layer of cheesecloth (or use a nut bag) and strain the almond milk into a bowl, pressing on the almond meal to remove as much liquid as possible. Discard the solids. Transfer the almond milk to a mason jar and store in the refrigerator for up to 3 days. Serve chilled.

Almond Milk

BREAKFAST
FRUIT BOWL
UNITED STATES

A bowl of fruit for breakfast is popular all over the United States and most parts of the world. This recipe can be customized with any available or preferred fruit options and topped with yogurt and/or Granola (page 110), nuts, and seeds.

Preparation time: 15 minutes
Serves: 1

· Cut fruit of your choice
· Granola (page 110)
· Nuts and seeds of your choice
· Plain yogurt

Add the yogurt to a bowl and top with granola, nuts, and/or seeds

PAPAYA
AND LIME
UNITED STATES

Adding lime juice to papaya or any tropical fruit, like pineapple or mango, gives a bright citrus note to this morning meal. This is also a popular addition to fruit in Southern California and Mexico.

Preparation time: 5 minutes
Serves: 2

· 1 papaya, halved and seeded
· 1 small lime, halved
· Grated lime zest, for garnish (optional)

Squeeze the lime juice over the halved papaya. Garnish with lime zest for color, if desired.

Papaya and Lime

GRAPEFRUIT HALVES WITH BRÛLÉED SUGAR
UNITED STATES

A grapefruit half with the addition of brûléed sugar was popularized in the 1980's and is considered a breakfast staple at hotel "continental breakfasts," diners, and on brunch menus.

Preparation time: 5 minutes
Cooking time: 5 minutes
Serves: 1

· 1 grapefruit, halved through the equator
· 2 tablespoons turbinado or light brown sugar

Preheat the broiler (grill) to high. Place the grapefruit halves on a baking sheet. Pat the cut surface of the grapefruit to dry slightly. Sprinkle evenly with the sugar. Broil (grill) until the sugar has melted and browned, 6 minutes; be sure to watch closely to avoid burning. Serve warm.

AÇAÍ BOWL
BRAZIL

This is a frozen blend of banana, açaí (the fruit from an açaí palm tree), and guarana extract (a caffeinated fruit). In the 1970's the açaí pulp was squeezed fresh by migrants of the Amazonian delta to Northern Brazilian cities. In the 1980s, JiuJitsu master Carlos Gracie froze the pulp (for a longer shelf-life) and added it to the training diet of the fighters in his gyms. In Rio de Janeiro and São Paulo, the frozen pulp was sweetened and served like ice cream. Across Brazil, Hawaii, and Southern California, açaí is now served in a bowl topped with granola, coconut, and fresh fruit, often in beautifully arranged patterns.

Preparation time: 10 minutes
Serves: 1

· 1 (3.5 oz/100 g) pack frozen açaí pulp, cut into pieces
· 1 banana, peeled, sliced, and frozen
· 1 tablespoon honey or agave
· 2 tablespoons coconut water, Almond Milk (page 440), Orange Juice (page 432), or your choice of nut milk, juice, or water
· 4 tablespoons Granola (page 110) (optional)
· 2 tablespoons shredded coconut (optional)
· Fresh sliced fruit, such as banana slices, cut mango, and berries, for serving (optional)

In a blender, combine the açaí, frozen banana, honey, and coconut water. Blend until smooth. Pour the smoothie into a bowl and (if using) top with granola, shredded coconut, and sliced fruit.

Açaí bowl

INDEX

INDEX

C

V

W

X

Y

Z

Milk is always whole.
Cream is always heavy (whipping).
Eggs are always large (US)/medium (UK).
Herbs, unless indicated otherwise, are always fresh, and parsley is always flat-leaf.
Butter is always unsalted, unless specified otherwise.
Salt is always Fine Sea Salt.

Cooking and preparation times are for guidance only, as individual ovens vary. If using a fan (convection) oven, follow the manufacturer's instructions concerning oven temperatures.

To test whether your deep-frying oil is hot enough, add a cube of stale bread. If it browns in 30 seconds, the temperature is [350–375°F / 180–190°C], about right for most frying. Exercise a high level of caution when following recipes involving any potentially hazardous activity, including the use of high temperature and open flames. In particular, when deep-frying, add the food carefully to avoid splashing, wear long sleeves, and never leave the pan unattended.

Some recipes include raw or very lightly cooked eggs. These should be avoided by the elderly, infants, pregnant women, convalescents, and anyone with an impaired immune system.

Both metric and imperial measures are used in this book. Follow one set of measurements throughout, not a mixture, as they are not interchangeable.

All spoon measurements are level.

When no quantity is specified, for example of oils, salts, and herbs used for finishing dishes, quantities are discretionary and flexible.

Exercise caution when making fermented products, ensuring all equipment is spotlessly clean, and seek expert advice if in any doubt.

All herbs, shoots, flowers, and leaves should be picked fresh from a clean source. Exercise caution when foraging for ingredients; any foraged ingredients should only be eaten if an expert has deemed them safe to eat. Mushrooms should be wiped clean.

··

About the Author

··

Emily Elyse Miller is a New York-based food and travel writer with
features, bylines, and projects with *Vogue, Forbes, The New Yorker,
Lucky Peach*, WGSN, Tock, *Conde Nast Traveler,* and more. She is the
founder and creative director of BreakfastClub. Through restaurant
events that gather people over breakfast, her passion lies in
connecting cultures through breakfast, art, and community in cities
around the world.

Author Acknowledgments

Wherever I traveled, the topic of breakfast always created a sense of community. This book belongs to the many voices who graciously contributed their knowledge, techniques, stories, and kitchens to share a meal and conversation over breakfast. Thank you to all the remarkable humans I met while traveling, at my events and tours, or through digital means.

This book would not have been possible without the generosity and knowledge of these true lovers of breakfast: Akira Akuto, Miguel Andrade, Ron Arazi, Caroline Argirokastritis, Diane Argirokastritis, Stephanie Artner, Andy Baraghani, Marie Berry, Katja Bremer, Sharon Brenner, Julia Bullaro Rothman, Katie June Burton, Vindhya Buthpitiya, Andrea K. Castillo, Catrina Cortes, Juan de Dios Garza, Victoria Eliasdottir, Rachna Elhence, Gheanna Emelia, Cathy Erway, Youssou Fall, Marianna Fierro, Jill Fisher, Liv Fleischhacker, Camilo Fonseca, Ewa Fraiha, Nicole Franzen, Jade George, Rana Good, Yana Gristan, Nazly Hafez, Georgia Hobart, Jeppe Jarnit-Bjergsø, Maria Jarnit-Bjergsø, Shraddha Kamdar, Nancy Kim, Ryan King, Anita Klasanova, Aun Koh, Tuukka Koski, Priya Krishna, Spiros Lappas, Giuseppe Lacorazza, Merav Levkowitz, Katherine Li Johnson, Victoire Loup, Joel Malebranche, Olga Massov, Magdalena Matyskova, Anne McBride, Pereyra Murray, Shahla Naimi, Angelis Nannos, Leora Novick, Natalia Pascual, Natália S. Pereira, Lucila Quin Andy Ricker, Linda Sarris, Deana Saukam, Ethel Schuster, Ileana Selejan, Lucas Sin, Tracey Smith, Eva Stenlund Thorsen, Su-Lyn Tan, Pierre Thiam, Sofia Tomé, Philippe Tremblay-Berberi, Liz Vaknin, Anisha Vasandani, David Vasandani, Meena Vasandani, Raj Vasandani, Madelaine Vásquez, Shoshanna Vles Bennett, Trung Vu, Teng Wen Wee, Lindsay Weger, Steven Whiteman, Elena Yamamoto, Kentaro Yamamoto, and Wen-Jay Ying. Special thanks to: Breville, Bob's Red Mill, Staub, and Lodge for stocking a global pantry full of supplies and equipment.

To my editor and friend, Emily Takoudes: Your belief in my passion for connecting people through food is what led to this incredible opportunity. It's a true honor to be part of this prestigious collection of global cuisine. To Sanaë Lemoine: Your calming demeanor, encouraging words, impeccable taste, and talent for understanding just what I'm trying to say make you an incredible editor and friend.

To Brittany Bennet: Thank you for keeping me focused with your sense of wonder and respect for all things baked.

To Mom and Dad: Your early-rising mentality instilled in me a respect for the beauty of the morning hours. You have been an unwavering support of my unconventional career paths. Your encouragement has made me fearless and I wouldn't be who I am without it. To my sister, Alana, whom I feel I've finally converted to a fan of soup for breakfast: I've had more breakfasts with you than anyone. Your fierce palate and craving for culture is what connects us as sisters, friends, and roommates. To my Grandma Carol and late Grandpa Shelly: Thank you for encouraging me to try new things, for your kindness and infectious enthusiasm. To my late grandmother Mary (Nanny): Growing up with you put a veil of humor over life and helped me cook with confidence and freedom from judgement.

To my friends: Thank you for your unconditional support and taste-testing, for bringing me pork rolls from New Jersey, for spending hours on the phone with your mom to talk about the specifics of North Indian breakfasts, for reading and re-reading my introduction and recipes, and for letting me take over your kitchen to make muffins and scrapple. You feed my curiosity and humor my wildest ideas.

Phaidon Press Limited
Regent's Wharf
All Saints Street
London N1 9PA

Phaidon Press Inc.
65 Bleecker Street
New York, NY 10012

phaidon.com

First published 2019
© 2019 Phaidon Press Limited

ISBN 978 0 7148 7804 1

A CIP catalogue record for this book is
available from the British Library and
the Library of Congress.

Commissioning Editor: Emily Takoudes
Project Editors: Sanaë Lemoine,
Madeleine Compagnon
Production Controllers: Sue Medlicott,
Nerissa Vales
Design: Astrid Stavro/Design by Atlas
Layout: Luísa Martelo
Photography: Haarala Hamilton
Printed in China

The publisher would like to thank
Evelyn Battaglia, Kat Craddock, Jane
Hornby, Theodora Kaloudis, and Kate
Slate for their contributions to the book.